RUPERT GARCÍA

RUPERT GARCÍA

THE MAKING OF AN AMERICAN ARTIST
A Testimonio

MARIO T. GARCÍA

RUTGERS UNIVERSITY PRESS

NEW BRUNSWICK, CAMDEN, AND NEWARK, NEW JERSEY

LONDON

Rutgers University Press is a department of Rutgers, The State University
of New Jersey, one of the leading public research universities in the nation.
By publishing worldwide, it furthers the University's mission of dedication
to excellence in teaching, scholarship, research, and clinical care.

Library of Congress Cataloging-in-Publication Data
Names: García, Mario T. author
Title: Rupert García : the making of an American artist,
a testimonio / Mario T. García.
Description: New Brunswick : Rutgers University Press, [2025] |
Includes bibliographical references and index.
Identifiers: LCCN 2025012635 | ISBN 9781978844018 cloth
Subjects: LCSH: Garcia, Rupert, 1941– | Artists—United States—Biography |
Mexican American artists—Biography | LCGFT: Biographies
Classification: LCC N6537.G373 G37 2025 | DDC 769.92 [B]—dc23/eng/20250618
LC record available at https://lccn.loc.gov/2025012635

A British Cataloging-in-Publication record for this book
is available from the British Library.

References to internet websites (URLs) were accurate at the time of writing.
Neither the author nor Rutgers University Press is responsible for URLs
that may have expired or changed since the manuscript was prepared.

♾ The paper used in this publication meets the requirements
of the American National Standard for Information Sciences—
Permanence of Paper for Printed Library Materials, ANSI Z39.48-1992.

rutgersuniversitypress.org

To My Extended Family: the Cuevas-Atilanos;
Orozcos-Garcías; Fernándezes-Huertas; Avilas; Yrungarys.
And to My Wife Sammi Madison-García
—Rupert García

To Rupert García, a Great American Artist
—Mario T. García

The fact that I make art reminds me that I wish to live.
—Rupert García

If my work is not beautiful and critical, I don't do it.
It has to be both, hard to do.
—Rupert García

For me, the important question is how I visually
express [the] social dynamic between me
and the rest of the world.
—Rupert García

Contents

RUPERT GARCÍA

Introduction

Mario T. García

The phone rang in my History office.

"Hello."

"Mario, this is Rupert García. How are you?"

"Hey, Rupert! Nice to hear from you."

"I finally had a chance to read your book on Bert Corona and really, really liked it. You did a fantastic job!"

"Thanks Rupert. I appreciate this."

We went on and chatted about the event in Oakland a few months earlier in 1975 where I had a book-signing at a bookstore on my edited volume on Ruben Salazar. I had gotten permission from Rupert to use as the cover of the book his image of Salazar done in 1970 shortly after Salazar had been killed covering the Chicano Anti-War Moratorium on August 29 of that year. I think I had met Rupert before but I got to know him a bit better at the book event.

"Rupert, it's been great talking to you and thanks for your call."

"Yeah, I just wanted to congratulate you on the Bert Corona book and also the Ruben Salazar one."

"Thanks Rupert. Talk to you later."

After I hung up, I thought that Rupert was hinting that perhaps I might write his story. I already had plenty of projects going but a testimonio oral history of a major Chicano artist like Rupert intrigued me. Why not take this on and start interviewing Rupert even while I worked on these other projects? I called Rupert back a few days later.

"Rupert I was thinking that it would be great to work on your testimonio. How would you feel about my starting to interview you for it?"

"Man, that would be great! When do you want to start?"

We arranged for Rupert, who is not related to me, to come down from his Oakland home to Santa Barbara for a week and I would put him up at the UC Santa Barbara Faculty Club. We started our interviews at the Chicano Studies Research Center in the Spring of 1996.

"Rupert, tell me about your family background?"

This is how we started Rupert's testimonio—his oral history life story as told through me.

■II■

The concept of the testimonio comes out of Latin America in the 1960s when testimonial texts began to appear, the result of the cooperation between journalists or scholars and political activists including revolutionaries. While based on oral history, a testimonio goes beyond providing information. It is intended to have readers observe the social conditions represented in the text; to reflect on these conditions; and most significantly to act and attempt to change those conditions. This has certainly characterized my previous testimonios including figures such as Bert Corona, Fran Esquibel Tywoniak, Sal Castro, Rosalio Muñoz, Gloria Arellanes, and Raul Ruiz.[1] Rupert García through his art has exposed racism and oppression and his story and art calls upon on others to act on changing such conditions. Testimonios are liberationist texts and this includes Rupert García's story.

■II■

Rupert and I worked that entire week and covered a lot of ground. I found Rupert to be very open, direct, and expansive in his responses to my questions. Having done my testimonio of Bert Corona, a giant in Chicano labor and civil rights history, I was comfortable in starting my interviews with Rupert. Like the Corona testimonio, I aimed to do a chronological life-story with Rupert, which is why we started on his family history. The challenge for me was that I am not an art historian. My work has focused on Chicano history topics such as: immigration, leadership, civil rights, and Chicano Catholicism. I appreciated Chicano art but it was not my expertise. So why then do Rupert's story? I did it because the opportunity came my way and if I didn't do it who would? To date there has been no substantive study or biography focused on Rupert and his art. Besides questions about his family and his early life before becoming an artist, my approach was similar to the way I interviewed Bert Corona. I was able to acquire from Rupert catalogs of his most important exhibitions up to the early 1990s. I studied these, including other information on his work that Rupert provided, and came up with questions about his images and their meaning from his perspective. Rather than an art critic or art historian analyzing Rupert's work, he would do it himself through my intervention. Moreover, as a Chicano historian, I could locate Rupert's evolution as an artist by contextualizing his work within certain historical time frames.

That week proved to be very productive, and in addition Rupert and I had a chance to get to know each other better, and we struck up a good friendship. We became comfortable with one another, which aided in our interviews and conversations. This week, however, was not enough to cover all of Rupert's history, even though we covered quite a bit. I arranged for Rupert to return in October to give a lecture at UCSB, and we used some of this time to do a few additional interviews. Because we still had not covered all of Rupert's story up to that time, we decided to get together later that December to try to conclude our interviews. After Christmas of 1996, I visited Rupert at his home and studio in Oakland. I also met his wife Sammi Madison, and Rupert gave me a tour of his expansive studio. We worked that entire day and finished his story up to that time. In the process I not only learned about Rupert's life, but I learned much about his techniques as an artist and about the artistic process.

The problem for me was when to begin to write up Rupert's story. At this time in the mid-1990s I was already working on two other testimonios involving the stories of Fran Esquibel Tywoniak and Professor Luis Leal. Both of these testimonios would be published in 2000. In addition, I started to work on a book on Chicano Catholic history that would also spin off into a biography of Father Luis Olivares and the sanctuary movement in Los Angeles. To further complicate my workload, I commenced the testimonio of Sal Castro, including his role in the historic 1968 "Blowouts" or walkouts in the East Los Angeles schools.[2] Needless to say, my head was spinning. I had to make choices and unfortunately decided to put aside Rupert's story to attend to these other projects which, to be honest, were closer to my own research interests. These other works extended well into the first two decades of the new millennium. All along I felt guilty about not getting back to Rupert's testimonio. Finally,

around 2020 I began to write up his story, knowing that in the meantime I would still need to cover it from 1996 to the present, over two decades of Rupert's evolution as an artist.

I had not been in touch with Rupert for some time and so with some embarrassment and trepidation, I emailed him and apologized that I had not gotten back to his testimonio over the past number of years but that I was now starting to write it up. I was pleasantly surprised that Rupert was delighted to hear back from me and was excited that I was now writing his story. Over the next two years I wrote eight chapters covering his birth to the 1990s. However, I still had to cover everything since then. In the summer of 2022 Rupert agreed to a new round of interviews that would fill in this gap. Because of the COVID pandemic and logistical issues, I did phone interviews which I recorded with Rupert's permission. We worked the entire summer and we filled in those years. In a way it was fortuitous that I had put aside Rupert's testimonio, because now I could do a full-life story spanning over eight decades of his life and work. Based on these interviews, I was able to write the last chapter of the book, bringing Rupert's story up to date. All told we did fifty hours of taped interviews. It has been a very long journey, but I felt a sense of accomplishment in concluding the story. It is a remarkable story.

■◼■

Who is Rupert García?

Simply put Rupert García is one of the outstanding American artists of the second half of the twentieth century and the first decades of the twenty-first century. He is also one of the most significant artists of Chicano/Latino heritage in the United States. No other Chicano/Latino artist, male or female, in my opinion, possesses the stature and recognition as a premier American artist than García. No other Chicano/Latino artist, male or female, has had the national and international exhibits that García has had. And yet to date, as mentioned, there is no biography of García, and so it is my hope that this testimonio will fill that gap as well as bring Rupert García the artist to wider attention. But nothing that García has achieved was given to him. He earned his reputation through hard and committed work over five decades of evolving as an artist. He wasn't born Rupert García, he became Rupert García—the artist. His story is very much an American story and a human story.

He was born in 1941 in a small settlement outside of Stockton, California, called French Camp. On both sides of his family were immigrants from Mexico who possessed very little other than their hard work as farm laborers. He was also born to a military family, including his father who was a World War II veteran. Other uncles were also part of the "Greatest Generation," and some later served in the Korean War. But his family was also a divided one when his parents divorced after World War II. Rupert and his two other brothers were raised by their mother and their maternal grandmother, Guadalupe. It was also a Mexican American family who lived

in the poor Mexican American section of Stockton, but where other residents of color also lived. Rupert recalls at an early age playing with Mexican American, Black, and Asian American friends. It was also an artistic family. Grandmother Guadalupe in her own artistic way made figurines of people and animals out of tissue paper, a form of *rasquachismo*, making art of whatever material is available.[3] It was what some would call folk art, but it was not for sale to tourists; it was for the family, especially the children. Young Rupert was fascinated by what his grandmother made. His own mother was artistically inclined as were his aunts who also lived in Stockton. This gave Rupert a sense that art was naturally part of his family culture.

While Rupert liked to draw in his early years, it wasn't until high school that he began to do some more substantial drawing, including images of movie stars taken from the film magazines that his mother read. One of his drawings was of James Dean, who portrayed a young rebel without a cause in the 1950s and became a teen idol. By the time Rupert graduated from high school, he wanted to become an artist. Staying in Stockton and attending Stockton Junior College for two years, García majored in Art and took classes that introduced him to the basics of art techniques. After graduating from junior college in the early 1960s, Rupert felt that if he wanted to be an artist, he had to move to San Francisco with its vibrant artistic culture. Living with friends from Stockton who also desired to become artists, Rupert came to realize that it was one thing to want to be an artist and another to become one. He had no money to go to art school much less college, and hence had to work just to pay part of the rent for the apartment he and his friends lived in. His one shot at artistic "fame" came when the owner of a pizza place allowed him and his friends to exhibit what images they had in the restaurant. While Rupert showed some of his early drawings and was thrilled about his first exhibit, no one paid any attention to them in the restaurant. This was a difficult period for Rupert, who had to retreat back to Stockton when his money ran out. Returning home would change his life, or at least a portion of it.

With no job and no prospects, Rupert was convinced by an Air Force recruiter to join the Air Force in 1962. He served for four years including one impressionable year in Indochina as the U.S. military intervention in Vietnam escalated. Rupert was assigned as a security guard at a secret U.S. base in Thailand. From this base, American jet bombers participated in Operation Rolling Thunder, which involved the bombing of North Vietnam. His job along with other security guards was to protect the base from any possible enemy attacks. It was a difficult year for Rupert, but he adjusted and survived his assignment there. While he did little painting at the base, he did absorb memories that he would later transfer into his art, especially the contradiction of what he considered to be the aesthetically appealing shape of the planes he guarded with their

mission of destruction. In 1966, Rupert received his honorable discharge from the Air Force.

He returned to Stockton still with no job prospects and the psychological effects of his year in a combat zone. He would live with this trauma for a few years. He also lived with a reluctance to admit his Air Force service, especially the year in Indochina, because of the growing anti-war movement in the United States. It was not until he came out as being against the war that his psychological wound began to heal—but not entirely—and he would at times have setbacks when he heard the jet engine noises at airports.

During his four years in the service, Rupert never gave up his dream of becoming an artist. Fortunately, the G.I. Bill of Rights proved to be the catalyst for him to enroll at San Francisco State College in 1966 to study art. As a returning veteran, García had to adjust to a college campus and to being a student after several years away from school. The next few years would be crucial ones for him. He adjusted to the college curriculum, which included taking classes from radical professors, such as in sociology, which opened his mind to critical thinking and not accepting the status quo. And in his art classes, he benefited from professors who encouraged his artistic pursuits. These included classes for his BA in art which he concluded in 1968 and his MA in art which he finished in 1969. However, the most significant impact on him was the Third World Liberation Strike at San Francisco State beginning in the fall of 1968 and lasting into 1969. More than anything else, the strike politicized and radicalized García. He supported the goals of the strike to have ethnic studies added to the curriculum and to increase the number of minority students, including Chicanos and Latinos. Besides attending rallies and marches on campus, sometimes being attacked by the police, Rupert wondered about how he and other art students could better support the strike. Fortunately, a progressive art professor who had been in Paris during the student uprising there that spring suggested the art students could use their talents to make posters in support of the strike, as had been done by the Parisian art students.

This is what Rupert had been waiting for—a concrete response by him and other art students to better engage in the strike. To do this, he and the other students learned a technique that they had not been taught—silk-screening. They learned how to make mass posters from this process, one that would come to characterize Rupert's art for the next several years. Among the posters that García created during the strike were portraits of Che Guevara entitled *Right On!* The use of the classic Che image revealed the extent of radicalism that Rupert had undergone, especially influenced by the Third World Liberation Strike in which Latinos demanded a curriculum that was about them and their cultures instead of that of white Western civilization. If Che was the ultimate revolutionary, Rupert and the Third World students at San Francisco State were his followers. In addition to the revolutionary Che,

García added a portrait of the Mexican revolutionary Emiliano Zapata of the Mexican Revolution of 1910, the champion of peasants. One additional poster that Rupert made in support of the strike was one that he called *Down with the Whiteness*, which showed a Black activist calling out this slogan. What is notable about this poster is that Rupert was not saying down with whites, of which many supported the strike, but down with the whiteness of racism. He was attacking systemic white racism, not whites.

The strike was ultimately successful and ethnic studies, including La Raza studies, was instituted at San Francisco State. The strike had launched García's career as a committed artist—committed to human rights and social justice. This commitment was furthered by his embrace of the Chicano Movement in California and throughout the Southwest, where most Chicanos resided. The movement was part of the larger protests linked to the social movements of the sixties, which actually spilled over to the seventies. It is here where Rupert became a Chicano, a term that he was not familiar with in Stockton but which he now embraced, including the concept of Chicanismo or cultural nationalism focused on ethnic pride and empowerment. The Chicano Movement represented the largest and most widespread civil rights and empowerment movement by Mexican Americans in the United States up to that time.[4] Rupert was influenced by the oppositional character of the movement although tempered by the diverse Latino community in the Mission district of San Francisco that included not only Chicanos but Central and South Americans. Rupert, besides becoming Chicano, also became Latino with no apparent contradictions. They were all Raza. This is what Karen Mary Davalos refers to as "hybrid cultural nationalism."[5]

After the strike, Rupert was introduced to fellow Latino artists in the predominantly Latino Mission district of San Francisco. Here he became one of the founding members of La Galeria de La Raza, a collective of Latino artists including Rupert. This experience at La Galeria was also foundational for him, as he learned the importance of a collective art outreach to the community. García continued and advanced his silk-screen posters in support of the community and of oppositional movements. In 1970, for example, he created his poster *!Fuera De Indochina!* which he did to support the large Chicano National Anti-War Moratorium in East Los Angeles on August 29, 1970.[6] This poster also revealed Garcia's conversion to the anti-war movement. Although Rupert did not attend the historic moratorium, he like others were shocked at the brutal police response that led to three Chicano being killed, including the pathbreaking journalist Ruben Salazar. To commemorate Salazar's death, García helped organize a memorial show at La Galeria later that fall. For the show in memory of Salazar, Rupert made the show poster with an image of Salazar. This would become an iconic image.[7]

García's involvement with La Galeria would prove to be among the most significant periods of his art production, specifically with respect to poster art. In many ways, Rupert is still often linked with this period despite his own subsequent evolution as an artist. His images became part of what was referred to as the Mission Cultural Renaissance of artistic and literary cultural production. Among his silk-screen images is one of the first of Angela Davis, which also became the iconic image of Davis. Other images included those of the great Mexican painters Orozco and Siqueiros; his homage to Picasso who influenced Rupert; of Inez García who was a woman unjustly accused of murder when she killed her rapist; and contemporary Mexican revolutionary Lucio Cabañas. Rupert further painted one of the first images of Frida Kahlo in the United States. In addition, García produced powerful pictures on the prisoner uprising at Attica; against the deportation of undocumented immigrants; and a bicentennial poster with the image of a dead person of color. These images among others are often the most referenced ones in Rupert's career. Although García's artistic production would increase over the next few decades, many art critics go back to the earlier posters because, according to fellow artist Juan Fuentes, they are so powerful.[8]

Around 1975, García decided to leave La Galeria de La Raza as an active member, although he would still be an affiliate and participate in some events. However, he felt that while he had benefited much from his experience in the collective, he needed

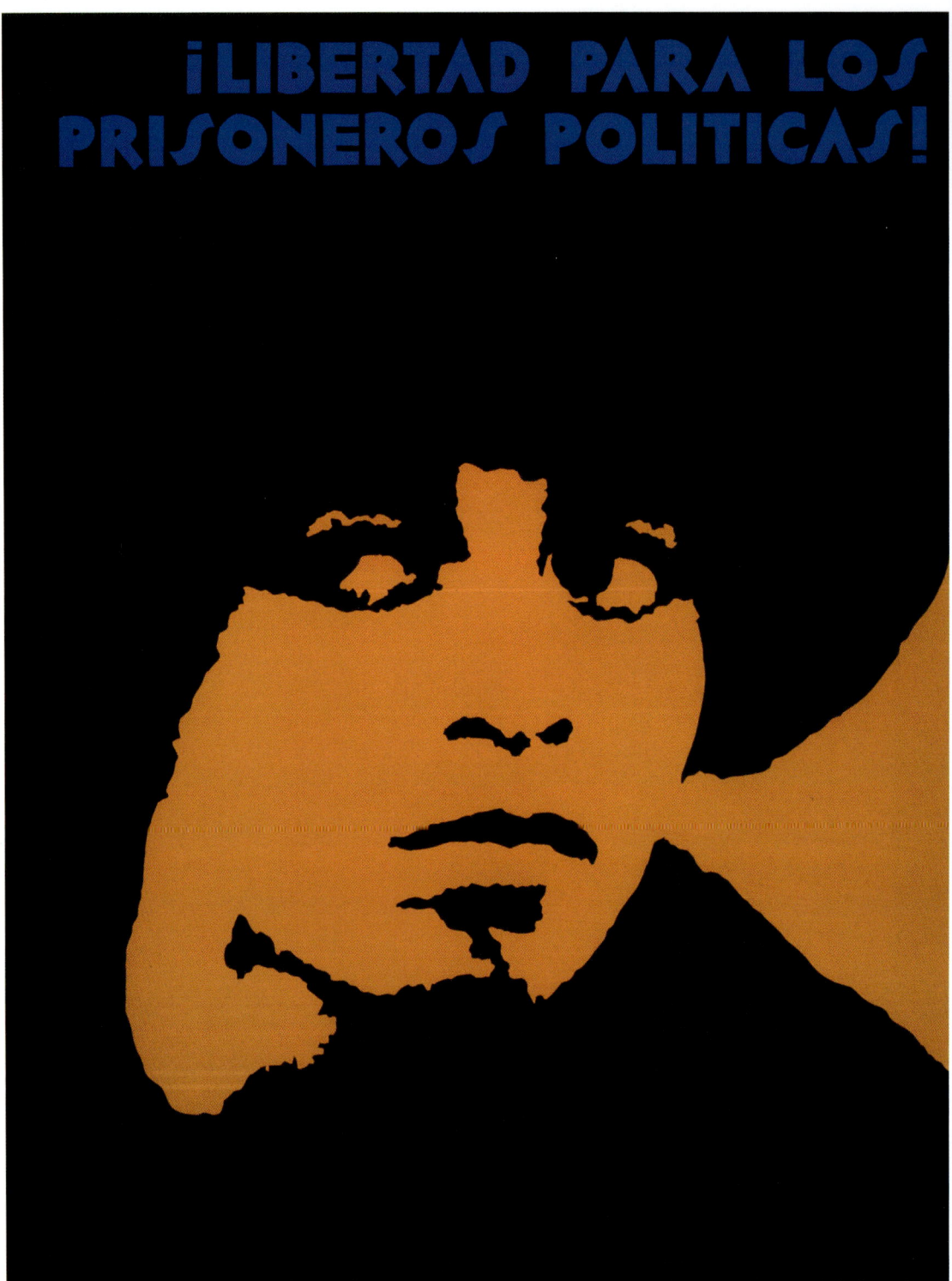

¡Libertad para los Prisoneros Politicas!, 1971. Color silkscreen on white wove paper, sheet size: 26 x 20 inches, image size: 24-5/8 x 19 inches. Copyright © Rupert García. Courtesy of Rena Bransten Gallery.

to go out on his own and experiment in other artistic venues. Juan Fuentes recalls that some other members of La Galeria felt that Rupert was abandoning not only the collective but his commitment to Chicano/Latino art.[9] Rupert felt otherwise. He wasn't leaving the Chicano/Latino movement but representing the movement in a different way. His leaving La Galeria also coincided with his minimizing silkscreen posters and images and instead turning to pastel as a medium. Pastel, he felt, provided him with more complex and diverse colors which would further enrich his pictures. To Rupert, color was central to his art. Perhaps his most striking pastels included *El Grito de Rebelde*, which depicts a Third World prisoner before a firing squad, and *Assassination of a Striking Mexican Worker*, which was based on a photograph by the great Mexican photographer Manuel Alvarez Bravo. In many of his pastels and even earlier in his silk screens, García based his paintings on photographs but took them to another level in his images. Other pastel pictures featured the portraits of the Flores Magón brothers who were anarcho-syndicalists in the Mexican Revolution; the Spanish painter Goya; Vincent Van Gogh; another image of Frida Kahlo; Bertolt Brecht; J. Robert Oppenheimer; Diego Rivera; Luis Buñuel; George Orwell; and his portrayal of the Virgin of Guadalupe which he titled *La Virgen y Yo*, an image I would use as the cover for my 2008 book *Católicos: Resistance and Affirmation in Chicano Catholic History*.[10] These are only some of the pastel paintings that Rupert did in the late 1970s and early 1980s. Although many of these images are not directly related to Chicano/Latino themes, García made no apologies for this. He believed that a Chicano/Latino artist should not be confined by his ethnicity, but that he or she should explore a myriad of subjects—which he did, but in some way always tied to humanism and social justice. He didn't care what others might say about his art; he painted, according to him, to please himself, not others.

García's pastel period also coincides with becoming the first Chicano/Latino to have an exhibit at the San Francisco Museum of Art in 1978, which included his earlier posters and the beginning of his pastels. In 1986, his art from the late 1960s to mid-1980s was featured in the exhibit *The Art of Rupert García* at the Mexican Museum in San Francisco. García became one of the first Chicano/Latinos who began to exhibit in art museums. Rupert believed that his art should not just be exhibited in the barrios but in museums where others could be exposed to it. For Rupert there were no boundaries as to where his art should be shown.

While García's pastels received much acclaim, Rupert felt he should not remain comfortable and static in this medium. He needed to push himself further. He turned to oil painting in the late 1980s and into the 1990s. Many believe that oil painting is the ultimate for an artist; however, Rupert discounts this. He notes that for him there is no hierarchy between his silk-screen posters, his pastels, and his oil paintings. He wanted to master all of these mediums, and he does so in beautiful oil images that cover a range of subjects but still with a critical edge to them. Rupert never abandoned his political principals based on critiquing oppression and violence and endorsing social justice. One example of this is his powerful oil painting entitled *Ominous Omen*, in which Rupert paints a beautiful bomber plane similar to the ones he protected in Indochina. However, in this striking image he paints the plane on fire before exploding. Rupert is destroying this beautiful image of mass destruction and violence.

It is also in his oil painting period that Rupert goes commercial by linking with various galleries and having agents represent him. While again some other Chicano/Latino artists may have criticized him for this, Rupert felt once more that his pictures deserved to be displayed in galleries that would do justice to his images and allow them to be purchased by the public. As part of this change, García was invited to exhibit some of his paintings in a Paris gallery, one of the first Chicano/Latinos to do so.

By the end of the 1980s, Rupert García had the distinction of being one of the most honored Chicano/Latino artists, with awards from various art entities. While Rupert liked to receive this attention, he did not rest on his laurels. He pushed himself further. He does this in the fourth period of his evolution as an artist when he employs digital art. Working with professional digital art technicians, he produces over the next three decades a variety of digital images that will be showcased in galleries and museums. Some of these pictures are borrowed from earlier periods but augmented by digital means. Many are striking and powerful new images influenced by García's political concerns, such as a series of depictions of torture committed by the U.S. military in the Iraq War, which Rupert opposed; and his images of Barack Obama, including perhaps one of his best paintings, digital or otherwise, done in 2010 entitled *Obama from Douglass* that involves a triptych of three images, one of Barack Obama and another of the great Black abolitionist Frederick Douglass, with black and gray lines in between them. Rupert is asking "what is the connection between the two?"

In one of his most recent exhibitions at his San Francisco gallery, Rena Branston Gallery, García returns to his experience in Indochina in a show entitled *Rolling Thunder*, which was the name of the mass bombing committed by the U.S. military against North Vietnam and partly operated at the secret base in Thailand where García served during the U.S. war in Vietnam. The theme of the show is war and the anti-war images that Rupert painted over the years. This includes a digital image of a young Air Force Private Rupert García based on a photo that he had taken of himself in Thailand. In the picture, Rupert takes the service medal he received from being in Thailand and places it over his eyes in the photo. He calls this picture *Hoodwinked*, meaning that he had been blinded and deceived along with many other Americans about the war in Vietnam. It was not a war to support democracy in Vietnam against the Communists but a war of aggression and imperialism on the part of the United States.

There is no way to do justice to the evolution of Rupert García the artist in this short introduction. This is only to observe some of this history that will be more fully developed in the text and where the images mentioned and many others will be presented. Rupert García is a complex and multidimensional individual and artist, and it is my hope that I have captured this in this book in search of who Rupert García is.

—||—

To understand Rupert García and his art, you have to place him in historical context. All art is political, even the most abstract kind, because artists relate in one way or another to their historical periods. Rupert García is part of the Chicano Generation, which is also my generation and of which I have written about.[11] Rupert, like me, was not born Chicano; he became Chicano. Having said that, it is important to observe that Rupert grew up in an extended family of Mexican Americans in Stockton. His family members were proud to be of Mexican descent. They were working-class Mexican Americans. Although they acculturated, they did not assimilate. That is, they merged or fused their Mexican cultural traditions with American ones representing different American groups. His mother and his aunts and uncles were part of what I call the Mexican

American Generation from the 1930s to the 1950s. I have also written about this generation that is characterized by its transculturation. They became bilingual and bicultural. They did not assimilate, because assimilation means that one wants to give up one's parental culture in order to be accepted by the dominant culture, in this case Anglo American or white culture.[12] As a result, Rupert grew up with no shame of being of a Mexican background that included Mexican cuisine, speaking some Spanish, and attending Mexican cultural events in which his family member participated, such as performances by the local ballet folklorico whose costumes female family members made. Although his name Rupert was English, he was partially named after his maternal grandfather Ruperto. In high school Rupert recalls being aware of and being to a degree influenced by pachuco culture. Pachucos were young Mexican Americans who, feeling alienated by both American mass culture and their own Mexican parental culture, created their own counterculture—pachuco culture with its own dialect called *caló*.[13] Rupert was not a pachuco but admired their swagger and countercultural aesthetics in their appearance.

Yet the 1960s was Rupert's coming of adult age and the times he could better reference. He was a Vietnam veteran who had participated in the U.S. war in Vietnam from his base in Thailand. When he returned he witnessed the expanding anti-war movement. But more significantly, he became caught up in the student protests of that decade when he supported the Third World Liberation Strike at San Francisco State.[14] It's during this experience and becoming aware of the Chicano Movement in California and elsewhere that he becomes Chicano. He refers to himself as Chicano. For Rupert, becoming Chicano meant participating in a social movement such as the Chicano Movement to bring about social change through direct action politics—protests in the streets. As a result, the stimulus for Rupert's early works lies in the protest politics at San Francisco State and in relating to the Chicano Movement in general. At the same time, as a result of the strike and then becoming involved in the Latino Mission district, Rupert likewise expands his identity to include a Third World consciousness and support of Third World movements of liberation both in the United States and in the Third World of Latin America, Africa, and Asia. As part of this larger perspective, Rupert further develops a pan-Latino one by working with La Galeria de La Raza and in the Mission. As he explains it, you could not be a strict Chicano nationalist, because the Mission and La Galeria involved not just Chicanos but people and activists who derived from other Latin American backgrounds, such as from Central and South America. From this, Rupert complements his embrace of Chicanismo or Chicano cultural nationalism with a pan-Latino one, and he saw no contradiction in this.[15] His early and even later art reflects this by not only including Chicano images but also pan-Latino and Third World ones.

Deriving his politics from the social protest movements of the late 1960s and 1970s, Rupert García and his art will always have an oppositional and challenging character. It is what Goldman and Ybarra-Frausto call "engaged art."[16] Despite his later showings in prestige museums and commercial galleries, García never abandons his humanist and social justice views. His art is always challenging the status quo politically and culturally. In the 1980s, for example, he paints images against U.S. policies in Central America involving the U.S. effort under the Reagan administration to overthrow the Sandinista revolution in Nicaragua and in support of brutal dictatorships in El Salvador and Guatemala. His art continues to oppose racism in the United States. He supports the liberation and anti-apartheid struggle in South Africa led by Nelson Mandela. Later through his pictures, Rupert will oppose the U.S. intervention in Iraq by the Bush/Cheney administration and the use of torture in Iraq by U.S. personnel. In one of his last exhibitions, as previously mentioned, *Rolling Thunder*, García comes full circle from his Air Force role in Thailand to reasserting his subsequent anti-war position and reconsidering his own role in the U.S. war in Vietnam.

Rupert García is an artist but one who speaks to his changing times. His work rather than being ahistorical and apolitical is instead historical and political. He is an artist of his times and one who continuously opposes racism, sexism, colonialism and neocolonialism, and imperialism. Although working in a capitalist society, Rupert is not a capitalist and contributes through his art to the struggles to change capitalism and to imagine a society where people are liberated and equal.

◼▮◼

In working with Rupert over the years, I am struck by certain social characteristics of his art. First and foremost is that he has a social conscience that guides his work. His selection of what to paint is influenced by his concern for social justice and for human rights. Second, he is a subversive artist in that his work challenges the status quo both with respect to his social themes and by challenging the false concept that Western art is the epitome of superior art. He started his art education believing in this, but his involvement in the Third World Liberation Strike and his subsequent involvement with La Galeria de La Raza confronted this view and instead promoted Chicano/Latino art as well as that of other minorities and of the Third World. A third characteristic that flows from this is that he challenges the mistaken notion that only Western art is universal. Rupert notes that this is a racist concept that denies the universality of non-Western art, including Chicano/Latino art. He observes that his art is as universal as any other art because it touches on the human condition and spirit. A fourth characteristic is that while Rupert was influenced by the cultural nationalism of the Chicano Movement, he at the same time is an internationalist. He is influenced by art from many areas including Western

art. He is not a provincial or dogmatic nationalist. Many of his themes are internationalist. One could say that Rupert is a post-nationalist artist. As such, he does not romanticize or essentialize "Chicano/Latino culture." Through his evolving art he expresses the contradictions, ambivalences, and ambiguities of this culture or cultures. He agrees with Karen Mary Davalos when she observes that a romantic and nostalgic view of Chicanos/Latinos cannot "account for divergence and complexity."[17] A fifth characteristic is that Rupert brings history into his work by producing images that speak to their times. He is aware of history and incorporates it into his work, such as his images that pertain to the Mexican Revolution or countering the jingoism of the American Revolution in his bicentenary image. I would say that a sixth characteristic is that Rupert is an intellectual and calls himself an intellectual. By this he means that he thinks about his art. He thinks about its meaning related to ideas. Above all, he challenges people to think about his art. What does it mean and what does it mean for you? He doesn't want us to just feel his art, he wants us to think about it. A seventh aspect of Rupert's work by all accounts is that it is complex and sophisticated. You can come to no other conclusion by seeing his art over the years. I will leave it to art critics and art historians to technically address this characteristic, but I believe the consensus is that Rupert García is a master artist.

Last is the question of whether Rupert García's art is political and that he can be said to be a political artist. "Don't call me a political artist," Rupert tells me. By this he means that he does not intentionally do his art to politicize others. Politics, Rupert insists, does not determine how he paints. It doesn't mean that politics are not involved, but that it is more complex, including his aesthetic approach to his art. Art and politics come together. This combination is what art critic Terezita Romo refers to as "aesthetics of the message."[18] García says that he does his art for himself. He is his audience. On the other hand, he observes that if you see politics in his work, then that's okay because he has no control over how we react to his art. If you are moved politically, that is your choice. Rupert's disclaimer that he is not a political artist is controversial, and I have wrestled with this in doing his testimonio. I think that he says he is not a political artist for two reasons. First, he does not want to be seen as a kind of propagandist. Second, he does not want to be pigeonholed as only being a political artist. He admits his initial work making posters for the Third World Liberation Strike and his work at La Galeria might be his most overtly political art, but he notes that he is more than that—more meaning that to analyze his work, you have to include the whole spectrum of his work. I'm sure that others will have a different take on this issue of Rupert as a political artist. If we agree that all art is political, then Rupert is a political artist. Rupert agrees that all art is political ("All art is protest," he has

said) but insists that he does not deliberately try to change opinions and consciousness through his art. "I make art to please myself," he proclaims, "and what you get out of it is your business, not mine." In my opinion, Rupert is an artist of social consciousness and social justice, and if that makes him a political artist so be it, but I will leave it to readers to come to their own conclusions.

◼◫◼

Art critics and art historians touch on some of these characteristics of Rupert García's work. While my survey of those who have written on García's work represents only a sample of such writers, certain themes emerge. First there is the theme of human dignity and humanism embedded in Rupert's pictures. Bill Berkson writing in the late 1980s observed: "The objective message—consistent in García's images then, and amplified more recently—is human dignity, which needs no ideological buttressing."[19] Robert Flynn Johnson adds:

> Despite the often serious content of García's art, it is far from being dour or distancing. On the contrary, García's posters and prints, vibrant in color and composition demand attention. The full range of human emotion from laughter to grief is explored in these works. The art world is fortunate to have an artist such as Rupert García in its midst, who examines and reflects upon the issues of our turbulent times. He proves that even

in our modern society art still has the power to move emotions and heighten our awareness of the world around us.[20]

As noted, social justice is a key concern of García's art. Lucy R. Lippard acknowledges this by writing:

García's posters and prints are not merely "mediated"—the product of a once-removed experience of the world. They are informed by his own life, which is in turn journalized or re-visualized emerging in a series of ferociously cropped and dramatic closeups that have been called the "ideological portraits." These are images intended to bring injustice and radical change to life, to bring the face of history's Third World protagonists up on the screen of the dominant culture.[21]

Carla Stellweg adds about García: "His composition precisely relays his message of social justice on a 'pseudo' mass level. For García, art and politics intersect and are played out within the context of art historical discourse."[22] In commenting on García's newest work on digital art, Claudia E. Zapata writes of Rupert: "His artwork with Magnolia Editions reflects artistic adaptation and curiosity in new techniques that afford a newfound speed, but most importantly it highlights García's ongoing efforts to address themes of social justice he has touched upon since the 1960s."[23] Writer Maxine Hong Kingston, who went to school with Rupert in Stockton, adds a personal touch to her acknowledgment of his focus on social justice through his art. "Rupert is a plain-speaking man," she writes. "I asked him if viewers have any trouble understanding his work. 'No,' he said. 'People understand my work right away. But sometimes the message is unbearable to them.' It is a passion for social justice, and whether hung in galleries or distributed in the streets, Rupert García's art is powerful and beautiful."[24]

García's focus on social justice is complemented by his social concerns and of using his art to stress social issues linked to social consciousness. For example, Karin Breuer in commenting on Rupert's employment of digital art states: "For García it is a search for new ways of making art to move emotionally and heighten our awareness of the world around us."[25] Poet and art critic John Yau concludes: "In a very real sense García is concerned with visual literacy, history painting, and how images can contribute to public discourse and debate."[26] Art historian Ramón Favela stresses that "through his [García's] inventive forms and colors, he still seeks to move the viewer to consider important ideological and social questions."[27] Part of consciousness-raising for García is getting viewers of his art to think about the meaning of his art and in so doing hopefully develop a critical consciousness. Harry S. Parker III and Robert R. Littman comment on this aspect of Rupert's art: "With refined technical skills and unusual sensitivity, García eloquently demonstrates the necessity for thinking critically about the human condition."[28] Critic and novelist Alicia Gaspar de Alba places García's social concerns within the orbit of the Chicano Renaissance of the Chicano Movement. "Rather than 'art for art's sake,' which was the modernists manifesto in mainstream American art, art of the Chicano art movement was an art of social relevance; its purpose was consciousness raising, empowerment, and affirmation."[29]

García's art is also oppositional and revisionist. It opposes the status quo in art and politics and it revises prevailing art forms to produce an oppositional art. The program notes for García's first digital art show at the de Young Museum in San Francisco have this to say of his work: "Most famous are his posters protesting war, racism, and exploitation that incorporated images of Che Guevara, Angela Davis, [and] Emiliano Zapata."[30] Peter Orsi observes that García opposes noncritical pop art with his images of opposition and resistance. "[García's] message is fundamentally 'anti-pop,' a criticism of mainstream American media, society, and culture. Close-up portraits of political figures and scenes of oppression, resistance, and affirmation comprise much of Garcia's subject matter."[31]

Not only does García oppose; he revises. This is especially the case with pop art. At San Francisco State, he was influenced by the advent of pop art as displayed by Andy Warhol. He admired Warhol and other pop artists who focused on everyday material life and transformed it into art. However, as Rupert became radicalized, he saw that pop art was not very critical and

in time was co-opted by the commercial market. It didn't challenge the capitalist system. Rupert utilized pop art techniques but he wanted to revise them to really serve the public and especially the marginalized. He made pop art—Chicano style—into the art of resistance to racism, colonialism, and other forms of oppression. Littman addresses García's revisionism this way:

> Working primarily with silkscreen technique, he developed a bold style, appropriating many of the pictorial devices and premises of Pop Art, but subverting them from a Mexican American and Third World perspective to serve his own aesthetic and ideological ends. . . . Much of Rupert García's graphic work is clearly intended to challenge the viewer's social and political perspective. His themes are universal—the struggle for human rights and for economic, social, and political justice.[32]

Favela adds to this by noting that García became an "anti-pop artist" whose purposes "were very different from the cool detachment and politically disengaged 'neutrality' of Anglo-American pop artists and their legacy, the contemporary post-pop 'image-scavengers.'"[33] To Favela, García was "creating an inverted art of cultural resistance—resistance against Anglo-American cultural imperialism, which is one of the principal definitions of Chicano art."[34] In this sense, Rupert was creating along with other Chicano artists in the movement years what Jennifer A. González calls a "counterdiscourse."[35] Peter Selz agrees when he perceptively observes,

> García was influenced by the Pop artists, whose work was omnipresent at the time. But, instead of a blank acceptance of things as they are, García takes a critical stance. He does not, as Jean Baudrillard would have it, substitute commodities for values. Whereas Pop artists justified the status quo by appropriating its reified images, García deconstructs the advertisement, frequently using a text to leave no doubt about what he is communicating. In general, mainstream American painting of the 1970s—be it Pop, Colorfield or Photo-Realism—lacked political commitment as much as it lacked passion. García and a few artists whom he admires, such as R. B. Kitaj and Leon Golub, were among the exception.[36]

García's revisionism likewise extended to mass media and mass culture such as television and print media, especially photographs, which he used extensively over the years as the foundation for his early posters and later portraits and other images. Stellweg notes that "not only does Rupert García appropriate from mass culture, he subverts it."[37] Favela seconds this subversion by quoting García himself when he stated:

> My art is committed to the paradox that in using mass media I am using a source which I despise and with which I am at war. In using the images of mass media I am taking an art form whose motives are debased, exploitative, and indifferent to human welfare, and setting it into a totally new moral context. I am, so to speak, reversing the process by which mass-media betray the masses and betraying the images of mass-media to moral purposes for which they were not designed; the art of social protest.[38]

Although García insists he is not a political artist, despite his protestations about this, most critics consider him to be a political artist. By this they mean that his concerns for social justice, his anti-racism, and anti-imperialism as well as other social concerns permeate his art. It further takes on, as Davalos notes, the role of power in the art world.[39] Critics, at the same time, are quick to acknowledge the sophistication and complexity of his art. One is not divorced from the other. García, himself, has noted that he loves the relationship between ascetics and politics.[40] As noted, García has stressed that he can't control how people interpret his art and as such most critics and scholars see his art as political in the best sense of that term. They believe that Rupert's politics only makes his art more powerful and relevant. They agree with artist Malaquías Montoya that Chicano art including García's became the "art of liberation" and the "art of protest."[41] Along these lines Mark Van Proyen wrote in 2007: "For over three decades, García has been creating politically charged images . . . all responding with intelligent indignation to the historical moments which conceives them. Throughout, he has pursued the genre of political art in a uniquely vital way."[42] Taya Wyatt notes that political concerns have characterized García's work beginning with his poster art. "Through his art," she observes,

> García focuses on the mistreatment of Latinos in the United States by emphasizing the legacy of colonial violence. . . . García has been an artist who supports activism since the start of his career. García was ahead of his time in his experimentation with posters as a vehicle for political art. Rupert García is Mexican American, and as a minority in the United States he has used his platform as an artist to spread positivity and power to the Latinx community. From protests to posters, García has been coined as one of the most important artists in the last 25 years.[43]

Critics further note that while García's art has evolved over the years, these changes in mediums still retain a political bent to them, though perhaps in more subtle ways. Thomas Albright positively characterizes Rupert's portraits as "radical political portraits—a genre that seems uniquely his own."[44] Of his evolution to pastels, Lippard observes, "The subject of the pastels are sometimes much more personal and art-oriented than the posters, but they are also as politically powerful."[45] Linda Nochlin addresses García's movement to oil painting in this way, "Although Rupert García's recent works on paper may in some respects be less overtly political in their implications than the earlier posters and portraits, his social commitment is still present in the expressive intensity of this more intimate and reflective vision."[46] Writing in 1991, David Levi Strauss puts García's political art in perspective:

> Rupert García has been raising hell and imagining heaven for twenty years now. From his early silk-screen posters for the Third World student strike at San Francisco State in 1968 to recent prints deploring the U.S. invasion of Grenada in 1987 and Panama in 1989, García's work has given vivid form and color to the struggle for peace, human rights, and social justice. . . . This is fully realized political art with a passion.[47]

Finally, I think that Katherine Cook puts it best when she writes the following:

> If the role of art is to not change its society but only—at least—to act as an irritant and a contraposition to power, then García has succeeded. . . . Art's power is not in its ability to answer questions but in the degree to which it ruptures the social conscience. Art is at best a subversive act. . . . Hence, the art of Rupert García remains an implacable witness to the function of art in late-Capitalist America, where it not only acts as an irritant to the power structure but summons its audience to greater awareness of the profundity of its own existence as human drama.[48]

Part of being an artist with a social conscience, García is historically minded. Many of his pictures reflect history or respond to his own historical time. This historical awareness is both personal and political. William Henning in 1988 on the occasion of Rupert's Distinguished Artist exhibit at The Haggin Museum in Stockton observed the following:

> Though born and reared in the Stockton area, García will undoubtedly shock some fellow Stocktonians with work often characterized by raw color, semi-abstract design, and social-activist themes. Genteel it is not! Yet many will see displayed—passionately, cryptically, ironically—vestiges of a California boyhood, a Mexican Catholic upbringing, ethnic self-esteem, strength of family, and, not insignificantly, the creative heritage of the great Mexican muralists.[49]

Ramón Favela notes García's interest in the history of the Mexican Revolution of 1910 and in particular the work of Los Tres—the great Mexican muralists—composed of Rivera, Siqueiros, and Orozco. "In particular," Favel writes, "the Mexican muralists and graphic artists about whom he [García] read and whose work he studied in illustrated books revealed to him that art in the service of a political as well as a cultural revolution was not only possible but a personal imperative for him as a fledgling Chicano artist with a growing social consciousness."[50] And Neery Melkonian concludes: "García uses historical references and art-historical cross-references not as false clues but rather to look at events critically."[51]

It is in the late 1960s that García enters history more boldly with his celebrated posters. Lippard recognizes this when she asserts that "García's posters read like a history of the political events and causes that have marched through our lives from the sixties through the eighties."[52] Some of this history has to do with Chicanos/Latinos as well as other minorities. One writer reflected this in 1993 by acknowledging that "García has been a major force in the art field since the '80s. His achievements are a particular source of pride to young Latinos. His paintings and drawings are a reflection of the events of his time, often depicting revolution, repression and anti-establishment themes."[53] In writing about García's pastel exhibit in Paris in 1987, Peter Selz declared that Rupert's "references are to history as well as current events."[54] Part of García's history and that of his generation was the U.S. war in Vietnam. Although a veteran and perhaps because he was a veteran from the war, he became strongly against this unfortunate part of American history. In writing of Rupert's anti-war exhibit *Rolling Thunder* in 2028, Lowery Stokes Sims emphasizes that "the glaring fact that black men and those of Latino heritage represented a disproportionally high number of draftees in the war is particularly relevant as we view the work by Rupert García in this exhibition."[55] Finally Geno Rodríguez and Andrew Perchuk get it right when they declare that the art of Rupert García is not just part of Chicano/Latino history but of American history! Rupert is an American artist. "His career," they write, "is proof that artists who are not enfranchised in our society because of race do not create or exist in a context unconnected to American history, but rather that these artists and individuals have always been creators of American history and culture."[56]

Although Rupert identified as Chicano and embraced the Chicano Movement, he was not an ethnic nationalist. "You can be nationalistic to a point, "he warns, "and then you can possibly become fascistic."[57] Here, the influence of the Third World Liberation Strike is significant. He became Third World before he became a Chicano. Rupert's embrace of Third World liberation movements reflected in his art made him an internationalist, as critics note. Tatiana Reinoza and María del Mar González stress that García downplays Chicano nationalism in favor "of creating hemispheric connections."[58] Peter Selz likewise brings attention to the internationalism of García's art: "The work is informed by occurrences in the world and the artist's responsible reaction to these matters as well as his need to render a visual record of the often-abhorrent reality. [García's] theme is generally Third World struggles for economic, social and political liberation but his prime engagement is in creation of art."[59] And Rodríguez and Perchuk add further to what they consider to be García's internationalism: "When his work says 'Basta Ya' (Enough is Enough) he is not just speaking to the issue of a particular community on the West Coast but to the world our New World Order is creating."[60]

García's internationalism in a way feeds into what some critics consider to be his universality reflected in his art. García, himself, has often responded back to those critics who don't consider Chicano/Latino art to possess universal appeal because it is too "ethnic." Rupert has argued back that the issue of universality has been monopolized by Western art to marginalize Third World art, at the same time reflecting the racism of Western critics. All art, he asserts, is universal if it speaks to the human condition. For García art is also universal because it is made by human beings.[61] Terri Cohn agrees and points out that it is the "beauty of García's disturbing images that enables them to speak across time and place."[62] And Harry S. Parker and Harry H. Littman are even more direct about García's universality when they write, "Much of Rupert García's graphic work is clearly intended to challenge the viewer's social and political perspective. His themes are universal—the struggle for human rights and for economic, social, and political justice."[63] García, himself, forcefully counters the stereotype that ethnic art including Chicano/Latino art is not universal. "I always thought my work to be for anybody who ever sees it," he said in 1991,

and those who do not see it as being universal or transcendental are revealing their myopic vision, not my open vision. Those who say one's work is culturally bound are really just disclosing their xenophobia. In other words, both Michelangelo's *David* and the Aztec *Coatlicue* are universal. How we look at them and give them meaning is determined by the social, cultural context in which we live. So, in other words, it's relative. That doesn't mean that the Aztec piece or any other piece made by any other human being on the globe is not universal, because we are all human beings manifesting various kinds of stuff to be called culture and we all have something to say, either emotionally or intellectually, about existence. Consequently, everything is universal because it's all going to add up to help us figure out where we are, where we come from, and maybe where we're going. But if we separate these things—that's not universal, and that is universal--we will never be able to add up the puzzle to understand the human position in this galaxy. If we maintain a continuing separation of peoples by race, sex, and age, ethnocentrism—all these "isms," if we continue down that line, we are doomed.[64]

While García was not born on the United States–Mexico border and his images are not mainly about the border, one critic still sees him as a border artist, especially based on his 1973 poster *¡Cesen Deportación!* Of this poster, Antonio Prieto comments:

While the first examples of Chicano art in the late sixties took up issues of land, community and oppression, it was not until later that graphic artists like Rupert García began to explicitly depict the border in their work. García's 1973 silkscreen "¡Cesen Deportación!," for example, calls for an end to exploitative treatment of migrant workers who are allowed to cross the border and are then deported at the whim of U.S. economic and political interests. The image boldly highlights the barbed wire that spanned most of the borderline. . . . The wire's black thorns over a solid red background becomes a symbol of unfair violence toward the Mexican immigrants, and also evokes the colors used in Mexican strike flags as well as César Chávez's UFW banner.[65]

Lastly in this section, I want to note how some critics assess Rupert García's artistry. Sophistication is the commonly used term. Examining his techniques and manipulation of mediums including silk-screening, pastels, oil, and digital, critics and scholars praise García for the mastery of his art. They note his ability to skillfully combine the political and social issues in his images with the skills of a master artist. Linda Nochlin quotes Rupert on this challenge. "It is very difficult to marry politics and technique, difficult to make it work. But I like to work that fine line." Nochlin in writing about Rupert's 1997 exhibit in San Francisco concludes, "García, at a high point in his career, has walked that line—and it is fine indeed; fine in every sense of the word."[66] Lippard concurs: "Both branches of García's work—dynamically activist on one hand and esthetically innovative on the other—are finally interwoven and inseparable, each gaining from the other. Together they prove definitively that art and politics do mix, that in the hands of the gifted their marriage can produce marvels."[67] David J. De la Torre adds that García couples refined skills with an "essential humanism."[68] Terri Cohn comments that the "visual and conceptual sophistication and force of García's images enable them to state their case in eloquent ways."[69] Robert Flynn Johnson contributes his assessment of García's artistry by noting that "García has bridged the usually uncrossable chasm between a truly accessible art for the people and compositional and artistic sophistication."[70] Finally, art critic Alfred Frankenstein writing in the *San Francisco Chronicle* on García's first major exhibit at the San Francisco Museum of Art in 1978 had this to say about García's artistry: "He has a genius for saying the essential thing without a line, a gesture or a touch of color more than necessary."[71]

Because of his sophisticated art, critics also note that over time Rupert García has become one of the finest American artists of his time. Here three quotes are apropos. One is a statement from the Smithsonian American Art Museum in 2022 that concludes:

García has proven himself to be not only one of the most important artists of the last twenty-five years, but an important political force as well. Most of his work has dealt with issues of racism and the mistreatment of Latinos in the United States. His style is direct and powerful; he seeks to be both forceful and readily accessible to a wide audience. Keeping these goals in mind, both García's graphic art and paintings display a skillful unification of the Mexican tradition of Rivera, Siqueiros, and Orozco, with elements learned from European artists and those of the American Pop art movement. García's art has evolved stylistically throughout his career, but he has constantly maintained a strong balance of graphic and "fine art."[72]

Art historian and curator Terezita Romo has this to say:

Throughout his career, García has honed a clarity of vision and a commitment to the exploration of visual elements to deliver powerful multilayered artworks. Distilling various art historical periods and significant cultural touchstones into his work, his art complicates their meaning through his skillful juxtaposition of graphic traditions and painting techniques. The result is a mastery of what I have termed an "aesthetics of the message," in which García seduces the viewer with his artistry while challenging them with the artwork's multivalent references and meanings. As an iconic artist, his body of work has succeeded in simultaneously ignoring and expanding Chicano and American art canons.[73]

Let me conclude this section by quoting from the Godmother of Chicano/Latino art Shifra Goldman when she writes that "García's message, and the skill with which he delivers it, has gained him international renown."[74]

━❙❙━

Besides his art, Rupert García was also a university professor. With his BA in Art, he taught some classes in the early 1970s in La Raza studies and in art at San Francisco State. Later he taught other classes at the San Francisco Art Institute. His more extensive early part-time teaching was in ethnic studies at UC Berkeley. This was after he received an MA in art history from Berkeley. Rupert enjoyed teaching college classes, but these were all part-time. In 1988 he got a chance to be a full-time professor when the School of Art and Design at San Jose State offered him a tenure track position. Not earning enough from his paintings, Rupert accepted it and commenced as an untenured associate professor teaching both undergraduate and graduate classes in oil painting and drawing. In a short time, he was promoted to full professor with tenure. Although teaching full-time affected his painting, he learned to focus on teaching on the days of his classes and then devote his full attention to his painting on his nonteaching days. Full-time teaching did not affect his productivity as an artist. He notes that his teaching provided financial stability for him and his wife. Rupert enjoyed his classes and working with primarily students of working-class background, including some Chicano and Latino ones. He retired from San Jose State in 2010 after twenty-two years.

As a university art professor, García, by his own admission, displayed certain practices with his students. First, he brought to his students a sense of intelligence. By this he means that he stressed using your mind as an artist. "I wanted them to think not just paint," he emphasizes. He wanted them to think about the purpose of their images. He wanted them to be intellectuals and artists. Second, he preached the integrity of the artist, meaning that you should never compromise your principles and values as an artist. You needed to be true to them and not sell them out. Third, you should be proud of being an "image maker" and respect the long history and tradition of other artists. "Don't be ashamed of being an artist; it is an honorable profession," he told his students. Fourth, in working with Chicano students, he told them to avoid in their work stereotyping Chicanos by simply reproducing images of Chicanos as Aztec warriors, for example. "Being a Chicano artist both men and women is not replicating what Chicano artists did during the Chicano Movement. That was then and this is now," Rupert stressed. "You have to be true to yourselves and to your historical moment. There is no or there should not be a prescription about being a Chicano artist." "I gave them 'tough love,'" he says, not only about his Chicano students but all of his students.

When I asked him about his teaching legacy, Rupert responded that "I impressed upon my students that art is serious, very serious, and being an artist can be a very serious way of life if you choose this route." He further added that "my legacy is that I gave all to my students and encouraged them to do the best they could and more." Not only was Rupert García an outstanding artist, but by all indications he was an outstanding professor and teacher.

Just as Rupert García was cognizant of his historical time and reflected this in his art production, it is incumbent on me to add a word about placing Rupert himself in history. There is no question but that the Rupert García that we know or should know is the product of the Chicano Movement and other protest movements of the sixties and seventies. These movements made and continued to make Rupert García the artist. It's true that without these social protest movements, García would have still become an artist, but he would not have become *the* Rupert García. The movement or movements radicalized and encouraged a critical consciousness on García. His initial oppositional silk-screen posters gained attention because of the movements. The Chicano Movement laid the foundation for new opportunities for Chicanos and other Latinos. It opened the doors, for example, to more Chicanos/Latinos attending college. As such, it led to an increase of Chicano/Latino professionals and increased the Chicano/Latino middle class. Into the eighties and further, the legacy of these movements including the Chicano Movement laid the foundation for real Chicano/Latino political power as more were elected into office and more voted. The Chicano Movement made Chicanos into national political actors. This did not mean that racism and inequities affecting Chicanos and other Latinos were eliminated, but it does mean that Chicanos/Latinos had flexed their political muscles and their agency and there was no going back. This protest culture in one form or another continued as it continues today.

Rupert García benefited from these changes. Indeed, he as an artist was part of making these changes. Because of the newfound status of Chicanos/Latinos during the latter part of the twentieth century and into the new millennium, García and other Chicano/Latino artists began to receive more recognition at all levels. Rupert became a nationally and even internationally recognized artist because of the power of the social protest movements. This does not take away from Rupert and other Chicano/Latino artists' talents, but it did assist in providing recognition and access to museums and galleries as artists. Rupert helped make the Chicano Movement and, in turn, the movement made Rupert García.

━ǁ━

The organization of Rupert García's testimonio is chronological. As a life-story, we first cover his childhood in Stockton in Chapter 1. We then discuss his school days through high school up to 1959 in Chapter 2. The next chapter deals with Rupert going on to Stockton Junior College for an AA degree in art and then moving to San Francisco in 1962 with friends in the hope of becoming artists, which does not work out due to financial reasons. Chapter 4 focuses on Rupert joining the Air Force in 1962 and being sent to Indochina, where as a security guard he is assigned to a secret Air Force base in

Thailand where bomber planes begin the bombing of North Vietnam as the United States escalated the war in Vietnam. The next chapter, Chapter 5, sees Rupert returning to the United States in 1966 and enrolling at San Francisco State that same year with the goal of getting a BA in art and moving on to become an artist. After he received his degree in 1968 and while enrolled as an MA student in art, the Third World Liberation Strike breaks out with Rupert becoming involved with it. In Chapter 6, Rupert describes his involvement with the Latino community in the Mission District of San Francisco, especially in helping to found La Galeria de La Raza. This is also the period when he produces his significant silk-screen posters. Moving on from the Mission, Rupert in Chapter 7 focuses on engaging in a new pastel medium and the images he produced during this time. Chapter 8 focuses on the fluorescence of his art during the 1980s and early 1990s when he turns to oil painting and becomes more and more recognized as a major American artist. Finally, we cover Rupert's development from the 1990s to the present, highlighted by his involvement with digital art. I include an Afterword to conclude the text.

I also want to call attention to what I refer to as inserts in Rupert García's testimonio. By inserts, I mean that within the text I have inserted quotes from art critics and art historians as well as quotes from some of Rupert's writings and from other sources. These inserts reinforce or add additional information on Rupert's recollections.

As such, additional voices are brought into the testimonio making it a multivoiced or polyphonous one. The testimonio by itself is already characterized by a double voice in that it is a product of oral history in which my voice as the interlocutor is also in the text but hidden. You don't see my questions to Rupert, only his responses. My questions determine the narrative. The addition of the inserts adds still other voices. I did a similar type of testimonio in my book on Sal Castro and the 1968 Blowouts or walkouts by Chicano students in the East Los Angeles public schools. In that text, I inserted at strategic locations of the narrative the voices of some of the students who walked out. For the Rupert García testimonio I have done the same.

I also want to note my process in creating Rupert García's testimonio. I recorded all of our interviews on a traditional tape recorder using cassettes. This is the way I have always done my interviews. The initial phase of interviews in 1976 were done in person. The second phase in 2022 were done via telephone interviews, which I recorded into my tape recorder still using traditional cassettes. As mentioned, we did fifty hours of interviews. For both phases I had the tapes transcribed. In the first phase, a professional transcriber did the work. In the second phase my undergraduate research assistant transcribed the tapes. I used the transcripts to write the testimonio, sometimes listening to the tapes as well. It is a testimonio because I not only interviewed Rupert but I wrote all of it. He provided me permission to do his testimonio. It was a completely cooperative process.

One further word on writing the testimonio is that it is not as simple as copying the transcripts into a readable narrative. The transcripts are the foundation or the raw material for the narrative, but the creative part of the text is my selecting what parts of the transcripts to include and not just automatically putting them on a page. Instead, I revise or rewrite the transcripts to make them more accessible and readable. In selecting what parts of the transcripts will undergo this process, in effect I am authoring the narrative. This includes inserting fictional dialogue but based on Rupert's story. I attempt to stay true to Rupert's voice, which is why I listen to the tapes as I go over the transcripts to have his voice in my head when I write his story. In so doing, I have to assume Rupert's persona. As noted, there is a dual authorship involved in writing a testimonio. Rupert's authorship is in the recorded tapes and in the transcripts. My authorship is the actual writing of the narrative into a book.

■-II-■

I want to conclude this Introduction by noting personal connections between Rupert García and me. Of course, we share the same surname, although we are not related. It has been an honor and pleasure to work with Rupert over all these many years. In the process, we have become very good friends and supporters of each other. I have also learned much about the art world from him. Doing Rupert's testimonio has broadened my range in testimonial writing. This testimonio has brought us together as friends and collaborators. We are also part of the same biological generation in that we are only three years apart in age. At the same time, we are likewise part of the same historical and political generation—the Chicano Generation. We became Chicanos due to the movement. As such, we share much of the same political and social views. I see myself as a liberationist historian in that I have a preference of working on the history of oppressed Chicano people. I consider Rupert to be a liberationist artist for focusing in his work on issues of oppression and racism. In my other testimonios as well as my other books, I have focused on people that I admire and have an affinity toward. The same applies to Rupert. Although I am not an artist, Rupert and I share being university professors with Rupert in art and me in Chicano studies and history. Both of us have a strong work ethic. We are always working on our projects and thinking of new ones. We are committed to our work. We further hold to high standards for ourselves and for our colleagues and students. Rupert sought to become the best Chicano/Latino artist and I sought to become the best Chicano historian. Finally, we have both been prolific in our work. Both our works spans seven decades and we are still working. It is for me an honor that one of these works is this collaborative testimonio.[75]

1

Stockton Boy

I have a long and involved family history. My becoming a Chicano artist during the Chicano Movement and of the other political upheavals and struggles of the sixties (spilling into the seventies) has a long evolution. But it certainly starts with my family.

My grandparents on both sides reflect different aspects of the Chicano experience. My mother's parents, José Ruperto Atilano Peña and María Guadalupe Cuevas Juarequin Atilano, are from Jalostotitlán, Jalisco, near Guadalajara. They were born around 1867. Jalostotitlán means Land of Sandy Caves in Nahuatl. On my father's side, my grandmother, Pascuala Orozco García, was born in El Paso, Texas, in 1903 while my grandfather, José Cruz García, was born in Fresnillo, Zacatecas, in 1891 and later migrated across the border. So, both families represent, on the one hand, the immigrant experience and, on the other, the U.S. born with deep roots in the Southwest.

It turned out that my grandmother Guadalupe was an artist in her own right. I learned later that this was a family tradition. As a boy, I remember that Grandma Lupe made figurines such as animals and people but out of Kleenex. She would sit on the carpet in the living room and my siblings and I sat around her. She would pull Kleenex from the cuff of her long-sleeved dress and start twisting it, and all of a sudden there appeared these animals and people. I was absolutely amazed; it was magic. I couldn't believe it. I never called any of this "folk art" because it's not. It was not designed to be sold at trinket stores or all that kind of nonsense.

So, art goes back in my family history, especially from my mother's side. I think this context really began to influence me as an artist.

◼▐◼

Eventually both sides of my family came to California. My mother's parents—my grandparents—were already married and they came in the early twentieth century fleeing the ravages and dislocation of the Mexican Revolution of 1910. They crossed the border as exiles from the revolution. Somehow, they wound up in Manteca, California, in the San Joaquin Valley.

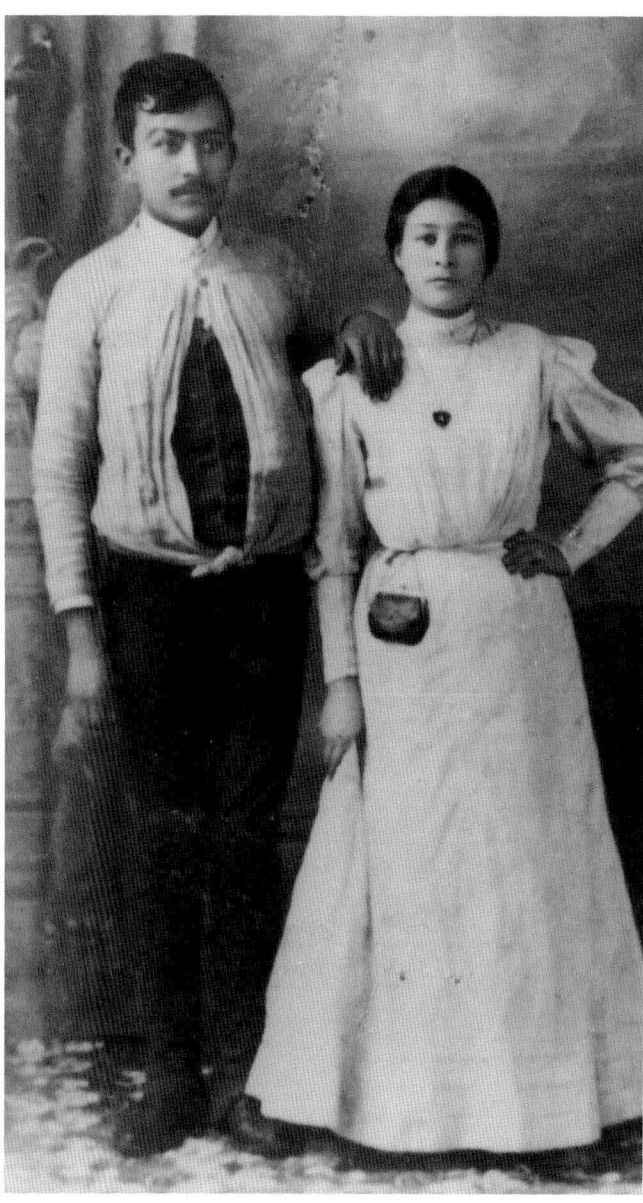

Rupert García's maternal grandparents, Ruperto Atilano and Guadalupe Atilano, Jalostotitlán, Jalisco, Mexico, late nineteenth century. Photo courtesy of Rupert García.

Manteca is near Modesto, which is near Stockton in the northern part of the valley. Stockton, where I grew up, was the larger town or city in this region.

But it was in Manteca where my grandparents started their family. There were five siblings including my mother Dolores Atilano García, but one of her brothers died as an infant.

So later my brothers and I were raised by three tías, Teresa, María, and Romana, and my tío Joe.

I know much less about my father's family because my parents parted shortly after my two brothers and I were born. My father, Francisco García, was born in Atwater, California, in 1920 but never played a consequential part of our upbringing. I never learned from him about his family history. All I know is that his father left Fresnillo, Zacatecas, and his mother left El Paso, Texas, for California. I'm not sure what my paternal grandfather did for a living in California.

My mother and her three sisters and brother attended elementary school in Manteca and then Manteca High School, and this was the extent of my mother's education which, however, at that time was actually a great achievement. I know little about my father's education.

My mother, like my father, was fully bilingual. However, my maternal grandparents did not speak English; they never learned it. They never spoke anything but Spanish. This later amazed me. It was just a fact.

My parents met either in Manteca or Stockton at some social function like a dance. They dated, fell in love, and married around 1938. They both were very attractive young people, just really good-looking people, as photos of them at the time show.

My older brother, Paco, was born one year later in 1939. His full name is Frank Cruz García Jr. Two years later, I came along on September 29, 1941. I was baptized Marshall Rupert García. Marshall was my baptismal name and came from some Catholic saint, I think. My middle name comes from my maternal grandfather, Ruperto. I never used the name Marshall. It just didn't seem to make any sense to me, and I didn't associate with it at all. I also never had a nickname, just Rupert, although some of my relatives called me Ruperto. Later when I was

in the Air Force they had to go by my full official name, and so I was Marshall García with the exclusion of Rupert. However, I told my friends in the military to just call me Rupert because "if you say Marshall I won't respond. Although if you have more stripes than I do or if you're an officer and you call me Marshall I will definitely respond!"

My youngest brother, Godfrey Joseph García, followed me. He was born in 1942. I believe we were all born in the public San Joaquin General Hospital in French Camp, located just outside Stockton. French Camp is as big as the snap of a finger. You go through it, and if you blink you miss it. That's where all the working-class families went to have their babies because it was affordable. Middle- and upper-class families—mostly Anglos— probably went to private hospitals in Stockton.

After my little brother was born, my father joined the Marine Corps on October 7, 1944, during World War II. I have no idea if my father saw military action. As I understand it, sometime before or after he was discharged on December 6, 1945, my parents separated. Besides my father, my uncles— my tíos—went into the military during World War II or the Korean War era, some in the Marines, the Navy, and the Army. Fortunately, my dad and my other tíos returned with no serious physical wounds, although perhaps psychological ones.

My memories of living anywhere begin when my mother moved us three boys and grandma Lupe from Manteca to Stockton. We lived in South

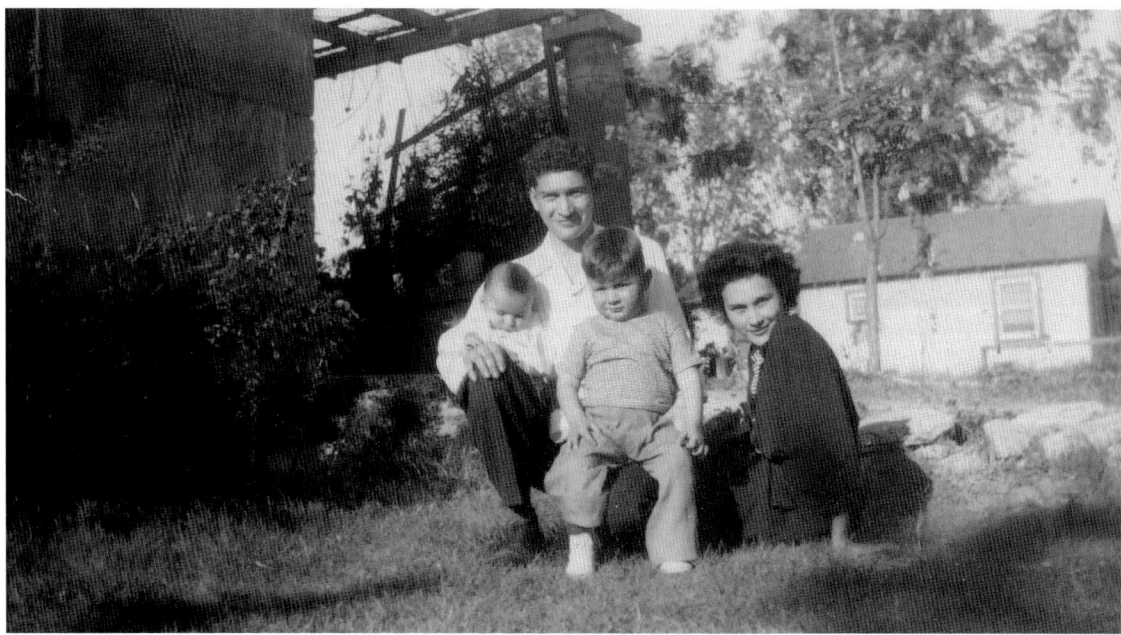

Rupert García's parents, Dolores Atilano García and Francisco García, with older brother Paco and Rupert, Manteca, California, 1941. Photo courtesy of Rupert García.

Stockton—referred to as the South Side and some called it Dogpatch—a very working-class area. Following the family move, my mother got a job at the meatpacking plant located near where we lived. We first lived on First Street in a very small house—very small. I'm amazed how my mother, my grandmother, three kids, and a piano could have fit in this tiny space.

Our small house was located near the railroad tracks. I loved hearing the sounds of the trains riding the tracks and the sound of their horns. To this day, I have an enormous affection for trains. The tracks were less than fifty yards away from our house and the railroad roundhouse was also nearby, and so as a kid, hearing the trains, seeing the trains, and then walking to the train roundhouse was just a part of

the natural environment as trees were. I loved going to look at the trains. I especially liked their sounds at night when I was in bed. It was wonderful and I loved it. I had a great romance with trains. It was as if I was going off to distant places.

While my brothers and I overall were good kids, we sometimes got into mischief. On one occasion my little brother and I were playing in a big field between our house and the railroad tracks. It was summertime and the grass in the field was dry and yellowish brown. I can still see the color of the straw-colored grass. Foolishly, we were playing with matches, and sure enough the grass caught fire. It was a hell of a fire. We had a great time watching the burn. We didn't freak out. Fortunately, we were able to put it

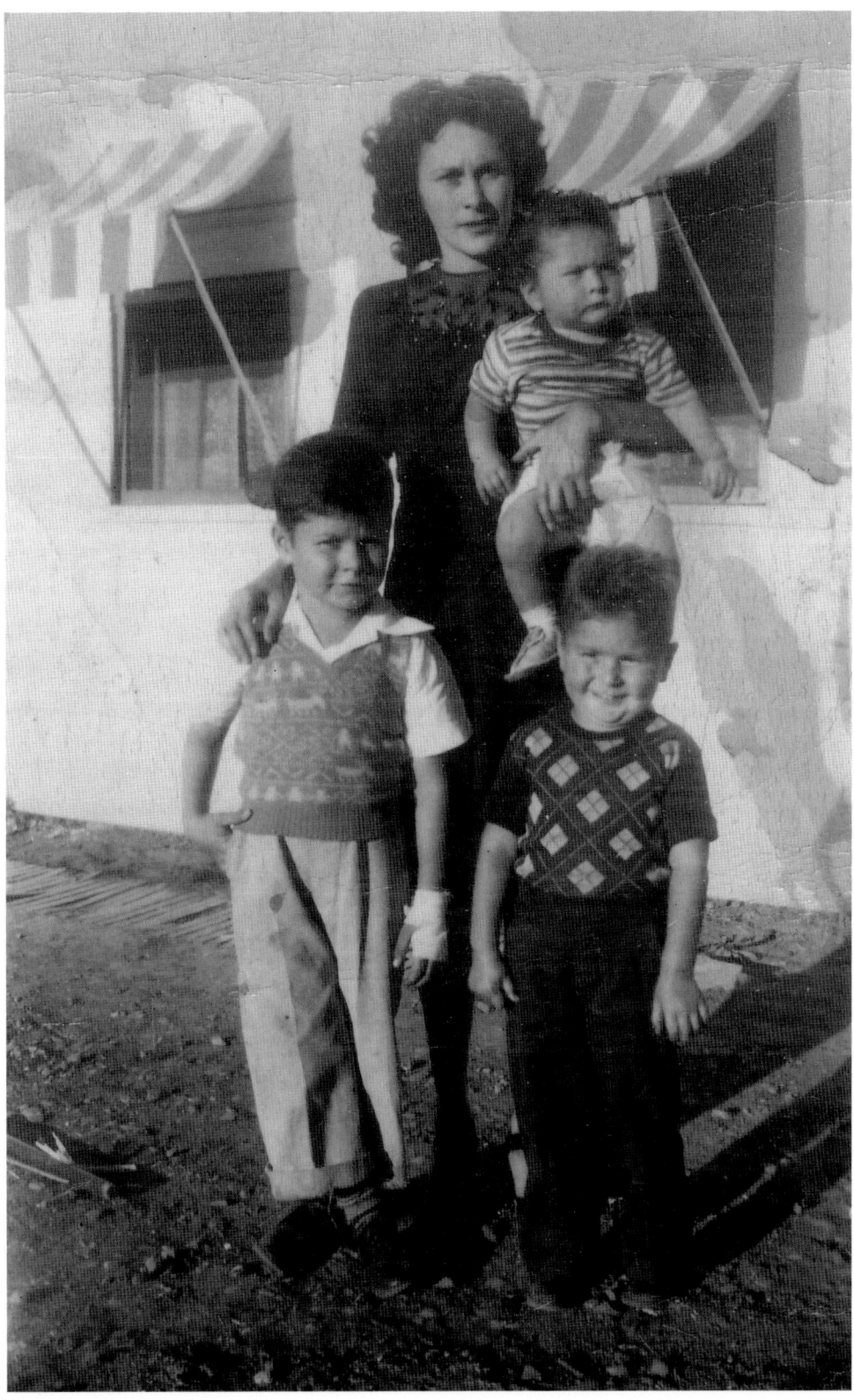

Rupert García's mother and Rupert on the right and brothers Godfrey (in mother's arms) and Paco (left), circa 1940s. Photo courtesy of Rupert García.

out before it spread to the entire field. In fact, my grandmother Lupe saw the fire from our house and quickly came to help us put it out. But, boy, did me and my brother pay a price for what we did. Still, I was fascinated with fire and the colors of fire, and this later inspired some of my art.

As a way of making sure that we did not get into trouble, my mother told us the story of La Llorona, the legend of the weeping Mexican woman who killed her children and wandered throughout the world in search of them at night. My mother's dramatic version went as follows: "You can hear her crying and wailing," she told us, "and you better be good or else La Llorona will come for you and take you away." She told this story not only to my brothers and me, but to the neighborhood kids as well. It put the fear of God or of La Llorona in us. She would tell us this story as it was getting dark. So, all of the other kids were afraid to go home, because who knew what might be out there. We, of course, were also scared. My mother was a great storyteller and told us other stories as well. She was amazing.

After we had lived in this very small house for a few years, we moved across the street to a larger house. By comparison, this new house, which we also rented, seemed palatial. Eventually, my mother was able to afford to buy a house at 58 West Sixth Street in southside Stockton.

Through these early years, we always interacted with our extensive family on both sides. We would often

visit with my father's parents and our tías and tíos and our cousins. My paternal grandparents lived in Stockton as did most of their children, while others lived in Modesto. In fact, these would be among the occasions when we visited with our dad. My mother never prevented us from visiting or being with our father or his side of the family. Never. But my relationship with my dad changed over time. At first it was good and warm, but then it became strained. My father was not one who openly expressed affection; he was guarded with his emotions.

—II—

As part of our extensive family on both sides, I was very close to some of my tíos as I grew up. I had several uncles and was influenced in different ways by each one of them. One was my Uncle David (Yrungary) who was married to my Aunt Mary, my mother's sister. David was the first in the family who went to college. He was a big man with curly hair and bronze skin. He was originally from Arizona. I always found him to be a very nice man, a gentleman, and very intelligent. He and Aunt Mary eventually cared for my grandmother Lupe.

One particular memory that I have of Uncle David that impressed me was when he built a barbecue pit for us in our backyard. He constructed it out of adobe bricks, hay, and water, which he made himself by hand. He mixed mud with straw to construct the bricks. He explained to me that this was an ancient Indian tradition in Arizona and other places as well. This struck me because in growing up, the only conscious acquaintance I had about Indians outside the family came from movies, television, cartoons, or comic books. These representations, I later understood, were racist and stereotypical. But here was Uncle David giving me a lesson in Indian artistry. No one had ever talked to me about architecture, especially that which came from Indigenous influences. This was very interesting to me. I later also came to understand that much of the food we ate at home such as tortillas, beans, tamales, and chili were also from the Indians. This affected my own sense of being Mexican as I moved on in life.

Uncle David and Aunt Mary later moved to Oakland where he worked as an engineer for the State of California, especially on freeway construction. I was sent to visit with them, and this was also impressive to me, because this was the first time I saw a big city. This was in the mid to late 1950s. Oakland at the time was a booming city. This was also the first time I saw San Francisco. They drove me across the Bay Bridge, and there in its entire splendor was the most beautiful place I had ever seen. I immediately fell in love with the city and vowed that I would live there at some time, which I would. San Francisco stole my heart, as Tony Bennett's famous song goes: "I left my heart in San Francisco." I couldn't believe what I was seeing. The physicality of San Francisco just gleamed before my eyes.

I was further impressed with David as an engineer. On my visits with him, he would show me areas where he was helping to build the freeway. What was impressive to me was not the actual construction but that my uncle was building it. It gave me a sense that members of my family, such as Uncle David, were important people and who through their talents were contributing to society. He and my other tíos and tías were hardworking people. They, like Uncle David, became role models for me. This was, as I look back on it, important to me, for I had loving, strong, smart, and diligent male and female role models.

Another uncle who I was impressed with was Uncle Fred. He was married to my Tía Teresa, another of my mother's sisters. Fred worked at the local cannery in Stockton as a mechanic. He was an excellent cook, especially with Mexican food. He had a great smile and a great laugh. He always cut his hair short like a porcupine, which is in style today. His friends called him "Porky." He loved baseball and played it very well. He played for the Stockton team in what was called the Mexican-American League, consisting of Mexican American teams from the San Joaquin Valley. Some of my other tíos and later my older brother played in this league. I especially liked when Uncle Fred drove me and my brothers to the mountains to play in the snow during wintertime. My mom didn't drive, and so our uncles like Fred would take us in their cars on family excursions. Just great!

As I was growing up, I was also impressed by this richly colored Mexican blanket in Fred and Teresa's home. It was beautiful and stunning. It had all of these unbelievable colors: blue, red, yellow, and green. These were solid saturated colors. Some of the colors were what one could describe as florescent. They dazzled my eyes. I have always been moved by color, and I would later employ rich colors in my art. I think this influence in part came from this Mexican blanket in Fred's house. I would also see these colors at local Mexican *jamaicas* or fiestas and on piñatas at family birthday parties. My Grandma García also made colorful dresses for the local Ballet Folklorico. But the most colorful was Fred's blanket. Whenever I see a similar sarape, I think of Fred.

As a boy my tío John Xavier Fernández, whose sister was the legendary Dolores Huerta, spoke to me in a very serious tone. He discussed with me man's inhumanity to man. I didn't quite grasp it, but I knew it was of consequence. John married Romana, my mom's sister.

All of my tíos influenced me in one way or another, including my sense of aesthetics, style, discipline, and love of colors. However, this influence went beyond this. Not only were they father substitutes, but they and my aunts created a wonderful extended family culture and atmosphere that I appreciated and still do. I was from a "fatherless" family but never a broken family, because they compensated for this through their presence and their love. We were *familia*.

━ll━

But I was also influenced by my tías, my aunts on both sides of the family.

They were particularly special because I got more of my creative sense from them. I received from them the practice and discipline of making things, all the way from making food to designing and making clothes and feathered hats to singing, dancing, and making images. This was part of their everyday lives, and it influenced me very strongly. The men were creative, of course, but they weren't as openly creative the way the women were. I was close to the women, my tías. I just let myself be open to their various creative acts that struck many chords within me.

My tías on my mother's side of the family intensely influenced me. For example, Teresa Atilano Avila made clothes for her family. I remember watching her make design patterns for a shirt or a dress or a blouse. She then used multi-pattern and colored raw cloth with which she used her paper patterns to produce clothes. Wow! I was beside myself. From seemingly unrelated elements, she fabricated a shirt or a dress. Simply amazing! Tía María Atilano Yrungary created hats out of feathers. Yes, hats out of feathers! As I recall, she made a lot of them. I would watch her completely focused on her task. Feathers of all sizes and colors, not dyed. I only stayed watching her for just a few minutes. A few hours or sometimes a day later or so, a hat was made. Like watching their mother, grandma Lupe, I was surprised by the transformation of different materials into an object having its own defined presence. Tía Romana Atilano Fernández, the youngest of my mother's sisters, was a very good singer in the style of Ella Fitzgerald. She sang a lot and I loved it, and I couldn't believe how wonderful and pure she sang. Sometimes she would sing in Spanish. It was a sound coming from within her to my ears and heart. Really great!

On my father's side, the tías were equally creative. This included the act of cooking, which was very important, exciting, and rich in the ways they approached it. Some of my aunts also danced, especially Mexican folkloric dances. My grandmother García was also involved in the local Ballet Folklorico. She would make all the outfits by hand and produced the dancers' colorful wardrobes with intricate designs. Just absolutely marvelous stuff. Whenever I visited grandma García, I would always look for the dancers' exciting wardrobe. The backyard had a raised dance floor where the troupe practiced. Sometimes when I made a visit, they would be rehearsing in full-dress colors; very exciting to hear the music and see the dancing bodies and moving colors. The best dancer was my tía Bambi (Aviviana), a nickname she picked up from the Walt Disney film. With this kind of creative family influence, it just seemed natural for me to get involved in something artistically. It was so natural that I didn't even think of it. It just happened because the context was such that it just made sense to do that. As a little boy, I felt that it was important to make art as opposed to understanding it. Later, I understood what it was about, but as a young person, it was just a strong feeling of wonder and magic.

Part of the influence from my tías and from the women in my family had to do with the production of food. I later had a better sense of the genealogy of food. Where does it come from? What does it symbolically represent? What my tías were expressing in their cooking was that this food is Mexican. But not only is it Mexican, it is significantly Indigenous. That has always been something very important to me. This food we ate kept us alive, yet it was not only about sustenance. Metaphorically and symbolically, it represented the history of a people. The food acknowledged one's heritage, one's legacy, and that rang very deeply for me when I began to reflect on this later in my life. As a child it was just food, but it became something much more important to me later.

But even in growing up, this food influence affected me in positive ways. I was never ashamed that my mother made bean burritos for my school lunch even though the Anglo kids had baloney sandwiches on white bread. Feeling bad about the food I ate such as frijoles and arroz would mean that I felt bad about my family. But I didn't. Mexican food was a way of life for me but in a very positive way. I never hated myself for being mexicano. I called myself Mexican as did everyone else in our families and friends in the neighborhood. It was in school that I became American, but never at the same time feeling negative about also being Mexican. I think I avoided this self-hate because there was no reason to. The strength of my extended familial cultural context and how this nourished me not only physically but spiritually and creatively helped to make me accepting of myself.

—II—

Outside of my mother, my maternal grandmother Guadalupe was a major influence on me. She was a very slight woman. I don't think she was more than four foot tall. She wore her hair pulled straight back in a ponytail with a bun. I wear what little hair I have left like this now. She always wore full dresses with long sleeves. They were plain in their pattern designs and color, nothing very exciting. I never recall seeing the skin of her legs. She always wore stockings that were opaque and light caramel in color. She never wore nylons. In skin color she wasn't very dark or very light but somewhere in between. My grandmother Lupe also had a great smile. She had glaucoma and had to wear these dark glasses that looked really chic. She, however, contrasted with her husband, my maternal grandfather, Ruperto, who was dark-complected and taller than her.

Grandma Guadalupe lived with us for many years after tío Ruperto died and always had her own room for privacy. In her room she had an *altarcito*, a home altar on top of her dresser. She was a devout Catholic who always seemed to be praying. Every night she gathered me and my brothers to pray with her in Spanish. I found her home altar to be very visually impressive. It had candles and pictures. Later I became aware that her altar was a homage to her husband, my grandfather. She never remarried. She never lost

her love for him and prayed for him or perhaps to him. She had a picture of my grandfather on the altar, although the main picture in her bedroom was that of Our Lady of Guadalupe, the patron saint of Mexico and Mexicans wherever they are. After she died, I got her picture of Our Lady that she had brought from Mexico, and I still have it. It's in my home studio. Because my grandmother's name was Guadalupe, I conflated her with La Virgen. I used to think that my grandma was Our Lady of Guadalupe. My grandmother was very saintly. Little did I know then that I would do my own pastel painting of Our Lady called *La Virgen y Yo* (1984). It was my own homage not just to La Virgen but also to my Grandmother Guadalupe.

Grandma would also take me to the movies. There were two Mexican movie theaters in Stockton that showed Mexican films in Spanish. We went to the one located in Stockton's skid row. She liked to see comedies such as those starring Tin Tan or Cantinflas, the Mexican Charlie Chaplin. We'd ride the bus downtown to where the theatre was located. We went on Saturdays. It was just wonderful being with her. She only took me and there is no doubt that among me and my two brothers, I was her favorite. She'd buy us some popcorn with a soda, and we watched these characters go crazy on the big screen. It was just amazing. I always felt very, very close to my grandmother. It was a treat to sit in the theater next to her. I loved seeing the blown-up figures on the big screen, and this may have influenced the size of my paintings later. I particularly liked Cantinflas. I couldn't say what especially drew me to him beyond the fact of how he looked with his little mustache and his funny hat and hair.

Interestingly, right across from the theater was where Alice Richards lived and where she owned and operated a small hotel largely for transients. Alice was the mother of Dolores Huerta. Her mother's first married name was Fernández and she was originally from northern New Mexico. We all knew each other so before or after the movies, my grandma and I stopped to visit. The hotel fascinated me. From the perspective of a little boy, it was large with all of those rooms. Once as Alice and Grandma were talking, I stole away and opened the door to one of the rooms. Thank God that no one was in there. It was amazing to see how this one guy lived and what he had in his room. But it seemed like a sad room for a sad guy.

Grandma Guadalupe, like my tías, was a creative person. She made those figures out of tissue paper. I think what really affected me in these early years was a sense of the magic of transformation, of how they could make something almost out of nothing. It was like magic. Magic became very important to me. My mother told us those stories of La Llorona as well as other magical and mysterious stories. Then my aunts and grandmother created magic through their creative abilities. I didn't know then more about all this, only that it occurred. I couldn't intellectualize or explain this. It was never knowing about how or even why. Just

the fact that it happened and you were deeply moved was enough. This was wonderful because of what it allowed me to do, which is to believe in magic, mystery, the inexplicable. I'm thinking of the art my tías, my grandmother, and my mother created. To this day I have faith in the mystery of real magic, and I just accept it without questions or being analytical about it. I didn't find this same magical and mystery experience in the Catholic Church with all of its rituals and ceremonies. There is also no mystery or magic to the causes of social injustice, racism, economic inequality, and so on.

I think all this made me see life as extraordinary. I still have that strong feeling that whatever the circumstances are, that it's an extraordinary experience. Just talking to someone I get that feeling. I can't totally understand it and I don't care. It's just amazing nevertheless, and this goes back to my childhood and seeing my family culture, especially the role of the women, in extraordinary ways. Life is amazing and they gave me that sense.

━ǁ━

But of all the women in my family and of everyone in my family, my mother was the most important person in my life. She gave everything to me and my two brothers. She loved us dearly and we loved her dearly. My mother was a good mother and person. She raised three boys, and we could be difficult, and took care of her mother, Grandma Guadalupe. At the same time, she had to work full time to provide for us. All this was very hard for her, but she did it and did it without complaining. As children, my mother never let on that anything was financially or personally troubling her. As far as I was concerned, I was living a good life, trouble free.

She worked at the local meat plant and was probably among the first women to do so, because meatpacking jobs were traditionally for men. Her work was not clerical, it involved working with meat in various capacities. It was also a good paying job and she further had access to all the meat that she could bring home. We always had steaks and other cuts of meat. She did tough and menial work, but she was a good, hard worker. There wasn't a lazy bone in her body.

Despite her work, she carried out her family responsibilities. She always gave us clean clothes, enrolled us in school, came home and made dinner, paid the bills, told us stories, and helped us to learn how to play the piano. Despite her divorce from my dad, she never spoke badly about him. She never discouraged us from loving him. No matter how strained her relations with my dad, she never cussed him. I always loved her for this because whatever reason caused them to split, it was beyond the control of me and my brothers. The divorce was between my mother and father and not between him and us. She never encouraged us to hate him, and that was really wonderful. My mother was also a very attractive woman, always stylish with long hair and makeup. She would go out dancing with her friends.

My mother loved to read and always had books around the house, and she encouraged us to read as well. She also liked to draw, as I did at an early age. In fact, early in her life, my mother wanted to be an artist. My mom used to help me draw; we used to sit together and draw. I loved doing this with her. My mother made it "cool" for me to draw. She always encouraged us about what interested us, such as sports or schoolwork. She was always positive. The only time that she was discouraging had to do with anything that might have a bad influence on us. This particularly had to do with drugs in the barrio.

"You're never to do drugs," she told us as we grew up.

Drugs were a problem. It was mostly marijuana, but there was also heroin and cocaine.

"If you start doing drugs you will not be able to control your life," she said and said it strongly.

This really hit me. Like, wow, I don't want to do anything that will overwhelm me and get me out of control. My mother just wanted to make sure that we knew her point of view on drugs, and it stuck, boom. None of us three kids ever did hard drugs. Yes, later in high school, we did a little pot but not that much. We always had my mother's warnings in our ears.

However, my mother did more than warn us; she disciplined us when she had to. As a kid I could be *travieso* or naughty. My mother had no problem in spanking me or my brothers. She was no-nonsense about discipline. At the same time, my mother was open to things we wanted to do as long as they weren't self-destructive or destructive to our family. Otherwise, she was very open, and I always felt free to think and feel what I wanted to within certain boundaries.

My mother likewise influenced us in language. We spoke Spanish to grandma, but my mother insisted that we speak English with her. She was completely bilingual, but she probably had had some bad experiences in speaking Spanish at school where kids were punished for doing so, including being paddled. This was common in the segregated "Mexican schools" of the Southwest. These were segregated and inferior public schools in Mexican American barrios. "Americanization" or assimilation was the name of the game at this time. In Manteca, my mother attended an integrated school. However, Mexican Americans in these schools were also punished for speaking Spanish. My mother didn't want us to have such bad experiences, and so she made sure we spoke English before we went to school and spoke it well.

At the same time, she didn't have anything against us retaining some of our Spanish. Obviously, we spoke it with grandma at home. However, because of our mother's promotion of English, we began to lose some of our facility in speaking Spanish. It got to the point that I was embarrassed to speak Spanish to some older Spanish-speaking relatives or family friends who spoke mostly Spanish. I didn't want to embarrass myself with them. Still, I tried to do so and was relieved that none of them ever berated me or my brothers for our lack of facility in Spanish. They never complained to my mother about our lack of Spanish. That was wonderful because if they had, we would have felt bad about ourselves and might have developed insecurities and self-hatred. I much later remember reading Richard Rodriguez's now classic memoir *Hunger of Memory* and how the young Richard was frowned upon by Spanish-speaking relatives when he could not speak Spanish to them or spoke incorrect Spanish. Richard grew up not too far away in Sacramento.

Nothing Mexican, including Spanish, was ever denigrated in our home. We were made to feel good about ourselves. My mother's own command of Spanish and her bilingual abilities later helped her move out of the meatpacking plant and get a job as a saleswoman and an interpreter at the local J.C. Penney department store.

My mother, like my grandmother, was also very religious, and this affected us. She wasn't as extreme as grandma, but she was in her way very devout. She was Catholic and attended church a good deal. She made sure we were baptized, made our First Holy Communion, and received Confirmation. We always attended Sunday Mass. We first attended Mass at St. Mary's in the downtown area until they build St. George's closer to where we lived.

I'm sure my mother wanted us to go to Catholic schools, but she couldn't afford to send us, or at least not all of us. The exception was Paco, my older brother. He was an extraordinary athlete, and I think my mother made some kind of agreement with the local

Catholic high school in Stockton, St. Mary's, for Paco to go to school and play sports. The coaches really wanted him. The school apparently waived the tuition, or most of it, for him. Paco was very special. He was very handsome, a killer in good looks. He became a star player for the school in all of the major sports. After he graduated, he joined the Marines. On his return, he went to community college and got his degree. I was and am so proud of him for doing that.

My mother was religious, but I personally was not as religious. I never felt that the Mass was particularly special, at least to me. I remember even as a kid rejecting being told in Catechism class that only Catholics would be saved in heaven. That didn't seem right. I had some friends who were Chinese and Japanese. I was very close to them. They were my friends. I couldn't understand why Jesse Oji and Jim Young were evil or bad because they weren't Catholic. I couldn't accept this and didn't. It just didn't seem right. It really began to turn me off to organized religion. How could I be faithful to a religion that was hypocritical? At the same time, Catholicism didn't accept and validate different religions.

What did make sense to me, religiously, was Our Lady of Guadalupe. I identified her with Grandma Guadalupe. By contrast, Jesus meant little to nothing to me. Jesus was like, I don't know what that is. But La Virgen was strong and powerful. I didn't think of her as the Holy Mother of God. It was La Virgen de Guadalupe and her connection with my grandmother. This is

why La Virgen was special to me. She became something I could really feel deeply about. It meant something. And she was everywhere, in my grandma's bedroom and in the Mexican churches in the barrios. She, to me, was more vital than Jesus Christ. I was amazed by her image. By contrast, I found the image of Jesus unexciting. I loved the colors of the Virgen image. Wonderful blues, yellows, greens, pinks. No doubt part of my attraction to La Virgen was visual; it was spectacular. I loved that little angel holding up La Virgen. It's magical and amazing. I didn't question this image. I questioned Jesus Christ but not La Virgen. Many years later I visited the basilica of La Virgen in Mexico City and found it mind-boggling. To see the purported actual image displayed and to see all these penitents and pilgrims venerating her and some entering on their knees was incredible. It just reinforced my love affair with La Virgen, which I have never lost.

Actually, after my brothers and I were confirmed, my mother told each one of us: "I have raised you as Catholics and I hope you will always be Catholics. However, you can now make your own decisions about going to Mass each Sunday. That's up to you."

I appreciated my mother giving us this freedom and not insisting that we had to continue going to Mass. I felt in fact liberated. From then on, I rarely went to Mass and don't now.

As part of my own creative development and influenced by my mother's cooking and that of my tías, I at five years of age made faux tamales out of mud. I was assisted by my brother Godfrey and cousin Gus. Instead of the *masa* used for real tamales, we used mud. We also grinded together red bricks to make a red powder, which when mixed with water looked like *mole* or red sauce. It was like paint. We then tore off the covering of corn to use to hold our mixture together. It was exciting to see what we were creating. It was magic. Of course, we didn't eat our "tamales" but played with them. Many years later I recounted this experience to a journalist, and I told him: "I think that early experience really put me in touch with the profundity of the imagination to have the ability to investigate or to create without being inhibited and it was just a wonderful thing."[1]

My mother was a wonderful and loving person. She had overwhelming love for her children, and she went the extra mile for us. She was very special, and I loved her deeply.

My mother as a mother was perfect, but as a person she was capable of making what I saw as errors. This especially involved her remarrying. It wasn't that she should not have remarried, but that I felt she married the wrong guy. She married a white guy when I was in high school. The issue wasn't that he was white, but that he was troublesome.

My mother asked my two brothers and me, "Would you boys mind if I remarried?"

But we didn't know how to respond. Part of me wanted my mother to be happy, but the other part of me didn't want to lose her to some strange man. Whatever we said or didn't say, she married him anyway.

She had a daughter from this second marriage, my sister Trudy. But her new husband turned out to be a difficult man and heavy-handed, and this had nothing to do with his ethnicity but just who he was. He didn't know how to be around independent teenagers as we were then. He tried to rule with an iron hand. He didn't physically abuse me, but he made life miserable. I and my brothers started to stay away from him and our house as much as possible. He eventually made my mother's life miserable. I don't think he ever hit her, but he verbally abused her. The only good thing out of this marriage was Trudy. She is great, and I love her very much.

When I began to get interested in becoming an artist and started drawing and painting at home, my stepfather confronted me.

He roughly asked: "Why are you doing this stuff for anyway? How is this going to get you a job, a real man's job?"

I said, "Screw you man. I don't give a shit what you think!"

I must have replied so strongly that he just turned and walked away.

Unfortunately, it took my mother twenty years to finally break with this guy and divorce him. She should have done this much earlier. She lost so many precious years. But at least she had Trudy.

One thing about my mother that I didn't really know or appreciate until much later was how much she was involved in the Mexican American community. She had leadership qualities and put them in support of the community. During my high school years in the mid to late 1950s, my mother was the president of a group of Mexican American women called *Club Azul y Oro* (Blue and Gold Club). I knew of the group, but I thought for years that it was just a social group of women in the barrio getting together for tea. I later learned that it was much more than this when I found an old newspaper clipping with a picture of my mother announcing that she had been made president of *Club Azul y Oro* and of their community activities. I realized how much my mother was conscientious about racism and discrimination toward Mexican Americans, including immigrants like her parents. Learning later about this side of my mother helped me when I became politically involved in the Chicano Movement and Third World movements. Discovering my mother's commitment to social justice provided me a reference point for my own activism. It ran in the family. But for some reason she never told us how much she was involved in her own social movement with these other women.

—||—

When I look back at my early years in Stockton, I also remember going to the carnival and the county fair. These were exciting events with the colorful lights and the rides. The county fair was very big, and thousands attended from the surrounding area. We got to see farm animals and tractors. They also had horse racing. I likewise remember as I got older going to the big palatial Fox movie theater. You walked in and all the furnishings and rugs were kind of baroque. It was exciting just to be there let alone see the movie. The screen was huge, which complemented the enormity of the theater. Stockton had many other movie theaters, including the Mexican ones plus the drive-in-theater, which me and my friends also called the motor movies. All this before there was TV or at least before we had a TV. Me and my buddies would sneak into the drive-in theaters. This was when I was already a teenager. Once we snuck into one of these theaters because they were showing a Bergman film. We had no idea who Bergman was, but we had heard that foreign films were nasty and we were going to see a lot of naked women. We were happy that a movie finally came to Stockton so that we could have some nasty thrills. We began watching the film with high expectations, but we found ourselves waiting and waiting for these thrills which never came. Nothing happened in this boring film. We were very disappointed. I still remember these Stockton stories.

—||—

With all this a part of my background as a Stockton boy, I began my formal education, although my education had already begun and would continue with my family influences. Still, I looked forward to being in school.

2

School Days

In September of 1948, I started my formal schooling. I began in first grade. There was no kindergarten in the elementary school closest to my home on First Street in Stockton. I was excited to be in school but nervous at the same time. One advantage that I had over other Mexican American kids was that I already knew English. Those kids who were children of Mexican immigrants still spoke mostly Spanish and struggled when they entered school since they didn't know English. Of course, there was no such thing as bilingual education. All the teachers were Anglo Americans.

—||—

My first school was Grant Elementary that went from first to fourth grade. I then attended Jackson Elementary near our home for fifth grade. However, when we moved to Sixth Street, I attended McKinley Elementary for sixth. This was middle school, but it wasn't called as such then. All these schools were what today would be called multicultural schools. They were also multiethnic and multiracial schools, because the students came from diverse backgrounds. There were Anglos of different European backgrounds such as Irish, Italian, and Portuguese. It's actually ironic to refer to the latter two as Anglos because Italians and Portuguese were not fully accepted by the "real" Anglos, those of English, Irish, and German descent. I don't think we even considered the Italians and Portuguese as Anglos. They were somewhere in between Anglos and Mexicans, Asians, and Blacks.

Most of the students including the Anglos were also from working class families such as mine. This diversity had a significant impact on my early life and one which continued to influence me as I grew up. Many of my friends besides being Mexican were also Japanese, Filipino, Black, Portuguese, and Italian. Some of the Japanese Americans were born in the relocation or concentration camps as part of the racist Japanese internment in World War II. This experience gave me a realistic view of the multiplicity of people who exist and occupy the world. It made me avoid being exclusionary and instead inclusive of all peoples.

It's this diversity that I remember the most about these early school experiences. The rest is fuzzy, and I can't think of particular ways that these schools had a specific impact on me. I did fine in my school subjects and learned more English and how to do math and learned something about geography and history. Yet, nothing really seemed to capture my imagination that I can look back and say that it influenced my life, other than the diversity of the students. Overall, it was a positive experience, and there were no major tensions or problems. I do remember two teachers that made some impression on me. There was Mr. Hershel who taught sciences. He was always very supportive of me and other students. Then there was Ms. Esplin who I'll never forget. I'll never forget her because at McKinley in the sixth grade she chose me to lead a group of other students to do a class mural. She taught art as one of her classes, and she at one point talked about the murals in Mexico. I don't remember that she mentioned the great muralists such as Diego Rivera, David Siqueiros, and José Clemente Orozco, but these are the ones she had in mind. This was the first time I had ever heard about artists in Mexico. I had heard from my aunts about the Ballet Folklorico in Mexico, but nothing about art, literature, sculpture, or architecture there.

Ms. Esplin for some reason assigned me to direct the mural. I shouldn't say that I didn't know why. The fact is that I had leadership skills as a kid, and I guess she recognized this in me and had me direct the project. I have

no memories of what we painted or how I directed it. We did it on sheets of butcher paper, maybe three or four sheets that were about six feet high. We must have used a ladder to paint the top of the mural. We did use some kind of paint, and I can't remember the colors. But it was poster paint, not watercolors. I can say that this was one of my first paintings, but the thing is that this mural left no impression on me, and that's why I can't remember the images on it. All I know is that I was made to direct the project, and we did it for better or worse. I had perhaps already shown some inclination to draw but not so much that Ms. Esplin would notice. What I did like about being selected to direct the mural was the attention. Like someone's taking notice of me. That was attractive to me.

It wasn't that I wasn't creative already. I certainly had all those creative influences from my family. I also remember that as a kid I displayed my own creativity. I redesigned my mom's jewelry, and I would take toys apart and put them back together. I also carved little sculptures out of wooden clothespins. It was just that in these early school years before high school, I hadn't yet found my niche. This would come later.

One creative thing that I did do was apply for a job at Walt Disney Studios as a kind of early teenage intern over the summer. To apply, I had to submit a drawing. I chose to draw one of the Walt Disney cartoon figures. I don't recall if it was Mickey Mouse or another character. It was a pencil drawing. The fact was that comic books and

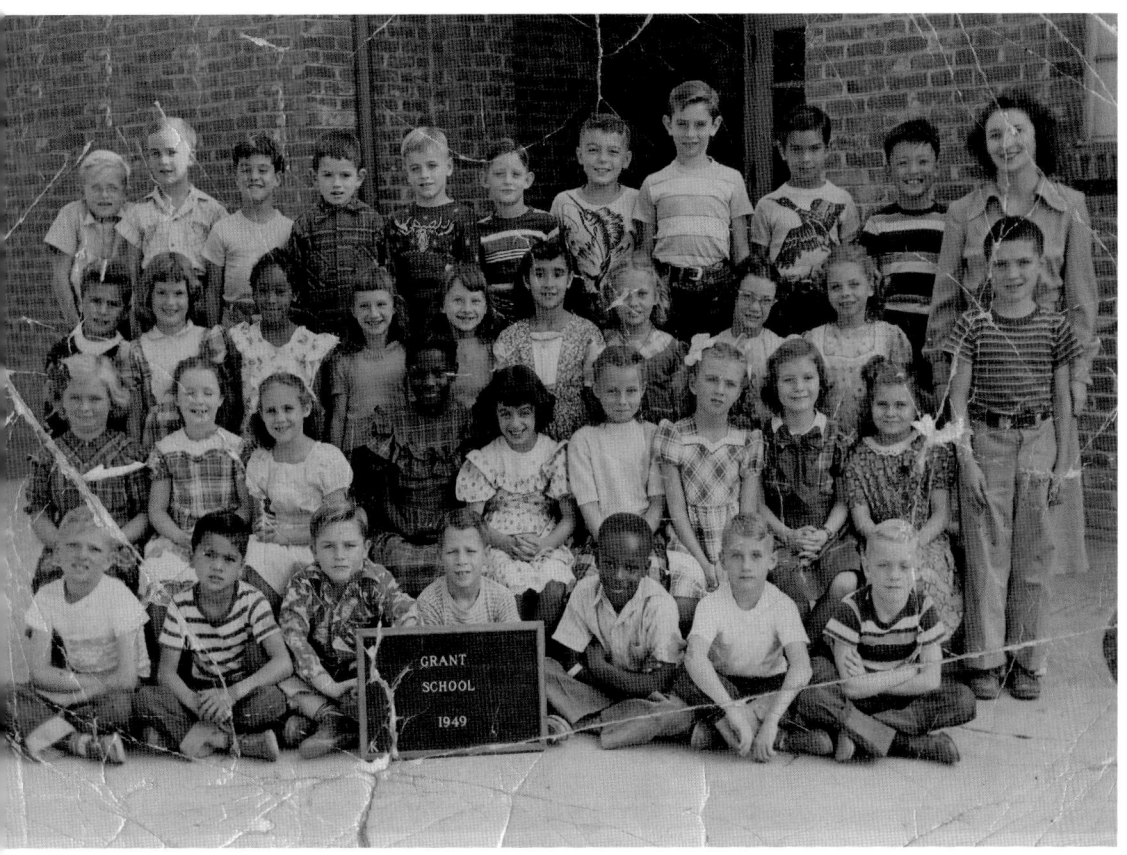

Rupert García, second row from top far left, at Grant School, Stockton, California, 1949. Photo courtesy of Rupert García.

cartoons were very important to me then as a kid for various reasons. For one, I thought the colors of the cartoons especially were beautiful and the clean shapes were exciting plus the unusual sounds made by the characters. I also found exciting the exaggerated behavior of the animated characters. I had high hopes when I mailed off my drawing.

A few weeks later, I received this large manila envelope with my name on it. Wow! It said Walt Disney on the left hand-top corner. I've struck gold I thought. I opened the envelope and I pulled out a letter written to me by none other than Walt Disney. I forget the exact words, but it basically said encouraging things about my drawing and that I should keep it up. Although I realized that it was a rejection letter; what I liked was the encouraging tone of the letter. In addition, they sent me two black and white eight by ten glossy photographs of Donald Duck and another of the Disney characters. I framed them and put them on the walls of our house. I felt good that someone outside the family, outside school, and outside of Stockton responded to something I had made. I was very proud of myself. This encouraged me to think that drawing and making images was of value.

As a kid, I was totally in awe of cartoons that I watched at the movies and of my comic books. It was not only visual but to me it resonated with truth with a small "t." In other words, they seemed real to me. I identified with them. In comic books, I preferred exaggerated characters such as Batman and Superman. There were also a lot of World War II figures and comic books, but I never favored them. I wasn't really attracted to war kinds of things, even though I watched many war movies growing up. What interested me about comic books was the graphic nature of the images, especially the use of color. I found the contrast of black against bright colors striking, which was the intent. They're to charge the viewer's eyes with the immediacy of using flat or one color and contrast color. This got to me visually. As a matter of fact, I would say that my early responses to that kind of aesthetic of comic books and animation have strongly influenced my work. What I loved was that there was no subtlety of the colors; there's no in-between. It's just these bold colors of red, black, blue, yellow, green, and orange. I was impressed by these rich colors. Much later, as I developed as an artist, I also employed such strong use of color. This type of aesthetic was very attractive to me. I was a child of the aesthetics of comic books and animated cartoons. There's no question about that.

As a kid there was also radio and then television. I was fascinated by the radio. I loved the sounds of the radio programs I listened to, the voices and the audio props such as the sounds of galloping horses, water running, and people applauding. I listened to Jack Benny and the Gangbusters. These programs as well as others were fantastic because of the way they sounded. The sounds made you want to listen. But what I also appreciated about radio was that you had to use your own visual imagination in conjuring up the radio stories. I found this very exciting because you were allowed to use your imagination to complete the story. I came to appreciate listening to the news, especially during the Korean War between 1950 and 1952. The news of the war was frightening and disturbing. Listening to music on the radio was a passing thing that you enjoyed and had fun with. But the news on the radio left a mark on me and a lasting impression. The news was real.

By contrast, I wasn't as excited about TV. We first had a black and white set as most people did until color TV came in. Television had both visual and audio, but I have always had an ambivalent feeling about it. For me, television cuts short the asking of one to use the visual imagination, if not imagination in general. We're not asked to use that part of our brain. TV shows do all that for you; there is no dialogue between the TV and the viewer. TV puts no demand on you other than turning off the set or changing the channel. That's why I've always preferred radio. Having said that, I should likewise note that at least black and white TV had the effect on my love of black and white photographs, which would influence my later art. Black and white TV at least allowed me to fill in the colors in my imagination.

Watching cartoons, reading comic books, and listening to radio was part of my informal education. As for the formal part, I liked school. I wasn't alienated from it. I also had school friends. My best friends were Chinese and African American. But it didn't matter to me. Actually, minorities were the majorities in these schools and so almost all of my friends were kids of color. I also liked school because as I grew up, I began to like girls. I didn't have a girlfriend. I was too young for this. However, I did have my first kiss. This must have been in third or fourth grade. I still remember her name, Cheryl Atwater. I walked her home to the corner of her house and then kissed her. This came to nothing, but you don't forget your first kiss.

In grade school we had the usual school experiences. For one, I joined the Cub Scouts. I was about eight years old. Later, and because of racism, I was not allowed to join the all-white Boy Scout troop; I had to be put in an Asian American troop. But something else that I remember in elementary school was reading about the killing of Emmett Till, a Black teenager in the South. He was from the north but in a visit to family somewhere in the South, he was accused of whistling at a white woman. White racists were outraged, and they assaulted Till and killed him. I remember being in the eighth grade around the mid-1950s reading about this in the local newspaper and being shocked that something like this could happen. That you could be killed for whistling at a white woman. Till was my age, so I identified with him. It disturbingly introduced me to racism in this country, which made me more aware as I grew up about race in my own community.

◼ǁ◼

From elementary school, I moved on to Edison High School, which was the closest one to where I lived. It included the seventh and eighth grades as well, which is where I started. Edison was one of three high schools in Stockton. Edison was on the south side; Franklin High was on the east side; Stockton High was on the north side. The south and east side schools contained mostly people of color and were where the white working class lived. The north side was where the rich white folks lived, and they sent their children to Stockton High.

Overall, my high school experiences were positive ones, and I had a great time in these years. At the same time, I was in high school when the civil rights movement began to really surface in the South and other parts of the country, including California. Racial tensions were building up in the country, and my school and Stockton were not immune from them. This included Edison. It involved Blacks, whites, and Mexicans. This puzzled me because I didn't understand why there were these tensions between Blacks and white kids and Mexican kids. It didn't make any sense to me. Why did

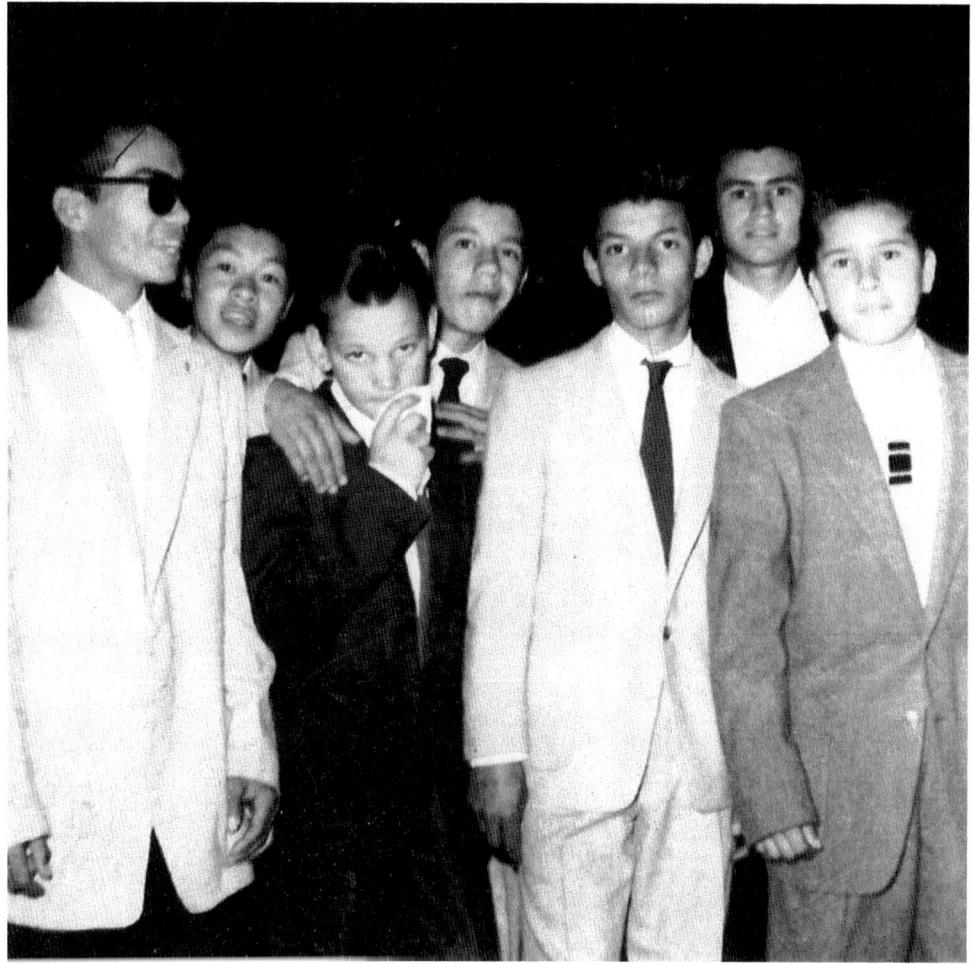

Rupert García, second from right top row, at Edison High School, Stockton, CA., circa 1950s.

we have disruptions from time to time based on race?

It wasn't that such tensions occurred all the time. These were occasional ones that led to shouting confrontations, although never really fights. But you could feel the tension. I always knew about racism, and I always couched it in terms of white supremacy and folks of color. This was understood. However, what I couldn't comprehend were internal bigotry among folks of color. This was confusing to me that Blacks and other minorities such as Mexicans would have negative views of each other and at times confront each other. What was this all about? Why would these groups fight against each other since they were all in the same subordinate position? What are you fighting for? I couldn't see what the prize was.

But having said this, my high school experience was 99 percent positive. For one I had a lot of friends. I always hung around with a multiracial group of Mexicans, Filipinos, other Asians, and some Blacks. I was also a good student—not a great one, but a good one—and I improved from year to year. I was very outgoing and giving to others. I became quite popular and was even elected class president my senior year. I also played sports including football and track, but I was not a star player. Sports were quite the big thing in high school.

There was no question but that sports reigned at Edison as it did in most high schools. At the same time, I was impressed that some students also received recognition in other activities such as art. Some got awards for being artists. I knew some of these guys. One, Raul Mora, got an award. I got the impression that art was an area where you could also get recognition, although this paled by comparison with athletics. While I didn't do a lot of art yet in high school, I hung around some of these artists, including some who were in drama. Many of them were Mexicans and Filipinos. These were nice guys, but they were not my exclusive friends. I also hung around some of the "bad" kids, the kind that stole cars and other bad stuff.

As in most of the other high schools, there existed a tracking system, although I didn't know it by this name. At first, I was put in lower-level classes and not the college prep ones. However, I did well enough in these classes that I was transferred to the more challenging ones. I could feel the shift especially in math and science classes and even in English. I initially struggled but soon got into these classes. In English, for example, what artistic inclinations I had helped me. I especially loved diagramming sentences. It was like drawing language with lines and breaking down sentences into subjects, predicates, adverbs, and adjectives. All of this was a visual way of understanding language. I found it amazing and very exciting. I also did well in my other classes such as Algebra, French, and Spanish. I wasn't a brilliant student, but I did well.

◼️❙❙◼️

In high school, I began to show more interest in art. I had dabbled in this at home where I would make drawings from my mother's movie magazines. These were pencil drawings. I think in my sophomore year I took a class at Edison that was like an introduction to art. I was serious about the class but soon realized that this class was actually a babysitting one for unruly kids so that they could pass some of the day away and not be disruptive in regular classes. These kids were unmanageable. To add to this the teacher, Ms. Campbell, was frightening. She was there not because she knew a lot about art, which she didn't, but to maintain order in a harsh way. If any student got out of line or defied her, she was big and strong and she kicked the butt of such a student. Still, despite this inhospitable climate, I managed to do some drawings. I did a self-portrait in pastel. I liked it but have no idea what happened to it. I didn't understand what I was doing technically, but that wasn't the object, and besides the teacher seemed to know just a little about art techniques.

I later also took a course in mechanical drawing that helped me learn some art techniques. And then in a French class I did a watercolor of the Eiffel Tower, which I still have. The teacher liked it, and she hung it up in the classroom for awhile. It looked nice with pleasant colors, and it resembled the Eiffel Tower. I also started to do some watercolor paintings on my own at home. I was starting to get a little bit more into my interest in art. I also had some friends at school who also liked to draw and paint. We supported one another. With my other friends, they never teased me about it or suggested that it was not "manly" to do art. In fact, some of them were themselves into music, and so they appreciated the arts. Instead, I got positive support that also included my mother. It was all saying "go, go, go." No one said "stop, stop, stop."

At the same time, I have to say that in the art classes I took in my junior and senior years there were no teachers who had any particular influence on me. In fact, I learned a lot on my own. And not just on my own but by interactions with other students interested in art such as Martin Izquierdo, Maurice Rapisura, and Ida López. We along with a few other kindred souls became a tight group.

But the fact was that in high school, I had no real art training as such. The only introduction I had in terms of making things was in industrial trade classes such as woodshop, metal shop, and a couple of courses in drafting, which I enjoyed. That was it. The rest was on my own.

Influenced by my mother's magazines, I started to do portraits of movie stars. One of the best I did was of James Dean, who became an icon with my generation. Films like *Rebel Without a Cause* and *East of Eden* displayed him as an alienated countercultural figure that at some level we could identify with. Certainly, I did. I still have this drawing and it has been featured in some of the art catalogues on my work. I did drawings of other movie stars as well.

I also did a drawing of one of my fellow students that unfortunately got me into trouble. This was a portrait of Beverly Chan, who I had a great crush on. I adored her but unbeknownst to her. I thought she was the sweetest and the finest looking young woman on the earth. As did most of the guys. She was tall, elegant, and beautiful, but she also had this air about her that said, "look but don't touch."

Beverly and I were friends but not close. Somehow, I got her picture. She must have given it to me, but my mind is fuzzy on this. From the photo I drew her image. She had no idea that I had done this, and I never showed it to her. It was like my own private drawing and a way, I suppose, of expressing my feelings toward her. Feelings that she was not aware of and that I was too shy to reveal to her.

But whatever feelings I had or expectations I fantasized about Beverly came crashing down in my senior year when I made a fool of myself at the junior prom. I went as senior president of my class. I went with Lillian Moquiete. We double-dated with my good friend Jim Young and his date Linda. After we settled into our table, Jim and I went outside, where we each proceeded to drink a pint of mint gin. When we walked back into the dance, I spotted Beverly at a reception table. She looked stunning. Why couldn't I be with her? When I sat down all of a sudden, I really felt that gin going to my brain. I was smashed but I felt great. This gave me the false courage to excuse myself and I walked over where Beverly was sitting. But I could feel that I was not walking straight. I reached Beverly and tried to say something, but I couldn't talk straight. Nothing came out correctly. My speech was all garbled. I'm sure she was thinking "what the hell does Rupert want?" I was just so drunk; it was awful.

The next thing I'm aware of is the school principal, Mr. Carl Baker, holding my arm and walking me out of the dance.

"Rupert, you're drunk. You can't come back into the prom. You better get someone to take you home. I'll deal with you next Monday in my office."

The only thing I remember next is walking over to my friend's car in which we had come to the prom and getting in and falling asleep. I don't know how long I slept, probably not very long, because Jim and our dates got into the car and drove me home. I was so drunk. I don't know how I got into my house.

When I woke up the next morning, I realized what a fool I had made of myself. Not only with everyone at the prom, including my date, but especially with Beverly. I knew that any

hope I had or dreamed of a relationship with her was now gone forever.

That Monday I reported to Mr. Baker's office to hear about my punishment.

"Rupert, you really embarrassed yourself and the entire school. I have no recourse but to suspend you for two weeks and to strip you of being class president. I hope you learn your lesson."

"Thank you, Mr. Baker. I know I made a fool of myself, and I understand my punishment. It won't happen again."

When my mother heard of what I had done and my suspension, she was livid and disappointed in me. But there was no need to punish me further; she knew that I had already been punished enough. I promised her also that this would never happen again. And it didn't.

As for Beverly that was the end if there was even a beginning.

Beverly was one of many Asian American students in the school. I was friends with many of them because we all lived close together. Asian Americans were part of the significant diversity of the school as well as of the Stockton community. Many had been farmworkers and some later owned their own farms. Some owned restaurants and other small businesses. One Asian American that I knew, although not well, was Maxine Hong Kingston. She would go on to become a major writer. Maxine was a year ahead of me although her sister was in my class. Maxine was brilliant as a student. We came to know each other better years later when we both became better known as artists. We reminisced about our Stockton years and about Edison High. We observed that the multicultural makeup of both Stockton and Edison better prepared us for the larger and diverse world we would encounter when we both moved to San Francisco. We were multicultural before people even used the term.

◼ǁ◼

Through my art classes or on my own I began to draw and paint and began to learn how to use various materials. Besides using pencil and paper, I also began to use watercolors on paper and oil on paper. My first drawings like the one I did on James Dean were pencil and pastel on paper. I did a lot in the late 1950s with pastel, which is like a colored chalk. It is a little softer than ordinary pencil and allows you the ability to make clear lines and to blend colors because it is so soft. There is hard pastel, but I used soft pastel. I learned how to use pastel in that unruly high school art class despite the distractions of the class.

I was also developing an idea of what it meant to be an artist at this time. I didn't yet know that I wanted to be an artist, but I was attracted to what I thought artists were all about. For example, I became attracted to the beatnik movement of the late 1950s. I liked their countercultural style and behavior. It was kind of a bohemian culture even though I didn't know that term then. I began to romanticize what an artist was all about. I started to mold an image of what artists are supposed to be like and do. Much of this I now know was a myth, but I didn't

know it then. It was the myth of the artist wrapped up in themselves; the myth about the troubled soul; the myth about the artist in the ivory tower; and the myth about the artist against society. It's not that this was all myth, but that I was only thinking of this in very superficial ways. My views of an artist also became conflated with my growing attraction and love of jazz. Jazz and art for me seemed linked, which in a way they are, but again this was not something I was delving into at a very deep level yet.

This view of an artist influenced how I first began to paint and how other students in my later junior college art classes painted. We assumed the identity of painters like Picasso and others and attempted to paint like them. But we weren't them. We were merely copying them. But that's all we knew, and we didn't have the sophisticated art teachers who would get us beyond this. In effect we were copiers of art history, not artists. We were simply replicating the art of other artists and thinking that this was art. But it was not. It was a pretense. We were not doing art but art history. Art history meant just reproducing the images of other artists such as Picasso and Van Gogh. It was like taking a photo of their art; it wasn't really painting. I remember painting the image of a clown from a famous artist, but all I was doing was painting a facsimile. It wasn't me. It was the artist I was trying to emulate.

I didn't understand yet that when Picasso did a painting, he was not only expressing his views and feeling, but also of the world around him. But it was his world, and it could not be mine, and my feelings and views could not be his. But we didn't know this. We thought art was doing paintings that looked like da Vinci instead of paintings that looked like us and the world we lived in. This type of awareness would come later in my life when I truly set out to be an artist. Still, what I was doing or not doing in high school or junior college was a beginning. It was the onset of a long road to be an artist named Rupert García.

—||—

Although we didn't have gangs in high school, the real hardcore ones existed in the south side and east side. These were Mexican gangs, and they were tough. Among the Mexican gangs there were two types. One consisted of the older gang members who went back to the pachuco years of the 1940s and early 1950s. They were the veterans or *veteranos* of the barrios. They were old time *batos locos* or crazy dudes. These guys were in their late 30s or in their 40s. They were still angry guys and could impose violence if you messed with them.

Then there were gang members more our age who were the most violent. You didn't mess with them. One particular gangster, Bobby García, was notorious for his use of violence. He'd kill you, or shoot you, or stab the shit out of you.

I had no interest in getting involved with these types of gang members much less joining them. I knew that some guys were getting killed by these

gangs and this violence was increasing. I began to realize that gang behavior, including what we were doing, didn't make any sense. It really didn't add up to anything, and I guess I wanted something to add up for me. So, I moved away from all of this, and I'm so glad I did.

At the same time, part of gang activity in Stockton, although not all of it, was a pronounced drug culture. It was primarily of four kinds: pills, marijuana, heroin, and cocaine. I was involved very marginally in pills such as amphetamines (uppers and downers). On the other hand, some did marijuana or weed. The hardcore druggies did heroin. The gang *vatos* usually did all four and especially heroin. At my high school, some of the kids did weed, but it wasn't rampant and there was no selling of it at school, but you knew guys on the streets who sold it. I first experimented with pills as a freshman, although my first "drug" was alcohol, usually wine or beer. From pills, I started on marijuana. I even foolishly but briefly inhaled white gasoline, which wasn't a very good high, but you did get one hell of a buzz. But in all of this, I was not heavily involved in the drug culture. It was something cool to do especially with the other guys, but in the back of my head was my mother's warnings about drugs, and so I always checked myself.

However, I did know some guys in school, although not in my immediate group, who did get heavy into drinking and drugs. There was one kid who somewhat hung around us who got strung out on heroin. He wound up in the joint, and he eventually died of overdosing. They just got too far into it and got hooked. Years later when I returned to Stockton to be inaugurated into my high school Hall of Fame and when I was presented with my plaque, I dedicated it to all of my friends who had died of drug overdoses or who had gotten run over or shot.

"These were friends of mine," I said, "and we should not forget them."

Gangs in Stockton were also associated with the pachucos, although not all pachucos were gang members. Even so there was some correlation. Pachucos, whether gang members or not, were young Mexican Americans who were countercultural and street dudes. They expressed alienation from both Anglo and Mexican culture. They were rejected by Anglo society and yet became acculturated enough to also rebel against their parental Mexican culture. They sought a third space, their own space. These were the pachucos. My friends and I called ourselves Mexicans or mexicanos. Chicano was a term that I would discover and adopt much later.

As part of their counterculture, pachucos invented their own language, caló. Caló was a language that was neither Spanish nor English. It was not Spanglish. Some believe that caló derives from indigenous influences or Spanish gypsy ones. No one seems to know. There are actual glossaries of caló terms. For example, pachucos would use the word calcos for shoes. Where did this come from? Not from Spanish, where shoe is zapato. I knew caló that I picked up from the pachuco

gangs. I didn't personally use it a lot, but still I thought it was great, interesting, and exciting. I liked it because it was different and countercultural, and I was beginning to see myself as partly countercultural, which was part of youth rebelliousness of the late 1950s—the beatniks, rock and roll. I liked the aesthetic ring of caló in my ear. It seemed like music when you heard it used, but a different kind of music. I saw it and the pachuco syndrome as a more complex way to comprehend the world and to articulate it. It provided more layers of feelings. It attempted to capture the complexity of a situation. Maybe it was because pachucos were not socially accepted by both Anglo and Mexican society that I was attracted to them or at least to their style.

Part of this style was how they dressed on a day-to-day basis. There was, of course, the zoot suit made popular in the 1940s, but not all pachucos dressed in the zoot suit, and it was not used very much anyway by the late 1950s. The pachuco style instead consisted of khaki pants, a Pendleton plaid shirt—it always had to be a Pendleton, which wasn't cheap—and big calcos or thick-soled shoes or boots. It's identical to what contemporary cholos wear and who are the descendants of the pachucos. To an extent, I emulated this style during my first two years of high school, but then shifted to a more contemporary California style that I saw in some men's style magazines such as Gentleman's Quarterly. I became a real clothes nut. I was always interested in clothes from an aesthetic perspective, even though my taste in clothes changed.

Pachucos or gangs are synonymous with graffiti; however, in Stockton at least, there wasn't that much graffiti or *placas* which are the symbols of different gangs. Placas are like the badges or markers of a gang. By contrast, there was more graffiti on the bodies of pachucos, meaning tattoos. Some pachucos had elaborate tattoos, including the ever-present one of Our Lady of Guadalupe. But the most common tattoo was the cross tattoo on one hand. I was impressed with this, and while I didn't necessarily want a permanent one, I first tried just to make one on my hand with a blue ballpoint pen. I dug it deep into my skin so that it might look permanent until one of my tíos said to me when he noticed what I had done, "Rupert, if you ever expect to get a good job, I suggest you get rid of that tattoo because employers don't want to hire pachucos and that cross identifies you as a pachuco."

I took his advice to heart as I always did from my tíos and tías. It wasn't easy to remove the cross tattoo. I had to dig into my skin to destroy it, but I finally succeeded even though it left a bit of a scar on my hand.

The other noticeable feature of pachucos and wanna-be pachucos was the ducktail hair cut. Talk about aesthetics! These were beautiful creations. Pachucos all with dark black hair would first put on a lot of hair cream such as the then popular Three Flowers and rub it all over their hair. They would then comb their hair straight back. Then the art came in. With a comb they would part the hair in the back into two parts with a straight line right down the middle. It was called a ducktail supposedly because it looked like the back of a duck. But the pachuco ducktails were beautiful. They were all basically the same with some variations. Some pachucos would also have a strand of hair in the front coming down their forehead. This was cool. I tried to also emulate this hairstyle but with mixed success. Still, I admired the aesthetic of the pachuco hairstyle.

The difference, however, that I had with the pachucos was that I was not alienated from my Mexican culture or family. I didn't call myself a pachuco but a Mexican. In my family we were proud of being Mexicans. I still spoke some Spanish at home, but more importantly I identified with my Mexican family culture. There was lots of love in this culture. The one thing that I did not identify with was the sexism or machismo displayed by some of the men in my family. This always bothered me. I didn't buy into the notion that women should only be relegated to their own space. My mother didn't accept this either. I didn't have this particular Mexican image of how to be a man.

◼ǁ◼

I was interested in girls in high school. I liked girls of different ethnic backgrounds, including Mexican, Filipino, Italian, and African American. They all were great, and I developed strong friendships with some of them. However, I never had a steady girlfriend. I would have liked to, but I was too shy and scared to death to ask a girl to go steady with me. There were some girls who stole my heart, but I couldn't ask any one of them to be my girlfriend. I was too damn shy and just fell over myself.

On the other hand, some of the guys I hung around with had steady girlfriends or they dated much more than I did. Some, as far as I know, also had sex with their partners. There was little to no sex education in school. You just learned it from others or from older siblings. There was also no effective birth control. The pill had not yet been invented in the late 1950s. I don't even know if the diaphragm had been invented. Of course, there were prophylactics, or the rubber, but most guys ignored using it. This was stupid. It wasn't like everyone was having sex. The 1950s was still a very restrictive period with respect to sex out of marriage. But it did occur in high school, and it could lead to serious consequences. My good friend Bobby Ruiz who had real musical talent messed up his future by getting his girlfriend pregnant. His hope of a musical career was shot; it just tore him apart as it did his girlfriend. He married her and had the baby. He later sold clothes in San Francisco. Other guys were equally irresponsible and wound up having to drop out of school or not going beyond high school in order to provide for their babies.

Given my own shyness with girls the thought of having sex with them was beyond me. I was scared to death of the thought of having sex and getting a girl pregnant. I was a virgin and as I look back on it, I'm glad I was. If not, it would have changed the whole course of my life and any desire to be an artist.

◼▮◼

By my senior year in high school, I knew that I wanted to be an artist. It's not that I had a lot of good art mentoring then, but I just was attracted to the idea of being an artist. It was something of my own countercultural tendency. Of course, as noted earlier, I did take some of the art classes available at school, and I learned something, although not a lot, but enough to encourage me to move in this direction. In these classes, I enjoyed both the drawings and paintings that I did. By my senior year there was no question but that I wanted to become an artist. Absolutely.

Part of this encouragement was that I was beginning to get some positive feedback. This included winning two art contests sponsored by art groups in Stockton, not my school. The first award was I think in my junior year, and I don't recall much about it. However, the one that I will never forget is the second award. This was an art contest for high school students, and I entered it. I submitted an oil painting of a seascape. I used a pallet knife to paint it and it was a decent-looking painting for an 18-year-old. It looked fine. I couldn't tell if it was good or not because I didn't know what really looked good, and so I was surprised that I won. I painted an imaginary seascape with the shape of a boat. Around this time is when I first saw San Francisco when my Tío David and my Tía Mary drove me across the Bay Bridge, and there it was—San Francisco! I just fell in love with it. The city made me feel excited, tingly, and gave me a sense that fun things were happening there that were not happening in Stockton. By then I knew that I would soon leave Stockton. I didn't feel fulfilled there. I also knew that if I stayed in Stockton that instead of becoming an artist, I would wind up working at the cannery like so many others did, especially Mexicans. I knew that I would first go to Stockton Junior College but would then leave and go to live in San Francisco.

The award that I won for my seascape was for the 17–18-year-old category. I just took my painting down to the location of the contest, filled out some forms, and left the painting. I don't remember how I found out that I had won, probably I received a letter. I don't even remember if there was a ceremony. The prize was a coffee table book on Monet, which I still have. I was absolutely thrilled. The large color plates in the book were dazzling. This was my first real art book.

My seascape picture was one of my first oil paintings, but I didn't have a sense that this was a big deal that I was moving from drawing with chalk to oil painting. It was just something we did in art class. But a lot of this was trial and error, since frankly the art teachers were not very good. For example, I decided to do an oil painting of a clown, but I used an old canvas that already had an image and I just foolishly painted over it to do my clown.

Over the years this painting began to peel because the bottom surface which I painted over was itself peeling. I didn't know that you're not supposed to paint over an already existing painting, but my teacher didn't say anything about this or warn me. He probably didn't know himself. I learned this in one of my junior college art classes. All I knew then was that by using oil I could do a much brighter painting.

I have no idea what happened to my award-winning seascape. The contest returned it to me, but I don't know what I did with it. I might have given it one of my relatives. All I know is that by the time I graduated from high school, I had been turned on to the idea of being an artist.

—II—

I have to say that I was not very impressed with most of my teachers in high school. Only two left some kind of impression on me. One was Mr. Peckham, who was kind to me when I came back to school after my suspension. But I also appreciated him because he was so enthusiastic about science and math, which he loved. The second teacher was Mr. James Reilly. He taught social science and history. I don't know the actual course I took with him; it could have been California history. He was a good teacher, and I did pretty well. He once wrote on one of my exams, "Rupert, you did a very good job and you're also a good-looking kid, but don't rest on your laurels."

I felt good about what he wrote, although I don't know what my looks had to do with my exam. I also didn't know what "laurels" meant. What the hell is a laurel? I went and looked it up. "Oh, wow," I thought. For a teen-age kid to read what Mr. Reilly wrote made me feel good, especially since it came from a teacher that I respected. I thought this was pretty heavy stuff, about not resting on my laurels. I've never forgotten this. He in effect was telling me don't rest on your past. It's what you're going to do that counts. That was deep. It really struck me at the same time that it scared me. It was scary because it meant to me that what you don't know yet is what's going to be important, not what you've already done. If you just rest on what you've already done, this will soon fade away. It's what you still need to do that is im-portant. I took this to heart and have never rested on my laurels. Mr. Reilly was in my ears saying, "That's good Rupert, but what are you going to paint next?"

—ıı—

Graduation finally came in the spring of 1959. It was the end of a decade in which I had grown up in and just be-fore the beginning of a new decade—the 60s! Little did I know what would happen to me in this new decade and how my life would be shaped by it. Graduation day was very special to me, although I can't remember much of the actual ceremony. It was held on the north side at Stockton High School because their auditorium was much larger than ours and could ac-commodate all of the families that would attend. My mom and many of my extended family were there. I had felt that I was never going to be out of high school. At one point, it felt like I would be there forever. This was probably true for many others of my classmates. But the day finally came, and I really enjoyed it because most of the friends I had in high school were graduating with me. We were all going to leave together as close friends, even though I would drift apart from most and some I have never seen again since that day. But you don't think about this when you graduate, you only do so years later when nostalgia hits you.

3

Junior College and the City

After graduation from high school, I stayed and enrolled in Stockton Junior College. I didn't know that much about college, and so it wasn't like I had choices. Nothing. I went to Stockton Junior College because it was in Stockton. The fact is I had no money to go to any college outside of Stockton. My universe was Stockton. I was defined by the parameters of Stockton, physically and culturally by its environment. Even then going to Stockton Junior College was a big leap for me.

It was made easier because in my senior year after my mother remarried we moved to the north side where the college was located. We found ourselves living adjacent to the College of the Pacific. This was a private college and there was no way I could attend it. Besides it was a Protestant school, and I was Catholic. But Stockton Junior College was also very close to where we now lived, so close that I could walk there, which I did.

Moving to the north side was a very different experience. I could have

transferred to one of the north side schools in my senior year such as Stockton High. However, I decided and my mother agreed for me to stay in my high school and graduate from there. I would have never transferred; it would have broken my heart to do so. Still living in the north side was an alienating situation. I didn't know anyone. It was a very white neighborhood, in fact exclusively Anglo. I didn't feel like I belonged there. It was a strange feeling. Our new home, on the other hand, was a nicer one than where we had been living. It was larger and newer. I was going to school with one of my teachers who lived on the north side; he gave me a ride to school each day.

Living in the north side was completely different. There were sidewalks here where in our older neighborhood there were few. There were streetlights, where there were few in the south side. The houses were bigger in the north. It was like living in a dream but not my dream. Still, I had no choice but to live there with my family and my stepfather, whom I didn't get along with.

—||—

Attending Stockton Junior College also further brought to my attention the class and race differences in Stockton that were reflected at the college. This was especially illustrated in a class on layout and design that I enrolled in my first semester. The students were primarily whites. You could spot them not only by their race, but how they dressed, how they wore their hair, how the girls put on their makeup and did their nails. All of this was a code saying to me and other minorities, "you are not me and you'll never be me." You will never be me and we don't want you. This was a strong realization of differences, and it really hit me hard in this one class but at the school as a whole. This was the first time I had ever felt that I was the "other." This was disturbing to me, because I couldn't fully understand why I would be pushed aside. It made no sense to me. It was an abstraction that I had a hard time grasping and giving form. It wasn't something that they said or did, but just a behavior toward me. It was exclusionary. It was strange, and it outraged me.

I had felt that by attending junior college, this hostile sense of alienation from rich white kids would go away or level out, but it didn't. Actually, it intensified the differences. There was some ethnic diversity at the school, but it was a diversity that seemed not to be wanted or accepted by the whites. It

was like, "this is our college and what the hell are you doing here?"

In the end over my two years at the school, I got over the hurt and just said "fuck it" and did my own thing.

At the same time, I did have one good friend, Ron Cooper, with whom I grew up on my side of town. We went to school together through community college. He was also an art major. I didn't have many other close friends, and I didn't date during this time. I was really focused on studying to become an artist.

—||—

I, of course, wanted to focus on art at junior college; however, I also had to take some required courses. I was not a genius, but I did okay in these classes such as biology, algebra, and sociology. But there was one class where I really struggled. This was a Western Civilization class. To this day, I don't know what the hell I read in that class. I don't remember a thing about the class except that the guy who taught it was a very wise old man. He was brilliant except that I didn't understand him. I remember sitting in the class and looking at my big old textbook and saying to myself, "what the hell is this about?" But it wasn't just the book but the professor as well. "What the hell is he saying?" It was like he was speaking another language. His ideas were so abstract that I thought "am I crazy or am I brain damaged that I can't understand him?" I think looking back the problem was that I didn't have a good grasp of language or at least at his level or that of the book. I just couldn't get it. Fortunately, some how I passed the class.

Although I had to take these other required general ed classes, I was in seventh heaven when I started my art classes. Although I had some so-called art classes in high school, they were anything but art classes. I didn't learn much if anything, for example, about technique. It wasn't until I started at Stockton Junior College that I really began to learn about art. I took a variety of art classes that included drawing, oil painting, ceramics, jewelry making, color, layout and design, and art history. I loved all of this, and it was so much fun. It was a very good experience. In these classes, I was with my friend, Ron, and a new friend, Jerry, who was also an art student. We had a great time together, and they were very talented. I learned from talking to them as well as from other students in these classes.

One professor that I learned a great deal from was an older woman. She wore a lot of clothes, curly reddish brownish hair, glasses, and always seemed to be self-absorbed. But she taught this class on color that was an eye opener for me. It was an absolute, fantastic introduction to the science of color, of how color works physically. It was just so exciting to me. I just couldn't believe it. I worked like crazy in that class because I was so enthusiastic about the material. I didn't need anyone to assist me in getting involved in that class. I was there and I did very well in that class.

What I learned in this color class, among other things, was that there are two ways of making color. One is using artist's pigments like oil paint, pastel, and watercolor. Second is how you can mix various colors using that material. You learn how to make values, tints, and shades. Values are dark and light. Tints are achieved by mixing white with dark and light. Shades is a way of darkening that color. For example, if you have a red but it's a dark red, that would be considered a shade of red. If you have red and you mix it with white, you get kind of a pinkish color that would be called a tint of red. And then you can mix other colors. I learned about primary colors which are red, yellow, and blue. Then you have the neutrals, black and white. You also have secondary or tertiary colors and so on. I learned how colors behave and how they interact with each other. We learned about complementary colors, simultaneous contrast, split complements, and more technical stuff.

This approach also interested me in science. I always had some attraction to science, but it was piqued in this color class because it had scientific connections. The mixing of colors had a scientific component, but it was also magical. That you could mix yellow and blue and get green! My God! But you could also react in a more scientific way about why scientifically you can mix yellow and blue and get green. All this was fascinating to me.

We also had different kinds of projects on how to apply these different theories of color. I had a great time doing this. This could be a bit tricky. Some students tended to become pre-occupied with the science of color and forget that as artists there is also, and even more importantly, a subjectivity of color. I never separated the two. I came to appreciate the theories of color and yet not forget how color or colors affected me personally, the sub-jective side. Color has always moved me both intellectually and emotion-ally. How color works and makes me feel. How it makes me think and imag-ine things. I didn't overly indulge in color theory. I didn't try to make art based on theory. I learned how to use theory about color to solve problems of how to achieve different colors, but not how to paint.

The professor of the color class was great, because she didn't discourage either of the two approaches to the use of color. She encouraged me to do what I did. She never said, "it's only this way." It was never a denial of one at the benefit of the other, which I'm grateful for. I'm grateful because I was attracted to color even before the class, but it became even more important to me after the class, not only in my work but in everyday life. I learned an awful lot, and it laid the basis for my own future work where color plays a very vital role.

Another art class that I had to take for my major was jewelry and ceram-ics. I liked it because I liked bending metals and using semiprecious stones. I always had an interest in jewelry. As a kid, I used to take apart my mom's jewelry and make new things out of them or at least try to. I also used to carve human figures out of wooden clothespins as a child. That's a direct link with my grandmother who made figures out of tissue. I had an interest in using my hands and working with jewelry. I even thought I might become a jeweler and design rings and brace-lets. But it was a passing thing. I found that making jewelry and ceramics wasn't enough for me. The way these mediums occupy space and the way you manipulate the materials wasn't me. I preferred to work on a flat sur-face that seemed to offer me more than spatial art.

An additional class that did deal with a flat surface was on watercolor. The instructor was a master water col-orist and was a great instructor. He knew how to move the watercolor. It was just amazing to watch him work. I did okay in the class, but I also found that watercolor was not my thing. I found it difficult to paint using water-color because of the amount of water utilized. It would move on the paper as if it were alive and had a life of its own beyond me. I did some nice lit-tle paintings, but I knew that water coloring was not my field. However, I enjoyed the class very much and had a great time. I loved the transparen-cies you can achieve with watercolor. I also loved the brushes used in water coloring; they were nice and soft. Still, it wasn't for me.

Another class I had to take was called lettering and layout. It was a design class. It taught you how to hand letter for the sole purpose of doing commercial work. I enjoyed this class also. I liked learning how to use a lettering brush and how to do different kinds of typefaces and learning about the proportion and the character of letters. I learned about negative and positive space. Letters are usually in black on a white surface. What is black is called the negative space; what's positive is the white open space. This led me to understand that everything counts when you make a picture. The background is as important as the foreground; the positive is as important as the negative. There's no hierarchy between the two. They both must be attended to equally. All this was very difficult work which required a lot of discipline. But I loved it and I was getting results. It was wonderful to see how you grew from when you began the class. Part of our classwork was to design some travel posters for tourists. I picked London, Japan, and some other country to design travel posters. We had to come up with a design using words and color. I used very simple shapes that would suggest, for example, Big Ben for London. I would add words to it and colors that would be attractive to the eye.

This class on lettering and layout would have an influence on me later when I did political posters using silk screen. The class taught me how to design, how to think about shape, color, composition, and how to use the amount of space that your paper provides. In other words, I came to know and become aware of the physical ingredients in order to make a poster.

Lettering and design for commercial purposes didn't interest me, but still I learned a lot in the class.

━┃━

In the end and maybe even the beginning, what attracted me the most as a budding artist was oil and oil painting. This became my passion then and until today. I have to credit Professor Bruce (I can't for the life of me remember his last name) who worked with me on oil painting in his class. He always was a great supporter and really encouraged me. My attraction to oil painting goes back even earlier and has to do with a flat surface. As a kid, I made drawings and little paintings all on a flat surface. This began my fascination with flat surfaces. So, for me, if it ain't flat, it ain't real, at least in terms of producing art. In Stockton College the importance of working with a flat surface became more pronounced. This is what seemed to bring me fulfillment. Unlike water coloring or ceramics, I felt that I had more natural control and affinity with a flat surface. Things worked better for me in this way, and it's still true today.

But a flat surface is only the beginning. It was oil that I became obsessed with in my development as an artist, beginning in junior college. The way in which I could manipulate the paint with the brush and knife was fantastic. With oil, I could achieve an intensity of color and a variety of color. The physical properties of oil painting became important to me not only in terms of seeing, but also in terms of smell. It smelled right. Smelling oil is like smelling a flower. The bouquet is fantastic. I love it. The physicality of oil painting is very important to me.

The physical properties of oil painting were all-consuming in my case. I mean everything about it was incredible. This included the tubes of paint, the brushes, the canvas; all those things started to become a part of me. Then I began to internalize the various elements and qualities of making an oil painting. I began to think and feel and see as a painter working on a flat surface. All this struck a major chord within me. I believe that all of us respond to the world in ways that include seeing, smelling, hearing, tasting, and touching in movement of space. We all do that. That's how we negotiate everyday life. But for some people, certain areas of their faculties are more important than others. In my case, it's the visual and it's the flatness of human experience. It's the way of representing experience or investigating experience. The spatial was never that important to me. I appreciate sculpture very much as I do motion pictures, music, photography, and all of the arts. But as a maker in these art forms, I have no interest. By contrast, seeing in a certain kind of way on a flat surface and using paints was the faculty that seemed to allow me the most in order to answer questions and to raise questions.

As I became more involved in oil painting, I also became more influenced by certain painters who used oil, such as Van Gogh and Picasso. In fact, I began to paint like Van Gogh and Picasso. It's not that I knew much about their paintings, but because they were part of a litany of painters who are popularly known by most students and others. They knew Michelangelo, da Vinci, Picasso, Dali, and Van Gogh. I knew these names. But in school, especially in junior college, I began to learn more about them and see more of their works. Of these painters, I found Michelangelo and da Vinci boring. I was much more attracted to Van Gogh and Picasso. I liked how they made their images and how they used color and their sense of composition. Picasso and Van Gogh and some of the abstract painters became my models. I was most profoundly affected by their work, which struck an emotional and intellectual chord within me. I loved how they used color. Both loved colors. The way Van Gogh used color was a bit more expressive in comparison to Picasso. With Van Gogh you could see the way he put the paint on; you could see the trace of brush and the various ways that he applied color and the intensity of color. The colors vibrate against each other. There is an incredible personal and emotional presence in Van Gogh's paintings that really struck me. I didn't so much think about his paintings as much as I responded to them. Man, I thought, this guy is for real!

What I loved about Picasso was the way he composed; how he fragmented his subject matter; and how he so carefully used color attracted me not just emotionally, but, in a way, more intellectually. He seemed to think a lot about organizing his painting, the shapes, what he wanted to break up in fragments, and where the different pieces were going to go. It all seemed carefully considered. It's not that his reflection strangled the emotional impact of the painting. Not at all, but at the same time, you can see that there's intelligence behind the painting as well as an emotional thrust.

So, in junior college, the work of Van Gogh and Picasso were very important to me. They represented to me the meaning of art. Consequently, at the time, I made pictures that looked like Van Gogh and Picasso, thinking that this was the way art was supposed to look. I also did a couple of abstract paintings, since I was also drawn to this style. I learned something about the abstract expressionists in New York. I copied this style but not knowing what abstract painting was about, just that it was supposed to look like something unrecognizable. I did also learn, however, that abstract painting does represent something very specific and concrete and that there is an inner experience that the artist wishes to convey. I learned to appreciate abstract painting, but I instinctively knew that it was not for me.

For me what is important in painting is the image. The image as recognizable has always been important to me as far back as I remember. When I carved those wooden clothespins, I aimed to produce an image of people. Even in my early stages, I was not concerned with making something nonobjective or totally abstract. I think I can explain my preference for recognizable images going back to my family. In family culture, things are pretty concrete and understood. Even in church, you can recognize and understand all the images. The same with motion pictures. I loved going to the movies and later TV, but both had images you could recognize. Magazines and comic books were the same. All of this culture was recognizable in some way. I came to favor the recognizability of reality. This was important to me and more so than something that was not objective or abstract. Having said this, there still is the resonance of abstractness to recognizable images, and there has always been a presence of this in my work. For example, as a kid working on the wooden clothespin, I'm trying to make a figure, but I'm also responding to the abstract elements of shape and of line that's always there too. I don't divorce that.

One form of reality over the years that has influenced me and that slaps me in the face and which I respond to very strongly are photographs. They have a presence of raw reality to them. I'm always dealing with something that is representational, and even if expressive representation is a bit abstract, you can still identify what the subject matter is in my work. I've always had this need to make things recognizable. It's not because I want someone to be able to understand my image. Not at all. It's because I want to understand the images.

The developing artist such as in my case has to base their style upon something. If you live in a tribal society, you learn style from a Master. Even if you live in New York today, you learn style from someplace such as an art book, gallery, museum, or magazine. You learn what art is supposed to look like, and you imitate it at first. For me it was Van Gogh and Picasso. With Van Gogh, I remember at first being influenced by seeing the movie *Lust for Life*, which is the story of Van Gogh with Kirk Douglas playing the artist. The movie had an impact on me. It influenced me as to how artists are supposed to look, act, think, and feel. Influences like this and then in art classes seeing the images of art produced by Van Gogh and Picasso further influenced me as to the meaning of art and that I should try to emulate it.

What also influenced me was that in art classes we learned that great art was made by Europeans. We never learned about art from Africa, Asia, or Latin America. We learned that in the context of European art, you go from representation of realism in Greek and Roman art all the way to abstraction art. There is just this definite line from ancient art to Jackson Pollack. You go from realism to abstraction in the visual arts, and there's no question about this. It's taught that it's not arbitrary; it's inevitable. We all bought this. We bought it because we weren't given any alternatives to understand the human production of culture. You just learned this myth, the modernist myth and the Eurocentric myth of culture. I just bought it all because that's what my teachers told me. You learn that this is the avant-garde, and you try to imitate it. But by doing so, you are also denying your family and its history. In my case, my Mexican

American family. It's as if they don't belong in art. They belong someplace, but not here. Still, I and others at first accepted this Eurocentric view of art.

However, what saved me was my strong attraction for representationism and for photographs and magazine reproductions. I kept going back to those ways of recording human experience and used them for my work, although not so much at junior college, but later when I discovered the myth that European modernism and all other great art only comes from Europe. I have always had a connection with the real world as captured in photographs. It might be a picture of a popular icon or someone of social importance or a photo of some historical moment. I think because I was so influenced since the 1950s with the photograph as being truth that that helped me realize the myth of modernism. This myth not only prioritizes European art but also developed the modernist movement of the late nineteenth and early twentieth centuries that considered great art to be simply the work of individuals not influenced by society. You can't bring in history, even personal history. Instead, you throw it out. The modernist canon considers itself to be universal and the only way to paint. By contrast, if you're doing work that's recognizable, then you're out of step. You are not in the line of progress, which tells us that we go from the image of representation to the image of abstractions almost in a Darwinian movement from the image of reality to the abstraction of reality. From emotion to intelligence. Modernism was not just restricted to art but applied to other cultural forms and to society in general. Modernism was progress or the myth of progress, and as such exists only in Europe or Western culture and certain of its territories.

I learned all of these myths at Stockton and for a time accepted them, and that's why my early paintings in my classes were more or less imitations of Van Gogh and Picasso. It wasn't my own art yet. Rupert García—the artist—did not yet exist.

—||—

While studying at Stockton Junior College, I lived the first year at home with my mother and my stepfather. My two brothers were in the military. However, things got so bad between my mother and her husband that I couldn't stand the fights and I moved out. Because I was working at the warehouse and making decent money even as I went to school, I could afford to do so. I felt that it was time to be on my own. One day, I just told my mother that I was moving out and I have no idea of how she felt about this. I didn't really care. I didn't feel guilty moving out, if anything I felt liberated. I wanted to get out of this shit with my stepfather.

I moved into an apartment in the middle part of Stockton, not too far from downtown. I moved in with this guy who also worked at the warehouse who needed a new roommate. The arrangement was okay except that this guy, who was not going to school, didn't respect my art. I had done this oil painting in the style of Picasso. It showed three musicians and it was a nice painting. I took the painting to my apartment and hung it up. One day, however, I came home and to my horror saw my roommate literally throwing darts at my painting. He had zero appreciation for my art, and he destroyed it. He was a big burly guy who was a dumbass. I didn't confront him because I didn't want any shit. I just took my painting down and put it in my room. I no longer have that painting and don't know what happened to it.

—||—

After two and a half years at Stockton Junior College, I graduated in the fall of 1961 with an AA degree in art. I chose not to go to the graduation ceremony. I don't know why, but I didn't. On the other hand, I was very proud that I was awarded the Frontier Award by the Art Department as the Outstanding Graduating Art Student. This came as a total surprise, and it was unbelievable. This was a decision by the faculty of the college. Every year they'd pick the outstanding science student, the outstanding music student, and so on. Then there was the one for the outstanding art student called the Frontier Award. I appreciated the award, but it wasn't that I needed someone to tell me that I was doing well. I knew I was doing well, and I already was convinced that I was going to be an artist for the rest of my life. I enjoyed doing art. I knew I wasn't great, but I knew I wasn't bad, so getting the award did help me psychologically. It told me that someone was taking notice of my work. At the same time, what was more important was how I felt about my work and that I was doing well. If someone doesn't like my work it affects me, but I go on because I have a sense of the value of my work. I felt good about the award and about graduating. This was an important accomplishment for me.

■II■

Shortly after I graduated from junior college, I made the decision to move to San Francisco to really become an artist—an "artiste"—even though I had no idea what this really meant or how to go about it. I had always been fascinated with the city and its special ambiance, including its artistic culture. So, when I learned that my friends and fellow art students Ron Cooper and Jerry Simpldurfer were themselves leaving Stockton and going to San Francisco, I said "I'm going too." Both Ron and Jerry had already applied to study art at San Francisco State. I couldn't afford to go to college then, but I knew I could become an artist somehow. In the meantime, I would find a job and paint on my own. The three of us agreed to rent an apartment and share the rent. By splitting the rent, this made it financially feasible for me to move in with them. We moved in early 1962.

I informed my mother about my plans, but I don't remember her reaction. She certainly didn't say I couldn't go or else I would have remembered this. What could she say? I was now twenty years of age, and I believed there was not much opportunity for

me to grow as an artist in Stockton. I don't think she knew what being an artist entailed. I'm sure she would have preferred for me to get a regular job or at least pursue what she would see as a more realistic profession such as law or medicine or even architecture. My mother's reaction really didn't affect me one way or another. I knew what I wanted to do.

I was a self-absorbed man. I just had this scenario of what I wanted to do since high school—to be an artist, a painter. This dream determined the scenario. I had to do this. Anything that would prevent my achieving my dream, I had to push aside or ignore. I had to be focused. So, it didn't matter what my mom thought; it didn't matter what anyone thought. All that mattered was what I thought and what I felt and what I had to do. This pushed me forward. I wanted to be an artist badly. I absolutely starved for it. Stockton couldn't provide food to satisfy my hunger. I had no regrets leaving my home town. I felt no remorse or sadness in leaving except that, of course, I would miss my family, but I wouldn't miss Stockton.

We found an apartment that we could afford in the Haight-Ashbury district before it became the "Haight-Ashbury district" later into the 1960s, when it became a haven for the hippies and other countercultural types. When we moved into the district, it was still basically a white working-class neighborhood. The hippies would force many of these people to relocate. Our apartment was near Golden Gate Park, and near the panhandle in this area later filled with homeless people. I, of course, found San Francisco to be beautiful. It was huge. It was exciting. I didn't know my way around very well, but I soon learned how to move around and what buses to take.

I was fortunate to quickly find a job as a dishwasher in a restaurant in the Mission District. I didn't know yet the history of this district as a place where many Latinos lived or would come to live as time went on. I just knew it as the Mission District. I worked in an Italian or semi-Italian restaurant where they served great steaks. I no longer remember its name, but it was quite prominent then. I had never worked in a restaurant before and had never been a dishwasher. But they taught me what I had to do, and it didn't take me long to learn the ropes. One thing that I learned was the class system in a restaurant or at least in the kitchen. The number one person is the chef, then there are the chef's assistants, the waiters, the bus boys, and finally there is me—the dishwashers. I also had to take out the garbage and mop the floors besides washing dishes. I took the brunt of everything, and I hated it.

I worked at the restaurant for several weeks which was as long as I could take it. I finally got fed up with the abuse of being a dishwasher. I didn't have an alternative job, but it didn't matter. I just got to the point where I didn't want to work there anymore. I had reached my tolerance level and I had to get out. However, before I quit, the owner of the restaurant, who I learned was a small-time gangster, told me,

"Rupert, come with me. I want to show you something."

We went to this building next to the restaurant that looked like a warehouse. He opened the door and we walk in and to my surprise it's filled with all of these clothes, suits, slacks, jackets, shoes, all kinds of mostly menswear. I looked at all of this stuff and said, "Oh, my God! What the hell is this?"

"What do you want?" the owner asked me.

"What do you mean?"

I thought to myself, "this is a small-time gangster world here. I have no interest in this because it begins with a jacket and it ends up with my owing him my life or doing something for him that might cost my life."

"Nah," I said, "nothing. I'm fine."

With that, I quit my job.

During this time, I checked out as much as I could of the art scene in San Francisco. I wasn't aware of galleries. I thought art was mostly displayed in museums. I would later learn the importance of galleries for artists. I went to the museums. I especially remember a particular exhibit at the Museum of Art downtown at Van Ness and McAllister. I found out that this was the place to show in northern California, a very important venue. It was what would be called a pop art show. I was particularly taken by an incredible piece of work by James Rosenquist, which was a front end of a Ford car with some spaghetti on it and a profile of a man and a woman kissing. Wow! What a painting! That painting just knocked me out. I loved the way Rosenquist used color and how he moved it around and his composition, a juxtaposition of elements that are not usually seen together. It was a fragmented depiction of reality somewhat reminiscent of how some of the cubist painters organized their paintings as well as some of the surrealists. That Rosenquist painting was an important moment for me as a visual experience because it registered with me. It made total sense to me when I saw it. It killed me. I couldn't believe I was seeing it. I kept looking at it and thinking "how did he think of this? How could he imagine this way of putting a picture together?" Aesthetically it was a stunner. So Rosenquist became a very important artist and influence for me as I evolved as an artist.

In between work or looking for work, I painted and drew. I did this in our small apartment. There was no room in this small space to set up an easel to paint. It was much easier to draw. I drew pictures based on photographs from magazines such as *Life*. I loved photographs although I had not done any paintings or drawings based on photographs at junior college. But here in San Francisco, I did. I used photos as my frame of reference. I must have brought my art supplies with me, because I don't remember buying them in the city. Since I was working at the restaurant during the day, I would draw in the evenings and on weekends.

My drawings were mainly black and white although I used some crayon. From photographs in magazines I drew mostly movie stars. I was attracted to the aura of movie stars although I

also did one or two historical figures. I drew Elizabeth Taylor and Gandhi. These were essentially portraits of popular icons. Unlike at junior college where I was imitating Van Gogh and Picasso, here I was developing my own style and doing pictures of people that mattered to me. Little did I know that I would go on to especially focus on the facial images of people, especially later of the Latino and Third World communities. I still have some of these early sketches and as I look at them, I love them. I think I did a good job and was developing my talent.

Ron and Jerry, my roommates, were studying art, so they also were making drawings and paintings. Somehow Ron or Jerry talked this owner of a pizza place called Papa's Pizza to allow us to exhibit our work there. I couldn't believe it! The pizzeria was right across from Kezar Stadium where the San Francisco Forty-Niner's football team used to play. During football season, the pizzeria was packed. It was great! Here I am showing in San Francisco and getting free pizza as well. It was fabulous! I don't think the owner allowed exhibits as a general rule, but he allowed this for us. This is 1962. It was my first exhibit outside of Stockton. I displayed some of my drawings, including one of Elizabeth Taylor and of some musicians. As far as we were concerned, we had arrived as artists in San Francisco!

Of course, no one except the customers and then only some paid any attention to our work. There were no announcements of the showings. I put up about five or six of my drawings.

I later was to learn more about how the art world works. It has a strong sociology. Back then and even today, showing your art in a pizza place or any restaurant was the lowest of the low of where to exhibit. No one seriously interested in art would go to such places to see art. It wouldn't enter their minds to go to a pizzeria to see anything of consequence. This would include art critics, museum directors, and curators, let alone gallery owners. But then we didn't know any better and it was fine. We saw no problem with this. In fact, we felt fortunate to just show our work even if it was at Papa's Pizza which, in a way, served as my first gallery!

I often tell my students about this experience in 1962 coming from a small town, Stockton, in the San Joaquin Valley to this huge monster of a city, San Francisco. I tell them that the showing at the pizza place to me was like showing at the Metropolitan Museum in New York. What difference did I know then? After all, the object, I remind the students, is to have your work seen.

Because I didn't have much money even when I was working, my social life left a lot to be desired. I didn't really meet many women around my age, and so I didn't date. However, I was able to reconnect with some guys that I had known in elementary school and in the Boy Scouts who were living in San Francisco, and so we had a reunion. These guys were attending San Francisco State. It was fabulous. It was wonderful seeing my old friends and hanging out with them. This included

Jesse, Tom, Denny, James, and a few others. We'd spend most of the time when we got together just listening to music, especially jazz. They were all, like me, interested in jazz. Occasionally, I would go to a movie, but not much.

I'm glad that I ran into these former friends because after I quit my job, I had to leave the apartment with Ron and Jerry. I couldn't afford my part of the rent. I had no money. Fortunately, my other friends from Stockton took turns allowing me to sleep at their apartments. They also fed me. This went on for a little while, but I knew it had to end. I couldn't continue to impose on them. I was wearing out my stay with them. Since I had no money, I made the decision to return to Stockton. I had no other choice. I loved being in San Francisco, and it was all exciting except for being a dishwasher. But I had done some drawings and even had some of my work exhibited at the pizza place. I knew I would go back to the city when I could sustain myself better there. It would be a while, but I was determined to return.

In the meanwhile, I went back to Stockton but didn't want to go home to my mother, because I couldn't stand my stepfather. Instead, I moved into my brother Paco's house. However, I wasn't able to get a job and so one day walking downtown, I passed the post office and noticed that inside there were different military recruiters. I didn't really want to join the service, but I went ahead and talked to the recruiters. In looking back, all of them lied to me. However, the Army, Marines, and Navy didn't seem right. I then ended up at the desk of the Air Force guy. This recruiter really stroked my ego and lied the best.

"Listen, Rupert, you're the kind of person we want in the Air Force. You're just what we need. You have two years of college and so you can go to officer's training school, da, da, da, da." And so, I joined the Air Force; it was a job. I didn't join for God or for country. Not whatsoever. This was the furthest thing from my mind. To me it was just a job, to work and make some money, and then maybe I would get the G.I. Bill and go back to school. Of course, in my family, all the men had been in the military. Although military service was part of my heritage, this was not the reason for me to join the service. I just needed a job. However, little did I know that in joining the Air Force, I was entering into a period of war—in Southeast Asia and in Vietnam. Oh, my God!

4

Indochina

After I joined the Air Force and said goodbye to my family, I had to get on a bus and travel all the way to San Antonio. I left Stockton in October 1962. I was assigned to do my basic training at Lackland Air Force Base. I was leery of being in San Antonio and in Texas because my Grandma García told me before I left, "Don't go downtown in San Antonio because they hate Mexicans; they beat them up." Of course, I had also heard that Texas was a bad place for Mexicans even if you were a U.S. citizen. I had a sense that Texas for Mexicans was like Mississippi for Blacks. As it turned out, I didn't have many opportunities to go into town anyway due to my intense training. Still, what my Grandma said stuck in my mind.

The drill instructors really kicked your butt; they trained you and they shouted at you, and they tried to deconstruct your ego and to give you another one, the one that they wanted you to have. But I saw through all that. I was twenty-one and probably the oldest airman in my squadron in basic training. There were kids that were young and just scared to death.

I just saw through the drill instructors' methods of indoctrination.

I did very well in my training, and so I was selected to be a barracks chief in charge of about a hundred young recruits. I did a decent job, although some of the recruits resented me. I heard that they were planning to "blanket whip" me. This involved overcoming you and covering you up with a blanket. They then beat you with a whip or stick, whatever they can get to strike you with. They use a blanket so the bruises won't show so much. However, I got wind of this and got a couple of other guys on my side to look out for me, so nothing happened because I was prepared for any assault. Thank goodness nothing happened.

But what was even scarier was being at Lackland when the Cuban Missile Crisis took place in October 1962. This was shortly after I arrived. Everything was tightened up several notches higher. I knew then that I was either going to be pushed into being a cook or in security. I just knew that because that's what is needed in times of war: food and security. I knew it was going to be either of the two. As it turned out, I was assigned to the Air Police and Security. I have to thank President Kennedy, Fidel Castro, and the Soviet Union for pushing me into security services. We were scared to death. Many like me had just arrived for basic training, and so nothing in our experiences prepared us to possibly go to war, especially a potential nuclear war. As a result, some guys just freaked out. I think I handled the crisis better. Thank God both the Soviets and the Americans pulled back and the threat of war abated. We were all relieved.

I was not trained to be a security guard in basic training. There are different ways you can be in security in the Air Force. One way was being an Air Force cop; I was not a cop.

—ıı—

After basic training, I was transferred to Malmstrom Air Force Base in Great Falls, Montana. I arrived after Christmas in January 1963. I had not been able to spend Christmas back home. What a shock Montana was at this time of the year. I arrived during the snowy season when it gets down to forty degrees below zero and the snow gets eight feet high. I was used to cold in Stockton, but not forty degrees below zero! We also didn't get snow back home, and so the bitter cold and snow was my introduction to Montana. But I quickly adjusted, and I actually learned to love it. I really came to like Montana as a place very much. It was beautiful. I liked the landscape, the snow, the cold, all of it. The summers are beautiful.

However, the people were not beautiful at all. They were very racist. They hated Indians and Blacks. With me, they didn't know what the hell I was. I went to one bar to have a drink with a white friend, and when he went to the bathroom, the bartender came over to me and said,

"What are you?"

"What do you mean," I responded.

"What are you?"

He was trying to get at me. "What kind of race are you?" is what he was trying to get at. When my friend returned to the bar, I said, "Hey, man, let's get out of here now. Let's go!" The situation was too intense.

As a result, I have a great fondness for the beauty of Montana, but I didn't like the people, or at least the white people that I met.

At the base, I was trained in security. The base was in part a secret base, or at least few people were aware that it was a base that contained nuclear weapons that could be delivered by the fighter bomber squads stationed there. My assignment was to help guard the base. To do this, I had to carry an armed rifle and sometimes a .38 revolver. I hated every minute of this. I just hated it. I despised being there. What was affecting me was a rumor that if you were stationed at Malmstrom Air Force Base, you would never leave for the duration of your enlistment. This really affected me. I didn't want to spend the next few years there. However, I also heard that the only way you could leave was to ask to be assigned to a place where few wanted to go.

I just wanted to leave, and so I volunteered for Special Forces that were like Blue Berets as opposed to the better-know Green Berets, the Special Force in the Army. Special Forces had the aura of romance and of swashbuckling, and in this case of fighting Communists. I worked with my sergeant, and I signed all the forms needed for my transfer. However, the more I thought about it, the more I questioned doing this. One day, I went to see my sergeant and said,

"You know, I've changed my mind. I don't want to apply for Special Forces."

"Airman García," he said with irritation in his voice and demeanor, "I filled out all of these papers on your behalf and now you're telling me, after all of this work, that you don't want to go?"

"Yeah, I don't want to go."

"Why not?"

I told him that if I went all my values would be changed. I remember saying something to that effect. I feared that I'd be altered beyond who I wanted to be. What could he say to that? Nothing much except cussing me out and tearing up my paperwork and throwing it into the garbage.

For the next two years, I remained stationed in Montana. I began to adjust more. I met guys from all over the country, and some became my friends. When allowed to go into town, I met a woman that I dated and had a good time with her.

I also used this time to do some of my drawings. I mostly drew models from magazines like *Vogue* and *Bazaar*. I did these using pencil and charcoal. My friends saw me doing this and asked if I could draw personal Christmas cards for them. "Sure," I said and did.

At the same time, I still wanted to leave Malmstrom. People began to talk about the increasing U.S. military role in Vietnam and surrounding countries. I volunteered to be re-stationed in Vietnam. I had no idea what I was getting into or how much more the United States would become involved in what came to be the Vietnam War.

—||—

Before I knew it, I got my orders to go to a secret base in what was called Indochina that included countries such as Vietnam, Cambodia, and Thailand. In my orders, I was not told where I was going or what I would be doing. I was just told not to mention my going to anyone. You can just say that you are being sent to Indochina.

Before I got dispatched, I was allowed to go home for a few days. Back in Stockton, besides visiting with my family, I also for the first time heard about César Chávez and the farmworkers movement. This was interesting but it had little to no connection with me at that time. I further heard about the free speech movement at UC Berkeley. My older brother was complaining about the students protesting, and I found myself defending the students even though I had no idea what the protests were about. I guess it just appealed to my own rebellious nature.

Since my father was now living in the Los Angeles area and I was to be deployed from there, I went to visit him. My father was living there with my stepmother. I had had my differences with my father, who had also been in the military. But on this visit, we spent time together, primarily drinking. On one drinking spree we drank a fifth and a half of whiskey or something like that. I don't remember everything we drank, but we drank a lot of it. Both of us drunk, we engaged in some serious talk. This was the evening before I had to leave for Indochina. I said a lot of things to my father, some good but mostly bad. All of these feeling just came out of me. Of course, the drinking no doubt influenced this. I blamed him for leaving my mother and his family and not supporting us. That he never sent my mother any money. I was very wrapped up in airing these emotions. I was self-absorbed and just needed to get off my chest all these resentments that I had about my father for years. My father seemed shocked about what he was hearing. I don't know what he expected to hear. After my tirade, he just got up and went to his room.

"You shouldn't have talked this way to your father," my stepmother who was listening said to me.

"Why not?"

"Because he's still your father."

"That doesn't make any difference to me, who he is. Because he's my father doesn't mean I can't talk to him in the way I just did. And I don't care what you think."

I was very stubborn this way and felt very strongly about my opinions, right or wrong. Perhaps morally, I shouldn't have talked this way to my father, but I just felt that it was the right thing to do.

The next morning with a big hangover, I went back to say goodbye to my father. He was still in bed but he wouldn't talk to me. It was like he was frozen in his bed. I think he was just shocked at what he had heard. I just said goodbye and left.

◾▮◾

I was flown out with other soldiers from Long Beach to Hickam Air Force Base in Hawaii. This was just a short stop and then on to Clark Air Force Base in the Philippines. During this short stop, I decided to call up a girl who lived in Hawaii and who I had written to as a pen pal when I was in San Francisco. She had placed her photo, address, and phone number in one of the newspapers, and I decided to write to her. We wrote to each other for a few months. We had a brief but very nice conversation. I told her I was being sent to Indochina, and she wished me well. It made me feel good to talk to her. I had even made a drawing of my pen pal from her photo. This was to take the place of the Beverly Chan drawing! Not really, but I enjoyed doing my pen pal's drawing, which I kept.

After arriving at Clark, my group stayed there for about a week training in marksmanship and weapons updating. We were going to be sent out as a security force. We were informed that we would be going to Thailand but not the specific location. The first thing that struck me about the Philippines was how awfully hot it was. Most days were over 100 and with unbearable humidity. We were drenched in sweat as we trained. However, we were allowed each day after training to go to the Airman's Club on base. It was huge but more importantly it was air-conditioned. It was unbelievable. You went inside and boom, the air conditioning hits and you're cool. You have an ice-cold San Miguel and you're in paradise. That's how I felt immediately. There's no question about it. I was in paradise.

From the Philippines, we flew out to Vietnam for a very short stop. We landed on an island that was being used as an American base as the United States escalated its intervention in Vietnam. When we landed and I looked out of the plane's window, I could see all these guys, guns, and encampments. It looked like war. It was war. "Oh shit," I said. "This is really serious. It's very serious. Where the hell am I going? What do I do now?"

We just refueled and took off again.

—||—

Our next landing was in Bangkok, Thailand. We were there for a few days, and that's when I encountered leprosy-infected people. A friend and I were walking around and didn't know where we were. Bangkok is a huge city. We wanted to go downtown, and as we turned a corner, we almost stumbled over somebody who seemed to be dying. His hands, fingers, and feet were eaten away. He had leprosy. We didn't know this right then but learned later that there was a leper colony nearby, and we were walking into

it. After seeing this man and his awful condition, my friend and I just looked at each other and we said together, "Man, let's get the hell out of here." We were scared. You don't encounter this kind of disease on the streets in the United States. At least, I never had.

A few days later, we were flown to our destination base in Ubon Ratchathani in up-country Thailand near the Laotian border. We had no idea where this was. We landed in a driving rain. You couldn't see anything outside of the plane. We didn't know where we were. We soon learned that it was a clandestine U.S. air base using a Thai Air Force base in conjunction with an Australian Air Force base as cover. Trucks transported us to where we would spend the night. On our way, we passed by fancy bungalows with air-conditioning. They had ice-cold water which we needed, because even though it was nighttime, it was hot as hell. We learned that this was a vacant officers' barrack especially for fighter bomber pilots. This place wasn't for enlisted men such as my group and me.

The next day when we arrived at our barracks, we found no air-conditioning, no windows, wire and sheet metal for the ceiling, and with bunk beds, classic World War II metal beds.

It was in this base that we learned what our mission was and what this base was all about. We were air policemen, and we were sent to secure this base. But it wasn't just any base; it was a secret air base. We learned that the CIA was involved. This was 1965 and the United States was operating this secret air base to bomb North

Vietnam without admitting that these operations were happening. It was codenamed Operation Rolling Thunder. We were to be undercover. To add to this, we were given certain kinds of hats to wear, the kind the Australian soldiers used. We were supposed to be disguised as Australian soldiers. I had no idea why we had to hide the fact that the United States had an air base in Thailand. Looking back, it was because the Johnson administration did not want it known that the U.S. intervention in Vietnam had spread to Thailand.

The secret U.S. air base housed many jet fighter bombers whose job it was to attack North Vietnam. Man, there were a lot of these airplanes. Ironically, even though this was supposed to be a secret air base, the planes had the U.S. Air Force markings. I have to say that they were beautiful-looking jets, handsome pieces of kinetic sculpture. I was moved by the aesthetics of this war machine, even though I knew they were going to kill people, burn things. I came away with this double experience of war, of these jet fighter bombers. They were simultaneously beautiful and killers. There was and still is poetry and deadliness in these jet fighters. They took off every day and night. You could hear their engines all the time. They were loaded with bombs and other devices. There were also helicopters. It was a constant movement of planes and other air equipment. I would later paint images of these bomber planes.

We were in the jungle and the jungle was all around us. We were aware of it in our quarters and when we patrolled the base. The jungle was particularly eerie and threatening at night. It was so dark. Every sound it seemed was someone or something out to get you. We were always aware of the snakes, cobras, pit vipers, tarantulas, and worms long and thick. I had never seen such worms before. You could hear the sides of their bodies scraping against the grass. They were at least four-foot-long worms. Nature was scary in Thailand or at least at night.

I have to say though that the presence of so many trees, flowers, gorgeous flowers, still stick with me. There was one particular flower that smelled like honeysuckle; it was a beautiful smell. The same was true of other jungle flowers. I remember walking from the base to the small nearby town and just inhaling these wonderful aromas from the flowers that grew everywhere. Some of this, including the town, reminded me of walking from our Stockton house to visit friends in the southside part of the city that was still rural as Thailand was where I was stationed. This sense of familiarity made me feel very safe.

As military police, we had to guard the base against any attacks. We patrolled the perimeter of the base both day and night. We were there to protect the U.S. jet fighters who were bombing the hell out of North Vietnam as President Lyndon Johnson escalated the U.S. intervention to protect South Vietnam from "Communist" insurgency and from invasion by the North Vietnamese Communists. The Johnson administration in true Cold

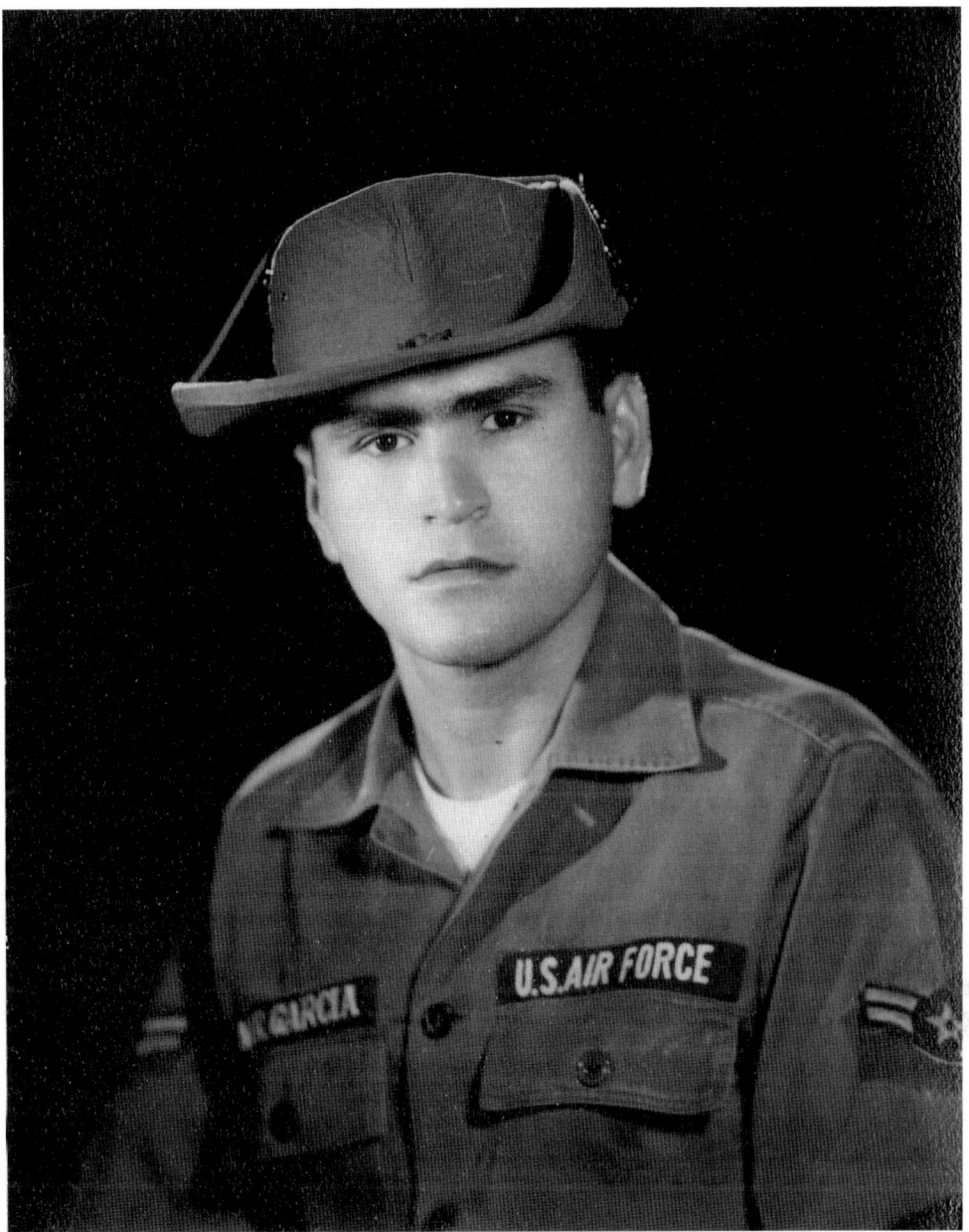

Rupert García in Indochina, 1965. Photo courtesy of Rupert García.

War fashion categorized what we were doing in Vietnam as stopping Communism.

I later realized that all of this was nonsense, but at the time I completely accepted the argument. I felt that we were there for the right reason, to hold back the Communists, and our secret base in Thailand was part of this battle. After all, I had grown up with this constant anti-Communist propaganda for years. I was a victim of it. It was black and white. We're good and they're evil. So, what we were doing in Indochina made total sense. For a whole year, I lived with the sound of bombers taking off, not knowing if they would return. All of this later became a problem for me when I got out of the military. But at the time, I just accepted my mission.

The base seemed immense, and so there was a lot of ground to patrol surrounded by fences to keep others out, especially those who might want to attack the base. What I dreaded was going out on patrol on the periphery of the base located miles from the actual site containing the jet fighter bombers. Each patrol consisted of two men. A truck would drop us off at a certain location and then go on to drop off more of our guys to patrol another area. It was scary because we patrolled day and night. Each patrol was for eight hours. It was strange being out there. It's all jungle. The nights were the worst because you couldn't see anything, and we were not to use flashlights so we wouldn't be detected. Every sound was potentially something out to get you. You could get paranoid because you couldn't see what was beyond five inches of the fence. No idea. All this was insane. I was scared to death. To add to our fears, we were not allowed to carry any weapons such as M-16s, nothing. Why? Because it would reveal that we were American soldiers patrolling what was supposed to be an Australian base. But everyone knew we were Americans. Even though we wore those Australian hats, we had Blacks and me as a Chicano who hardly looked like white Australians. Who was kidding who? Yet

to allow the myth that this was not a covert American base, we were not allowed to protect ourselves by carrying weapons. It made no sense and put us at risk.

To protect myself at least physically in case I was attacked, I worked out a lot to make myself physically strong. I biked around the inner base. I took karate. Man, I was ready for anything and anyone at anytime to take care of myself. I just thought of wanting to get back home safe and sound and to do that I had to stay in tip-top shape, which I was.

I also broke orders by carrying a knife when on patrol. I figured if I can't carry a gun or rifle, at least I can carry a knife in case I'm attacked. I hid the knife inside of one of my boots and strapped it to my ankle. I thought it was nonsense that we couldn't openly carry weapons even though within the base we had tons. I said, "to hell with this; I ain't crazy!"

◼◼◼

During my year at this covert air base, I did get a chance to meet and mingle to some extent with the Thai people who lived in the closest town to the base. The one thing that stuck out immediately was how beautiful the Thai women were. I got to know some and even dated a few. However, I have to admit that my first encounter with these women was in the bars catering to American military personnel. These were prostitutes. The families in the town didn't want their daughters dating Americans. If you wanted to be with women, the only recourse were the prostitutes. These were my first introduction to Thai women.

At the same time, as I and others were visiting bars, we were warned by base doctors about the threat of contracting venereal disease. They showed us a film that I'll never forget. It was a classic film. It showed you what a healthy penis looked like and then how it looks when you get syphilis. What a difference! It scared the hell out of us.

On base, getting clothes custom made was very cheap. I got shirts and suits and even shoes made for me. I actually designed the clothes I wanted. I would draw a design and take it to the tailor who would measure me and make the clothes. The tailor was Indian but married to a Thai woman. He knew some English, but his son who worked with him knew much more. As I did business with them, they got to like me and introduced me to the rest of the family, including one daughter whom I instantly fell in love with. She was beautiful! I got to see her a few times but under restricted conditions.

I enjoyed drawing the designs for my clothes and shoes but other than that, I didn't do much drawing that year. I only drew two things. One was of a typical Thai house on stilts and the other was of a man wearing a turban. I still have the drawings.

I also went to some Thai restaurants. I loved it. It was the closest thing to Mexican food. They used a lot of chili *picantes*, some that I had never seen before, and they made different kinds of salsas. The food was great. I was in heaven. I also tried some pizza in the town, but it wasn't very good.

On the other hand, there was an Australian restaurant where the specialty was steak and fries. I frequented this place a lot because the food was good. I had these meals with ice cold Thai beer that was fantastic. It reminded me of San Miguel beer in the Philippines.

By comparison, the food served on the base was boring and tasteless. The food was the same as they served in the Montana base and just as bad. It was like going into Woolworth's and getting mass-produced food; it was like campus cafeteria food. They made a lot of food, shoved it on your tray, and you sat down and ate it. Nothing very interesting.

What helped in my diet is that my family would occasionally send me a care package of Mexican canned food. Once I got a letter from my Aunt Mary, my mother's sister, who was a great cook. She told me that she was sending me some homemade tortillas made by her. I couldn't believe it! Homemade flour tortillas! I could hardly wait. I even told some of my buddies that I would share the tortillas with them. They finally arrived after a couple of weeks or so. They came in a packet, and when I opened it I saw that the tortillas were wrapped in aluminum foil. I could hardly wait. My mouth was watering and my stomach began to growl. As I opened the foil, I couldn't believe what I saw. The tortillas had green and brown spots—all of them. They also had mildew. Oh, my God! What happened to Tía Mary's tortillas? They were no good. I couldn't smell them because they were putrid from the few weeks of being delivered thousands of miles. It was terrible, and what a disappointment to me. I apologized to my buddies. I could look at the tortillas and only imagine what they would taste like if they were fresh. I could hardly wait to get back home and have some of them.

—||—

Drugs were an issue at the base as it would be among American troops throughout the war in Vietnam. We did hard, dangerous work, and some guys tried to deal with this by using drugs. Marijuana and harder drugs were the norm. You could easily get it in town. Guys would go out on patrol loaded. Some guys would even contemplate suicide under the influence of drugs. One day I was in my bunk resting and this other guy next to me begins to cut his wrists. "Goddamn it!" I said as I jumped up and grabbed him to stop what he was doing. I don't remember if he thanked me later, but it didn't matter to me. Drugs and drinking were a serious business. Some guys would go to work loaded with drugs and booze. This included those who secured the fighter bombers and prepared them for their next flights. I could see the guys just wheeling back and forth because they were loaded. It was a mess. I remember thinking, "this is too much, but that's the way it is." I'd be on patrol and some of the guys with me were either loaded or drunk and they're supposed to protect me and others. The intensity of the drug culture grew and grew. Outside of some pot, I shied away from the hard stuff. I also only got drunk once and kept in good

physical shape. All of this was indicative of the attitude of many servicemen who had no idea what we were doing in Indochina and just wanted to get the hell out of there. I didn't blame them.

This drug culture affected both whites and Blacks. I hung around mostly with the Blacks and a couple of decent white guys.

—||—

One interesting experience while at the base occurred when one of the jet fighters who went on a bombing raid over North Vietnam had not been able to release one of its bombs. The pilot on his return tried to disengage the bomb over the Laos jungle, not knowing whether it would explode. He succeeded in releasing it, and it didn't go off. The base command was obligated to find the bomb and return it to the base. We didn't want the bomb to go off and possibly kill or wound Laotian people. This would not look good for us. My sergeant announced to us, "We have a situation in which there is a bomb that was disengaged, and it didn't fire. It's located in some swamp near Laos, and we need some volunteers to fly in and find the bomb and protect it until we figure what to do with it. Any volunteers?"

"I'll go Sarge," I raised my hand. I don't know why I volunteered other than it was something different to do from the monotony of our patrols. I also liked the idea of flying in a helicopter. I don't think I was scared. Boom! Let's go.

Two other guys also volunteered and away we flew in the helicopter.

We had no idea if we were going east, south, west, or whatever. We just knew we were flying over all this jungle. After awhile, the helicopter began to swoop down and we were told to jump off as the helicopter hovered. We jumped off onto a little bump of land in the swamp. Our orders were to stay there and guard it and make sure that no one else came close to it. Of course, we didn't know if it might go off on us.

The helicopter then flew off, and we were left alone. On top of this, we had no weapons, thank you very much! Soon some people came by with their animals and looked at us with great curiosity. There's nothing we could do except make sure they didn't come close to the bomb. I finally said, "Let's go to sleep. We can do nothing. We're outnumbered and who gives a shit?"

We went to sleep, and fortunately nothing happened. After several hours we heard the chopper coming in to change the guard. We jumped on the helicopter and were flown back to base.

That was my experience with a live bomb. It was all crazy. It was fun in the helicopter, but the rest was crazy. We weren't scared about the bomb. In fact, it all seemed romantic to fly in and secure it. It would have been scary if we had had to stay there at night, but we were there only during daytime. If it had been dark, that would have been another story. I learned one thing in Thailand, "go where there's light!"

—||—

Race was another issue at our base. There were many tensions between whites and Blacks. I was the only Chicano there, and I mostly hung out with the Black soldiers. There was a Filipino guy there who had attended my high school. Everywhere I went in the military, there were race problems. In fact, back in Montana there had been a mini-race riot between whites and Blacks. These feelings were transported to the secret base in Thailand. I think that part of the race tensions had to do with the civil rights movement led by Dr. King that we were hearing about. This made Blacks in our unit feel empowered, while it made the whites feel threatened and resentful. In fact, the white guys were just terrible. They acted as if they owned the world. They expressed their racist feelings not only to the Blacks on the base, but also to the Thai people. They were absolutely disrespectful to the people who lived there. I was embarrassed to be an American. I had to leave some bars and other places where I witnessed such racist behavior. I just couldn't bear it. I just couldn't.

At the same time, we were hearing and reading about the growing anti-war movement back in the states. While I was sympathetic to the civil rights movement, I was opposed to the anti-war movement. I and other security guys at our base said that they should send us back home with M-16s to shoot the students who were protesting. Just shoot them all. I was very adamant about this. This was my mentality in 1965–1966. I think we resented the college guys who had deferments from being drafted while we were out there in the jungle fearing all the time we might be killed. This feeling on my part was augmented by a feeling that I was never going to be able to leave Thailand. I felt that my year of duty would never end. I felt that I was going to be stuck there, and that this was going to be the end of my life. Like other American military in Indochina including Vietnam, I would count the months, the weeks, and the days before my tour of duty would end. It seemed endless. Everyone counted.

-II-

After a few months in Thailand, I wanted out. I applied to be sent back to the United States. There was an option available that if you were nearing the end of your entire service, as I was, and you had a job waiting for you or if you were going back to school, that you could receive permission to be released earlier. I knew that I wanted to go back to school and pursue a degree in art, and I also wanted to go back to San Francisco, so I applied to San Francisco State. While in Thailand, I got the good news that I had been admitted into the school. On this basis, I applied for early release from Thailand. My request was granted, and I was delighted. I had had enough not only of Thailand but of the Air Force. I was released with a few months to go in my service and flown back to California. I was discharged as an Airman Second Class. Unlike other veterans who now are returning to Vietnam to visit where they fought, I have never felt this need.

The thought of reenlisting never entered my mind. I had no interest in a military career. The only reason that I had enlisted was because I had no job and being in the service gave me that. I did my job including going to Indochina, and now that job was over. I wanted to move on and fulfill my dream of being an artist.

I looked forward to going back to school. I had saved some of my military pay, which would help, and I also learned that I was eligible for the GI Bill that would also provide funding to return to school. In addition, when I was stationed in Montana, I took some college courses offered at the local college and received credits for my general education requirements at San Francisco State.

-II-

I got my honorable discharge from the Air Force in May of 1966. This was back in California. On the flight back, the plane stopped first in Seattle. The first impression of coming back to the United States was seeing white women, glass doors, and doorknobs. This hit me right away. This was because where I was in Indochina there were no white women, no glass doors, and no doorknobs. I later thought about how strange this was that this is what first impressed me about being back in the States.

From Seattle, I was flown to Sacramento where my buddy, Jim, picked me up. I had known Jim since high school. Jim had also joined the military and was in the Marines. He was a brilliant guy. He picked me up in his Porsche, and I was still dazed. But I was happy that I was out of the goddamn military. I really felt happy, just joyously happy. It was over and no more, man. That was it. It was like when you graduated from high school. You get your diploma and you're free. You're not going back, and you don't have to go back. It was the same thing with the Air Force when I got out. I knew it was over. I no longer had to wear fatigues. All that stuff was over. Man, it just liberated me. At the same time, I experienced an internal quietness and reticence about my military experience. It was not something that I was proud of. I never wore my uniform back in California because I was afraid of being harassed by anti-war protestors. I had heard that many returning veterans experienced this, and I wanted to avoid any harassment. I just wore my civilian clothes that became a kind of shield for me. I didn't want people to know where I'd just come from.

Jim was kind enough to drive me back home to Stockton to see my family. Since school didn't start until September, I stayed and worked at the cannery to make some money, and I lived at home.

━┃┃━

I have to admit that my four years in the military and especially that one year in Indochina had emotional and psychological impacts on me, some of which lingered for many years. This is true of all vets in combat situations. I wasn't directly in combat but close enough to undergo strong reactions. One thing I experienced was how intensified racism is. It was very blatant

in the military. It was something that was hard to escape in a military confined environment. I was especially struck by the behavior of American GIs of all colors and their abusive behavior toward the Indochinese people. It was horrendous. I'll never forget this. It had a lasting effect. It really highlighted the reality of the ugly American.

Another effect, not necessarily bad, was how my sense of loneliness developed, especially that year in Thailand. It involved being alone for hours and hours. Alone. I had to come to grips with that. It made me become more aware of my physicality and my environment. It meant hours of silence, nighttime and daytime. I would have to be on patrol by myself for long stretches. I couldn't talk to anyone. It took discipline to be alone. What do you think about? How do you occupy yourself in a way you won't go crazy or fall asleep? I actually fell asleep once on patrol in Thailand. I was on the midnight shift, which went from midnight until seven the next morning. We were out there standing between jet fighter bombers and securing the perimeter, and I was really tired. I was very exhausted. I decided to lie down and just close my eyes for a few seconds. That's all I needed. I fell asleep. I woke up and saw these black shiny boots with clean pants, and they go up and there is the sergeant of the guard.

"García! What in the hell are you doing? Are you crazy? Don't you know that somebody could come in here and blow this place up?"

What could I say? He was absolutely right. I said aloud "oh, shit!"

I felt it was over. I was going to be court-martialed. He was going to shoot me, and he had every right to do so. You were never to fall asleep while on guard, especially protecting the planes. It wasn't just the planes; it was also people's lives. I had nothing to say. Thank God, the sergeant let me go. He said,

"I'm not going to report you but don't let me ever catch you again asleep while on duty."

"Sir, you will never catch me doing this again. Never!"

And he didn't, because I knew that the next time would be curtains for me. He would either shoot me or I would be court-martialed and sentenced to jail. It was very big of the sergeant to not report me, as much as I hated his guts. He was a complete redneck, as were many of the other sergeants. Still, he let me go.

What also affected me for many years was being gun-shy. At the secret base in Thailand, we were fired at a few times by insurgents. The sound of this firing resonated in my ears. Upon returning to the United States, every time I heard what I thought was a gunshot, I cringed and wanted to hit the ground. The sound of jet planes also triggered a psychological reaction. I had heard so many jets take off from our base, and this sound haunted me for many years. I would start sweating and get paranoid at these sounds for a long time.

This fear of jet noise especially affected me once when I was invited to participate in a summer youth program at Loyola University in Los Angeles.

This was many years after the war. They invited me along with other college teachers who taught art, as I did, to work with these exceptionally gifted high school students. I went down and they put me in a hotel near the campus. Loyola is adjacent to LAX. It turned out that my room faced where all the jets took off. This triggered my panic attacks about jet noises of the kind I had heard consistently at the base. For two nights, I couldn't sleep, and I started to sweat profusely and felt sick. I was having these delusions of being back in Indochina, and I was starting to lose it. I felt really vulnerable. I felt terrible. I didn't know what to do. I called my wife who told me to get out of there and come back home.

I also called Oliver Stone, the filmmaker, who I knew because he had bought some of my paintings. He knew that I was a veteran and had spent a year in Thailand. I knew he had been in Vietnam and by then had made his epic film on Vietnam, *Platoon*. Oliver had invited me to dinner the following night at his home in Santa Monica. I called him and told him how I was breaking down.

"Oliver, I'm in a bad state, man. I'm really bad. It's terrible."

"Come on over right now," Oliver said, and he gave me his address.

Before going, I withdrew from the program and then took a cab to a downtown hotel. From there I went to Oliver's house. When I walked in and met Oliver, he announced to his other guests who had arrived for dinner, "This is Rupert García and he's having a very difficult time." He made this announcement as if it was no big deal. There were other Vietnam veterans there, and they understood. Everyone was very welcoming, and this helped put me at ease. Oliver got me a drink, and we later had dinner. It was just what I needed. It helped me get out of my emotional trauma. I had a great time and Oliver brought attention to my paintings hung on his walls. He was showing me off, which made me feel great and wanted. Oliver gained my respect and love forever.

━┃┃━

Sometime before this incident, I encountered another very emotional experience tied to the war. This was in the late 1970s at the San Francisco International Film Festival where I and Tim Drescher went to see the premier of the documentary *Hearts and Minds* that was very powerful and critical of the U.S. role in Vietnam. As the film started, it didn't take long before I started crying. I was all messed up psychologically. I didn't know what was happening to me. I was almost frozen. I was like this all through the film. After it was over, they had a Q and A with the producers of the film. When they asked for questions, I stood up to make a comment, but I could barely talk. So, they said to me, "come up on stage." And so I did and tried to talk about the film, but all I could do was cry. This cathartic situation was taking place in front of hundreds of people. But I didn't care. Finally, I found my voice and talked about how the Vietnam vets were not being given adequate psychological care. Saying

all this was painful, confusing, and disorienting, but, at the same time, exhilarating because I felt something happening to me. I could actually get these feelings out that I had been hiding for all these years.

I was further paranoid about having served in the secret base in Indochina. For a long time, I wouldn't tell anyone about this experience. I didn't want to be attacked by anti-war protestors and others who opposed the U.S. war in Vietnam and Indochina. But this experience at the theater finally allowed me to face the fact that I had been running away from. I had denied that I was involved in the war, making it possible for bombs to be dropped that killed people and burned their homes, trees, and crops. I now felt I could admit all this. I felt liberated and it was wonderful for me to go up there on the stage as a vet and do this. It felt great.

After the discussion, people came up to me and thanked me for my words. One of them was Daniel Ellsberg. I said, "I am very proud of what you did in releasing the Pentagon Papers." We had a very nice chat.

But I couldn't have spoken out as I did without my friend Tim who went with me to the film. He was very helpful, and the fact that I knew that he was there allowed me to really let go. If Tim hadn't been with me, I don't think I would have spoken out. I don't unnecessarily put myself in dangerous situations—except for going into the jungle in Indochina, of course.

I mentioned on the stage the failures of the Veterans Administration with respect to Vietnam vets. It was disgraceful. Many vets suffered from their exposure to Agent Orange in Vietnam. Many vets were homeless. Of course, like myself, many had psychological and emotional issues. Many were jobless. Some became drug addicts, which they had started to be in Vietnam. Many had to deal with the trauma of having killed people, including innocent Vietnamese. You had to live with this. So how do you justify that you took people's lives? That you burned their homes and their crops? That you destroyed their animals and water supplies? How do you justify all this? You almost can't. It's difficult because you gave up a year or two in Vietnam. You don't want to say that it was a bad thing because if you do that, you blame yourself. And if you blame yourself, how do you deal with that? How do you justify that? If you blame your country and government, then you become very embittered, and how do you handle that? In addition, you have to deal with your family and friends, some of whom opposed the war and some who supported it.

All this is really powerful and complex, and it continues to be powerful and complex. It's insufficient to have the Vietnam Memorial in DC. That memorial helps U.S. citizens but not the GIs. The vet who goes to the memorial, of course, breaks down and cries. I was never involved in hand-to-hand combat, but imagine those who were and the trauma they live with. Their situation isn't altered by the wall. The memorial is poetry, a poetic gesture, but it has nothing to do with profoundly helping the vet who was in

Vietnam. It doesn't put money in his pocket; it doesn't help him get a job; it doesn't help put his family together. It does none of that. I'm not belittling the memorial and I have never been there, although I don't know why.

◾◾◾

I returned to Stockton in May 1966 after four years in the Air Force. Because of the tensions I had with my stepfather, I didn't stay with my mother. Instead, I stayed with Alicia Arong and her husband and dear friend Bonifacio who had been in the Marines. Alicia was a long-time friend since the sixth grade and was the sister of Dolores Huerta. At the same time, my family did give me a big welcome home party. This included my mother and my siblings and various friends at the home of my oldest brother. It was a wonderful event; however, if you see the pictures, I'm trying to be happy, but you can see that, at the same time, there's a certain sadness or hesitancy on my face. I was struggling with the effects of my years in the military, especially that one year in Indochina. Part of my anguish was that I couldn't tell anyone about my mission at the secret camp in Thailand. I was sworn to secrecy when I agreed to go there. My family and friends knew I had been sent somewhere in Indochina, but they didn't know where or what I was doing. This pained me and forced me to keep all of these feelings about my experiences there inside of me. That wasn't a good thing.

At the same time, I was pleased that I would be going to San Francisco

State in the fall. I knew that with what I could save from working the cannery during the summer plus my GI Bill of Rights financial assistance, I would be able to afford my tuition and living expenses in the city. I looked forward to taking art classes and learning more about becoming an artist.

That summer I also had an interesting meeting with Dolores Huerta, whom I had known while growing up in Stockton. She, of course, had become a major leader along with César Chávez in organizing the farmworkers into a union and struggling for their labor rights and self-dignity. At Alicia's house Dolores talked to me about becoming part of the union and putting my skills as an artist on behalf of the union.

"You know, Dolores, my dream is to become an artist. That's what I want to do and that's why I need to go to San Francisco State."

"Rupert," Dolores replied, "I love you for this. Go do it and do your best."

Dolores was totally encouraging. Many years later a big party for Dolores to celebrate her sixty-fifth birthday was held in San Francisco. I was invited to produce a poster for the event and to attend and say a few words about Dolores. I talked about that time when Dolores without any reservations encouraged me to pursue my dream, which I did.

"She did this from her heart. She was pursuing her dream as was César of organizing farmworkers, and she wanted me to follow my dream. She could have guilt-baited me about my obligations to El Movimiento and to La Raza, but she didn't. She was very supportive and loving to me. I needed this encouragement, and Dolores gave it to me. Dolores, I love you!"

With her encouragement, I set off to a new chapter in my life.

5

San Francisco State

I went to San Francisco in the fall of 1966 to study art at San Francisco State (SFS). I was assisted in this by the GI Bill of Rights, which helped to pay for my tuition and other expenses. I found an apartment near the Haight-Ashbury district. The Hippie movement was just beginning then. I knew little about them. I was alone and I was scared to death to go back to school. I'd been out of school for five years. I also found the SFS campus to be huge and threatening. When I first went there, I was hit by all these things going on that were largely foreign to me. This included the anti-war movement; civil rights; the Black Student Union; the Black Panthers; and the farmworkers movement to name a few. All of these things were happening and there I was with this shield around me. My eyes and ears got big just absorbing all of this campus activity. It was an incredible introduction to returning to education.

—ıı—

Another big challenge for me was just understanding how to enroll and which classes to take and where to pay my fees. It was all hectic with no one to help me and other students. I consulted the college catalog, but this was of no help. It made me even more confused. The language seemed all mixed up. I said to myself, "What the hell is this? What's a semester unit? What's a GPA?" All this was strange to me. I had a hard time. It took a while to get a hang of all this.

Somehow, I found the Art Department, and they were helpful in answering my questions and guiding me to enroll in my first classes with my designation as an art major. Although I had fulfilled some of my general education requirements at Stockton Junior College and while in the service, I still had to take some at San Francisco State. In taking some of these classes, my mind was blown. I was being introduced to critical ways of seeing life and society. This was in keeping with the political climate of the 1960s—the sixties—and a new critical approach to the curriculum especially in the humanities and social sciences. Through these classes I became politically conscious. This included classes in sociology, social psychology, anthropology, philosophy, and even my art classes. In fact, I planned to minor in sociology. I was becoming aware of how societies are put together. I was becoming aware of what it means to have class consciousness and what it means to talk about race and the structure of racism and how it's connected to other parts of organized society. I was also becoming aware of the role of war in history and who wins and who loses.

I was learning how human beings really function. For example, I took a course in which we read a book called *The Social Construction of Reality: A Treatise in the Sociology of Knowledge* by Peter L. Berger and Thomas Luckmann. I read this book and others too and began to understand how human beings define who they are. How they give meaning to human experience. On the one hand, there are things that are instinctual. You have to eat. If you don't, you die. We think. We respond to the world. But how you do that is socialized. It doesn't fall from the sky. You learn this.

Peter L. Berger and Thomas Luckmann:

> The basic contentions of the argument of this book are implicit in its title and subtitle, namely, that reality is socially constructed.[1]

The book was an eye-opener on how people develop who they are and an understanding of the world and how society evolves. I learned that since the world is a social construction defining what is true, what is false, what is good, and what is not good, we can reconsider these values. Since we constructed this, we can deconstruct it. I had never heard information like this until I read this book, which made all these things clear. It was amazing. I didn't follow step-by-step what I read in the book to make a painting; however, it was always on my mind consciously or unconsciously.

I had this great desire to learn about how society works, how individuals work, and understanding the role of history and economics. In this way, I got insights into helping me understand how we got to Stockton. Why did grandma and grandpa come to the United States? Why did we live where we lived on the southside? Why did we live on First Street in that little house? Why didn't we live in a mansion on the northside? Why didn't we have a Mercedes-Benz parked in our garage?

I began to understand other aspects about what I was doing. For example, I was learning about the role of propaganda during the Cold War and how this molded my mind in believing in a Communist threat. How watching World War II movies really affected me and prepared me to almost unknowingly join the Air Force. Something had to prepare me to think this way as if it was just natural. I came to understand that this was the role of how symbols come into play. Knowledge and information, whether literary or visual, are symbols that tell you what to think and what to do and how to behave. I had taken everything for granted. I assumed that everything was in the correct position, and so I never questioned this.

Well now through my experiences at San Francisco State, both in classes and outside of classes, I began to question everything. Everything was up for grabs. So, when the Black Panthers happened, when the farmworkers struggle happened, when the student movement happened, and when the anti-Vietnam War movement happened, I began to understand them completely. I understood and became totally sympathetic.

I began to adopt a more critical perspective, because I intellectually understood what was happening. I was still emotionally turning inside out. It was torture. But I was understanding intellectually the dynamics of how people were socialized even though this didn't explain my emotions. My emotions were still there.

I was absorbing this through my classes and my readings. Someone gave me a copy of Mao Zedong's book on culture, and I just devoured it. Mao talks about the role of culture and the artist, and that forced me to critique the role of the artist as I had learned it. Mao's definition was counter to the self-absorbed individualized concerns of the bourgeois artist. This really challenged me.

I was also influenced by political actions. This was brought to my mind when the Black Panthers went to Sacramento with their weapons and went inside the State Capitol. I watched this on TV and I was thinking, "right on!"

I was beginning to read various Marxist writers that I discovered by hanging out at this progressive bookstore, Modern Times. I began to understand how Marxism related to capitalism. I learned about Marx's analysis of the capitalist's control of the means of production and of the workers who make the products but don't control them. The workers are paid a dollar, and the product is sold for fifteen dollars. The owner makes all that money, and the worker who made the product can't even afford to buy it. I had never heard of these things before.

Marxism helped me to understand class society. However, I found Marxism problematic on race and culture. I thought that Marxists tended to have a reductive understanding of culture as merely reflecting the base. This was a kind of easy way of understanding a very complex process of how history and culture take place. I critically reacted to seeing art images from both Russia and China that supposedly represented revolutionary cultures and, in particular, revolutionary painting. I didn't buy this because they were so unexciting aesthetically and they robbed the imagination. This was socialist realism which I rejected. It was very boring. You could replace images of Russians with Chinese, but the image remained the same with no exciting aesthetic. To me, it was insulting to my eyes to see this kind of art that was supposed to be revolutionary art. They were very simplified representations of complex human behavior. The images were all about the ideal worker and the revolutionary soldier. It just gave me a headache. This was Stalinist aesthetics, which I didn't accept. I accepted Marxism as a way of critiquing capitalist societies such as the United States. However, Marxist aesthetics as represented by socialist realism was not for me.

As part of my new education, I became very conscious of advertising and how advertising as a system of signs and symbols tells us what to buy and for what reasons. I took a seminar on advertising with a newly minted PhD who looked at advertising in a kind of symbiotic way. He utilized a theory of signs of information which attempt to convince you that you need something. He looked at how advertisers examined how human beings biologically function and how they built upon human needs and desires. They, in turn, link these to certain products to sell us. They're really tapping into our real needs, but they're hooking it up to lipstick, perfume, cologne, cars, or clothes. Through this class, I began to see how corrupt advertising and corporate America is and how they don't really have our interests at heart. They superficially do; however, in essence they're more interested in turning a profit, and a big one at that.

Along these lines, I read Marshall McLuhan, who became a kind of mass media guru in the late 1960s. Actually, I knew his son, Herbert, who was in the Air Force with me. At that time, I had no idea who his father was. Well, years later, Marshall McLuhan's name was in neon lights everywhere. He coined that wonderful catchphrase, "The Medium is the Message." I related to this because being an artist and working with the medium of art, I came to better understand the significance of my art in conveying messages. McLuhan also got me to think of the importance of technique in art making, such as silk screen, which has a message in itself. It's saying something. I stretched McLuhan's theme.

This critical approach I expanded to other fields and other aspects of human life. Art history, philosophy, and every other discipline had to be reexamined. I came to know that I couldn't take anything for granted. We had to look at what was going on behind what was apparent. I needed to understand what was behind it. What was the mechanism behind it? What were the values and ideology behind it? What was really being said? What was really being asked of me? These are some of the changes in consciousness that I began to experience by being at San Francisco State. This critical consciousness would become part of my approach to my art.

I learned so much and so fast at SFS. It was overwhelming but not debilitating. Learning all these things saved my life. It did so because it helped me understand a lot of what I just took for granted. I learned how to formulate questions. I obtained the tools to do that, to be critical, but also to not be dogmatic. I learned to be as open as possible because no one answer is going to give you a complete answer. I really believe that. I think part of the reason I didn't become dogmatic or at least not very dogmatic, in part, goes back to my Catholic training and my questioning of it even at an early age. Catholic doctrine then insisted that only Catholics could go to Heaven. But I had friends who were not Catholic, and I couldn't accept that they were going to hell. How could Jesse and Jimmy go to hell? I didn't understand this. In addition, at SFS I dabbled a bit in Hinduism, Buddhism, and Daoism. I didn't become a follower as did many young people in the 1960s, but I took some things away from these religious influences. I mostly read about these practices. They seemed to possess a true transcendence that I didn't think Catholicism had. Also, unlike the Catholic Church, these other beliefs seemed to be nonhierarchical. That is to say, everyone, even those you hate, will go to heaven or a heaven. No one is going to hell. That's some of what I got from these faiths, which influenced my more nondogmatic view of life.

—||—

Part of my developing political consciousness was becoming aware of Third World movements both domestically and internationally. This included the Cuban Revolution, China, Vietnam, and social movements such as the Black Power Movement and the Chicano Movement. I began to realize that there was a relationship between them. Both were fighting for liberation. The affiliation became clear to me. Crystal clear. We have a domestic war and an international war. So, in addition to developing a critical consciousness, I was also developing a Third World consciousness.

This is when I read Frantz Fanon's *The Wretched of the Earth* and how he forcefully lays out the relationship between the colonizer and colonized. What happens to the colonizer and,

more importantly, what happens to the colonized—the wretched of the earth. He writes about culture and the national bourgeoise and the inequities of a colonial condition. Here was this psychiatrist from Martinique who was doing his best to understand his own colonized status. That's what was so strong for me. I felt that I could relate to Fanon as if he was speaking to me. Through him, I came to understand the need for decolonization not just in the Third World, but in the United States. The Chicano, the Black, the Asian American, and the Native American, we all represented colonized people within the United States.

This new way of thinking began to likewise affect how I saw art. I recognized that much of what I had learned about art was mostly European art. But where was Mexico? Where was Africa? Where was Asia? There was very little representation, if any. I really began to think about art history and to reexamine it. Why was I just being fed art that included the Greeks, the Romans, the Middle Ages, the Renaissance, the Impressionists? This art was supposed to represent the best of human culture. But I was starting to wonder, was this true? I didn't think it was true. I was gaining the intellectual tools to analyze this, critique it, and look elsewhere. I began, for example, to teach myself the art history of Mexico.

I had always had an attraction to art history. I always found it interesting and exciting. But when I became critical about it, I realized how literally whitewashed I had been in terms of what I had been presented as being art history. I began to discover the art history of the Third World. I remember taking a class on the history of philosophy of Mexico, which blew my mind. It was taught by Roberto Rivera, who had a PhD in philosophy from one of the UC campuses. I took it because it sounded interesting to me. I had never heard of Mexican philosophy. I learned the world view of the Mayans and the Aztecs and the evolution of thought in Mexico from the colonial era to the twentieth century. It was amazing. We read philosophers such as José Vasconcellos, Samuel Ramos, and Octavio Paz. I particularly was impressed with Paz, especially his book *The Labyrinth of Solitude*, which many Chicanos were reading at the same time. His study of the pachuco I found very interesting, along with his general view of the world. I especially liked when he quoted someone asking him "are you a Mexican philosopher?" His response was "I'm Mexican and more." I would later very much accept this view. All of these exposures to Mexican philosophers were eye-opening, because they allowed me to become aware of such things as Mexican thinking and Mexican thought, and they emboldened me because of that. There was plenty of Plato, Aristotle, and Kierkegaard defining human thought, but Mexican thought also existed and was of particular consequence for me. I thought it was terrific. I said to myself, "there's a whole intellectual culture here that is absolutely profound. And I wasn't taught any of it, none of it. And here it is. This is me."

━II━

Not only was my political and ethnic consciousness developing at San Francisco State, but so too was my development as an artist beginning with the first art classes that I took. When I returned to school in the fall of 1966, I hadn't made a picture in almost two years. When I started art classes, I didn't know what to make paintings about. I almost went back to school with a blank slate. All I knew was that I wanted to take art classes and to become an artist. One of my first classes was in intermediate painting. It was a drawing and painting class. Some of my first pictures in this class were kind of vague. They were done technically well because I was learning technique—how to use a pencil. In painting, I began to learn how to use acrylic, which was a hot item then. It was fairly new, non-oil based, water-based, nontoxic, and when it dries you can wrap it, twist it, and it won't break. You can thin acrylic with water, but it's not watercolor. Unlike watercolor, acrylic, because it has a plastic base, won't peel or crack. I used acrylic because it was the fad of the day. But I didn't like how it looked then. It dries and lacks a certain kind of visual presence. All of this is in comparison to oil which I prefer. The attraction of acrylic was that it dried fast and gave you a great surface that was really bound to the canvas. On the other hand, it doesn't have the luster that oil does. I did some of my very early paintings in this class.

However, I wasn't just learning technique. I was beginning to seriously think about the role of painting and of the artist. Some of this began almost by accident. In the apartment building where I rented, the owner of the building, Robert Clutton, was an artist from Wales. He had all of these art magazines in his front office, many of them from London. I had never before seen an art magazine in my life. I didn't know that they existed. I began to look at them. I was just stunned because I was looking at visual thoughts and feelings that began to raise questions in me about seeing. For example, I saw in one of the magazines my first René Magritte picture. The article was about Magritte with illustrations. I hadn't ever heard about Magritte, and so I learned about him. The one picture of his in the article that I really got into was a drawing of a chopped tree and the roots of the stump were choking the hatchet that chopped it down. The tree was getting revenge. I was looking at this image and I was thinking, "my god, how could this happen? How can the hatchet that chopped down the tree be strangled by the roots of the chopped tree?" It was a puzzle, an enigma. I just looked at that picture for a very long time, and it made me think of the pictures I had done before going to college and the ones I was doing in school. It made my pictures seem insignificant, because unlike the Magritte picture, mine lacked the intellectual inquiry that his picture had. Magritte's image was a thinking one.

The tree was nature, and the hatchet was culture, and so nature was struggling with culture. I said to myself, "Jesus Christ! What the hell is happening?" I had never thought about that kind of stuff and never seen a picture like that one. Magritte's work had that kind of thinking process where things were topsy turvy. This image helped me in developing a sense that the world doesn't have just one way of existing, and that there are many ways to think about human experience. Encountering Magritte's image was an eye-opener.

I also came to know more about the Dadaist movement in Western Europe during the early twentieth century. The Dadaists such as Marcel Duchamp identified Western culture, civilization, and bourgeois culture as the cause of World War I. They deconstructed high art; they reconsidered it. The Dadaists were mostly anarchists and nihilists with some political radicals They made what was called anti-art, meaning that their procedures and constructs didn't look like the way art had looked before they started making their art. For example, Duchamp put a urinal in a gallery and said that it was art. He used everyday objects, manufactured objects, to make a statement about society and culture. He and other Dadaists challenged traditional art. For me, Duchamp and the Dadaists represented a reexamination of what art is and who decides what is art. In a way, this was the direction that my art was taking me. The Dadaists were to me an expression of freedom in the arts.

John Gutmann was a very important professor of art for me. I got him as a drawing instructor because I asked some other art students,

"Who do you recommend for an intro drawing class?"

"Whoever you take don't take John Gutmann."

"Why?"

"Because he's hard. He makes you work too hard."

"Well," I said to myself, "that's why I'm here."

I took Gutmann and boy did he work me. One day in his class, I was working like crazy and very intensely on a drawing, and Gutmann walked by me and pointed one finger to my drawing and said,

"What is that for?"

I stopped drawing because no one had ever asked me that question. I'm thinking "what the hell does he mean?"

"It's a drawing," I awkwardly replied. "It's art. What do you mean what's that for?"

"No, no, no, tell me what that's for!"

I was thoroughly puzzled. I was wishing I wasn't in the class. I felt so challenged and didn't know what to say.

At that point, Gutmann walked away.

"Oh, man," I thought, "what the hell is going on here?"

It took me a while and more time in Gutmann's class to realize what he had meant. He had asked me this question to suggest that nothing should get in my drawing or painting that did not belong there. I had to be alert to all the marks and smudges that you can make and make sure that they belong. Don't include something that will get in the way of the overall picture. I reflected on the Magritte picture where everything was seemingly thought out both emotionally and intellectually.

Gutmann introduced me to the notion of thinking about making a picture. You need to use your intelligence when you make a picture. Although your intelligence doesn't necessarily drive the picture, still you need to use it. Thanks to Gutmann, I began to consider that art, in part, is about thinking. It's a view of the world that is presented by whoever is making the art object. This was fascinating to me. I had never thought about this before. I had believed that art was about individual expression, but never with the question of "what for? To what end?" Art is about self-expression, but it's more complex and more layered than this. I began to really get into the notion of the complexity of making a picture.

What I was learning from Gutmann and other professors such as Robert Bechtle and Richard McClean was the importance of being an artist. I didn't know exactly why it was important or how it was important, but I knew there was something to being an artist that was of significance. There's a reason why we remember today some artists from centuries ago. There are reasons why they stick around. But I never knew why. They were called masters, but at first this only meant to me that they were very good painters. That's all it meant. But now with my formal training, I began to understand beyond this simple notion. They are masters, I learned, because their art has ideas, imagination, and feeling. It can affect people whether the artist intended to or not. It doesn't matter. I liked that. It has never been important to me to make a picture for an audience or a viewing. It was an avenue for me to organize my thoughts and feelings, to make a statement, or raise a question. Still, I've never had the idea of being conscious of an audience. I'm the audience. I'm the client. I'm the one who has to be pleased and satisfied with whatever question, statement, or investigation had prompted my work. It's like this even today. It is a form of self-absorption that I had even as a kid.

I owe a lot of my thinking about art to John Gutmann. He was not only my professor and mentor, but also a good friend. I loved this man because he was no nonsense and didn't bullshit. He talked to you about your work always with the intent of helping you make your picture better. We would have deep conversations. He was the only professor who really did this with me.

John Gutmann never said art is to be made this way or that way. He never imposed limits on you, but he did insist on discipline and that you learn your tools and the materials you painted on. John and I kept in touch over the years after I graduated from SFS. He knew that I became part of La Galeria de La Raza in the 1970s. He sometimes visited me at La Galeria. John felt good about how I was developing as an artist. By the 1980s I had lost contact with John Gutmann, but I credited him as my mentor, especially in those years at SFS.

Some of what I was learning both as technique and a more critical approach to art was visible in some of my class paintings beginning in 1967. One of my first was an etching on white wove paper. It is simply listed as *Untitled*. However, in parenthesis I added "fragmented nude." Here I was influenced by painters such as Rosenquist and Magritte, whose images have a sense of fragmentation; however, they weren't really divided spaces that were clearly different from each other. I expressed myself in this way because I, myself, felt fragmented. I felt very fragmented being back in the United States and very puzzled about being in Indochina and reacting to the protest movements around me, such as the anti-war one. America was being critically analyzed, and it was like I was in bits and pieces. I wasn't quite whole yet. I was still trying to figure out how I felt and what I thought. My painting reflected this.

Another image that I did that same year is titled *The War and Children*. It's also an etching on white wove paper. It is divided into two parts. The upper one shows two soldiers with a cross behind them. The lower part is of a young Vietnamese girl crying out. This two-part image I patterned after some other artists whose work Gutmann introduced us to. I and the other students just went crazy seeing them. To me these types of images represented an artistic language that made emotional and intellectual sense. I was very excited about the duality of the images and attempted to emulate them. But the inspiration for my image came from having been in Indochina. On one occasion, I was patrolling the perimeter of a bomb arsenal. There were villagers nearby and sometimes kids came up to us on the other side of the gate. Once this little girl came up and she had fallen and hurt herself. She actually approached me. I took out my first-aid kit and cleaned her wound. I thought of this encounter with the little girl when I did *The War and Children*. I thought about when I became aware of how people were being killed in Indochina. The image of the young girl was inspired by this encounter. The soldiers in a way represent me and the other military personnel at the base. The cross is not a reference to Christ or Christianity. I put it in there because it was a fascinating way to divide the space of the two-part image. I did knowingly place the cross but, on the other hand, I always leave open the unknowingly because I don't know everything that happens.

I also did two pictures both entitled *Black Man and Flag*. Both are allusions to the American flag as well as allusions to prison bars. I was confronting the myth of the American flag. While for some the flag can represent freedom, for others such as Blacks and Latinos the flag represents imprisonment. Metaphorically, the African American male in both pictures represents prison and not real freedom. In both pictures, I use the image of prison bars, although in the second one the bars are in red as I experimented with colors. I was inspired to do these pictures because at the time I was taking a course in criminology where the professors presented a critical perspective on prisons and linked it to racism.

Tatiana Reinoza and María del Mar González:

> The etching and collagraphy *Black Man and Flag* is representative of his [García's] period of active involvement with the Third World Strike at San Francisco State. . . . García's vertical flag appears to be mourning with deep stripes resembling prison bars and the red silhouette of a Black Panther activist.[2]

In another course I took on advertising, I was influenced by pop art such as that of Andy Warhol and how he did those paintings about commercial products. The professor in this class also had a critical and radical perspective about advertising. We examined a variety of ads such as the Marlboro man one and others. He also referenced the pop art depiction of ads. I was impressed with pop art because it reminded me of the cartoons that I enjoyed as a kid. I liked the aesthetics of pop art, especially the use of very flat and bright colors and shapes that were very clean and very sharp and very obvious. At the same time, I felt that there was something lacking in pop art. Influenced by my own more critical view, including a Third World consciousness of anticolonialism that I was experiencing, I felt that pop art was unfulfilling, at least for me. Pop art lacked a critical perspective or it wasn't critical enough for me. For example, it didn't reference racism, the

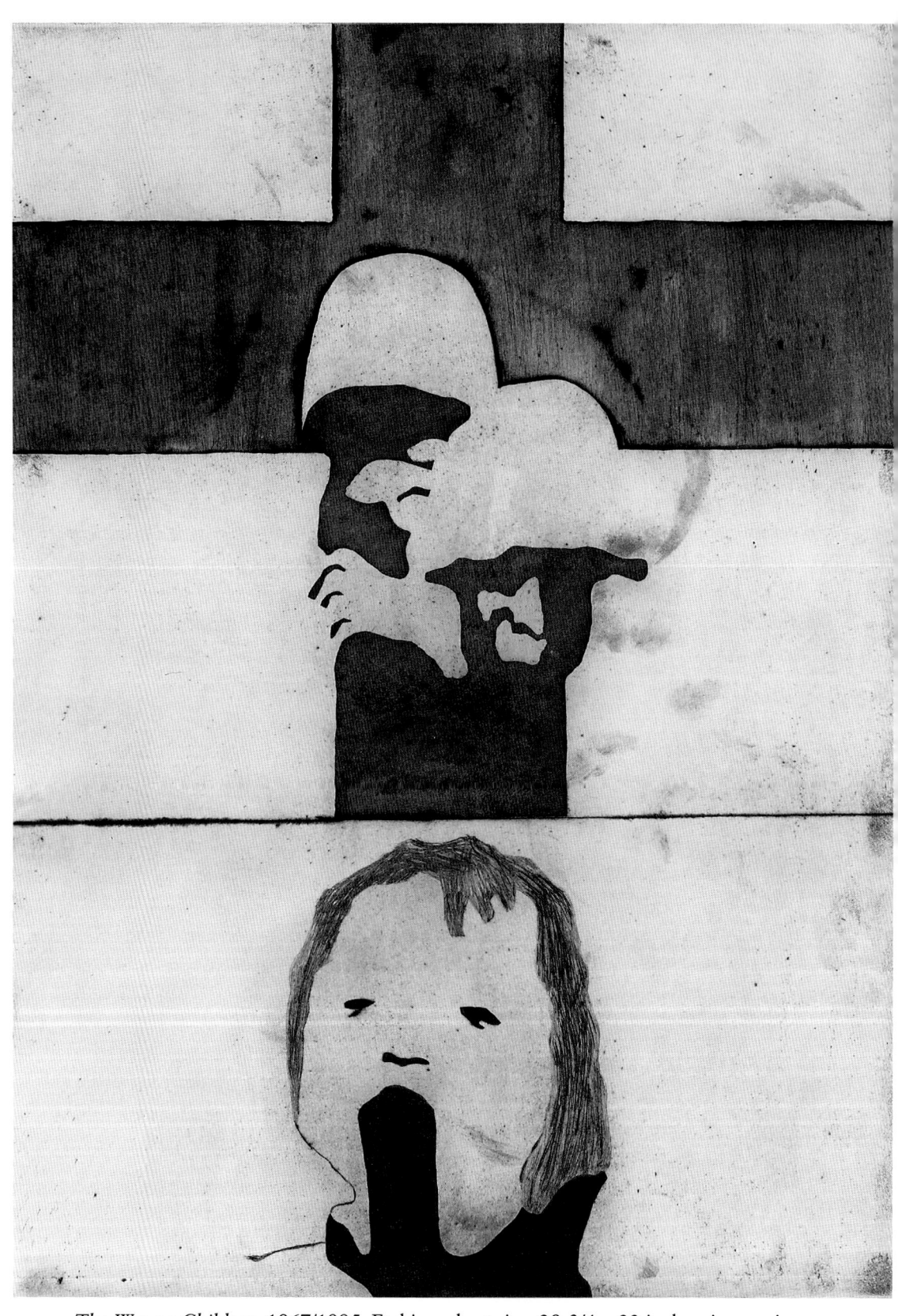

The War on Children, 1967/1995. Etching, sheet size: 29-3/4 x 22 inches, image size: 15-3/4 x 11-1/8 inches. Copyright © Rupert García. Courtesy of Rena Bransten Gallery.

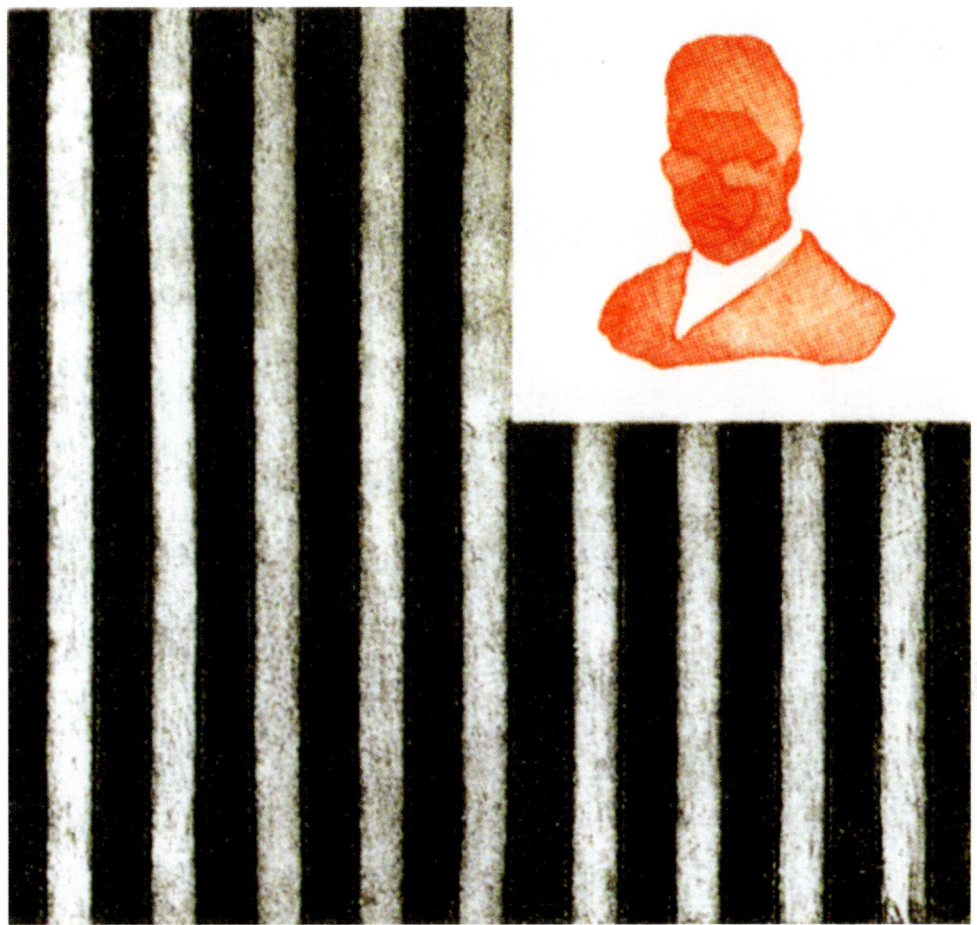

Black Man and Flag, 1967. Etching and collagraph on Rives BFK paper, sheet size: 21-3/4 x 22-1/2 inches, image size: 17-1/4 x 18-1/2. Copyright © Rupert García. Courtesy of Rena Bransten Gallery.

U.S. war in Vietnam, or Third World revolutions such as the Cuban Revolution. It paid no attention to sexism. Perhaps pop art did this through allusions, but I wasn't interested in allusions which became illusions.

Having said this, I allowed myself to be influenced by the aesthetics of pop art. Not only by how something looks, but also what the pop artists chose to be interested in, which were everyday commodities that we find in stores and marketplaces. And so, I began to look at everyday life, which I was already doing back in the 1950s when I was looking at comic books, cartoons, and Hollywood photos of movie stars. It made sense to me to deal with the here and now, but with a different perspective than most of the pop artists that I had seen, including Warhol. I began to look at images, for example, such as the Cream of Wheat package. I made a picture of it. However, under the image of the Black chef holding a steaming bowl of Cream of Wheat, I inserted "No More of This Shit," which became the title of the work. I

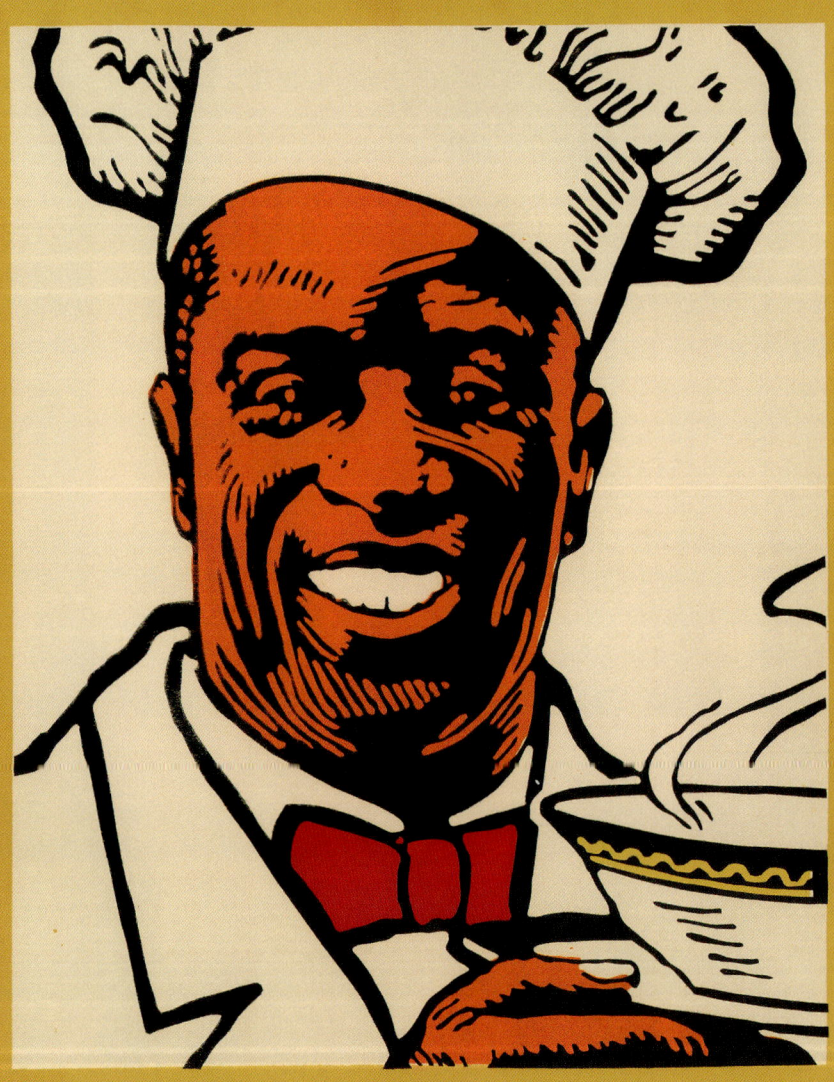

NO MORE O' THIS SHIT.

No More O' This Shit, 1969. Color silkscreen on white wove paper, sheet size: 24 x 18 inches, image size: 17 x 13-5/8 inches. Copyright © Rupert García. Courtesy of Rena Bransten Gallery.

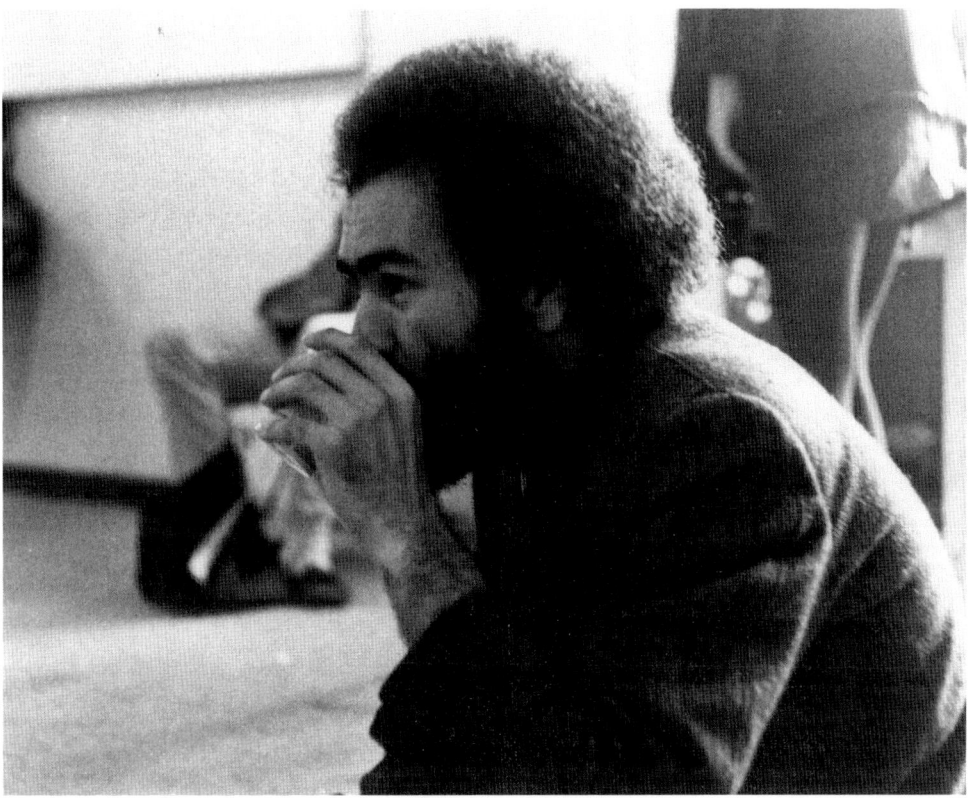

Rupert García at San Francisco State, 1967-1968. Photo courtesy of Rupert García.

did this one as a silk screen on white wove paper. I did this in 1969, which reflected my increased radicalism. Like the pop artists, I did this as a silk screen which could be mass produced but also contained a kind of pop art aesthetic. I was already doing other silk-screen images. I liked the clean flat shapes and bold colors that I could apply. It had the visual immediacy of a poster, which is what many of these were that I began to do. But unlike pop artists, I was interested in other things. I was interested in something more, such as the rise of the Black civil rights movement and Black Power, which I never divorced from the civil rights of others such as Chicanos and the farmworkers.

Carla Stellweg:

Not only does Rupert Garcia appropriate from mass culture, he subverts it.[3]

An important journal for me at that time was *El Grito* published in Berkeley. It was the first journal of Chicano intellectual and cultural analysis linked to the developing Chicano Movement. I knew one of the editors and writers, Nick Vaca, with whom I had gone to high school in Stockton. He also attended SFS, and that's where we reunited. This was around 1969. He was already working with *El Grito*. He told me about it and suggested that I give him some of my pencil drawings to possibly publish in the journal. "Absolutely," I replied. In fact, it published a portfolio of my drawings that I was producing. Some of them I had made back in 1967 and 1968. I thought they were quite good and I really appreciated that *El Grito* published them. I read the journal and was impressed with it. Its chief editor and publisher was Professor Octavio Romano, an anthropologist at UC Berkeley. I met him once later. I found the journal interesting to read because the writers were raising questions about things that I was thinking concerning challenging stereotyping of Chicanos and the assertion of Chicano culture and identity. I later referenced some of these essays in my MA thesis.

Still another key publication that I discovered was *La Raza* published in Los Angeles. Its chief editor was Raul Ruiz, a key activist in LA. I also subscribed to it. I learned much about the Chicano Movement in Los Angeles. In addition, I discovered other movement newspapers that were springing up all over California and the Southwest linked to the movement. All of this provided me a Chicano perspective as I began to identify as a Chicano.

I was going through so many changes at SFS. However, much of this became crystalized by the Third World Liberation Front (TWLF) Strike on campus in the fall of 1968. The strike and its ramifications would change my life and career.

—‖—

I was also able to participate in the strike because I remained a student in the fall of 1968. I graduated with a BA in art in the spring of that year. Because I had attended community college and took college courses while in the Air Force, it only took me two years to graduate. I didn't get an MFA because there was no such degree at San Francisco State, and I had never heard of such a degree anyway. I was very proud of myself for graduating. I had done it! I was the first in my family to obtain a college degree. I really felt that I had learned something in those two years. My classes and the politicized environment at that time made me feel that I had undergone profound changes. When I graduated, I knew that I wanted to stay at SFS and work on an MA in art and particularly in painting. My drive to become an artist was enhanced by graduating. I wanted to continue to study about becoming an artist. This was the fire in my belly. I applied for the graduate program and was accepted in the studio art program. I wanted to take my education as an artist as far as I could take it. I first and foremost wanted to be an artist, although I also considered teaching art as well. This is where I was when the strike began.

The Third World Liberation Front Strike, which went from November 1968 to March 1969, did not occur in a vacuum. It's not like we returned to campus that fall and all of a sudden there was a strike. There were issues laid out in previous semesters as well as national and international happenings to feed into the strike. So, when the strike happened it was no surprise, at least for me. It logically occurred given past grievances that the administration did not adequately address. Moreover, the anti-war protests and the rise of Black Power, and even by then the Chicano Movement, all set the stage for the strike. Having become more politically aware during my first two years at SFS, I personally felt prepared for the strike. I wasn't shocked.

There were a number of issues and demands put forward by the coalition of Black, Latino, Asian American, Native American, and white radicals. Together, they formed the Third World Liberation Front (TWLF) that along with the Black Students Union called for a student strike to stop classes until the administration agreed to negotiate with the Black Student Union and the TWLF. El Renacimiento, a Mexican American organization, was part of the coalition. Students called for a more humanistic approach to higher education. They dissected the Master Plan for the Cal State University system (CSU) and noted it primarily aimed to fit students into the marketplace. You went to school to prepare you to plug into society as it was. The Plan said nothing about social change or social justice or about racism and sexism. Instead, it upheld the status quo. I read the Master Plan and was not impressed by it. Students were seen as cogs to fit into this wheel to keep it going as it had always been going. However, I knew that it could not go on as it had been. It needed to be changed. This feeling of change was very intense among the students, or at least those who went on strike. We did not feel alone in our protest because

similar student strikes were happening at other campuses in the country and in other countries. All of us were influenced by the mass student strike in Paris that spring. We were not alone.

NOW IS THE TIME FOR ALL GOOD MEN TO STAND WITH US, FOR A COLLEGE FREE FROM RACISM! FOR A COLLEGE FREE FROM POLITICAL TYRANNY![4]

One of the prime demands of the SFS strike was to establish Black studies and ethnic studies as a way to offer formal knowledge which had previously not been available to students, including students of color. Ethnic studies to me made total sense. I could identify with the call for this new type of curriculum. I had already concluded that art history, for example, had to be reexamined. It was predominantly the history of Western art. That's why I had to teach myself on my own the history of Mexican art. Why did I need to do this? Why wasn't there a class on Mexican art in the Art History Department? For that matter, the art history of the Third World—Africa, Asia, and Latin America—was downplayed. This had to change. If the departments refused to diversify the curriculum, then at least this knowledge should be taught in ethnic studies. The call for ethnic studies was not to have one large department, but to set up a Black Studies Department and a School of Ethnic Studies which would include La Raza studies including Chicano studies, Native American studies, and Asian American studies.

What was also important about ethnic studies was that it would be a way for students to learn about systematic or institutionalized racism in American society. Some of this was being addressed in other departments such as sociology, but it was still important to learn about racism with respect to its impact on different racialized groups.

A related issue was affirmative action and the diversification of the student body. The fact was that there were not many Blacks and Latinos on campus. We needed to change the process in which students were admitted in order to recruit more underrepresented students. Affirmative action, as we understood it, was not to give minority students certain privileges; it was to give them a chance to show that they could compete and succeed in college. It would include programs like academic counseling to ensure that these students were able to compete. Looking back, this was the most important demand to set up a pipeline from minority schools to San Francisco State.

Still another issue was to protect minority faculty who not only were supporting the strike, but who in their classes were critically examining American society. One such professor was George Murray, who had been fired by the administration because he was a member of the Black Panther Party. Murray was the only Black professor in the English Department. One of our demands was that Murray be reinstated.

These and other demands only contributed to my own political consciousness. I saw the student strike as part of a larger critique of society that

needed to take place. The strike was not just about San Francisco State, it was part of something larger and more profound. The fact is that the whole world needed to be changed. I didn't know how this change would occur; I just knew it had to be changed. I also knew that I had to change as well. Some issues were being raised that I had never really looked at seriously. Years later I told an interviewer that during the strike, "I listened to what the students were talking about in terms of colonialism, imperialism, new words, new ideas—what the hell did I know about these things, but I began to read the leaflets and began to listen and it all began to fit."[5]

To press the demands and issues, various demonstrations occurred on campus. The emphasis was for students to boycott classes and bring a stop to campus activity. Initially, many students heeded the call; however, as the strike continued, many students went back to classes, especially by final exam periods. I went to most of the demonstrations. On the picket lines, students shouted out "On Strike! Shut it down!" Most were peaceful, although in some the campus police backed up by the San Francisco city cops intervened and some students were hurt. Police arrested both students and supporting faculty. The cops entered the campus with their billy clubs and some rode in on their horses. I saw some with their guns drawn. Thank God, no one was killed. Each day you could see the police assembling just outside the campus. However, some physical conflicts occurred when more conservative (mostly white) students attacked the demonstrators. This resulted in fistfights. I had a strange reaction to the demonstrations. I would sometimes get sick to my stomach or have butterflies in my stomach. It was a combination of fear and exaltation about the protests. It was an up and down situation for me. I think perhaps my military experiences influenced my reaction in some way.

The administration's reaction to the strike was to condemn it as a radical and even Communist-led one. For the early months of the strike, they refused to negotiate the demands by the Black Student Union and the TWLF. President Robert Smith tried to reach out to the students but failed. He was fired and Professor S. I. Hayakawa replaced him. Hayakawa at first refused to speak with the striking students. He made a big media show of standing up to the students that became national news. He got a lot of mileage out of the strike. He described the students as the scum of the earth and said we didn't belong on campus. He said that we didn't deserve an education. With his attacks, he became a big media star and later banked on it to become a U.S. senator.

But his attacks had nothing to do with what our intentions were. I'm not trying to paint a picture that every person in the strike was an angel. They weren't. However, in general, I felt that what we were trying to do was absolutely correct. Hayakawa was painting the opposite image.

During the strike I was also aware of the major leaders, and I became

friends with some. They were all part of the Third World Liberation Front. Although I never actually joined the TWLF, I served as a liaison between the Art Department and the Front. I think that I didn't join the TWLF because I felt that the leaders and their ideological views were way beyond me and that I wouldn't be able to effectively participate in discussions. And to be honest, I did feel that some of the leaders, both Black and Latino, were a bit abrasive and perhaps felt superior to the other students. At the same time, I tried to be involved and went to many meetings of the Front. These were big meetings that included not only the TWLF, but also other major student groups as well as political ones like the Black Panther Party and the Progressive Labor Party. These meetings were very intense and exciting. I would also get nervous at them not knowing what to expect. I don't recall speaking out at these meetings.

I was familiar with the main artist of the Panthers, Emory Douglas, whose work I liked. He made the drawings for the Panther newspaper as well as posters which influenced my approach to poster art. Emory's work was very flat like pop art. It was flat meaning his colors didn't interact with one another, and it was bold, colorful, and political. I liked the method that Emory was using and the fact that his images dealt with social change and Third World people, which was becoming important to me. Emory Douglas, as far as I know, did not go on to do art with a gallery. All of his work was with the Black Panther Party, but Emory was an important influence on me stylistically and politically.

As I was hearing all this critical discourse, God, it was just amazing. I was listening to all this stuff, and no one really knew me. I was looking around and listening and trying to make connection with what was happening on campus with what was happening off campus and what was happening throughout the country and around the globe in 1968. What the strike was talking about was being talked about in Paris and in Mexico City and in other places in the world. I began to see this global interconnection of these different movements of protest and critique and of the desire especially by young people to redesign the fabric of their societies. These movements were to define and produce a new human being. All this made sense to me—that something had to be done. I didn't know exactly what, but certainly something had to be done. I didn't necessarily subscribe to a particular ideology or group, but I believed in change and wanted to participate in the struggle beginning at SFS.[6]

Latinos were quite active in the strike. There were a couple of Latino organizations already on campus. One key Latino student leader was Roger Alvarado, who also worked as an Educational Opportunity Program (EOP) adviser. He likewise was active in the Mission District. Roger served as a main spokesperson for the Latino students during the strike. He was part of the TWLF. Although I didn't belong to the Latino groups, I identified with them as a Latino and Chicano.

The involvement of the Latinos, both men and women, in the strike was profound. Another key leader of the Latino groups was Dr. Juan Martínez, who was perhaps the only Latino professor on campus. He was in history.

My initial role in the strike was to keep the art student faculty and students, especially the grad students, informed of the strike and the efforts to negotiate the demands with the administration. I would go to the rallies and demonstrations and then return to the Art Department and report on them. I would help organize meetings in the department concerning how it could support the strike. Almost all faculty and grad students endorsed it. The main and most contentious issue that we discussed was supporting the strike by reconstituting classes. We wanted each class in its own way to address the issues of the strike and to address the discussion of the role of Western art in the exploitation of the Third World. We wanted classes to change their syllabus to include presenting competing Third World art. Not all faculty agreed, but enough did to get the ball rolling. Of course, we further discussed changing the curriculum to include Third World art and recruiting faculty of color to teach these classes.

On one occasion in a Western art class that I was taking, the professor was lecturing about certain European artists who had a critical view of art and life, and so I stood up and challenged her and the class.

"Here we're talking about this art history and how some of the artists were critical of their society and culture. Yet outside the door of this art building, there are students doing the very same thing about which we are studying. They are also being critical of our society and culture today. So, what do we do? Do we just sit on our asses here? Or do we go out and participate in this important decolonial struggle? Let's go! Let's get outta here and go out there!"

Some students joined me and some didn't. I didn't care. All I knew is that I went out!

At the same time, we the art grad students didn't want to just talk. We wanted to participate in the strike and use our skills as artists in support of the TWLF. "How do we as artists relate to the present moment on campus and the world?" was the question for us. We concluded we could do this by engaging in producing poster art in support of the strike. At one of our meetings in the Art Department, one of our professors said that he had been in Paris in May during the student rebellion there in the Spring and how important poster art was for this movement. Through images, it captured the zeitgeist of the movement, and he proposed that we do the same for our strike. This was great. This would be how some of us as art students could more effectively participate in the strike. We would design and make posters for the TWLF. Another professor, Barry McDowell, who did design, reminded us to not lose sight of the role of the image in a political struggle. He made it very clear. It convinced me that I needed to put aside my emphasis on easel painting and being a fine artist. The strike made me reexamine this. I wanted to be an easel painter more than anything, but the heat of the moment called for another art form—the poster done on silk screen to publicize the struggle. My easel painting was inadequate for the moment, and I had to really come to grips with that. I was doing a kind of pop art with surreal overtones. As a result of these discussions, some of us, both students and faculty, organized the San Francisco State College Student and Faculty Poster Workshop in the Art Department.

Few of us, except for me, knew how to do silk-screening, so we went to the department print workshop, and the professor in charge gave us a thumbnail sketch of how to do silk-screening. It was a different process, but we learned in an hour. Silk-screening is the process of pressing ink through a stenciled mesh screen to create a printed design. The ink lays down flat and beautiful. The colors are solid and very rich, and I found that very exciting. We made stencils to stick onto the silk screen. You could produce hundreds of posters in a short period of time, which was one of the attractions of using it to publicize the strike. It was a more democratic way of reaching a larger audience. Learning the technique of silk-screening is fairly easy. What cannot be taught, however, is the perfection of it. That takes practice. The technology of silk-screening became very attractive to me, almost as much as making the design and the poster itself.

━ⅠⅠ━

As we learned, we began to produce poster art. No one told us what to make; that was up to our own individual ideas, although we responded to the issues of the strike. Some of the posters that we produced were used in the various demonstrations on campus. Some were posted throughout the campus. Some faculty and staff put them on their doors or windows. At one demonstration, there was a major confrontation between the students and the police. Some seven hundred students were arrested. This was a major crisis, and so we did posters to protest police violence. Another way that we supported the strike was by selling some of our posters and donating the money to the TWLF as bail money for those arrested.

Prior to the strike, my pictures were somewhat abstract and surreal but readable. I think that the formal attributes of my work were coming along well, but what I was trying to say had not yet begun to take form. Conceptually, I was still exploring. Technically it was there. Well, the strike really brought the two together. It brought the conceptual framework and the technique—silk-screening—together regarding what I wanted to say with what I was thinking and feeling. Not only did my images change, but my whole understanding of what an artist is went topsy-turvy. My images began to become socially engaged and critical. I became involved in that which I saw and printed. I didn't distinguish me from it. I was it.

A few years later in 1976, I reflected on this change when I wrote: "Artists, if they wish to be authentically relevant, must come to re-realize that art is dynamic and that art exists within history and a socio-cultural context. To view art otherwise is to 'play ostrich' and is to continue being part of the problem art-life finds itself in today."[7]

The first poster that I personally did was one that warned about police violence against the students. I don't know where the inspiration of the image came from, but it shows a penis with the helmeted heads of two cops and the penis is ejaculating red or blood sperm. In red letters, I wrote "They're Coming!" Needless to say, this image elicited much comment as it was displayed on campus.

My second poster was my image of Che Guevara. I think it may have been one of the very first such images produced in the United States. Not my image, but similar ones with Che's face with the beret would go viral and soon became the image of revolutionary struggle, especially in Latin America. Che had died in 1967 in Bolivia where he was attempting to lead a revolutionary movement in that country as he had done in Cuba in the 1959 revolution with Fidel Castro. He was captured by the Bolivian military aided by the CIA and executed. Che originally was from Argentina. He became a worldwide icon. I had heard about him as a champion of Cuba and of international liberation movements against colonialism and imperialism. There was this romance about Che.

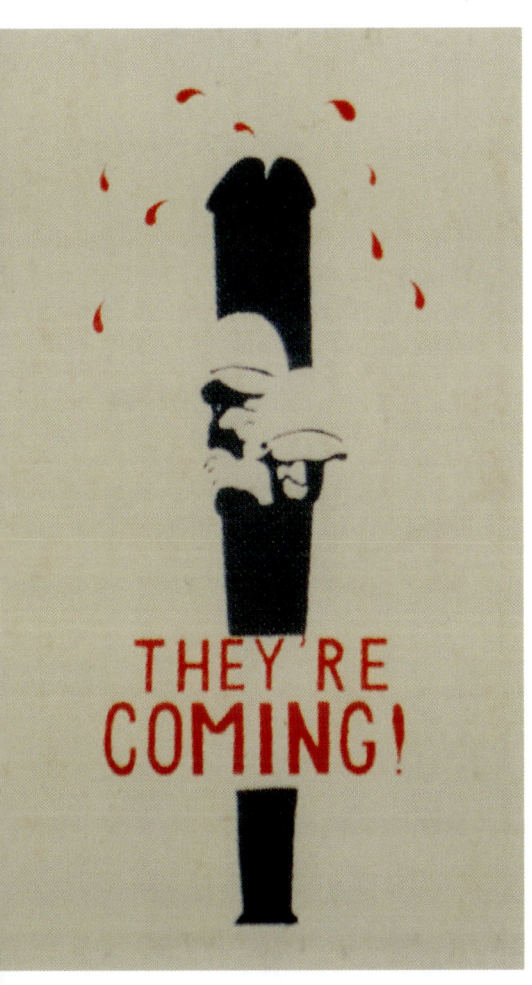

They're Coming!, 1968. Color silk-screen on white wove paper, sheet size: 35 x 23-1/8, image size: 23-1/8 x 9-5/8 inches. Copyright © Rupert García.

He was a very good-looking guy who was a medical doctor. My Che image was one of my first facial images that I started to do. Most of my images deal with real people or real-life situations. There's a need to have that element of reality to have me do it. It has to connect with me. I didn't do Che because it connected to a certain group's ideology. I did Che and later other historical figures because they connected in some way with me.

Many people were affected by Che. Some even tried to look like him. This involved the long hair and beard and wearing Army fatigues and a beret. I saw what became the classic picture of Che done by the Cuban photographer Alberto Korda in one of the radical publications such as *Ramparts* or perhaps the newspaper of the Black Panther Party. It was a very strong graphic image of Che, and it seemed to capture a lot of what I was feeling and thinking about change, including revolutionary change. He seemed to epitomize commitment and devotion to cause. So, my image is not original, but it's based on what was becoming the worldwide image of Che. I did it in black and white on silk screen. Underneath the image, I painted the words "RIGHT ON!" The first time I heard these words was at a demonstration in downtown San Francisco outside of City Hall. We were demonstrating and marching around the building and some people started crying out, "Right On, Right On!" This phrase stuck with me. "Right On!" Right on with change. Right on with what needs to be done. So, when I did the image of Che, that phrase just automatically came because "Right On" captured Che's dream and pursuit of social change. It all made sense. Che represented a certain kind of internationalism which further made sense to me. Che was also important to me because he was Latino. Several years later, I painted another image of Che for the Latino restaurant, La Peña, in Berkeley.

Terezita Romo:

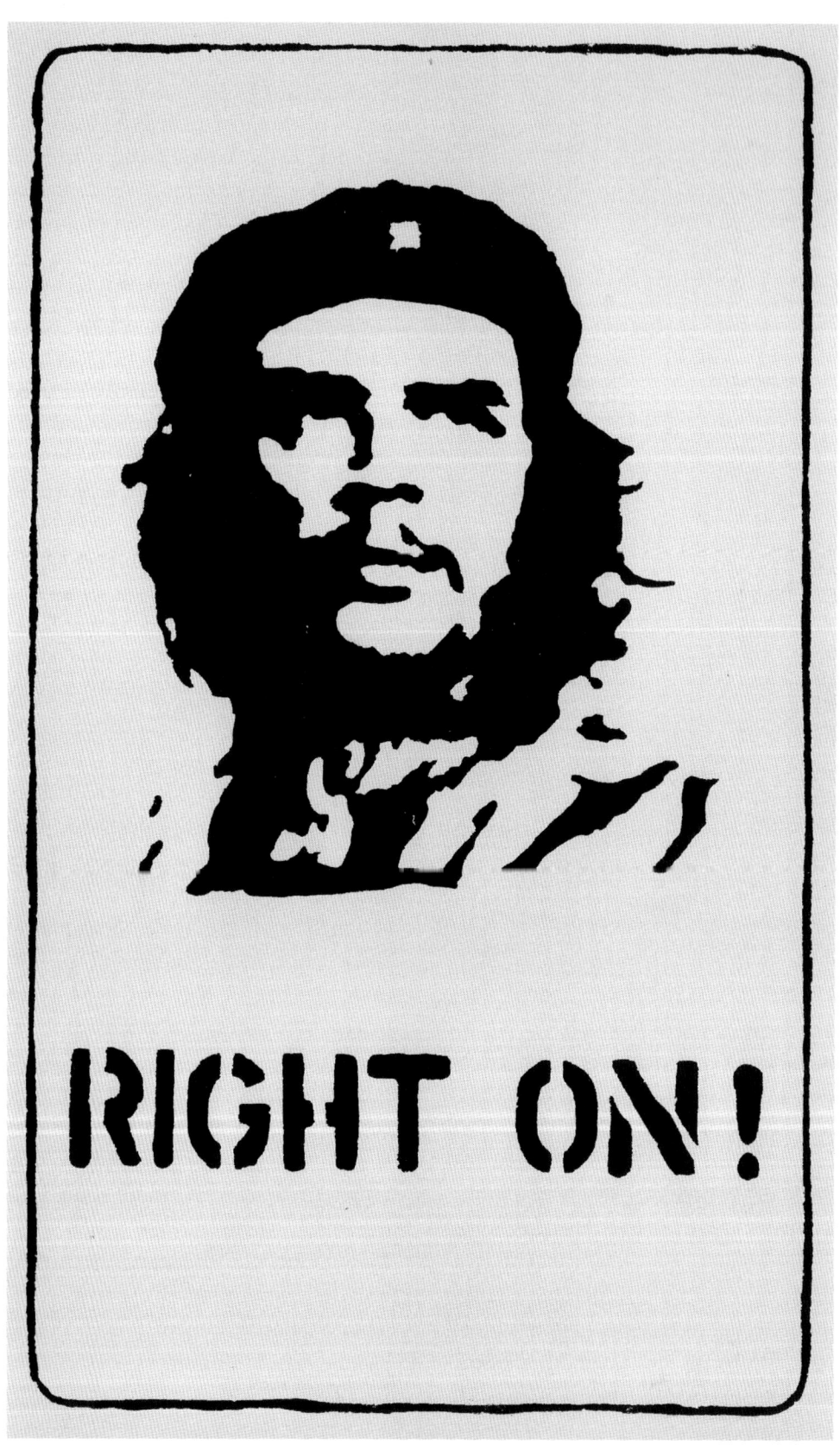

Right On!, 1968. Color silkscreen on white wove paper, sheet size: 26 x 20 inches. Copyright © Rupert García. Courtesy of Rena Bransten Gallery.

Though lacking the bold colors of his later prints, it reflects what would become García's graphic style: a blend of pop art sensibilities and strident political statements mixed with the technical acuity of Cuban graphics. Historically important, *Right On!* (1968) is one of the first works by an American artist to render homage to Che, who is now an omnipresent figure in Chicano/Latino and American art.[8]

It was at the time of the strike and my beginning to do my silk-screen posters that I become acquainted with Cuban poster art that strongly affected me. This was in addition to the influence of pop art and that of Emory Douglas's posters for the Black Panther Party. The Cuban posters were done in the 1960s by Cuban artists in support of the Cuban Revolution of 1959. I didn't see the posters in an exhibit but in radical U.S. publications. The posters were reproduced in full color. I found the Cuban posters fantastic, especially the work of René Mederos. They showed the relationship of the poster to society and of art in society. The incredible quality of the designs and the use of revolutionary experience moved me deeply. These reproductions educated me visually and intellectually and inspired my own posters.[9]

What especially attracted me to the Cuban posters was the simplicity of the image and text and the elegance of shape and color. I was drawn to the design composition, the shapes, and the brilliant colors. Some of the artists

for the Black Panther Party, especially Emory Douglas, were also influenced by Cuban posters, and so I was influenced by some of the Panther posters as well. What the Cuban artists were doing was amazing. I appreciated that their posters spoke to the historical moment. I decided that this was the way I was going to go, and I did. I'm very thankful for the poster makers of Cuba. I think they influenced the course of the world and set a new standard of poster art.

Carol A. Wells:

Because the Cuban Revolution had such an indelible effect on Chicano political discourse and artistic production, the importance of Cuban posters in the development of the Chicano poster cannot be overstated.[10]

Some of the other images that I did in support of the strike included one on Emiliano Zapata, one of the major revolutionary leaders of the Mexican Revolution of 1910. The farmworkers already were using images of Zapata, mostly photo images of him, set in poster format, and so this influenced me to do my own version. I had heard of Zapata, the leader of the agrarian movement in the revolution, beginning with my family and then when I started to learn on my own about Mexican history and art. Actually, I did the poster in part to support the strike but also in support of a Latino community newspaper in the Mission District called *La Prensa*. They had done an interview with me in the paper and then asked if I could do a poster for them to raise awareness of the paper to help with circulation. I agreed to do so, but said "let's give a copy of the poster to those who purchase a subscription to the paper." The editors were elated and agreed to this. I decided to do my image of Zapata as the gift. My image is the same as the photos of Zapata, except that I don't round out his face and separate it from the beginning of his torso. On the torso, I printed the famous *bandoleros*, the bullet cartridges that the Mexican revolutionaries carried on their chests. I did the poster in black and brown. I didn't print in a title but simply called it *Zapata*. Zapata was a hero to me and to the Chicano Movement. I did my poster based on a postcard that I received from a member of the New Left periodical *Leviathan*.

In 1969 I also did a poster in support of the farmworkers strike. It was to support the union's grape boycott. I was influenced by the image of the Mexican flag that shows an eagle with a snake in its beak. That image goes back to Aztec mythology that was the sign of where the Aztecs would build their main settlement of Tenochtitlán, which became Mexico City. In my image, I replaced the Mexican eagle with the union eagle and on the body of the snake I put in "Safeway," one of the main grocery chains being boycotted. In the poster, I added the words "HUELGA!" at the top of the image, and on the bottom I printed "BOYCOTT SAFEWAY." I did the image in black on red. I did a second poster for the farmworkers about the dangers of pesticides in fruit such as grapes, which

the union was focusing on. César Chávez and Dolores Huerta were early champions of environmental justice. I titled the poster *Protect the Consumer, Protect the Farmworker*. I did another pro-environment poster that same year simply titled *DDT*.

One of my favorite early posters was one I called *Down with the Whiteness* in 1969. I was interested in addressing white supremacy and white racism, so I found a photo of this Black man raising his arms with clenched fists and I liked it. It seemed to define this individual, but I was interested in the overall shape of that individual. As I printed it there's no detail, no eyes, no lips, no nose, none of that, just a flat image. The image of the man is in black although partly in yellow, which is the background color. The use of these colors was an aesthetic decision. But then I added the words "Down with the Whiteness" in black letters but within a white bubble emanating from the man. This is a cartoon bubble. I always enjoyed cartoonist and magazine artists and I just loved the bubbles indicating the voices of the cartoon characters. I liked the bubbles as a shape and as an idea. On one occasion, I went to an art event in Chinatown in San Francisco and took some copies of this image. A white couple passed by the stall where I had the image displayed and saw my picture and said, "that's terrific because it's not about white people; it's about what some white people think." I responded, "That's it. Thank you very much."

The slogan "Down with the Whiteness" was not a popular slogan which

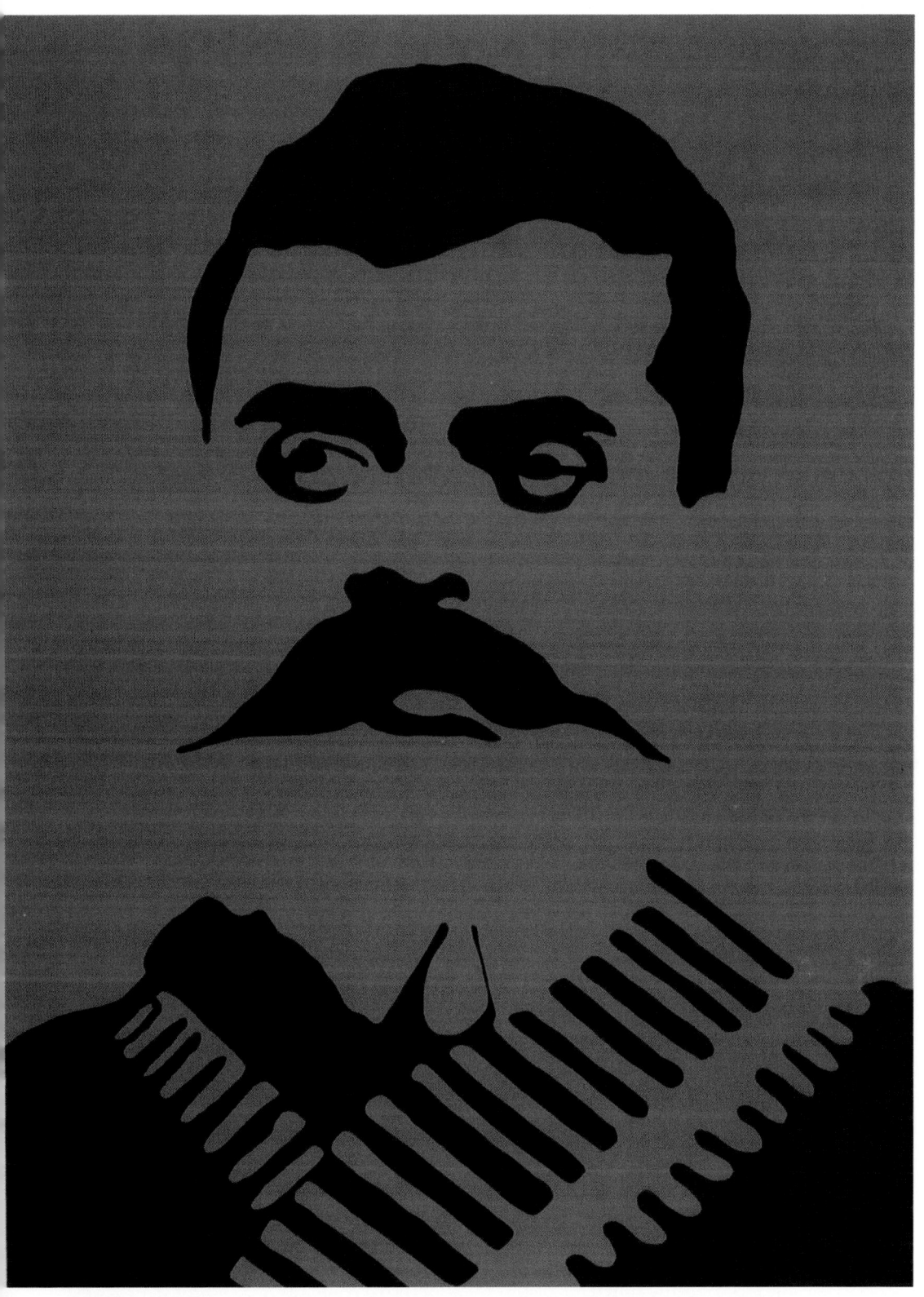

Zapata, 1969. Color silkscreen on white wove paper, sheet size: 26 x 20 inches.
Copyright © Rupert García. Courtesy of Rena Bransten Gallery.

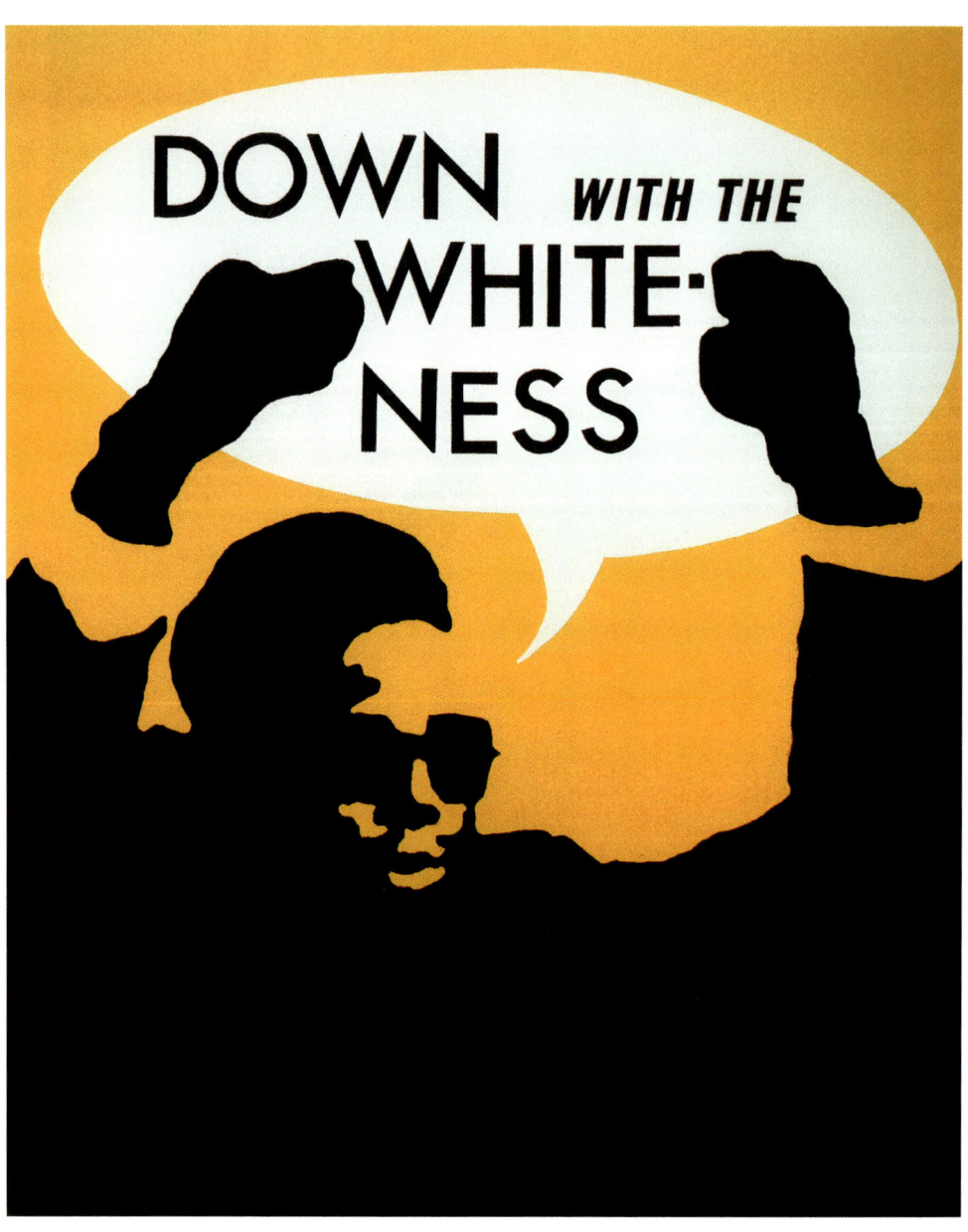

Down with the Whiteness, 1969. Color silkscreen on white wove paper, sheet size: 23-1/4 x 19 inches, image size: 22-5/8 x 18-3/4 inches. Copyright © Rupert García. Courtesy of Rena Bransten Gallery.

I borrowed. I came up with it just totally out of my imagination. It was something I was thinking about. I love that picture to this very day.

In all, I did about nineteen posters in 1969 and 1970, my first years of doing silk-screening. Poster art became my first major art form and displayed my now linking art to social causes and never looking back. It was clearly indicative of my becoming a Chicano artist and a Third World one as well.

Terezita Romo:

Though García's posters drew from pop art, including the comics and Warhol's iconic Campbell soup cans, they are "anti-pop" prints that counter the advertisement objective with socio-political content.[11]

During the strike, I was critical of the police, of capitalist exploitation. I did posters of Che, of Zapata, and other Third World leaders. As artists, we climbed down from the ivory tower. We abandoned notions that the artist was supposed to be against society, against people, be different, exotic, bohemian. It is in the workshop, not the classroom, that I really learned silk-screen printing. I also learned to work in a collective—critiquing, sharing, subduing one's ego. I had planned to be an easel painter, but the strike changed that.[12]

Luis Valdez:

I feel that somehow what the movement is about has everything to do with what art is about—which is human expression. And what art does for us is give us tools of expression. I believe in popular art. It should be close at hand—we can make art out of anything.[13]

By March of 1969, the strike came to an end. Despite all of his venom against the students, Hayakawa agreed to some of the demands. The most significant had to do with the establishment of a College of Ethnic Studies including a Department of Black Studies and a Department of La Raza Studies. In fact, I was hired in 1969 to teach the first art course in this department, which I called "La Raza Art Workshop." The second agreement had to do with affirmative action and the further commitment by the administration to recruit minority students. Although these agreements effectively ended the strike, for many TWLF activists the strike never ended and still hasn't. The strike and how it changed my life and art represented "the most important moment in my life." [14]

—•II•—

In 1969, I finished my MA thesis in the Art Department, although I received my degree in 1970. I also had to organize an exhibit of some of my work, which I further did in 1970 (see Chapter 6). My MA thesis was a major critique of the mass media, both in terms of how it rather cleverly seduces us to buy products and the importance of signs and symbols in mass media. The thesis was actually the text to complement my exhibition based on some of the pictures I had done during my MA years. In the thesis, I wrote about advertising and racism. I quoted art critics as well as social critics such as C. Wright Mills. The thesis reflected what was going through my mind at that time. One of the key points that I made was that the role of images about everyday commodities does something to us. There is information that is imbedded or is carried along with the way in which products are designed and packaged, for example, the images on the Cream of Wheat or Uncle Ben packages. Then there are tortilla wrappers with romanticized and really vulgarized images of Mexicanos. My thesis wasn't unique; others had written about all this. Still, I was thinking of how these everyday products mean something. I discussed the role of commodity images to perpetuate racist stereotypes and racist perceptions of different groups.

My thesis also focused on this seemingly innocuous area of cultural products of everyday life, but which are not innocuous at all. In doing my thesis, for example, I learned about how some corporations such as Ford were involved in producing components for the ABM missile system. In response, I made a poster called *ABM Ford ABM*. I made one image to represent the Ford logo; however, I made an accompanying one where instead of the word "Ford," I printed "ABM ABM." I was challenging how through advertising we are led to believe that corporations like Ford only produce products to better our lives. We fall for this because we can't see behind what they are doing due to ads on TV or in magazines or newspapers. You can't see truth behind this. So, my MA thesis dealt with issues like this.

■II■

The TWLF strike was a major turning point in my life and career. It not only further politicized me, but it critically increased my ethnic awareness of myself as a Chicano and as part of the broader Latino community in San Francisco. Above all it made me committed to my linking of my politics to my art. This linkage is visible in my turning to do poster art on behalf of political causes and social justice. The strike marked my becoming better prepared to now go into the community and place my art on behalf of the people—the Chicano/Latino people of the Mission District. I would now become a community artist.

George Lipsitz:

Within the Chicano Movement, poster production emerged as one of the important sites where insurgent consciousness could be created, nurtured, and sustained.[15]

Terezita Romo:

Chicano poster artists [in the 1960s and 1970s] functioned as the unofficial conscience of the country.[16]

6

The Mission Cultural Renaissance

My experiences at San Francisco State politicized me. That period of the late 1960s witnessed incredible political and social movements covering civil rights, anti-war protests, ethnic studies, the feminist movement, and the counterculture. All of these influenced me and changed my consciousness. But what really changed me was the San Francisco State strike. For the first time, I became politically involved in a movement to transform the traditional campus and curriculum to reflect the diversity of the community in San Francisco and the various ethnic experiences. From this politicization, I moved to yet another transformative period when I was introduced to the Mission District in the city. Out of this experience, I became fully Chicano and Latino.

—||—

Being from Stockton, I didn't really know all of the various districts in San Francisco. This included the Mission District, south of downtown, that was the principal Latino settlement in the

city. This changed in 1970 at the time I had completed my MA in art. What got me into the Mission was that I met a guy by the name of Francisco Camplis. At some point after the strike, Camplis was installing an art exhibit in the student union building which was adjacent to the art building. One day, I walked into the student union while Camplis was doing this. I was looking at the paintings, and he came over and introduced himself. I told him that I was an art major and was finishing my MA in this field.

"You should come down and meet us at the Artes 6 Gallery in the Mission. It's a group of Latino artists and we have a gallery and we run it," Francisco told me.

"Okay. It looks like you guys are doing some interesting work based on what you're exhibiting here."

So, I went to the Artes 6 Gallery which was on 18th and Dolores in the Mission. It was right across from Dolores Park and Mission High School. Inside the gallery, I found Camplis, who introduced me to some other artists such as Ralph Maradiaga and Rolando Castillon, and a few others. The gallery was a small place, a real storefront, but here is where they organized exhibitions by Latino artists. The exhibit that I saw was beautiful. I also learned of other cultural groups in the Mission such as Casa España de Bellas Artes. It turned out that Camplis was the art director of the Casa. I started hanging out at Artes 6 and began to meet other artists, poets, writers, and activists in the Mission. They were all very politically inclined in one way or another.

It was at Artes 6 that I decided to do my MA exhibit. Everyone completing an MA had to mount an exhibit. I chose to do it at Artes 6, which supported me. I needed that support because not a single one of my professors or other MA students attended the opening of my exhibit. I didn't care because many Latino artists did attend along with people from the community. My MA exhibit consisted of the various prints and posters that I had done mainly in connection with the strike. This included my images of Che Guevara, Emiliano Zapata, and my take on the Cream of Wheat box image. I consciously decided to have my master's show at Artes 6 because I wanted to demonstrate that the art I made can be shown anywhere I wanted to show it, and that at that moment I was working with these artists in the Mission and what I was doing was a political gesture.

What I showed for my master's exhibit was what I practiced in life. I wanted to marry art and life. There was no separation between them. It wasn't like I wanted to make art over here and I'd do life over there. Rather, they were merged. They were one. It was an attempt to embrace both.

One of the other things that I learned about the Mission was that it was a mixture of Latinos and Chicanos. It wasn't solely mexicanos, which to me was an eye-opener, because in Stockton it was only mexicanos. However, in the Mission there was a mixture of different folks from Latin America. This impressed me that there was more to being Latino than just being mexicano. It was very interesting and complex and began to influence my sense of ethnic identity to going beyond being Chicano and also identifying with being Latino.

It was from these groups and individuals that I became part of the most important influence on me as we moved into the 1970s. This was La Galeria de La Raza, which I helped found in 1970. It meant the gallery of the people or the people's gallery. It was organized by those artists from these other groups that felt they not only needed a larger venue, but a place to reach out to the community. I joined in this effort. I felt that in organizing La Galeria that we were trying to say a lot of things. We weren't just saying here's a place where we as artists can show our works, talk about them, and share it with the Raza community. That was certainly part of it. But more importantly for me was that La Galeria was a way of critiquing modernism, which was the kind of art I had studied. The kind of works that we came to do and were doing at La Galeria aesthetically and conceptually ran counter to the thrust of abstract modernism. We were using recognizable images. We wanted to marry art, society, history, ethnicity, and everything else you could think of with art. We weren't unique in this. To a degree, surrealism, the art movements in Mexico after the revolution, and art in Russia after 1917 were trying to bridge these themes. Even the pop artists to a lesser extent were doing this.

I was very aware of what we were doing in terms of this critique. It was to politicize culture and not pretend that it was free-floating in a vacuum that is disconnected from everyday life. On the contrary, it is this life which gives art its fire or should. Its juice is that connection with life. If art isn't connected to life in some way, then for all intents and purposes, it is connected to nothing.

I also was becoming more aware due to my connection to La Galeria and the Mission that the museums and galleries in downtown San Francisco had little to no relevance to us and to our art. Instead, these institutions proposed the marvelous myth based on Eurocentric views concerning what is significant about human culture. The traditional art critics considered Latino art to be too culturally bound. "You're too preoccupied with being mexicano, Chicano," they would claim based on ignorance. "So how can you be universal the way art is supposed to be?" That was the argument. I felt that we through La Galeria had to counter these kinds of faulty ideas about the work we were producing. We had to talk about it. I always knew that there was no contradiction between being whatever you are and being part of the human family. What I concluded from these critics was simply this: When they said that the work of someone was culturally bound, what they really were saying was that we don't identify your humanity with my humanity. That's what they were saying. Not that our work was culturally bound because, goddamn it, they could look at a painting from China or sculptures from Rome or Egypt and then write books about them. So why weren't they culturally bound by writing about Egyptian art? It's amazing how these critics play this game; this arbitrary game. I was privy to all this. This made me stick really strongly to my beliefs.

These biased and perhaps even racist critics are really saying: "I can't see me in your culture, so how can you be important if I don't see myself in your culture?" My response is: Because you don't see yourself in my culture doesn't matter, because I know my culture is universal. What kind of a shell game were and are these critics playing? I knew we were right and we're still right. There is nothing wrong with a people making images of themselves. Nothing wrong with that. You can question how we do it or about our technique, and even raise questions about our particular aesthetics, but you don't say it doesn't fit into some make believe notion of what's universal, which somehow conveniently excludes us. Something is wrong there.

René Yañez:

It [La Galeria] was an alternative to the system that existed at the time. Museums, galleries were not exhibiting Chicanos, so we felt we had to take our destiny into our hands.[1]

All this gave me the fire to plunge into being active with La Galeria. I knew that what we were doing was very important beyond merely the Mission District, beyond the Bay Area, and beyond California. It was the sound of trumpets to the world. This was not only true about La Galeria, but of the many other Chicano/Latino art centers throughout the country. There were regional differences, of course, and historical ones. Still, there was this overall thrust of *centros* to produce art that was relevant to the people and an art that was part of the Chicano/Latino movements. These centers simultaneously became negation and affirmation. But above all they were empowering.[2] I was proud to be part of this. It was a defining moment for me.

Some of the key people behind La Galeria were Francisco Camplis, Peter Rodríguez, René Yañez, Ralph Maradiaga, and Robert González. La Galeria really grew out of Artes 6. Artes 6 needed a larger space, and so it moved, although not immediately knowing that it would become La Galeria. The new location was at East 14th off of Valencia in the Mission. Later La Galeria moved to 24th and Bryant. After the initial move, we had serious discussions about changing the name. Artes 6 didn't seem to be adequate enough for what we hoped to achieve in the Latino community as an art collective. We went through all kinds of possibilities. We agreed that we couldn't call it mexicano or Latino or Chicano. These terms were not the ethnic reality of the Mission. The fact was that the Mission consisted of many people from different parts of Latin America including the Caribbean. To capture this diversity, we finally came up with La Galeria de La Raza. Using the term "La Raza" seemed to better convey the diversity of the Mission.

Clearly, men dominated La Galeria and many of the other cultural institutions in the Mission. Looking back, I can see the sexism involved. At the same time, female artists and writers were very active during this period of the early and mid-1970s. One such artist was Mercedes Gutiérrez-McCormick, who did installation art. Other female artists who exhibited at La Galeria or who assisted there included Graciela Carrillo, who was a painter. There was Patricia Rodríguez from Arizona, also a painter. Perhaps the best-known artist who exhibited at La Galeria was Ester Hernández, who is best known for her revisionist images of Our Lady of Guadalupe. Having said this, there is no question but that La Galeria was dominated by men. It didn't exclude women, but unfortunately at that time the men superseded the women. However, this changed into the later 1970s and 1980s, when women became much more central to the art collective.

■II■

La Galeria was primarily a venue to exhibit our art. However, we also provided art classes especially for young people. In fact, I became a mentor to those who wanted to learn silk-screening. This work was enhanced when La Raza Graphic Center was established in 1972. I shied away from labeling myself as a mentor. I didn't want to wear it on my sleeve. I saw it as work with friends, and I was careful not to be condescending. It was likewise a place to have discussions concerning a variety of political and community issues. As a member of La Galeria, I began to write brochures and catalogs as well as produce the posters for particular exhibitions. I also did the book covers for some of the Mission poets. In addition, I curated some shows. For example, I organized a show of student posters from Mexico concerning the 1968 student strike in Mexico. We not only featured U.S. Latino artists, but in a display of internationalism, we had links with artists from Chile and Central America. In time, we further tried to link up with Black and Asian American art groups. Although we were La Galeria de La Raza, we didn't turn our backs on others. Additional cultural activities sponsored by La Galeria included dance classes, film screenings, poetry readings, community exhibits, art conferences, and publications of hand silk-screened calendars and a coloring book.[3]

Being a collective meant that we tried to make decisions based on consensus. We fed off each other—the energies and ideas. One of the major decisions we made as a collective was to not have the kind of individual shows that we had started with.

Instead, we would now have no less than a two-person exhibition. This was to emphasize our collective efforts. We came to believe that individual shows represented a bourgeois notion of individualism which we critiqued and rejected. We wanted to be more group oriented. We wanted to demonstrate solidarity among artists.

One of the major shows we had soon after La Galeria opened was one on Ruben Salazar. Salazar was the most prominent Chicano/Latino journalist in the country writing for the *Los Angeles Times* and as the news editor of KMEX, the then only Spanish-language TV station in L.A. Salazar was killed by L.A. County Sheriffs after covering the historic Chicano Anti-War Moratorium on August 29, 1970, in East Los Angeles. Some 20,000 people, mostly Chicanos, demonstrated against the U.S. war in Vietnam, which was taking a death toll on many young Chicanos in the military. The August 29 demonstration was the largest one during the Chicano Movement. I was devastated about hearing of the attack on the demonstrators by the county sheriffs and the death of Salazar. I learned more about what happened that fateful day because I subscribed to *La Raza* published in L.A., and it had great coverage about the moratorium. I didn't know much about Salazar, but I learned about him through the widespread news coverage of his death. I later read some of his wonderful columns for the *L.A. Times* that he wrote during the last months of his short-lived life. I was deeply moved by his death.[4]

I knew about the demonstration even though I didn't attend. Still, I made a poster for the moratorium committee in L.A. and sent several copies of it to them. I entitled the poster *¡Fuera De Indochina!* I did the poster from a striking photograph of a Vietnamese woman shouting out. I don't know what she was shouting out about, but she was crying. I used this image and coupled it with the words "¡Fuera De Indochina!" To me the image and the caption are integral; they complement each other. One is not more important than the other. I try to make it such that they are equally important, and sometimes because of the scale of the image, I try to balance it with the text.

Los Angeles art critic David Pagel:

> If posters can be masterpieces, this one ¡Fuera de Indochina! is as fine an example as any.[5]

I don't know who suggested that La Galeria do a show honoring Ruben Salazar, but as a collective we agreed to do one. Many of our artists offered to do something for the show. My job was to make the poster advertising the exhibit and which would also be the centerpiece of it. I made the silk-screen poster based on a photograph of Salazar that had been reproduced in many newspapers. I used mostly red and black colors with the exception of Salazar's face, which I did in a brownish color. On the top borders of the image, I painted in "Ruben Salazar Memorial Group Show Opening Dec 12," and at the bottom I inserted "Galeria de la Raza." It was a striking image of Salazar. I did the picture in flat colors, which means that the color red that I used and the color black do not change or modulate; they are the same type of red and black throughout the image. There are no shades of red, for example. It's called continuous color.

I further decided to do an additional but more innovative image of Salazar for the exhibit. I decided to do a four-image picture. In four squares, using different colors, I painted the same face of Salazar. I also did this in acrylic. I did this type of image being influenced by avant-garde films that I was watching. At this time in the late 1960s, I was seeing many foreign motion pictures, especially films by Godard, Costa-Gavras, Pontecorvo, Buñuel, and the American Haskell Wexler. These films influenced not only my style but my themes. These films were political. Godard was consciously critiquing the bourgeois understanding of cinema with respect to structure, how sound was used, and using a kind of Brechtian aesthetics of breaking down the illusion of art and life. He and some of these other filmmakers used divided screens with multiple images. This amazed me. I appreciated this fragmentation of images on the screen. It challenged my imagination and intellect. Seeing two or three realities happening simultaneously on the screen was incredible! It upset one's comfort zone, and this was deliberate by the filmmakers. I was also reading books about the semiology of film and film theory. Semiology refers to the study of signs. This taught me about always being critical of what you see. Don't take it for granted.

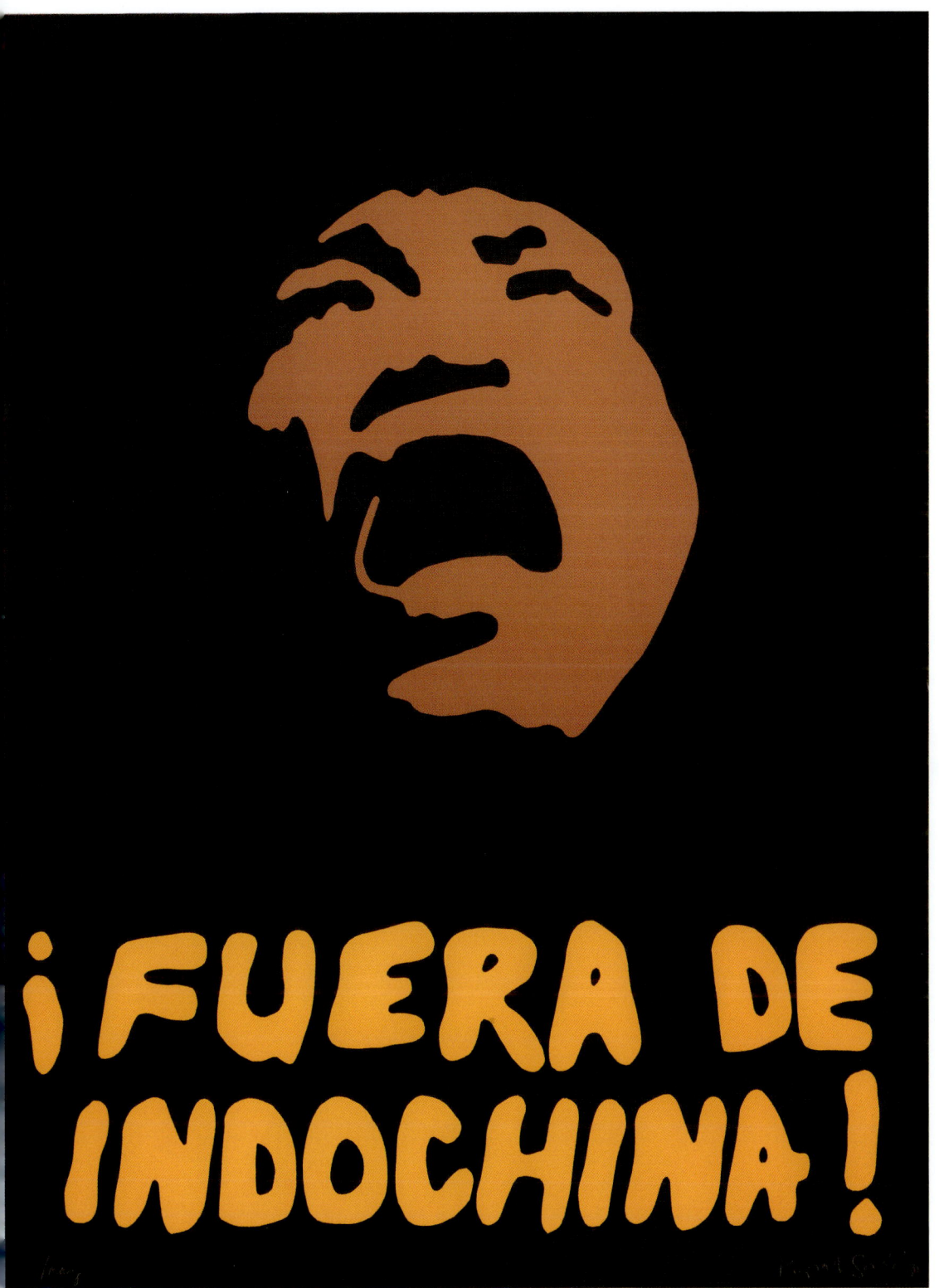

¡Fuera De Indochina!, 1970. Color silkscreen on white wove paper, 26 x 20 inches.
Copyright © Rupert García. Courtesy of Rena Bransten Gallery.

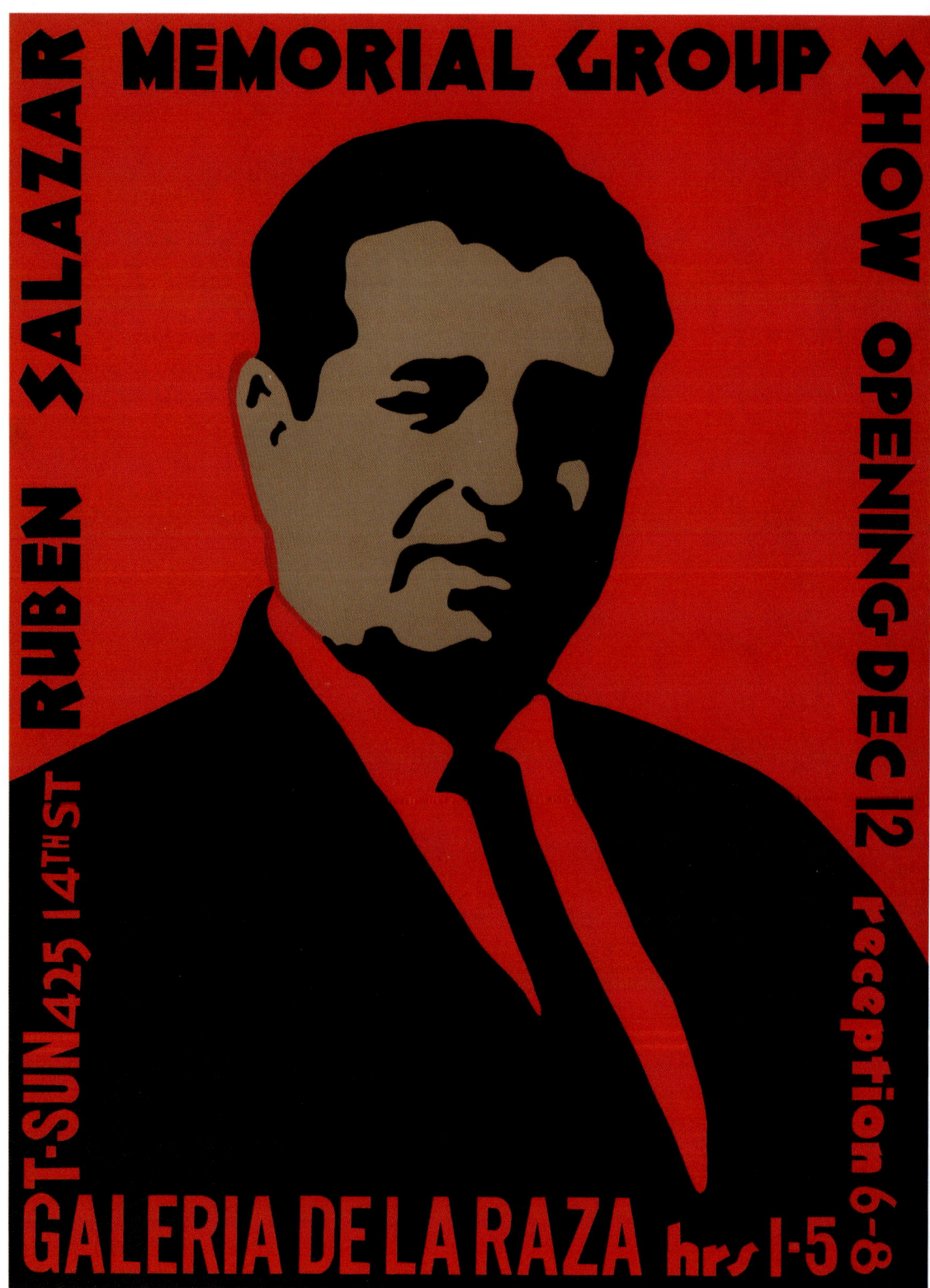

Ruben Salazar Memorial Group Show, 1970. Color silkscreen on white wove paper, sheet size: 26 x 20 inches. Copyright © Rupert García. Courtesy of Rena Bransten Gallery.

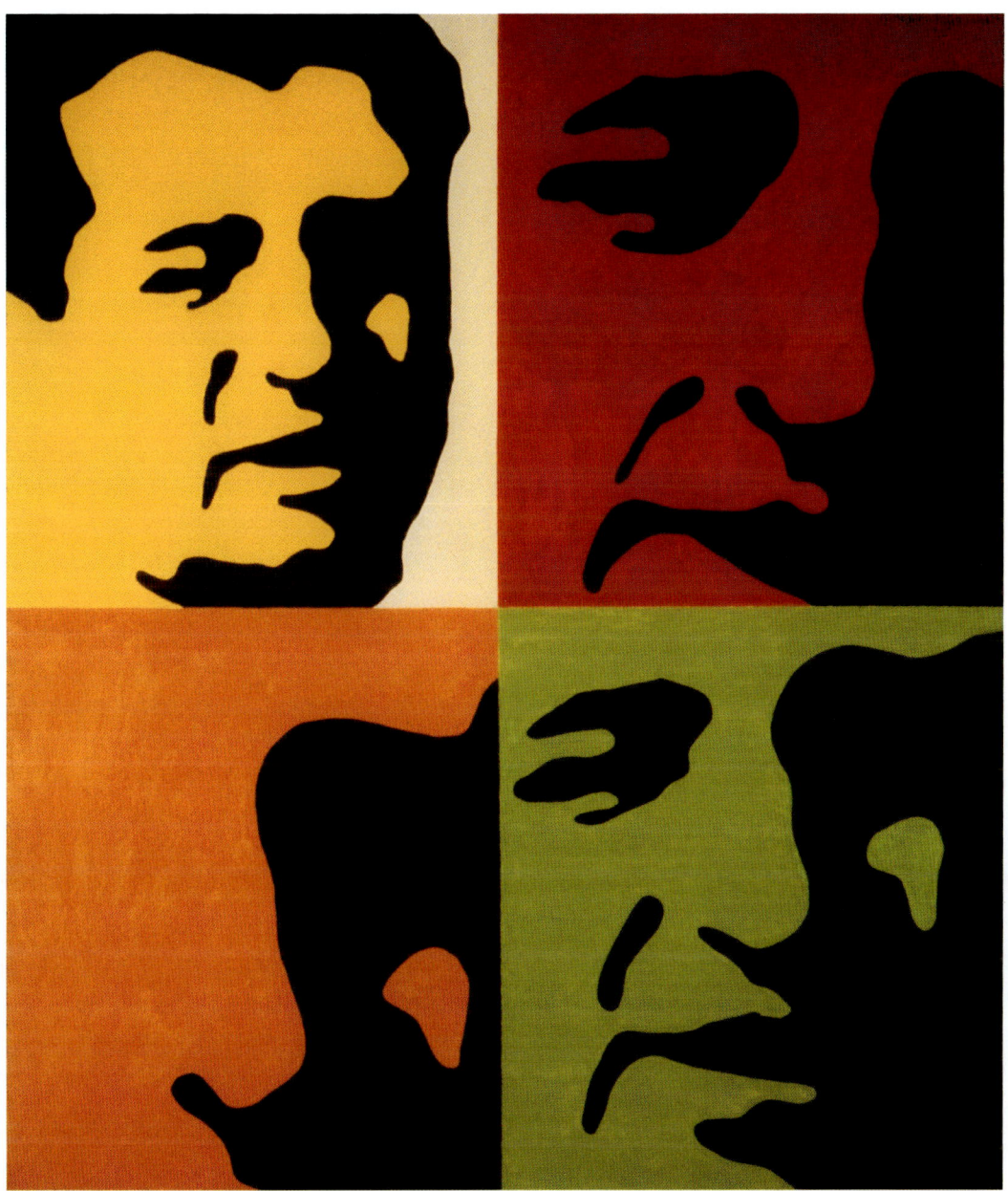

Ruben Salazar, 1970. Acrylic on Canvas, canvas size: 54 x 48 inches. Copyright © Rupert García. National Portrait Gallery, Smithsonian Institution Washington, D.C. Courtesy of Rena Bransten Gallery.

At the same time, I have to say that my images of Salazar were also influenced by Andy Warhol and his pop art images of movie stars such as Marilyn Monroe and Elizabeth Taylor. In a way, my images of Salazar were done in a pop art fashion.

All this influenced me in doing my fragmented images of Ruben Salazar in the additional painting I did for the special exhibit. Many people came to the opening of the exhibit and expressed interest and appreciation of my two Salazar pictures. The exhibit lasted for a month, and many more attended. My images of Salazar brought me larger recognition in the Latino art world. My Salazar portraits many years later in 2018 were permanently included at the National Portrait Gallery in Washington, DC.

—ⅠⅠ—

As I worked with La Galeria and continued with the silk-screen workshop, I evolved as an artist. Many Chicano/Latino artists at this time seemed to be influenced by *Los Tres Grandes*—the great Mexican muralists and painters: Diego Rivera, David Alfaro Siqueiros, and José Clemente Orozco. I was aware of Los Tres in my research, but in my case their influence on my work in terms of the aesthetics of how they made their pictures was for all intents and purposes limited. If anything, Orozco is the one who influenced me because of his expressive use of colors, paints, shapes, and composition. Rivera and Siqueiros are more of an intellectual influence in their use of art and culture in the context of post-revolutionary Mexico.

To be honest, I was and still am much more influenced in my work by José Guadalupe Posada. I first encountered Posada in the late 1960s. My girlfriend Liz's father was a lefty, and he was familiar with *arte popular* in Mexico. In his home library, he had all of these art books that featured Posada's work in the early twentieth century. I was stunned. Like everyone else, I was struck by Posada's *calaveras* or skeletons. I liked his plebeian point of view and his embrace of Mexican popular culture. In doing so, he was critical of the powers that be. His art was confrontational. He went from the "refined" based on his earlier training to the "vulgar" here, meaning not his style, but his embrace of the culture of the masses which is not vulgar. I thought that was great! He made a conscious effort to do this. He communicated with the masses in a kind of artistic vernacular language, both in terms of aesthetics and in his use of his characters, especially the calaveras. He made the skeletons come alive, talking and moving and dancing and poking fun and being critical of society and the bourgeoise. This was very exciting. His work is magnificent. Posada profoundly influenced every artist in Mexico following the revolution and even up to today. It's Posada who helps mexicanos figure out how to come up with an aesthetics of Mexicanness. He was incredible.

In addition to Posada, I would have to say that Frida Kahlo affected me and did so big-time. I also became aware of her in the late 1960s and early 1970s. Like Kahlo, I have done a lot of portraits. Hers are predominantly self-portraits. But there is that similarity of using the portrait in some way. That is one of the things that got me involved with her work. My initial impression of Frida was simply the unabashed honesty and frankness of her work, of herself, and what she was thinking or feeling right then and

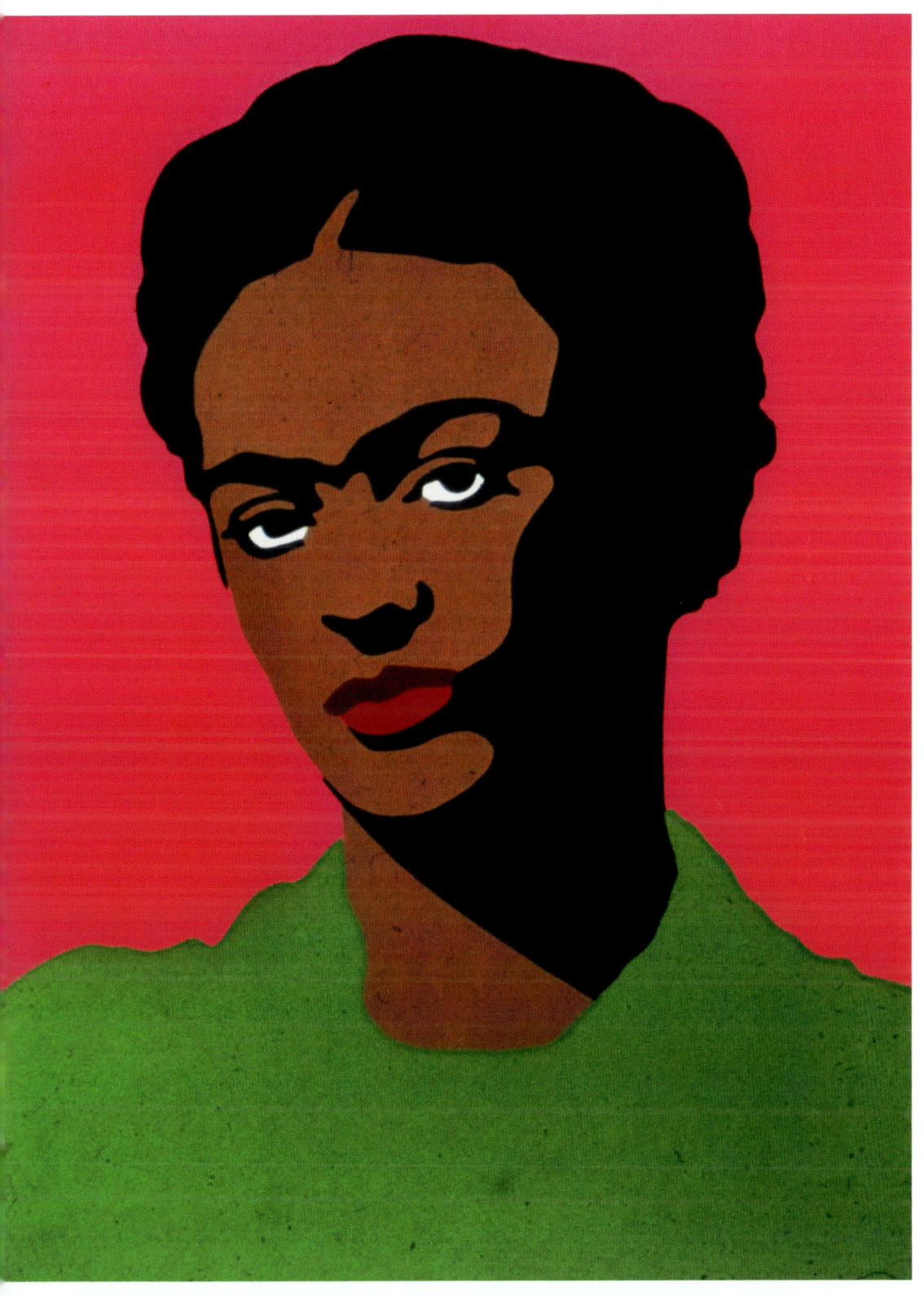

Frida Kahlo, 1975. Color silkscreen on white wove paper, sheet size: 23 x 17-1/2 inches. Copyright © Rupert García. Courtesy of Rena Bransten Gallery.

there. You couldn't escape it. She revealed in her paintings her honesty, pain, agony, and humor. She was a very funny woman. I think her work is sometimes hilarious, although always serious, too. I was drawn to the iconic organization of her self-portraits. They come to you. You don't have to meekly investigate the pain. It's there.

Other influences from Frida included her use of color, beautiful color. She also was not afraid of taking risks. She didn't censor herself. She really put out a lot of personal information. I love her use of animals, monkeys, birds, and even a deer. I further admired her politics that weren't always demonstrated in her work although if nothing else did express her embrace of Mexican nationalism or Mexicanness. She—like Rivera, whom she was married to, and Siqueiros—was a Communist. I admired that Frida and the other two were not bashful as artists in revealing their Communist and Marxist sympathies. I liked this because with other artists who were Communists, such as Picasso, their radical politics are often overlooked or downplayed by art critics. In the case of Mexican artists including Frida, their politics are front and center. I found this refreshing because in art departments, art and politics don't mix. They're separated. But not in the case of the mexicano artists. There is no separation between their art and politics. It's one in tandem with the other. I emulated this.

I also fell in love with Frida. She was a beautiful woman, very intelligent, and very funny. All this made me more attracted to her although I didn't know her. Part of my feelings toward her likewise had to do with her unabashed exposure of her body, which was very brave of her. In this sense, she was a true feminist with a capital "F." Her work is the real deal. That's why I became one of her early allies in the United States and especially among Latinos, even before it became fashionable to do so. In 1975 I did a silk screen of her that is, in fact, a love letter to her. It's a really passionate poster. I did it for one of the *calendarios* that La Galleria issued each year. I did her portrait from a photograph that I reduced to simple shapes and changes in the shadow a little bit. I simplified her look and I reversed the position of her face. I have done many other images of this remarkable artist and woman.

◼◼◼

I tell people that in San Francisco, there was no specific Chicano Movement. You couldn't have a Chicano Movement because of the diversity of Latin American people there, especially in the Mission. In Oakland and in San Jose, there was a Chicano Movement because of the greater Mexican population in those areas. But not in San Francisco. That's why we were La Galleria de La Raza. That's why at San Francisco State there was a La Raza Studies Department and not a Chicano Studies one. We couldn't pretend in these cases that we were only mexicanos and Chicanos. That would have been too divisive. It made absolute sense to use terms such as Latino and La Raza in San Francisco. I related to this. Even though my family was Mexican, I grew up living along-side other ethnic groups such as Asian Americans and Blacks. So, I knew about ethnic diversity, and this made it easier for me to adjust to the Latino mix in the Mission. I could be both Chicano and Latino without suffer-ing an identity problem. I understood the role that nationalism played in the Chicano Movement, and I supported that. However, what I rejected was the notion that if you didn't identify as a Chicano that you were some kind of traitor. I didn't understand this either/ or mentality, this binary. If you're not, you're out. If you are, you're in. I iden-tified as Chicano when I was among mostly Chicanos, and I identified as Latino when I was among people from different Latino backgrounds. So, what's the problem? This is what most people do today.

I had to deal with this to an extent when I was hired to teach the first La Raza Art Workshop class in La Raza Studies at San Francisco State in 1969. I think some of the people who inter-viewed me thought I would only teach about Mexican art. I challenged this when I told them:

> Look, if you want me to teach this class and if you're expecting me to turn out little Diego Riveras and little Orozcos, you have the wrong man. I wouldn't do this. I'll teach about Mexican art, but I will also include art from other Latin Amer-ican countries in addition to the work of Latinos here in the U.S.

My statement seemed to satisfy them and I was hired. But I didn't just say this just to be hired. The fact was and is that I approached Latino art in a very expansive and inclusive way, and I wanted to pass this on to my stu-dents. I wasn't interested in having my students think that their imagination and creative impulse was limited to Los Tres Grandes. This would suffo-cate their creative ability, and I didn't want to do that. I further rejected es-sentializing Chicano and Latino cul-ture as some in the movement seemed to be doing, but which had nothing to do with reality. Chicano and Latino cultures are heterogeneous and com-plex. They can't be simplified to some kind of core culture. This excludes the diversity of these cultures and peoples. I rejected this personally, ideologically, and artistically.

■11■

I need to say more about the term Chi-cano and my reaction to it. When the notion of being Chicano arose in the late 1960s with the Chicano Move-ment, I had no problem with it. I was never raised to feel bad about being Mexican. Maybe my Spanish language abilities weren't the best that they should be, but that was my problem. Still, I really subscribed to Chican-ismo. It wasn't that I had to deal with the whole roots issue that perhaps other Chicanos went through. I had a sense already of my roots through my family. I already felt self-assured about who I was. So, there weren't really major identity building blocks for me. Chicanismo just added fuel to the fire of my sense of myself. I began to call myself Chicano because I identified with the movement. The only qualification that I had with the term was when others tried to define it in very strict terms of who was Chicano, and by so doing leave many others out of the movement. I didn't have such a limited view of being Chicano. To me, Chicano is both particular and general. Moreover, it doesn't negate the human potential at all. You can be Chicano and be part of humanity.

Becoming a Chicano was a very conscious and sociopolitical act on my part. What it meant to be a Chicano at that time was very important for me philosophically. At the same time, I didn't go around wearing buttons saying "Yo Soy Chicano" or "Chicano Power." Someone has referred to this as the "button revolution." I felt wearing a button was forced. The movement wasn't about buttons. It was about contributing important ideas or getting involved in important activities that in some way bring about change. So, the wearing of buttons wasn't important for me, although I understood the importance of the button revolution, because in those buttons a cultural consciousness was manifested. You could look at the buttons as a visual statement about what people were thinking about and what they were feeling about. And we could see in looking at many buttons that what was emerging from these pictures was an ideology—Chicanismo. Buttons were important, but they weren't important for me.

To be honest, I had never heard of the term Chicano until the period of the movement. As part of the movement, the term was a political and cultural statement. It represented a different kind of consciousness about being Mexican in the United States. It was linked to the genealogy of you and your family as well as of other Mexican Americans in the Southwest. Being Chicano led me to better understand the role of racism and Eurocentrism. It broadened my understanding of the importance of neighborhood life and the community. It heightened my appreciation of the importance of sharing collectively in working with others. Being Chicano did a lot of good things for me, but it was never romantic or narrow. It was never that, because if I did perceive it as a strict form of nationalism, I couldn't have become part of La Galeria and worked with other artists and poets in the Mission who were not Chicanos.

As part of being Chicano, I also embraced the concept of *mestizaje* or the mixing of peoples and cultures as proposed by El Plan de Aztlán and Corky Gonzales's epic poem *I Am Joaquin*. Mestizaje noted that Chicanos were a blend of Spanish and indigenous background but stressed the latter over the former. However, I stretched mestizaje because Mexicans are not only European and indigenous; their hybridity also includes African and Asian. You can see this in parts of Mexico.

One part of Chicanismo, however, that I had problems with was the concept of Aztlán. Aztlán was the original homeland of the Aztecs before they migrated to the Valley of Mexico and established their empire. The belief is that Aztlán is to the north of present-day Mexico City. How far north is not clear. Some scholars suggest that it was along the Pacific coast of Mexico today but below the U.S.–Mexico border. Chicanos, in turn, proclaimed that Aztlán was in the Southwest where most Chicanos lived. This was a convenient way for Chicanos to state that therefore not only were they living in Aztlán, but they were the descendants of the Aztecs. I never bought this. This was romantic and poetic nationalism having little to do with historical reality. Few scholars believe that Aztlán was as far north as the southwestern portion of the United States. I have never referenced the term in my art or in my writing. I can't swallow it; it sticks in my throat. I do things about indigenous people, but not with respect to Aztlán. This form of cultural nationalism, in my opinion, limits the reality of the Southwest peopled by many different indigenous people who have no relationship to Aztlán. The concept is limiting because it's only applied to Chicanos. And so, I try to stay away from any involvement that has a very narrow notion of Aztlán. I also stay away from the obsession by some Chicano artists during the movement about pre-Colombian symbols that feeds this false narrative about Chicanos being the direct descendants of the Aztecs. I have included some of these symbols, but not to the extent of many other Chicano artists.

I know, on the other hand, that Aztlán was a way to politically and culturally organize Chicanos. I understood this because I was familiar with the role of nationalism from reading about other social movements in Mexico, Cuba, China, and Russia. I understand the role of nationalism, including cultural nationalism, which was central to the Chicano Movement. Nevertheless, I was and still am ambivalent about the concept of Aztlán. I'm ambivalent because of the intellectual and poetic stretch to make the Southwest the ancestral home of the Aztecs, which is not accurate. I became Chicano due to the Chicano Movement, but becoming Chicano for me didn't include accepting Aztlán as the historic homeland of Chicanos.

Rupert Garcia interview with Guillermo Gómez-Peña:

> I don't mind that people consider me a critical Chicano artist, as long as they understand the complexity of the term. To be "Chicano" is above all to be a concerned human, and to be this means to be complex and multifaceted. It is true that my work is sometimes explicitly and suggestively political, but I am also concerned with many other things. A democracy demands that its citizens be critical, political, and vociferous, or in my case, also visiferous.[6]

—||—

During the early 1970s and while I was affiliated with La Galeria, I witnessed as part of the Mission Cultural Renaissance the impressive mural movement in the Mission District. Young artists had discovered the legacy of the mural movements in Mexico spearheaded by Los Tres and attempted to emulate this in the Mission. In a few years, a number of murals were painted in the barrio. This was part of a larger muralist movement among other Chicanos/Latinos in the Southwest and Midwest. Hundreds if not thousands of murals were painted as part of the Chicano Movement in the Southwest including California, for example.[7] The muralists in the Mission, both men and women, left in some cases a lasting legacy. It was all part of the political and cultural upheavals of this period. It stressed even more directly that art and politics could coexist. Of this, art historian Tim Drescher and I later wrote: "Raza murals must be viewed in terms of the several relationships, artistic and social, they simultaneously embody."[8] We also added:

Like the "cultural revolution" of the Mexicans beginning [in] 1929, La Raza of Aztlán emphasized the Native American and mestizo heritage of its culture as well as the Mexican revolutionary heritage. Within this reawakening of La Raza's complex and profound history, art forms, including the mural, have been rediscovered, newly appreciated, and put to use.[9]

The mural movement further arose as a way to communicate with the Latino community in one of the few ways that Chicanos/Latinos possessed. Of this I wrote later in 1983:

One of the major roles of the Chicano artist was to publicly communicate, and in some instances rather quickly, the many critical issues of the Chicano Movement in the community. The Chicano communities' lack of control of the mass media to effectively articulate their needs on a mass scale led the Chicano artist to seek alternative methods of public communication. Among other avenues of creative production endeavored, many Chicano artists "took to the walls" of the community. Neighborhood walls and related surfaces were the only immediately public spaces available on which the community could see and "hear" themselves. Artists transformed these blank walls into "public speaking spaces" of vibrant colors, shapes and figures relating images and information of the Chicano Movement to the passersby. Like the artist in earlier periods of struggle, the working class Chicano artist pursued the media of their time not yet dominated by the corporate elite, the mural and the poster.[10]

La Galeria became the flame that fueled the mural movement in the Mission. This led to images on walls, fences, and garage doors as well as in schools, restaurants, and community centers not only in the Mission, but in other parts of San Francisco. René Yañez was one of our artists who got involved with other artists and started doing mural painting around 1971 or 1972 in a recreation center. They painted murals inside the center, and that really is the beginning of the mural movement in the Mission. La Galeria was directly responsible for the renewed interest in mural painting, which is really a community-based project. While you had more professional artists such as René, you also had many others who were not. Nevertheless, they all contributed to the making of murals. Besides encouraging this effort, La Galeria also raised funds for these projects. We applied for federal funds through the CETA program (Comprehensive Employment and Training Act) that in particular assisted young people to do community-based work. These were federal funds channeled through the city of San Francisco.

The murals were like vignettes. Themes varied from pre-Columbian motifs and myths to social criticism, Raza history, and solidarity with other struggling oppressed people. In 1975, one of the most successful murals was produced on a wall near the entrance to the BART commuter train station at 24th and Mission by Mike Rios, Tony Machado, and Richard Montes. The different images on the murals were interconnected through the design and color. Some muralists worked on one panel and others on another. Many of our artists affiliated with La Galeria participated. The locations of the murals were negotiated mostly with social services organizations, and the murals were painted on the exterior or interior or sometimes both. None of the murals were done in for-profit businesses. Of this, Drescher and I wrote: "Denied access to ruling-class dominated mass media, galleries, and museums, political artists turned to the walls of their own communities as forums for presentation of crucial issues."[11] I should also note that it wasn't only Latinos who were doing murals. Asian Americans, Blacks, and some Native Americans in their neighborhoods were likewise doing them.

The one exception of a mural done in a for-profit business was one done inside the Bank of America on 23rd and Mission that I liked. It was inspired by a mural that Diego Rivera had done in the early 1930s for the Pacific Stock Exchange in San Francisco. When questioned how an avowed Communist like him could justify such a mural within a capitalist institution, Rivera responded that he was not doing the mural for the Stock Exchange, but for the people who worked there. By the same token Latino muralists agreed to do the mural inside the Bank of America, which the people in the Mission referred as "La BoA," with the intent that the mural was not for the bank but for the people who banked there. Emmy Lou Packard, who worked with Diego Rivera, consulted on the La BoA mural. I wrote about the mural for *El Tecolote* and quoted Mike Rios, one of the artists, who added the following:

This mural is a great step forward for the struggling artist. A kind of mural this size (90 feet by 10 feet) hasn't been done in a long time. A lot of young Third World artists are getting turned on to the medium of murals. Murals are the strongest and commonest way to make everyday people aware of their art-conscious brothers and sisters who are trying to reflect the community experience through their artistic talent. We try to express their hopes, fears, and aspirations. In the murals, we are talking about our family.[12]

At the same time, I differentiated between what some call murals and what I call "wall art." To me the Mission murals are examples of the latter. When I think of murals, I conjure up the work of Los Tres in Mexico as well as other mural artists such as Tamayo. These professional artists didn't just do images on walls. They started with an understanding of a sense of aesthetics, of the architectural structure on which the mural would be painted, and of the social use of the space on which they would do the mural. They had a certain kind of vision about murals and the history of murals. One of the other characteristics of the murals in Mexico City, for example, is that almost all of the murals were sponsored by the federal government and done on federal buildings. All of the Mexican muralists were much older in age when they painted their murals than the Latinos who did wall painting in San Francisco. The Mexican artists were also much more trained in art, having studied both in art academies in Mexico as well as in Paris.

By contrast, the Latinos in the Mission, and the same could be said of other artists such as in East Los Angeles, painted pictures on walls. Did they do a mural? No, not in the sense in which we traditionally understand a mural. Some did but most did not. Many people get upset when I talk this way because they think that I'm denigrating an important cultural component of the Movimiento. But I'm not at all. I'm just saying that you can't in the same breath assume that a mural done by many Chicanos/Latinos is the same

as those done by Los Tres Grandes in Mexico. It's not the same. The difference lies in the complexity of doing genuine murals such as those done in Mexico City. When you do a mural, you must take into consideration scale, the specific site, the physical structure where you plan to put your pictures or the interior architecture. You must take into consideration who uses the space, how do people actually traffic the space, what is the space used for, and what is the best way to articulate the image on the surfaces inside this building. All these considerations are complex.

I'm not saying that our artists didn't think of these issues, but generally speaking they didn't. And it may have been because these were issues that were not important to them because the thrust of the Chicano/Latino mural movement had many other reasons for being. One was to have a space upon which to visually articulate your ideas, emotions, dreams, and protestations. So, you use whatever walls are available, including garage doors. I think, too, that our artists built on the tradition of graffiti or *placas*, which are gang symbols which made some people more familiar with using walls to make pictures. Moreover, making murals represented a social organizing tool to bring people together. It was also to visualize historical symbols and icons of one's history. It's not that the Mexican muralists weren't also reflecting their political and social views, especially with respect to the Mexican Revolution of 1910. The main difference then why I consider the images in Mexico to be murals and those in the Mission to be wall paintings is the difference in the training, professionalism, and experience of Los Tres compared to the Mission artists. Yes, Chicano and Latino artists were inspired by the Mexican muralists, but that does not make their images into murals in the way that I'm defining murals. Perhaps, we should call the murals done by Chicanos and Latinos "neo-murals."

Despite the importance of the "murals" in the Mission and elsewhere, what came to bother me was that many, Chicanos and non-Chicanos, were identifying "Chicano art" with murals and posters. Of course, my production of posters was part of this. However, Chicano art was not just murals and posters. Other artists were likewise doing a variety of other forms of painting. Still, murals and posters became regrettably synonymous with Chicano art. That to me was ridiculous. To me, it was problematic to limit the cultural production of the visual artist to only these genres. I don't believe in limiting the opportunities of Chicano and Latino artists to go in many different directions. Chicano art is whatever a Chicano artist wishes to do. We have to have an expansive understanding of what Chicano art is and not limit it.

I, myself, never worked on a mural at this time. I never thought that I could do a mural. I always thought about Los Tres as the model muralists, and I never felt that I could achieve their high standards, at least in mural making. I just didn't feel prepared to do a mural, and I never felt that I had to prove myself as an artist by doing

murals. The closest I came to working on a mural or wall painting at that time was when I was contacted by the Chicanos who were doing the murals in Chicano Park in San Diego. After a community struggle, the Chicanos obtained permission to do the images on the pillars underneath the Coronado Bridge freeway in the early 1970s. While local artists did most of the images, the organizers also invited additional participation in a very interesting way. They devised a method whereby artists outside of San Diego could participate without having to go to Chicano Park. I thought this was fascinating. The method consisted of the organizers sending me a slide of one of the *pilons* that didn't yet have an image. It was a blank slide. I then had to project the slide on a slide projector up to a certain size. I then drew my image right on that space and made a slide of it. I sent the slide to the organizers accompanied by a code for the colors I wanted on my image. At Chicano Park, they projected my slide on the pilon, and they traced my image on it adding the colors. I thought this was brilliant. I was happy to participate in this way. My image, which is still there, is one of Frida Kahlo surrounded by Los Tress of Rivera, Siqueiros, and Orozco. But this was my only involvement in wall painting. Of course, as part of La Galeria, I supported those who did work on murals. I also appreciated the political importance of the murals and the inspiration that they gave to the community. The mural movement was very much a part of the Mission cultural renaissance.

Sister Karen Bocadero, founder of Self-Help Graphics in East Los Angeles:

They [the murals] gave people a sense of pride and accomplishment.[13]

■ ❙❙ ■

The Mission cultural renaissance, of course, consisted of many other art forms. We had our writers like Roberto Vargas in both fiction and nonfiction. These included poets and music. The most famous musician that emerged out of the Mission was Carlos Santana. His music transcended the Mission and became an important part of the larger cultural renaissance of the Chicano Movement. In addition, in the Mission, many *salsero* groups emerged, reintroducing salsa music especially to the younger and more acculturated Latinos. Moreover, at this time in the movement, we were rediscovering our history and cultural traditions as Chicanos/Latinos. One of those traditions was the celebration of Día de los Muertos. Consequently, we at La Galeria sponsored this celebration beginning in the early 1970s. It particularly struck a chord in me. It had a link with the *calaveras* of Posada that I had discovered. It also had a link with Halloween as a kid. It further reminded me of the scary stories that my mother used to tell us. My grandmother also had a home altar where she prayed for the soul of my grandfather. But there were no *calaveras*. At the same time, in Stockton and within my family, we never celebrated the Day of the Dead. In fact, I didn't even know anything about it until La Galeria sponsored it.

La Galeria's promotion of the Día de los Muertos consisted of organizing an exhibition where artists were invited to do pieces on the Day of the Dead. Many artists contributed. Most did a version of the *calavera*. I wasn't very involved in these exhibits; however, I did do a poster on the massacre of prisoners at the Attica state prison in New York state centered on a *calavera*. This was directly related to Posada and the Day of the Dead.

For the 1975 Día de los Muertos show, I wrote out a short statement for the event. In part, I wrote,

The artworks in this exhibition depict, in a sense, each artist's struggle with death. Not only have these artists used a death-related symbol, they have also transformed their "raw materials" into a new esthetic experience. Within this process is expressed the essence of the dynamic of life and death. In transforming the artist's medium, clay for example, into a new object is the inseparable process of destruction and creation. The artist must "negate" the pliable, moist clay to achieve a work of art. The finished product demonstrates how the artist converted this medium. In other words, works of art depict the artist's never ending celebration of death—regenerator of life.[14]

■ ❙❙ ■

An additional part of the Mission cultural renaissance was the publication of *El Tecolote*. This was a major community newspaper. It grew out of the strike at San Francisco State. It then became part and parcel of La Raza Studies Department. Juan González was the driving force behind the newspaper. He was a major in journalism at SFS. Like me, Juan was also from Stockton, but I didn't know him then. Although the paper started on campus, it moved to the Mission community in the early 1970s and began a long history of publication for several decades. It was part of the ideology at the time which centered on empowering the community. The paper could not be done in isolation; this wasn't practical. It had to be in the community and for the community.

El Tecolote embraced the Chicano and Latino and merged the two in an early version of Latinidad. It recognized the importance of merging the experiences of the different Latino groups in the Mission into a new pan-Latino identity that still respected the individual character of the varied cultures. The paper serviced the community by providing information of what was happening in San Francisco and specifically in the Mission. It also had various features, including historical, political, and cultural ones. For example, it reviewed exhibits such as at La Galeria. All of its stories and editorials had a progressive cutting edge to them that included a left of center perspective and an international one as well.

My involvement with *El Tecolote*, which was part of my political education, was twofold. For one, I drew some of the illustrations for the masthead and for some of the articles. In addition, I wrote a bit for the paper.

Juan González talked me into this. I had never written for any publication before. I said, "yeah, sure, sure." It mostly included articles on Latino art exhibits such as on the mural movement. I wrote this one piece on La Raza murals in 1972, which was my attempt to develop a genealogy between the murals or wall paintings being done by Chicanos/Latinos in the United States with those produced in Mexico going back to pre-Columbian times. I had felt and believed then and still do to this day that there has never been a period when murals have not been produced since the Olmecas. There has been continuous production of murals by Chicanos/Latinos and their ancestors whether based on ancient rituals, colonialism, postcolonialism, revolutionary times, in Mexico or the United States, whether by the well-trained or amateurs. It includes murals painted in bars, meat markets, or other establishments in the barrios. I even saw murals in banks. Some of these paintings preceded the Chicano Movement. It doesn't matter the venue. This continuous production has never stopped. For this article, I also visited murals in East L.A. done by artists such as Félix Almaraz and Willie Herrón. In addition, I wrote on certain cultural events. I had a great time doing this writing and being involved with *El Tecolote*. I was allowed to write about whatever I wanted.

Beside *El Tecolote*, I also worked with another Mission newspaper *La Prensa* and with Ediciones Pocho-Che, which was a small publishing house started in 1971 in the Mission District

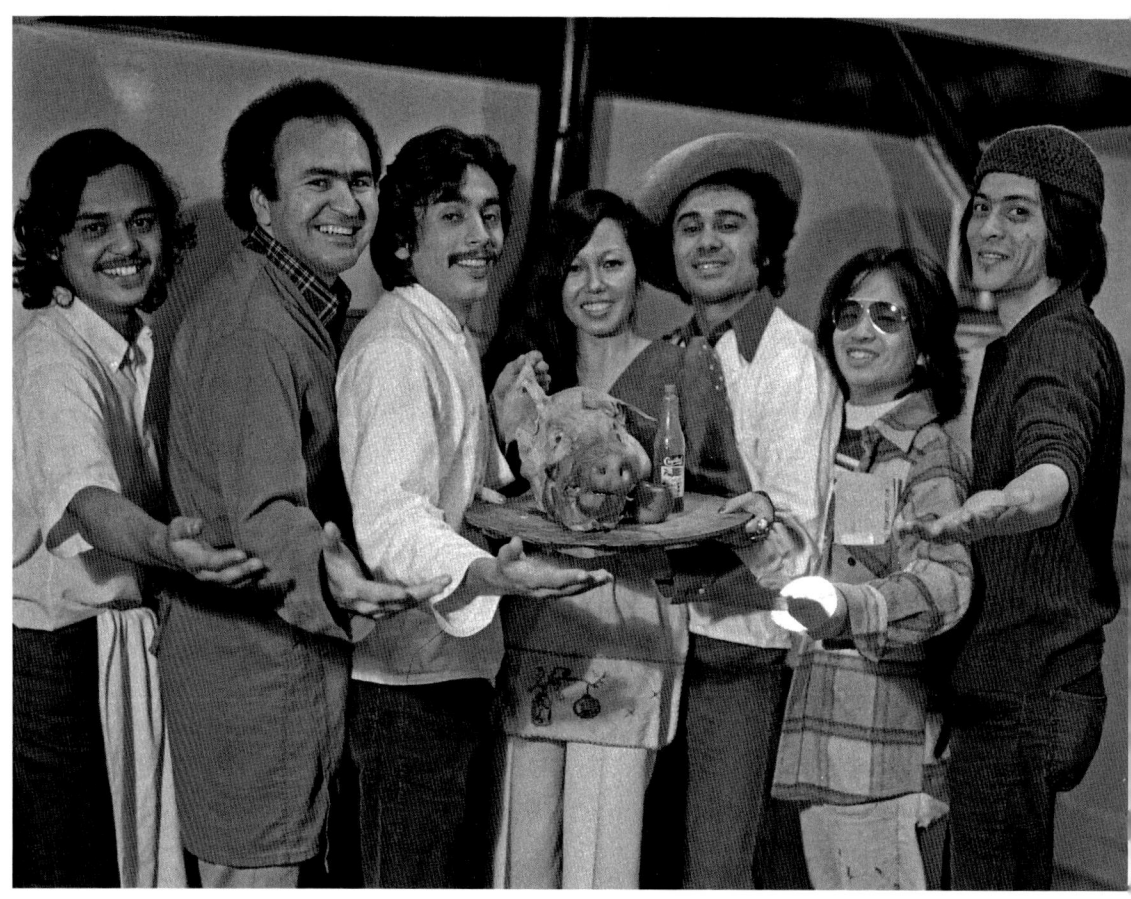

Rupert García, second from left, with other editors of publication *Time to Greez! Incantations from the Third World*. From left to right Joe Ramos, Rupert, Alejandro Murguia, Janice Mirikitani, Roberto Vargas, Jim Dong, Luis Syquia, Jr., 1975. Photo courtesy of Joe Ramos.

by Roberto Vargas and Alejandro Murguia. For *La Prensa* I made drawings and a Zapata poster. Ediciones Pocho-Che promoted poetry, politics, and social awareness. I served as art editor for a while. Ediciones published some books and tabloids such as *Tin Tan*. It was named after a famous Mexican comedian who portrayed a pachuco figure. I did an image of Che Guevara, both dead and alive, for the third edition of *Tin Tan* in 1976, which was a special poetry issue. *Tin Tan* was

a beautiful-looking publication. I also did the cover for a poetry book by Elias Hruska Cortes and Roberto Vargas published by Ediciones Pocho-Che. It was an innovative book because it was two books in one, and one side was upside down. Cortes's book was titled *This Side and Other Things* and Vargas's was called *PrimerosCantos*. I did the front and back covers painting the images of both Cortes and Vargas. Inside the book I included my images of Zapata, the Mayan Indian, Angela

Davis, Attica is Fascismo, and ¡Fuera De Indochina!

■ ❙❙ ■

In 1973 I had an opportunity to visit Mexico as an artist. I went with my then girlfriend, Liz Brown. It also coincided with my teaching a course at the San Francisco Art Institute. They had asked me to teach a class on the cultural and art history of Mexico. Liz and I went to Mexico City during spring break. The trip blew my mind. Of course, we saw the major murals by Los Tres and also by Rufino Tamayo. It was just so impressive seeing the murals. It was a profound experience because they were so accessible to people and so monumental. They're like visual operas. Big, colorful, dynamic shapes. The reproductions in art books that I had studied did not do justice to the murals. You have to see them in person. When you see the real murals, you're more aware of the actual scale of the work, the actual color, the actual surface of the wall, the actual brush strokes. That's very impressive. I was in awe of them. I was just as impressed with the Tamayo murals. I had always liked Tamayo's work. I never agreed with some leftist critics who felt that his work wasn't ideologically correct. That it wasn't Mexican enough. They also accused Tamayo of being too European and too Parisian. I disagree. In my opinion, Tamayo is the most Mexicano of all of the muralists. I just loved his colors, his transition of colors, and his abstract shapes. He just had a different presence of Mexicanness. While the other muralists were descriptively presenting things Mexican, Tamayo more or less offered you the feeling of Mexico with his colors and semiabstract shapes. There was always something in Tamayo's work that is readable. He didn't fully go abstract.

Besides seeing the murals, we went to see the pyramids in Teotihuacán. This was incredible. I had never gone to a sacred sight and really let myself go and feel that I was in a very special place. I never experienced the same feeling in a church, including the Basilica of Our Lady of Guadalupe, which we also visited. I don't want to sound too romantic, but the pyramids to me were transcendental. I knew that the pre-Columbian people also had their shortcomings and violence toward each other. Still, I couldn't help but be impressed with the pyramids. I was taken by just looking at the architecture and how they handled space. It was just overwhelming. I felt that these structures meant something; they were in touch with something spiritual. By contrast, I feel that U.S. buildings are in touch with money.

I had further profound feelings when we visited the Museo Nacional de Antropologia (National Anthropological Museum). I had never experienced anything like this before. I couldn't believe that I was seeing the famous Aztec stone calendar and the image of Coatlicue, a major Aztec goddess. When you study something, it's pretty abstract. You're removed and it's intellectual. It's not emotional. So, when you actually go and see the object that you were studying earlier, you almost forget what you have studied, because now you're in touch with the real object. I was very drawn into the stone calendar and Coatlicue. I was dumbfounded. I had to come back more than once. But the rest of the museum was just as powerful. It was fascinating to see the displays that showed the evolution of the Indigenous civilizations in Mexico prior to the Spanish conquest. You get a sense of the history of Mexico that goes back thousands of years.

What also struck me was the display on Indigenous foods. I couldn't help but make the link with my own family. These were many of the foods that we ate. This got me thinking a lot about *comida* or the meals we had at home that were similar to that of the Indigenous in Mexico. It was the same chili! In growing up, I had no sense of this history. No one explained this to me. But the connection was real; it wasn't make-believe. It also made me understand why we had cactus plants—nopales—in our backyard and that a nopal is more than simply a nopal; it is culture. At the same time, it made me think about how the controlling culture of the United States deprived me and other Chicanos of this connection and history. It aimed to deprive Chicanos of this and other aspects of their real history in order to better control and exploit us. A people without a history is a people who live in insecurities. It wasn't just this dietary link with the Indigenous that I and other Chicanos were deprived of, but also about the pyramids and the later murals as well as the language, music, and dance. Those who are colonized don't have a

great sense of self-esteem. However, if you have a sense of self-esteem and a sense of who you are, you get a moral, psychological, and aesthetic strength. This made me angry as I went through the museum. God damn it! Why wasn't I taught in school about this history that related to me and other Chicanos? I didn't even get it in college, including my art history classes. Why did I first identify with the Greeks and Romans and not the Toltecas and Aztecas? What's going on here? What really bothers me is that this is still going on today. We now have majority Chicano/Latino students in our K–12 schools in California, for example, but they are still being denied this history and culture that I discovered in the anthropological museum in Mexico City, to say nothing of Chicano/Latino history in general.

But I also had a profound experience in visiting Mexico City. I realized that I was not "Mexican." I recognized this by how people there responded to me. I was raised calling myself Mexican. However, when you actually go to Mexico where mexicanos live and breathe and eat, you realize that you may be of Mexico, but you are not Mexican. This realization made me feel puzzled. I really felt that something was wrong with me inside. I had failed or something. It even made me feel depressed, and it took some time for me to come to grips with this. I was Chicano and not mexicano. I later began to realize that in fact there are many Mexicos and many Mexicans. There are blonde Mexicans, mestizo Mexicans, Afro Mexicans, Asian

Mexicans, and Arab Mexicans. And then there are Chicano Mexicans. This diversity within the Mexican population on both sides of the border made me understand that in fact I was Mexican, but part of the diverse Mexican population.

My trip to Mexico City was well worth it, and I came back with many profound feelings about myself and what it meant to be Mexican or Mexican American. This influenced my identity and my art.

—||—

During this period of time, I never moved into the Mission. I continued to live in the Haight-Ashbury, although for a short time I rented a place near the Cliff House by the beach. I could hear the waves from my place. However, for the most part, I lived in the Haight. I never directly faced pressure from other Latino activists to live in the Mission. The only time this was raised was when I was interviewed by *The Bay Guardian*, an alternative Bay Area publication. It did an article on four Bay Area artists including me. I read the first draft of the article and it was very good and positive. However, I was shocked to see the printed article, which was completely different and very critical. Among other things, it raised the question of why, as a Latino artist who worked in the Mission, I did not live there. No one had ever asked this question except the idiotic people at *The Bay Guardian*, who had some kind of agenda. In the printed article, they also wrote about my "Mayan flat features with flashing Latin eyes."

I couldn't believe such nonsense. I couldn't believe a progressive publication could do this thing I thought was racist. The article was devastating. Having said this, there was some discussion among activists that those who were working with the community should be from the community and live in the community. That kind of ideology was floating around, but there was no pressure. No one ever raised this in my presence. I wish they would have, because I would have replied that how was my work going to be better or worse if I didn't live in the Mission? I didn't see the connection between good artistic work and where I lived. I could do lousy work and live in the Mission. I could also move away from the Mission and also do lousy work.

At the same time, there was discussion about the proper venue for a Latino artist. Some argued that Latino artists should only display their art in the barrio, in the Mission, since their art was for the people.[15] This was especially promoted by a fellow artist from Oakland's Mexican American Art Liberation Front. I never bought into this. I have always contended that there is no one place to show my work. My work can be displayed in any venue, and there's no contradiction between the various places exhibiting my work. I don't believe that my work or anybody's work should be shown only in one venue. This doesn't make any sense to me. Still, there was an ideological debate about the role of Latino art and Latino artists and where that art should be shown. To me, there were and are no boundaries. A venue is a venue is a venue. So, I have never shied away from showing in different places and I still don't. I later had exhibits both at La Galeria and at the Museum of Modern Art in New York City. I have also shown in Paris and other European venues. Nothing precludes where I show.

■ΙΙ■

Although at La Galeria there was much unity of purpose and all of us were friends, still there did surface some tension in the early years. One area of some difference was how overtly political we should be with respect to our art. I can say that I was the most political, although I never pushed a particular line or ideology. No one did that. But because of my personality, I thought that we should be more political. Rather than make pronouncements, I decided to let my art speak for itself as political art. For example, when I curated the show of posters from Mexico concerning the student strikes in 1968, that was my way of encouraging a more political art approach at La Galeria. This was a way of highlighting the politics of art without saying so. So, I let my work speak for itself rather than pushing a line.

There were also gender tensions. Some of our female artists felt that they were not being duly recognized. That's one of the reasons why some organized the Mujeres Muralistas. The fact was, unfortunately, that some of the local male muralists would not work with the women. This was a gender-based decision by the women to

work outside male dialogue or control. No question about that. At the same time, many of the female artists continued to support La Galeria and work with it. As Drescher and I noted,

> the Mujeres Muralistas did not paint solely feminist images, believing that the mere fact that they, as women, are doing the painting is a strong statement in itself. Their murals depict issues of importance to the entire Latino community in the Mission District.[16]

One notable mural done by Latinas in the Mission was titled *Latinoamérica* done in 1974 by Patricia Rodríguez, Irene Pérez, Consuelo Méndez Castillo, and Graciela Carrillo de López on the outside wall of Mission Model Cities at Mission near 25th Street. The mural is dedicated to the variety and rich cultural history and heritage of the Mission people including Mexicans, Central Americans, and South Americans. I was impressed with this mural. It was very different from the one done by the men. It had a very good design and great colors. It was a good use of social space. The Muralistas went on to do around eleven murals in the Mission District.

Karen Mary Davalos:

> Even at this early juncture of the Chicano art movement, art attributed to men was considered more political than art by women, who were frequently criticized for focusing on personal expression and private matters.[17]

While there were some tensions, there was also a kind of notion that all of our art was oppositional to mainstream culture. There was also the feeling shared by all of us that we were part of the barrio and part of El Movimiento, both with respect to the Chicano Movement and to other Latino-based ones. The sense of opposition to me was very important as well as always trying to do the best work I could possibly do. Pushing the envelope was something that I accepted and tried to encourage others to also do. So, there were tensions but also much that held us as artists together in La Galeria and in the Mission.

■ ‖ ■

In the early 1970s, I developed as an artist with a number of silk-screen posters. In fact, I was part of what I later called a renaissance in Chicano poster art. Many of these posters were portraits which characterized my early work. Not all were portraits, but many were, and these are the ones that brought attention to my work. In these portraits, for example, I merged art and politics. My selection of a given portrait was based upon two factors. One was what the individual represented politically or culturally. The second was how to represent this figure from an aesthetic perspective. Art and politics. Politics and art. These were the twin sides of the same coin for me. I never did a portrait simply as a portrait. There had to be other layers of meaning or reasons for doing the portrait which, in my case, was the political importance of the figure being depicted. I wrote the following in 1977 when asked in an interview what distinguished Chicano poster art; I noted that we as artists dialectically related to both the present and the past:

> On one hand, Chicanos, like other oppressed people, are involved in a struggle against centuries of domination, and the Chicano artist has been working within this militant context. This means that Chicano artists have an adversary in the protectors of "official bourgeois culture." These people and the millions who identify with them find Chicano or any other Third World cultural assertation threatening. The questioning of our art is ultimately directed at our existence—for a people have never existed without an Art which is identifiable to them. So . . . what is being asked is "do you exist?" This challenge that our art threatens the very oppressive, inhuman, degrading, social fabric under which my people have suffered since the making of the Chicano—that fabric woven with racist threads of capitalism, white male domination, and Anglo-European cultural values.[18]

Terezita Romo:

> Coming to prominence in the first decade of the Chicano movement, Chicano artists such as [Malaquias] Montoya and Rupert García mastered the special bond between art and politics and used it to shape a unique art form.[19]

One of my first images that I did in 1970 was not a portrait, but a poster to support the case of *Los Siete*, who were seven young Latinos in the Mission falsely accused of shooting and killing a cop. Activists rallied to their support and set up a legal defense fund called the Los Siete Defense Committee. These supporters came up with the name *Los Siete* or The Seven. This police profiling of these young men really affected me. It was not an isolated case. Such profiling was rampant not only in the Mission, but in most barrios in California and the Southwest against Chicanos and other Latinos. The cops were also harassing and arresting others who were involved in radical groups, including anti-war protestors. Those of us from La Galeria could easily have been the ones arrested. I knew one of the guys arrested because he worked at La Raza Silkscreen Center, and I used to talk to him every day. I also knew others who knew the men arrested. In addition, the *Los Siete* Defense Committee was located very near La Galeria on 14th and Valencia, and I met some of those working on the committee. I wasn't a member of the committee, but I decided to do a poster in support of the committee and *Los Siete*.

When I conceptualized the poster, I was being influenced by pop art and specifically an artist named Robert Indiana. He made paintings and silkscreen prints using words and numbers and simplified shapes of recognizable images using flat colors. Although influenced by Indiana and other pop artists, I consciously applied their art techniques to political issues. So, in my silk-screen poster, I printed a large red "7" and underneath printed "Free Los Siete." The poster was duplicated and used in rallies in support of the young

Latino men. Fortunately, they were found not guilty. I don't know how much my poster aided in their defense, but I felt good in helping the efforts to free them. Much later, I obtained some FBI files on Los Siete Defense Committee, which clearly indicate how the group was mischaracterized as violent in order to harass and persecute the members.

That same year, President Nixon sent U.S. troops into Cambodia, and this widening of the Vietnam War led to mass protests throughout the country, especially on college campuses. At Kent State in Ohio, National Guard troops fired on the students, killing four, all of them white. I found this incident to be horrendous. The students had no weapons and yet they were killed. This was a tragedy. The same thing also happened at Jackson State in Mississippi where National Guardsmen fired on and killed some of the Black students attending the school. This was equally horrendous. I was very moved by all this, and so I decided to do a poster on the Kent State killings. I lifted the photographs of the four students killed that appeared in the newspapers and reduced them to a simple black and white poster featuring the images of the four students. Most of the media focused on the image of a young female student kneeling over the body of one of the killed students. You can see her crying out in anguish. This became a classic photo. However, I decided not to use this image, because it had nothing to do directly with the killing of the four other students. It had to do with her

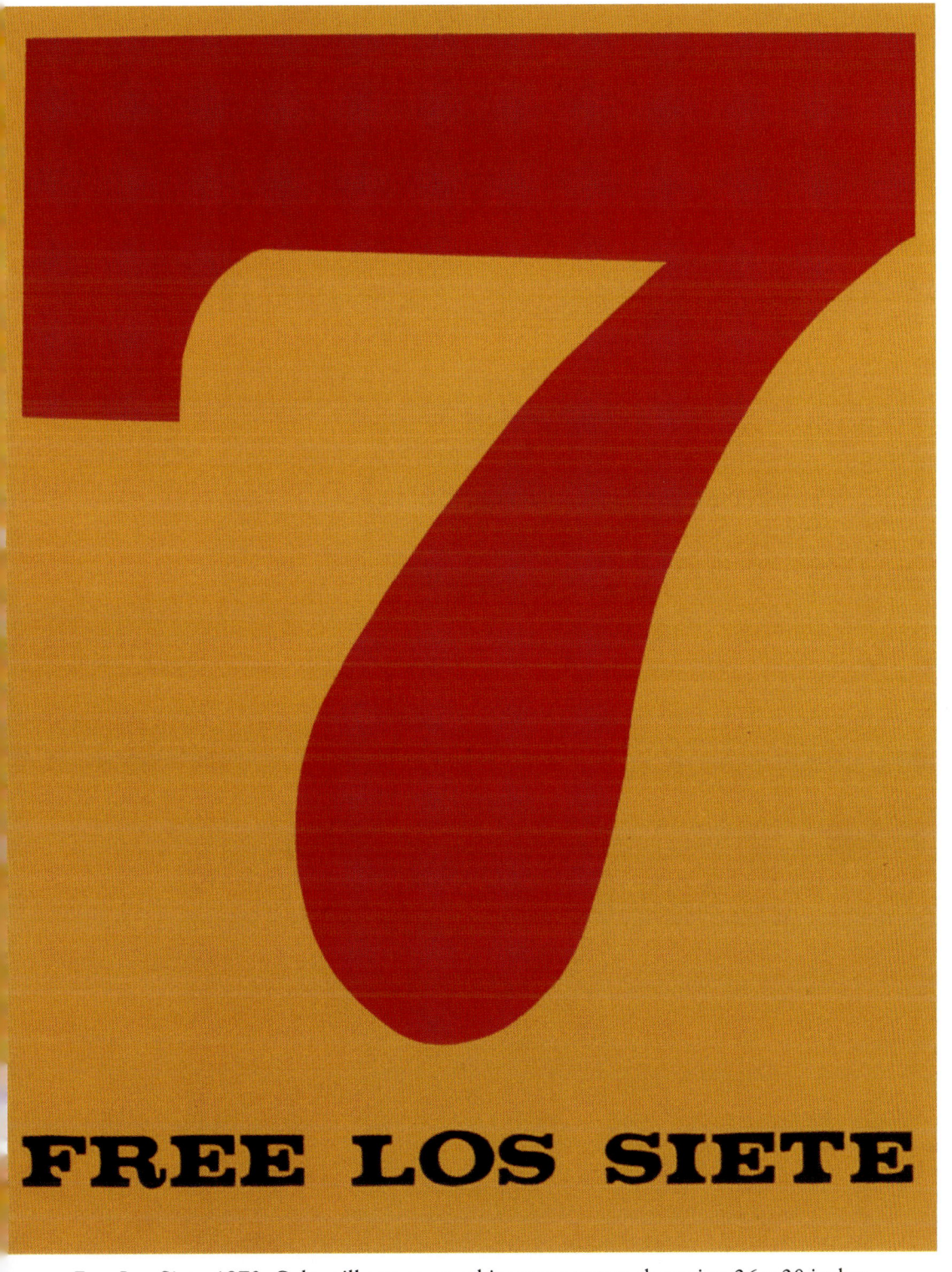

Free Los Siete, 1970. Color silkscreen on white wove paper, sheet size: 26 x 20 inches. Copyright © Rupert García.

response to the killings. This photo had been used so much that I didn't want to use it again. I wanted to bring more attention to the deaths of the four students. In my silk screen, I printed the faces of the two females and the two males. Underneath the faces, I inserted "Protest Kent Murders."

One year later, I did an image of Angela Davis that became one of my most noted and reproduced portraits. I had followed to a certain extent Angela Davis's political life. I especially reacted to her arrest on the grounds that she had tried to smuggle guns into San Quentin Penitentiary to free George Jackson, a Black prison activist. It seemed to me that the reasons given for her arrest were very weak. It was clear to me that she was a domestic political prisoner because she was a member of the Communist Party. Because of her arrest, I decided to do a portrait of Angela Davis. I saw a great photo of her in the British newspaper *The Guardian* and reduced it to a straight black and white so I could have simple shapes and use solid colors to really dramatize the issue of her arrest. I didn't want to do a caricature of Angela because she already had a fantastic face with her Afro haircut. She also has great and expressive eyes. So, there wasn't a whole lot to do on her image. I just wanted to pay attention to the integrity of the picture.

I did three versions of the image. One was in black and white; another in black and brown; and a third in black and yellow. At the top of each image, I printed in the words: "Libertad Para Los Prisoneros Políticas" (Liberty for Political Prisoners). I didn't need to insert Angela's name because she already was such a recognizable figure that everyone knew that this was her. I wrote this in Spanish to express solidarity with the Cuban Revolution. I wanted to link Angela's struggle and my poetic gesture with the struggle of the Cuban Revolution which I supported. It wasn't an effort to reach the Spanish-speaking community. Not at all. I've never thought about that in my work. I think about me. I mean, as selfish as this may sound, it's not selfish. No. I never think of an audience when I insert words into my pictures. I think of myself and how I want to express myself as an artist. I thought of an audience only once when I did my portrait of Nelson Mandela and placed words in three languages—English, French, and Spanish—because it was done for an international agency of the United Nations and it was going to be distributed worldwide. Having said this, I will note that my use of Spanish in the Angela poster was to express international solidarity between Black and Raza peoples, and the solidarity with our struggling comrades in Latin America. At the time, I recall thinking especially of the Cubans and their struggles.

After I did the Angela Davis poster, I got in touch with her defense committee and told them about my image and that I was going to send them copies which they could reproduce and use in anyway they wished. They did use them. That was fine with me, because it wasn't about copyright. It was about Angela Davis's life and I wanted to assist in freeing her, which she ultimately was. I had never met Angela until after she was freed, at someone's house. We became friends very quickly. It was very nice to meet her, and she was very warm and generous. She said that my portrait of her was the best thing that had been done on her. To me, it was a gesture of love. It was honest with no make-believe shit. I really had wanted to help her. It's one of my favorite portraits.

In 1971 there was also the massacre of prisoners at the Attica State Penitentiary in New York state. Prisoners went on a strike demanding better conditions. They took some guards as hostages. After several days of negotiations with no resolutions, Governor Nelson Rockefeller ordered state troopers to attack the penitentiary and put down the strike, which they did, but killing several of the prisoners. The day of the assault, I was listening to the radio and heard the news of what happened at Attica. It became a massacre and I just couldn't believe what I was hearing. This was fascism as far as I was concerned. It seemed like a heavy-handed fascist kind of attack. I heard that there was a defense committee. It was actually a union organized on behalf of prisoners' rights. I contacted them and told them I was doing a poster on Attica. In doing the poster, I took a bow to Posada and included a *calavera* with the words on top that read "Attica Is Fascismo."

In 1972 I did a poster on Ceylon Tea. I grew up drinking Ceylon Tea and Lipton Tea, both produced by the Lipton Company. The package for both featured an older white guy with a commander's cap and a bowtie holding up a cup of tea. I thought that there was something more menacing behind this allegedly benign image. I did some research and learned that there was a Sir Lipton and he was part of a British imperialist effort to control tea production in India. I also read a book on Lipton and said, "boy, I've got to let people know what I think about this guy." So, I reproduced the image of the box of Lipton Tea, but in a white ghostly color and above it inserted the words, "Ceylon Tea: Product of European Exploitation!"

I was angry and frustrated when President Salvador Allende in Chile in 1973 was overthrown by the Chilean military supported by the CIA and the Nixon administration. Not wishing to be captured, Allende shot himself. I along with many other activists supported the election and administration of Allende. Many Latinos in the Mission District in particular supported Allende. His election in 1970 had a very strong impact in the Mission. Consequently, his overthrow was devastating. That's why I did my poster on Allende. I used a photo profile of Allende with his eyeglasses. I did the image in black and white with the wording, "Allende 1909–73."

I didn't do the Allende portrait for any group. It was done for me. As vulgar as this may sound, I did it because I was struck by the overthrow of Allende and was very moved to do it. What I'm trying to say is that I want to get away from the myth of the socially concerned artist putting his ear to the

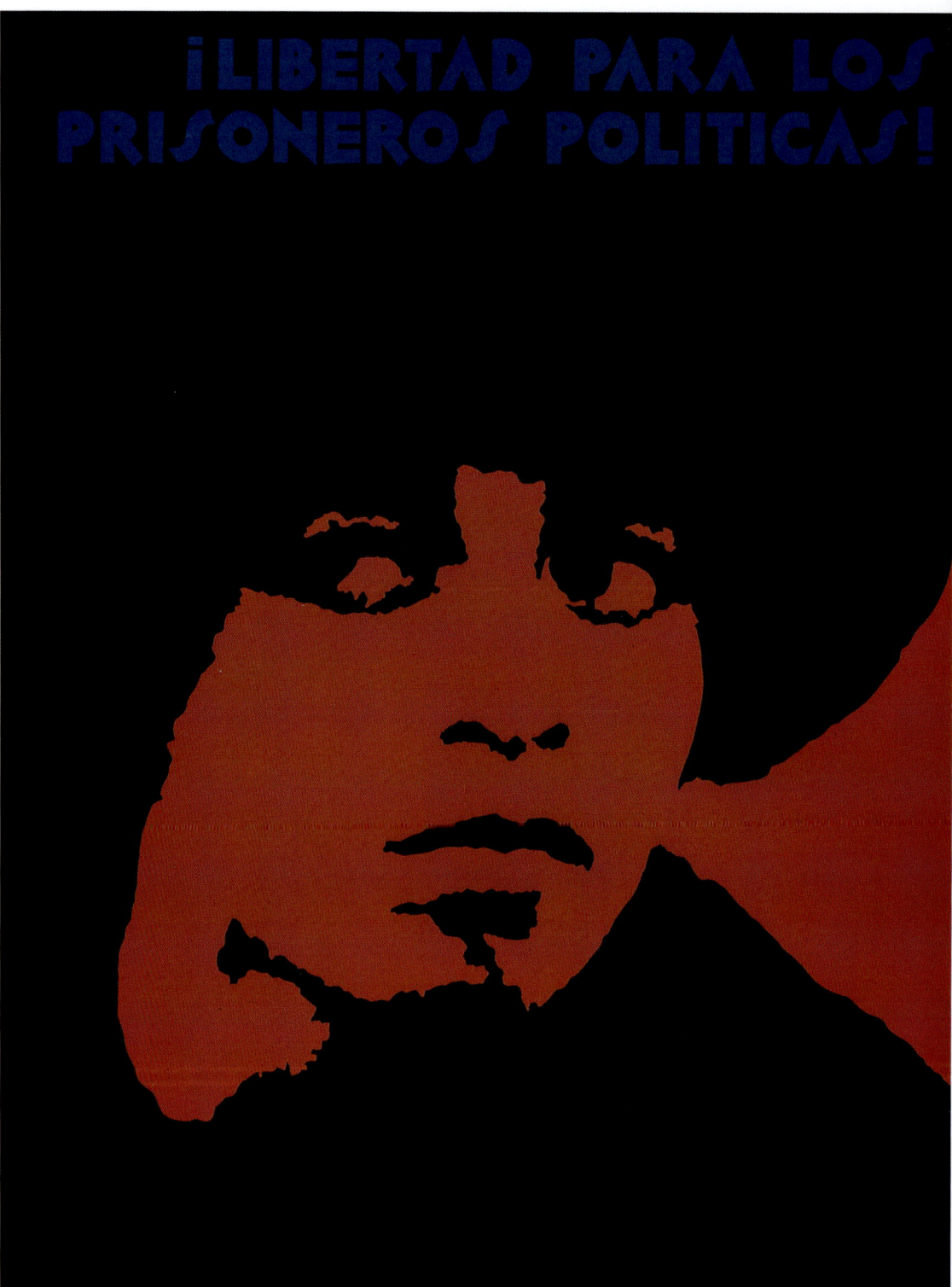

¡Libertad para los Prisoneros Politicas!, 1971. Color silkscreen on white wove paper, sheet size: 26 x 20 inches, image size: 24-5/8 x 19 inches. Copyright © Rupert García. Courtesy of Rena Bransten Gallery.

Attica is Fascismo, 1971. Color silkscreen on white wove paper, sheet size: 26 x 20 inches. Copyright © Rupert García.

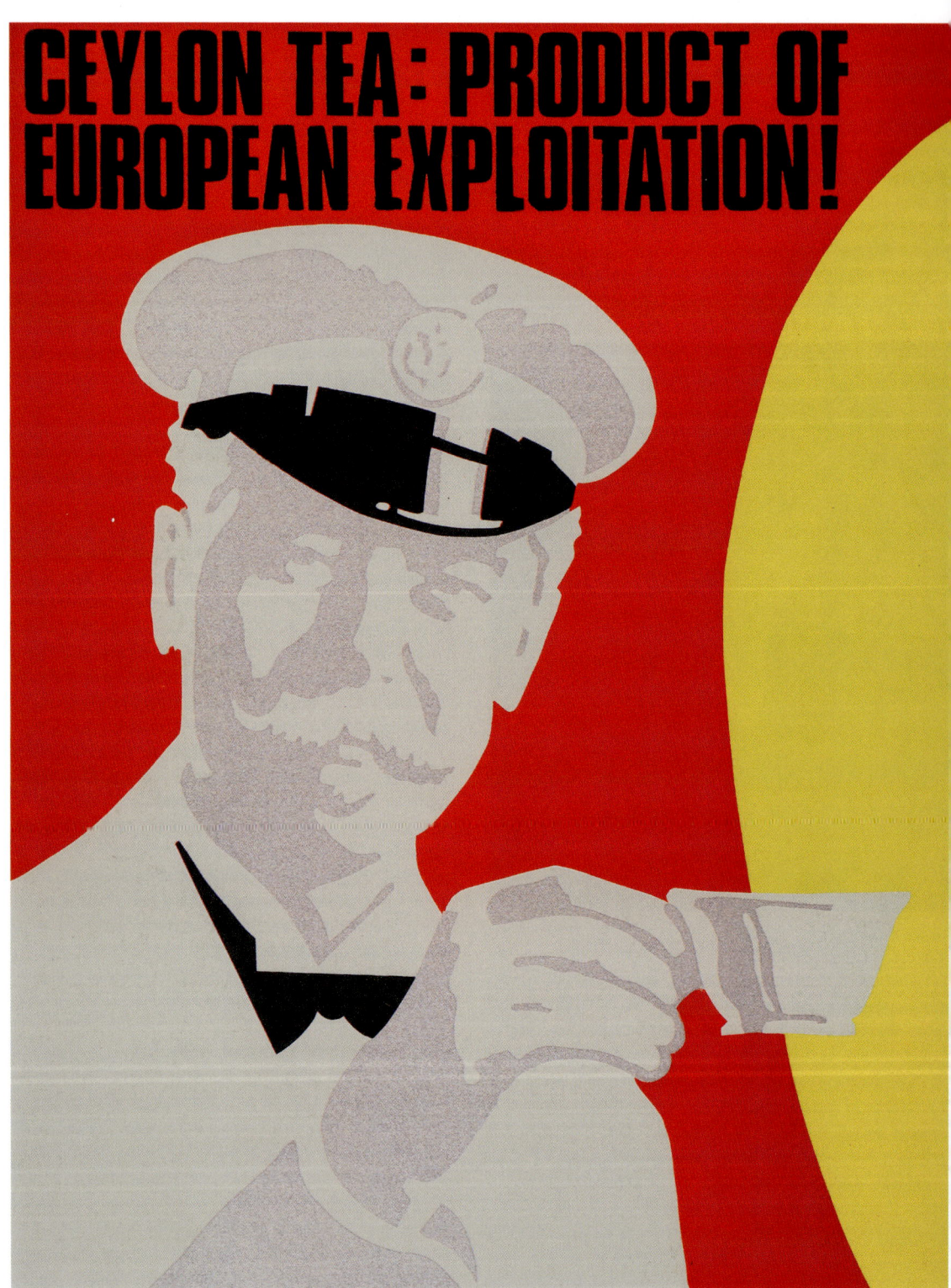

Ceylon Teas: Product of European Exploitation, 1972. Color silkscreen on white wove paper, sheet size: 26 x 20 inches, image size: 25 x 18-7/8 inches. Copyright © Rupert García.

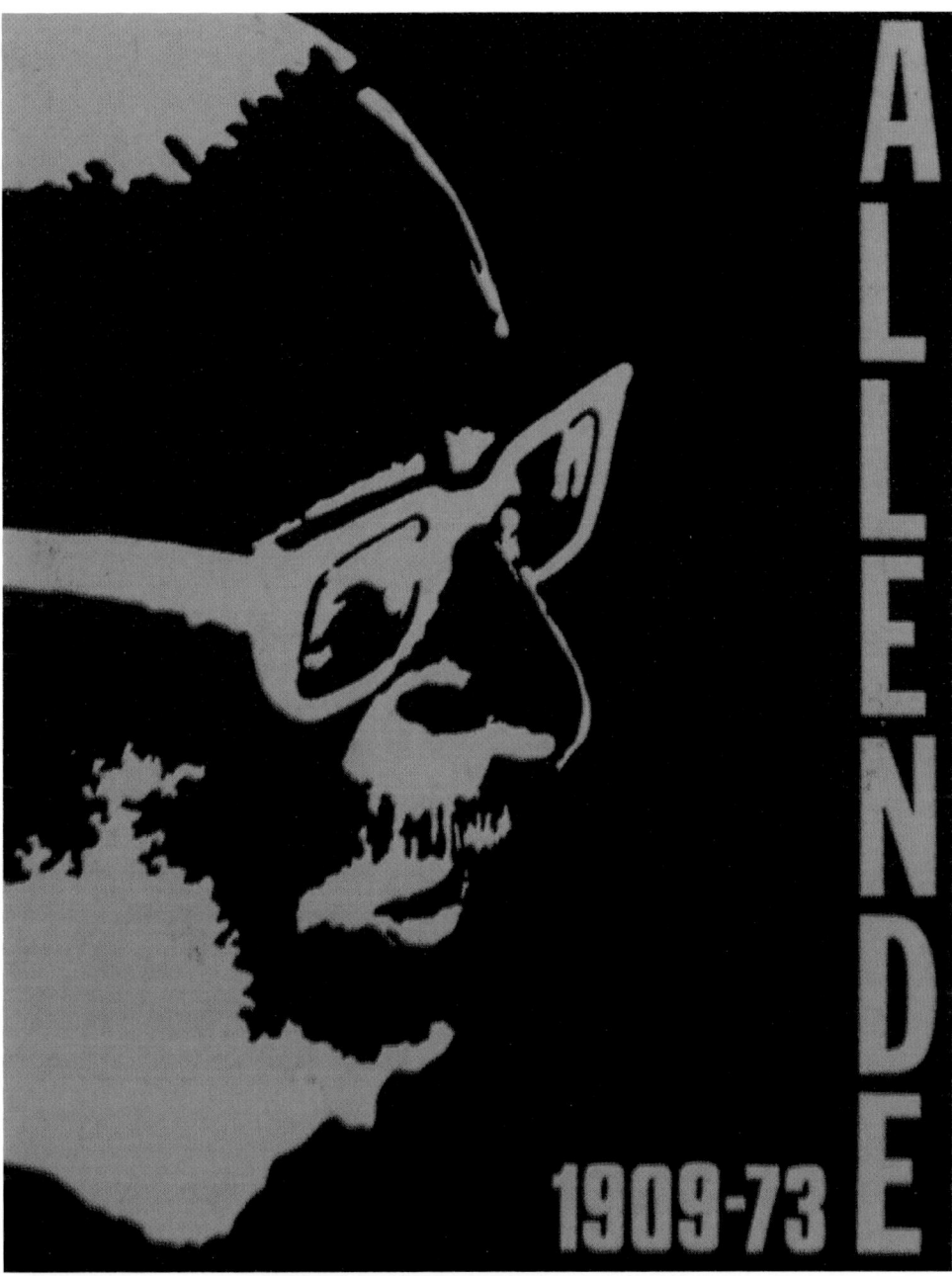

Allende, 1973. Color silkscreen on white wove paper, sheet size: 26 x 20 inches. Copyright © Rupert García.

ground and listening to the masses rebel and then making images about this. I put my ear to my own heart, and everything that I make is because I was deeply moved to do it. That doesn't mean that many others weren't also affected by Allende's overthrow, and obviously they were. It also doesn't mean that a lot of people didn't respond to my portrait. They did. But I didn't do it for them. I did it because I believed in the issue. That's very important to me that people understand that that's how I work, and that's why I have to make the best image that I can because it's for me. If the issue ain't real for me, then I can't do it. I have never fallen into the myth about the artist working for and getting lost in the masses. I don't know what the hell this means. I know who I am at all times, so how could I get lost? I can get lost in me and my friends, but I never get lost. I don't disappear.

In the early 1970s, as undocumented immigration from Mexico increased, federal officials through the Immigration and Naturalization Service (INS) intensified the deportation of such immigrants. It was affecting all communities, including the Mission. I decided to do a poster calling for the cessation of these deportations. When I did the poster, I thought about all the abuse that the undocumented faced in order to try to provide for their families and doing the "dirty jobs" that American citizens wouldn't do. I knew friends back in Stockton who were undocumented. My maternal grandfather and grandmother never became citizens. As kids, we made fun of "la migra"—the immigration officials. I brought all of these thoughts to doing my poster. I did it mostly in red and black and I included barbed wire. At the top, I wrote "¡CESEN DEPORTACIÓN!" I thought that it was an effective poster.

Pablo Picasso died in 1973, and so I wanted to commemorate his death with a poster. It was an expression of my thanks to him for what he did as an artist and how he influenced me and many others. In this one, I did a silk-screen edition and one with pastel over the silk screen. I was reintroducing myself to pastel as a medium. I made the image of Picasso's face dark on one side and so you only see the other side that I did in brown. I also did a follow-up picture of Picasso in 1974/1975 using the same facial image, but with different colors and also with pastel on the silk screen.

I also paid tribute to the great Mexican artist, José Posada, when I did the poster for the Posada exhibit that we had at La Galería in 1974. In this case, I did an offset poster, which is a photo mechanically produced, whereas my silk screens are all done by hand. However, when you do a mechanical offset lithograph as I did for Posada, you can produce a thousand prints in no time. We did 250 copies of the Posada poster to advertise the event, which was very successful. In the exhibit, we had a number of Posada's broadsides and some copies of his newspaper work. I had never seen so many original Posadas in my life. In the poster, I did a side image of Posada's face in black and brown.

Around the mid-1970s, I became aware with the struggle in Iran against the Shah. In fact, I attended a rally at UC Berkeley on this issue. There I came across a leaflet being passed out in support of the revolution. I was struck by the image on the leaflet. It was of a captured Iranian rebel who was being punished by being executed tied to a stake. When I saw that leaflet, man, I said, what a horrible and powerful

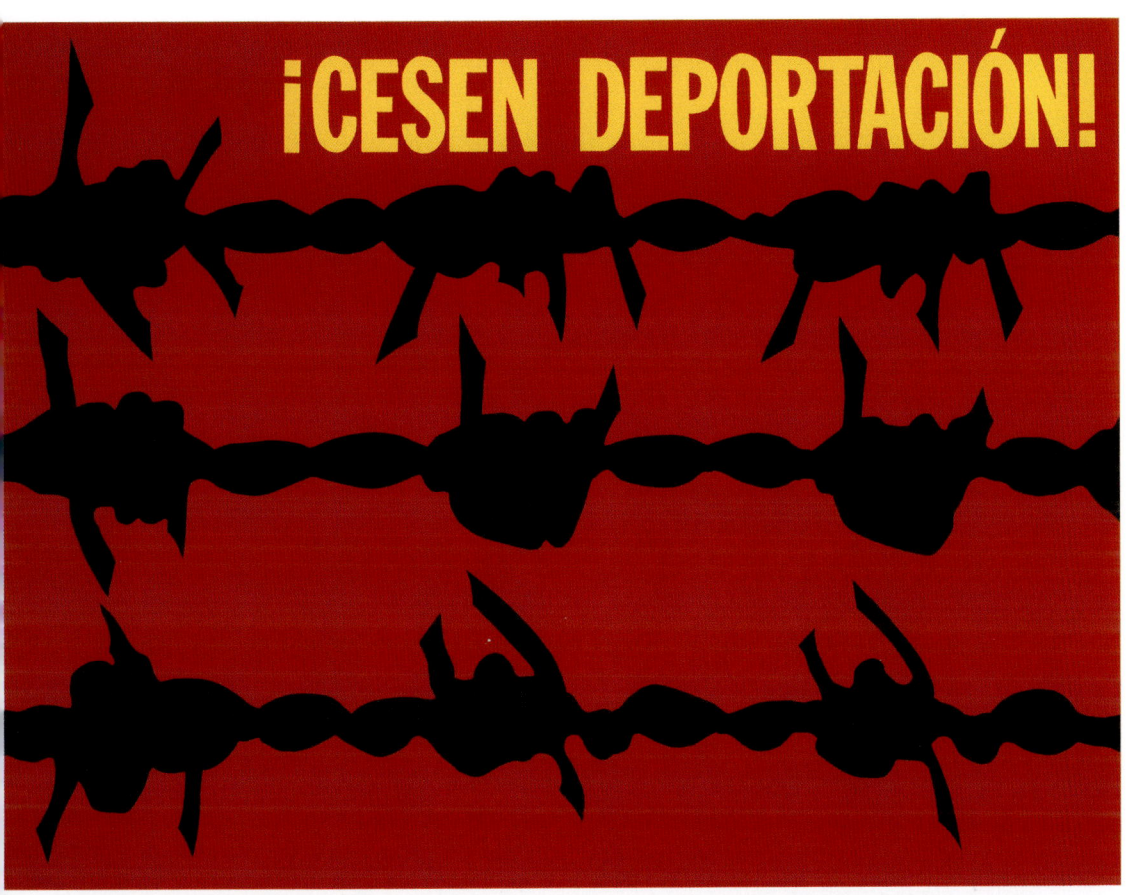

¡Cesen Deportación!, 1973. Color silkscreen on white wove paper, sheet size: 20 x 26 inches, image size: 18-3/4 x 25-1/8 inches. Copyright © Rupert García. Courtesy of Rena Bransten Gallery.

image. It spoke to the lengths to which a country such as Iran would go to silence protest for social change. I was so moved by that picture that I had to do something with it. So, I made a silk-screen print using that image and titled it *El Grito de Rebelde (The Cry of the Rebel)*. I could have made the image of the rebel who's tied to the stake in a very victimized way. However, I gave instead a lot of dignity to the rebel. He's tied but he's still yelling out. Even in his victimization, he is rebelling. The fact is that all of my work is not interested in the aesthetics of victimization. I'm interested in those who may be victims, but who retain their dignity and elegance as human beings. I used Spanish for the title of my picture for no particular reason; I was just playing around although conscious of using Spanish. Why not use Spanish? What the hell's the difference? I know what the title means and that's all that matters. It was also a kind of cultural rebellion on my part in terms of what is normally taught in art school but only in English.

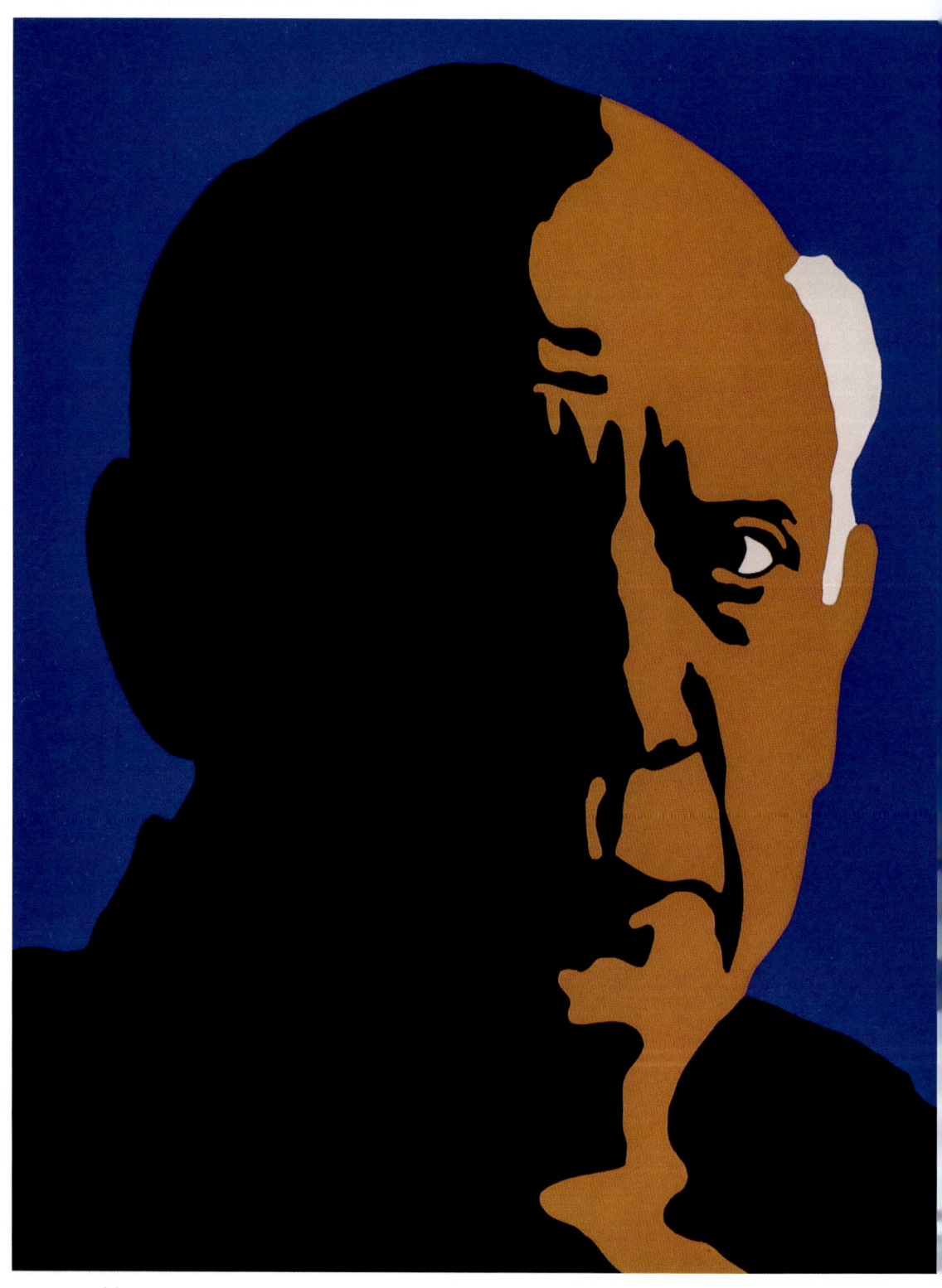

Pablo Picasso, 1973. Color silkscreen on white wove paper, sheet size: 26 x 20 inches, image size: 24-3/4 x 19 inches. Copyright © Rupert García.

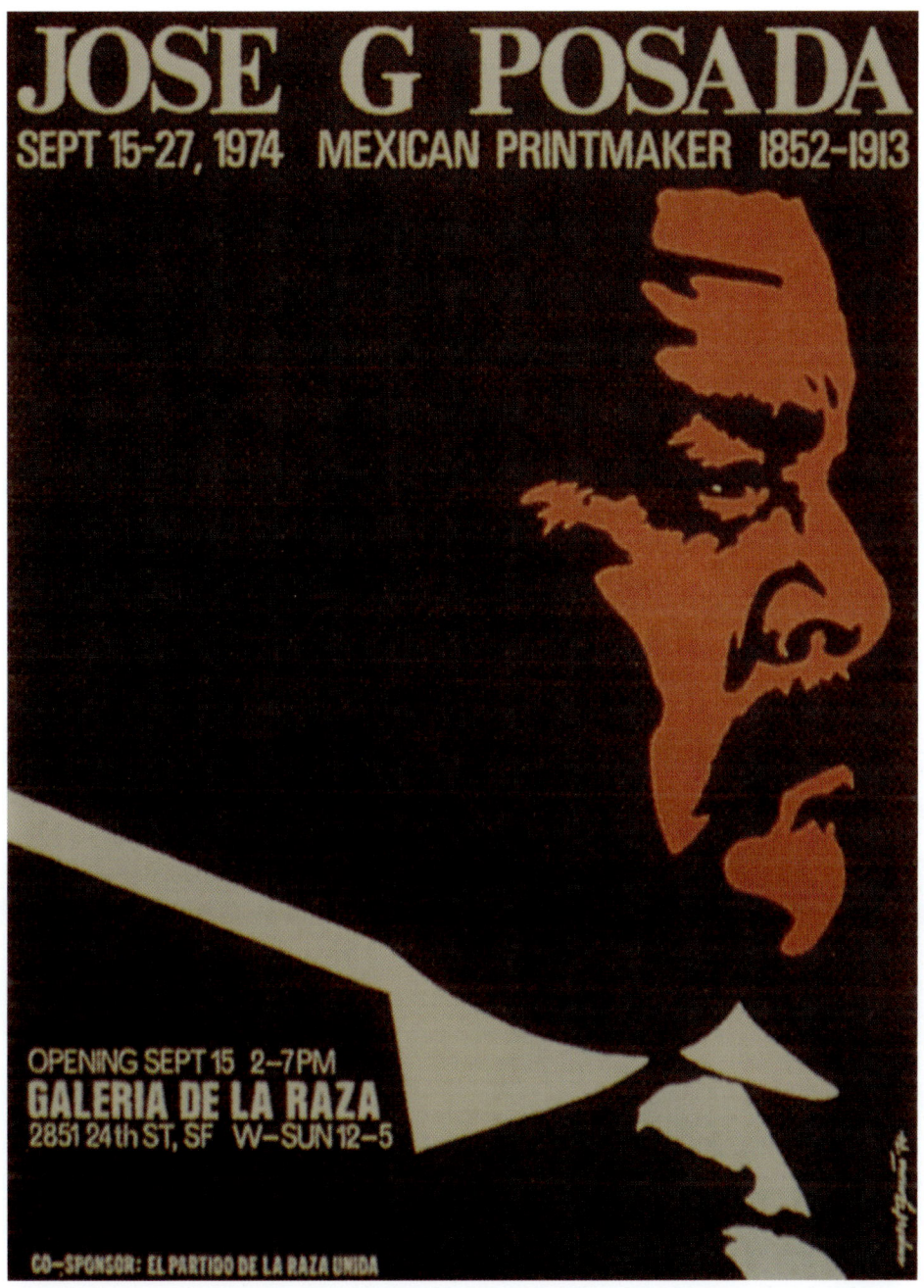

José G. Posada, 1974. Color offset lithograph on white wove paper, sheet size: 21 x 15-7/8 inches, image size: 20-1/4 x 14-3/4 inches. Copyright © Rupert García.

Finally, I want to call attention to my 1975 silk screen, which I did as an oppositional image to the celebration of the Bicentennial of the United States. One day I was walking in downtown San Francisco on Union Street and I passed by a frame shop. I looked in the window and saw these official posters on the Bicentennial. They were all very nice-looking posters

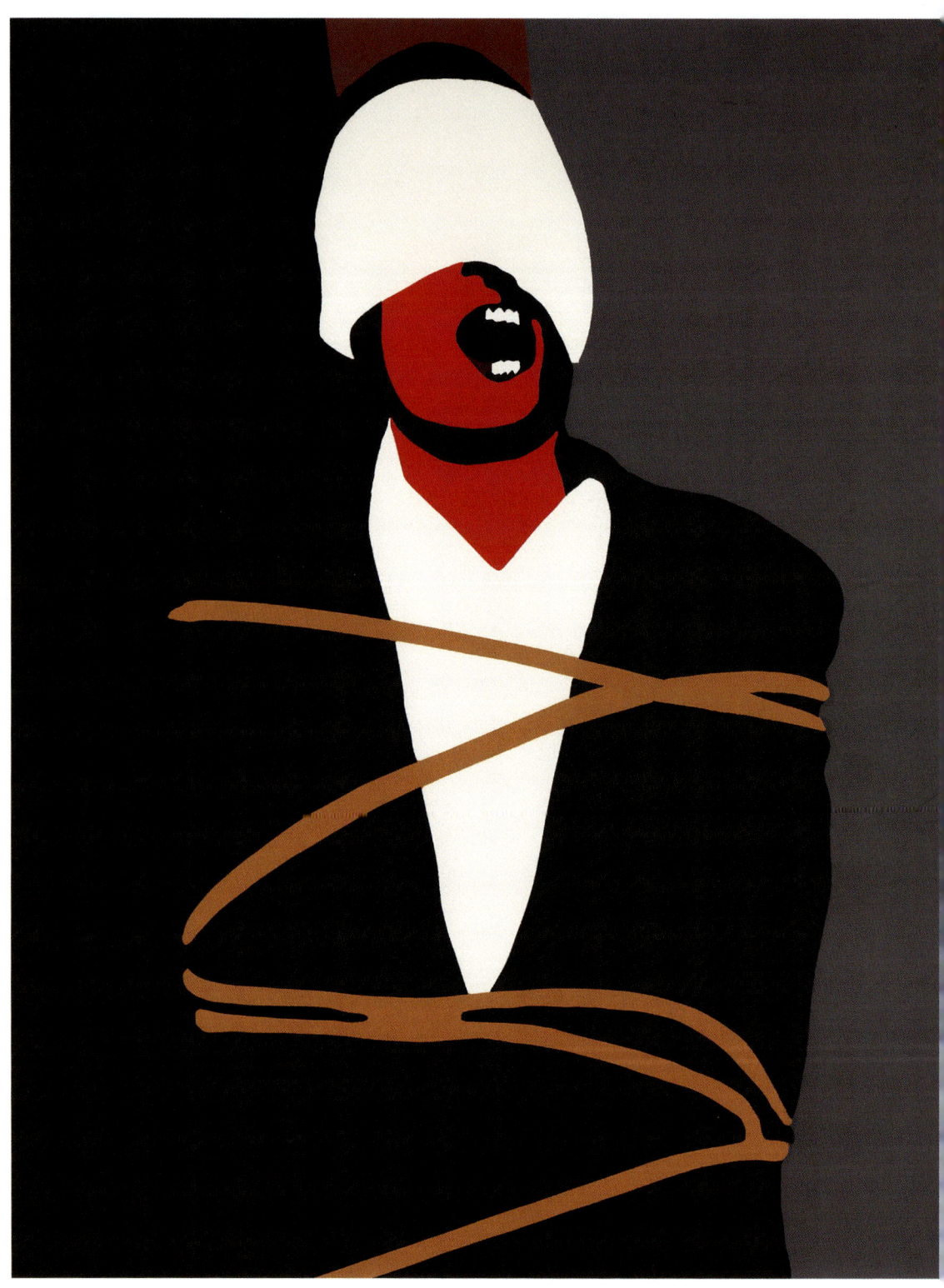

El Grito de Rebelde, 1975. Color silkscreen on white wove paper, sheet size: 26 x 20 inches. Copyright © Rupert García. Courtesy of Rena Bransten Gallery.

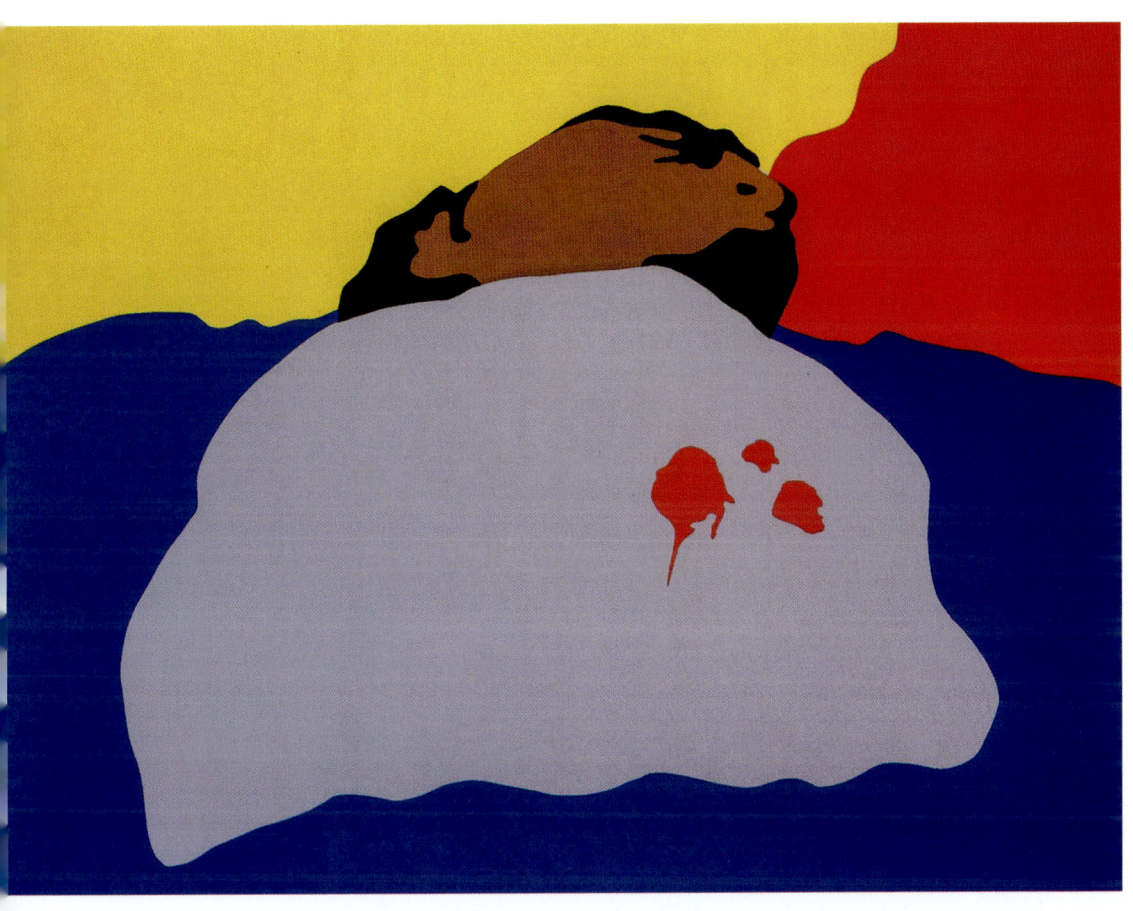

The Bicentennial Poster, 1975. Color silkscreen on white wove paper, sheet size: 20 x 26 inches, image size: 18-7/8 x 25 inches. Copyright © Rupert García.

done by outstanding artists. However, they were depicting only the wonderful things about the country. When I saw them, I said, "no, everything is not wonderful. The celebration of the two-hundredth year of the United States is not all wonderful." I thought about all of the violence that had taken place over these years as the country expanded from east to west. At the same time, I was familiar with a handbill by David Bragin depicting persons of color dead as a result of being shot and done in black and orange. I thought, wow, that would make a

great poster for a counter-Bicentennial image. So, I did this image in silk screen, but with different colors, and entitled it *The Bicentennial Art Poster*. It was my way of interjecting another point of view about the Bicentennial, which is a pretty bloody one and yet is done in an elegant and beautiful way with my use of color and shapes. In a way, I don't want to let the viewer think about this *pobrecito* (poor guy) who's been shot. I want the viewer to think about a different way of thinking about the Bicentennial. I don't recall any negative reaction to my image. On the contrary, those who saw it thought it was fantastic.

These pictures and others are historical but are ones that critique history and reassess it. I refer to Chicano posters as "historical documents" because in many cases they are the only existing recording of a historical event. They give history a different feeling. The poster, unlike the mural, is portable. It can be placed in multiple locations and different surfaces. Moreover, I didn't make them to be politically correct. I have never based my aesthetics on an organized ideology. Yet the image has to be provocative. It has to have some meat to it. Everything I have done is from something that I believe in or feel strongly about. For example, I made my poster of Zapata in 1969 because I believed in it and I wanted to see it.

Between 1970 and 1975, I did many other silk-screen images and too many to discuss here. This was my personal embrace of the portrait, which I would still do later. However, these five years are the most intensive ones with respect to this art form that I utilized. These pictures made me known as an artist and would help to define me in part. However, I would refuse to become comfortable with this genre, and so I went on to explore others as I evolved as an artist.

▬ıı▬

These early years in the Mission District were heady ones for me and for others. We became part of a movement and of a community. It's here and then that I really surfaced as an artist—a committed artist. I am proud to have been part of the Mission Cultural Renaissance. In a way, it was my own personal renaissance. These were defining years for me, and they continued to influence me in later ones. These were five very intense years, but by 1975, I was ready to move on and to challenge myself further as an artist.

7

Moving On

After five years of working at La Galeria and in the Mission, I felt the need to move on. The years 1970 to 1975 were critical years in my development as a Chicano/Latino artist. I felt I had contributed to the Mission Renaissance and to the community. However, I felt that I didn't want to be confined by this experience. I didn't change my politics, but I wanted to shift my life and artistic pursuits in new directions. I didn't want the movement to dictate to me what I should do. I wanted to make these decisions on my own. And I did.

Being involved in the San Francisco State Strike had opened up new ways of consciousness for me; it opened up all of these doors of how to view life and society. I felt the same way about working in the Mission. It was liberating both intellectually and emotionally. In a similar fashion after 1975, I felt another wave of liberation in my life and especially in my art. I began to shift my aesthetics. I had been doing silk-screening since 1968 and involved in the process of making a silk screen turn into poster art. I had learned from this and it brought me some notice as

an artist. However, this silk-screen process became too tedious, too laborious, too time consuming, and taking too god damn long to realize an image. Silk screen as a primary medium no longer held my interest. I needed something more spontaneous and immediate. I needed a new outlet, and this involved beginning to paint in pastels.

—11—

Pastel offered me the opportunity to make an image in a very expressive fashion. Painting with pastels to me represented a freer way to express myself that paralleled what was happening to me individually and socially. Pastels allowed me to articulate my ideas on a piece of paper with immediate results. The medium was like a metaphor for what was happening to me after 1975.

It wasn't that I wasn't acquainted with pastels. In high school, I did a self-portrait using pastel, but I only came back to pastels in 1976. After I stopped living with my girlfriend, I got a new roommate, Juan Fuentes, another artist. Juan used pastels and he had a bunch of pastels on his desk in the studio that we both shared in the apartment. One day I took a handful of the pastels and applied them to an old poster that I had on the wall. I began to make marks on it with the pastels. I couldn't believe how the colors vibrated and I felt this surge of excitement. And I said, "man, this is me! This is my next path. This is what I'm going to do!" A pastel is 98% pure pigment so it's almost pure color. I couldn't wait to start painting with pastels. The pigment is dry, which is pressed into a chalk form, and it's held together by gum Arabic, which is the binder which makes the chalk or crayon form. It was very exciting to paint like this. One advantage of pastel over silk screen is that you get more color and variations of color that you can't get in silk-screening, which are flat and of one dominant color such as red but with no variations of red. In pastel, I could get variations of red. All of this about pastel painting I learned by myself.

In using pastels, I also began to make much larger pictures. Whereas my silk-screen posters were usually two feet in length, my pastels went monumental to six feet by three. Some would be even bigger. I started to really change scale and I got more complex with my colors, using more layers of color and more subtlety in transitions from dark to light. The variety of color with pastels is incredible. With pastels I could get four to eight reds. It was the same with other colors. This allowed more complexity in my painting, and so the meaning and the feelings of my work also became more complex and multilayered. All this made me feel freer and allowed my imagination to soar. I didn't feel trapped as I was beginning to feel just doing silk screens. I could now achieve more expansive visual significance. With pastels I also went back to doing more fragmenting of images. I begin to use diptychs (double images) and triptychs (triple images).

These changes that I begin to experience in the mid-1970s came at a time when the intensity of the Chicano Movement and other social movements began to somewhat decline. One can ask if my personal and artistic changes have a connection with a lessening of the earlier political fervor of the late 1960s and early 1970s. This is a question that I can't quite connect with. It would take someone else to see that in my work; however, I did see that the high pitch of El Movimiento had begun to wane. Much of this or some of this had to do with the ending of the U.S. war in Vietnam and also with Nixon leaving office in disgrace due to the Watergate scandal.

Yet problems continued and my work continued to address these issues, although in a different way. I was still committed to social change and social justice. At the same time, I began to have a soberer realization of what social change entails and the time factor associated with such change. I could see that change wouldn't come right away or easily. It's really a major project to change the world. I began to realize how complex and how entrenched are the causes of the worldwide crisis including poverty, racism, capitalism, neo-imperialism, and on and on. These conditions will not be changed quickly. I also began to see how confrontational politics is not necessarily going to achieve these changes. When one says that you're going to challenge the U.S. capitalist and racist system, you're saying that you're going to challenge the U.S. Marines, the Army, the Air Force, and the Navy in addition to the FBI and CIA. So, what are you talking about? I came to a greater realization about the obstacles to social change, even though I didn't despair of it and hoped to still do my part to achieve it peacefully, but perhaps no longer with the romantic view that characterized many of the earlier protest movements.

This new awareness on my part didn't discourage me or depress me. I didn't lose any kind of faith in the struggle for social change. It's not that at all. I also didn't lose my excitement about being alive. I didn't feel lost or isolated, and I certainly was not cynical. I didn't have any of this. I just realized that it's a long haul to achieve progressive changes and you have to be prepared for the long haul. I might see some of these changes in my life and then again, I might not. I was still prepared to struggle but with a larger realization of what this would entail.

◼�«◼

Moving in a new personal and artistic direction also meant that I began to move away from my commitments to La Galeria. The art collective had played a very important role in my life. From both a political and artistic

sense, I grew up with La Galeria; we grew together. However, I outgrew my need to be part of La Galeria. It's like you grow up with your family and you need to be there for just so long and then it's time to go out on your own. In similar fashion with La Galeria, I needed to be there for a period of time, but then I had to go out on my own. It was wonderful to be with all of the other people that I came to know and even love, yet after a few years, I felt the need to leave. So, I slowly pulled away from my involvement with La Galeria. I had mixed feelings about this, but I did what I had to do. No one ever said to me, "gee, you're turning your back on the community; you're a traitor." At least no one ever said this to my face.[1]

As I turned to pastels, I now worked on the walls of my home studio which I shared with Juan Fuentes, an excellent artist. I pinned a paper to a wall and worked directly on the wall because I liked the hardness of the surface. I liked that firmness and could really feel it as I was moving the medium around.

◼«◼

It was also after 1975 when my family and I made a visit to Mexico, specifically to the state of Jalisco, which is where Guadalajara is. We went to visit tías and *primos* or cousins. I wouldn't say that this trip was part of my transition, although it was to further give me a sense of my Mexican roots. I don't remember whose idea it was to make the trip. It wasn't mine, although I supported it. It must have been either my

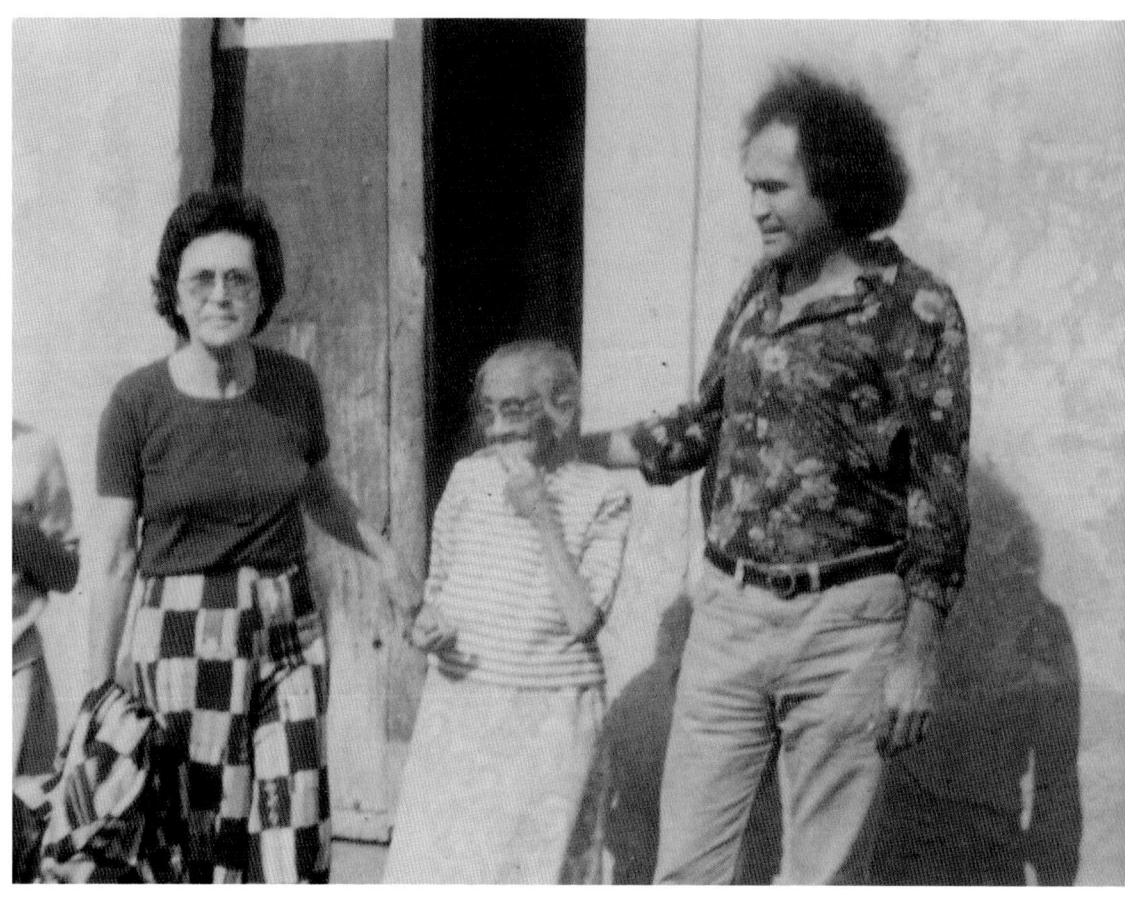

Rupert García with his mother and Tia Juana, Jalostotitlán, Jalisco, Mexico, circa mid-1970s. Photo courtesy of Rupert García.

mother or my tías in Stockton. We flew to Guadalajara and there visited with some of my cousins. This was very exciting and everyone was very kind and hospitable to us. I really enjoyed being in Guadalajara, especially when one of my cousins took me to see several murals that Orozco had done in his home city. He also took me to Orozco's studio, which is now a museum. This was just fantastic! Very, very exciting! After a few days in Guadalajara, we drove to the family home, which is this small *pueblito* or village called Jalostotitlán. It was there that we met

my great aunt, Tía Juana, the sister of my maternal grandmother. I had never met her before. I couldn't believe it; she looked and dressed just like my grandmother. It was spooky. She made these artistic paper figurines of animals and people, and when I told her that she was a great artist, she responded, "no, no, mijo, you're the great artist." It was wonderful to meet her and the rest of her family there.

■❙■

After working hard for about three years on my new pastel paintings, I got a good break in 1978 when I was invited to exhibit some of my new pictures at the San Francisco Museum of Modern Art. This was my first major exhibit outside of the Mission. This came about because Rolando Castellon, who I had met in 1969 and who encouraged me to work in the Mission first with Artes 6 and then La Galeria, had recently been appointed as a curator for the museum responsible for diversity issues. It was a way for the museum to make a token concession to the minority art community. Rolando was very much aware of this but used his position to sponsor exhibits by artists of color. I was one of the first artists that he turned to exhibit. It was a big break for me, and I am indebted to Rolando for making this possible. The San Francisco Museum of Modern Art is the place that artists aspire to exhibit in.

The exhibit allowed me to show my large pastels. The scale was three or four times that of my silk-screen prints and posters. They were pretty big. My pastels in subject matter were not significantly different from my earlier work, only that they were bigger and more complex due to the rich deepness of the colors. They are also very strong images of particular people.

The exhibit opened with a great reception that Rolando organized. There was a salsa band plus great food and great wine. The place was packed. We had a wonderful time. The people who came were many of my friends and those interested in Latino art. The more blue-blood people won't deign to attend a "minority" exhibit. These people are only into rubbing elbows with the famous, not the infamous. This included key people in the San Francisco art world. The ones who didn't see my show were the people who would go to an exhibition by Andy Warhol.

Even though I had turned to pastels, I was still mostly focusing on portraits. Some of these were in my exhibit. One portrait was of Inez García. It was one of my very first pastels. It was a very big piece, maybe five or six feet high and maybe four or five feet wide. Inez García was not a famous person. However, I was drawn to her story. She was a Latina in San Francisco who shot and killed a man who raped her. She was arrested, charged with murder, and put on trial. She pleaded self-defense. Regrettably, she was unjustly convicted of second-degree murder and served fifteen months in prison until the California Court of Appeals overturned her conviction. Many people including myself were outraged at her conviction. An international defense committee was organized to assist her. I wasn't a part of it even though I sympathized with the cause. In fact, I was pissed off. Rape is outrageous. This abuse of women by men is horrendous. Inez struggled with this guy and ended up shooting the son of a bitch and killing him in self-defense. To me, this made absolute sense. I'd shoot the son of a bitch too in self-defense. I was so moved by Inez's story that I decided to do her portrait based on a photograph of her in one of the San Francisco newspapers. I and many others were relieved when

Inez was declared innocent on the basis of self-defense. It was one of the first such cases that upheld a woman's right to self-defense, including the use of violence.

I was further moved when after her trial a friend of mine who knew about my portrait of Inez brought her over to my studio to see it. She was so embarrassed but very grateful. She said, "oh, my nose! I have a funny nose and you got it too good!"

"Why did you do this picture?" she asked me.

"I did it because I believe that what you did was right and I support you in this and this is how I decided to show my support."

Inez was just blown away with this. I was honored that she came to my studio.

Inez's portrait was one of the centerpieces of my exhibit. In the picture I show her not as a victim but as a very strong woman. I related to her strength because I grew up with very strong women, including my mother, my grandmother, and my tías. They were strong like Inez. This also influenced me to do Inez's portrait. It took me two years to do it, and that's why the title of the picture is *Inez García 1975–77*. I especially took my time in doing it rather than rushing to complete it. My intent was not so much to use it to publicize her case, but to honor her and her courage for posterity.

One of the other portraits that I exhibited was one that I did on Mao Zedong. This was around the time that he died, and so this was an homage to Mao. I had wanted to do an image of Mao for some time and finally did. I felt that Mao was one of the great revolutionaries in history. He fought against a reactionary authoritarian government in China and succeeded in a socialist revolution. This was a tremendous undertaking in a country that was still largely feudal. This is what motivated me to do the portrait. Mao may have done things later that weren't very savory, and we can condemn him for that. However, we can't condemn him, or at least I won't, for leading the revolution that brought better conditions for the masses of Chinese who lived in utter poverty. At the time that I did my picture, there was much tension between China and the Soviet Union, which I thought was unfortunate. That's why I inserted the hammer and sickle, which is on the Soviet flag, as a way of symbolizing that these two great socialist nations should come together. One newspaper reviewer who covered the exhibit wrote that I was an avowed Marxist artist because of my image of Mao. This was a ridiculous conclusion and was an attempt to stereotype me. I had never met this reviewer and so I don't know where he was coming from. For him, if you did an image of Mao you were a Marxist!

One of the other images in the show was entitled *Political Prisoner*. The image is based on a photograph of a Vietnamese woman who is shouting out with her mouth wide open. I forget the story that accompanied the photo in one of the newspapers. I used and changed the photo image to show another woman who wants to shout out

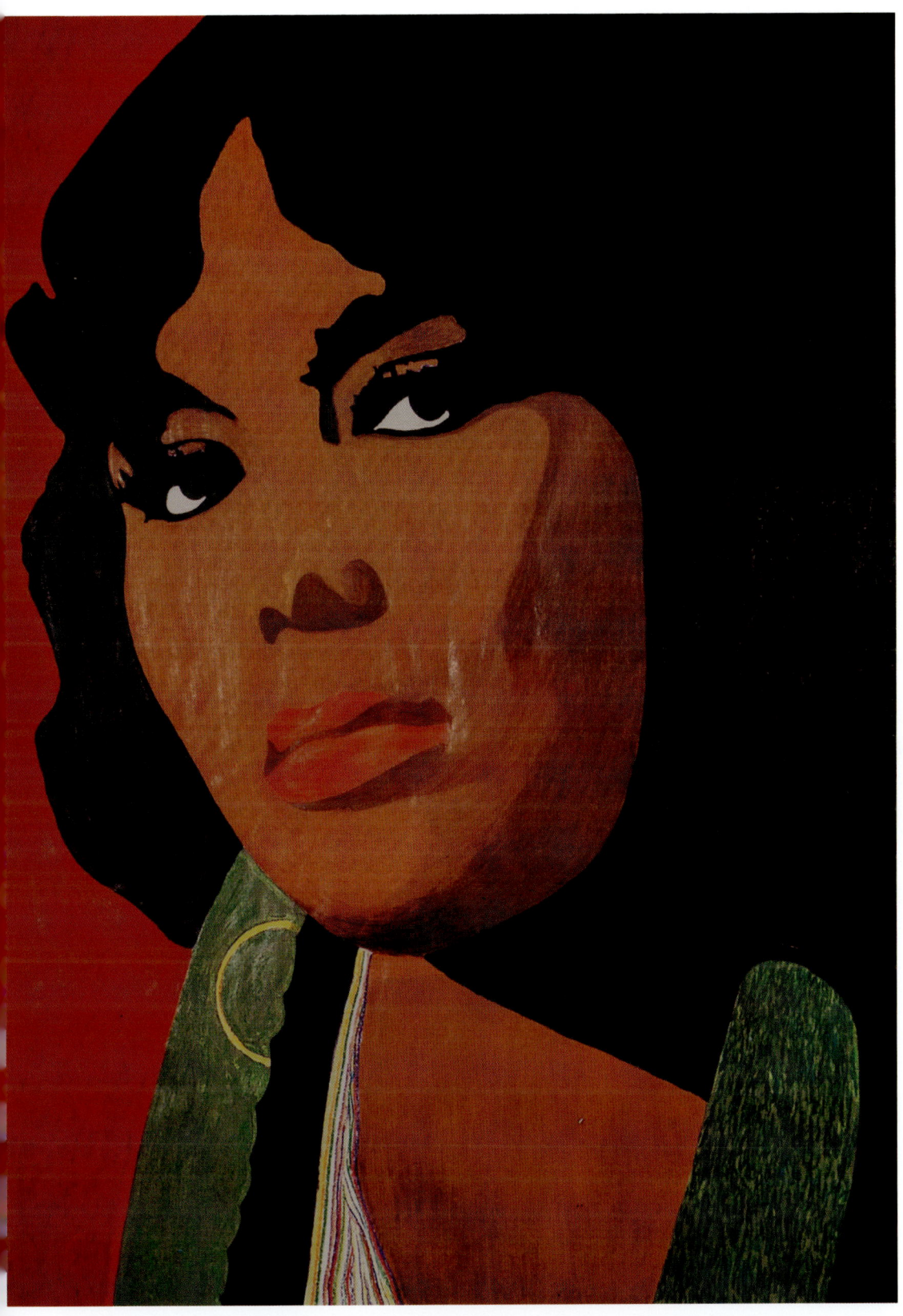

Inez Garcia, 1975–1977. Pastel and poster paint on paper, canvas size: 54-3/4 x 36 inches. Copyright © Rupert García.

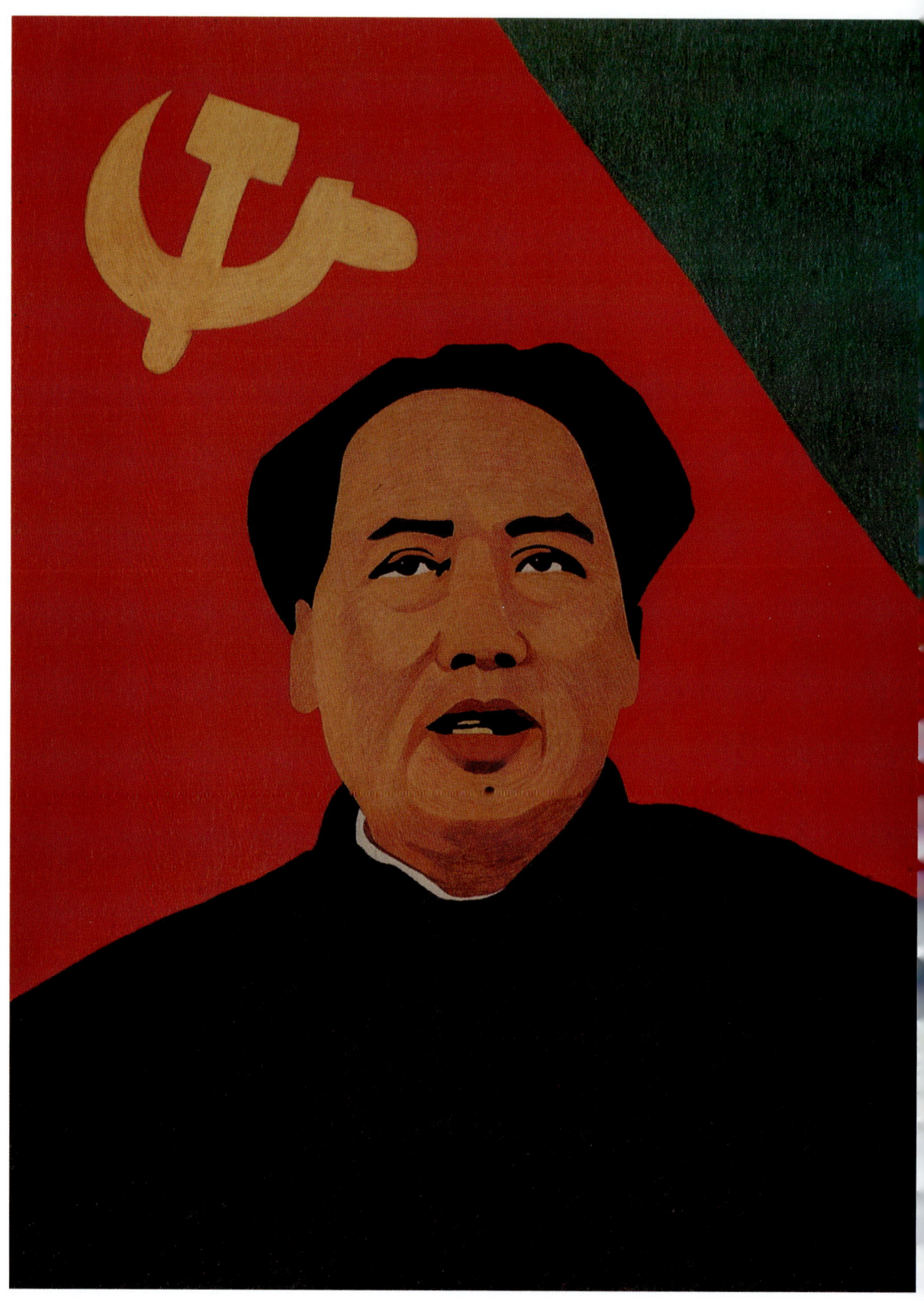

Mao, 1977. Pastel on paper, canvas size: 51 x 36 inches. Copyright © Rupert García.

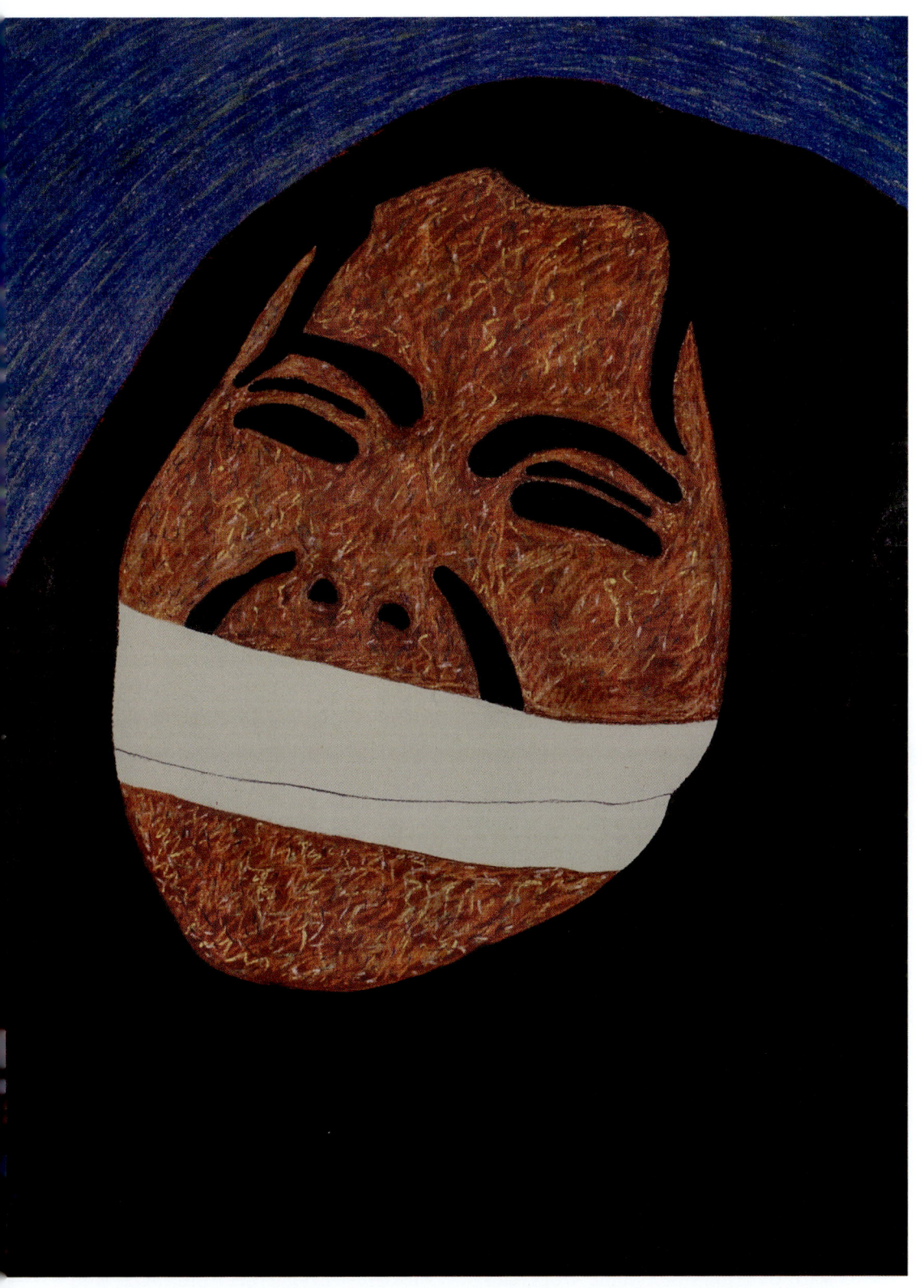

Political Prisoner, 1976. Pastel on paper, canvas size: 48 x 36 inches. Copyright © Rupert García. National Museum of American Art, Smithsonian Institution, Washington, D. C.

but can't because she is gagged with a white tape across her mouth. It is actually a representation of Olga Talamante, a Latina activist from the Bay Area who went to Argentina around 1974 to participate in the movement to restore democracy in that country. Because of her political activism, she was unjustly arrested. When word of what happened to Olga reached back home, an Olga Talamante Defense Committee was formed which petitioned the U.S. Congress and the State Department to intervene and get Olga released. This did not occur until two years later in 1976. My pastel was to show Olga wanting to cry out against injustice, but she can't because she has been gagged by the Argentine secret police. I borrowed the photo of the Vietnamese woman shouting and juxtaposed the image of Olga as a way of showing international solidarity. This painting later was obtained by the National Museum of American Art in Washington, DC.

I was very pleased with the exhibit, which validated my change to pastels and encouraged me to do more.

—II—

Although I was now focusing primarily on my pastels, I still had some contact and work with La Galeria. My last involvement was my participation in helping to organize the first ever homage to Frida Kahlo in the Mission in 1978. Frida was not yet well-known among Latinos at that time. Some of us as artists, including myself, were aware of Frida's incredible work and we read about her in art journals, but

we wanted to promote her to a larger audience and specifically to the Latino community of the Mission. In fact, I believe that our event was the first one ever done on Frida in California. The Frida exhibit also became part of La Galeria's Día de los Muertos events. The idea of a homage was not mine, but I think it came from some of the women associated with La Galeria such as Amalia Mesa-Bains.

The homage consisted of Latino and Latina artists doing artwork or writings or other ways of honoring Frida at La Galeria. There was no way we could afford to do an exhibit of her actual paintings; it would have been too expensive. My contribution was twofold. I contributed an image of Frida for the poster of the event and, second, I worked on a bibliography of publications on Frida, which we made available at the homage and which we later published in 1983. I'm very proud of this book; it is a gorgeous publication and I was very pleased that Chicano Studies at Berkeley published it. Of course, I had done a previous image of Frida for the 1975 calendar for La Galeria. I further wrote the Introduction for the publication. We also had educational sessions about Frida. People would come and learn about her and her work through slides and reproductions of it.

My image of Frida was done in silk screen, which I had never fully abandoned but only did occasionally by this point. I used a photo of Frida from the cover of a book on her published in Mexico. I exaggerated the image and cropped it to focus on her eyes, which

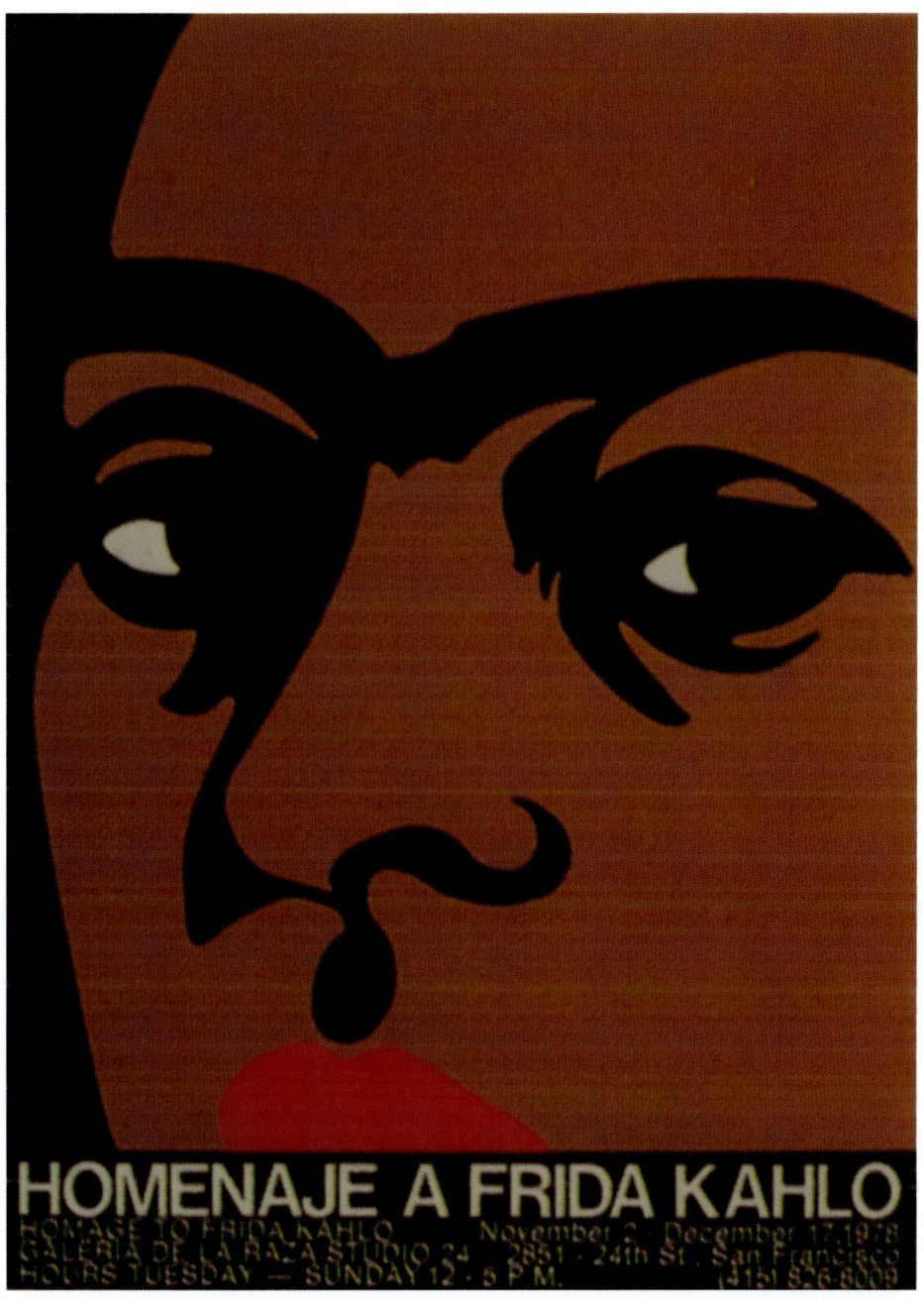

Homenaje a Frida Kahlo, 1978. Color silkscreen on white wove paper, sheet size: 23-1/8 x 17-1/2 inches, image size: 22-3/4 x 16-3/4 inches. Copyright © Rupert García.

I thought was the most important part of her face. I was intrigued also by how her eyebrows met and her sensuous nose. I then added my own colors and simplified the shapes. In my image, I didn't do her whole face, only from her lower forehead to her top lip, and thereby centered those incredible eyes, her eyebrows, and her nose. I painted her face a kind of caramel color.

The opening of the homage was packed with people mostly from the Mission. I had also heard that Hayden Herrera, a writer who was working on the first biography in English on Frida, was coming to our show. I had already read some of her articles on Frida and was very excited about her attending. I was especially thrilled that this Chicana writer would be joining us. There were as yet not many Chicano and Chicana writers, and so having someone like Hayden Herrera at our event was great. Her coming helped to stress the importance of what we were doing. At the same time, we were all wondering what she looked like, since none of us knew her. We also had heard that Hayden would be attending with Emmy Lou Packard, who was an American artist who had known Frida Kahlo and Diego Rivera very well. In fact, Emmy Lou assisted Rivera in doing one of his San Francisco murals. Her studio was actually in the Mission. I had met her and we became very good friends. I liked her very much. She was an older woman who was bright, caring, knowledgeable, and articulate. She became a treasure to us as Latino artists.

At the opening reception, I spotted Emmy Lou but not who I thought was Hayden. I was looking for a Chicana-looking woman. I asked Emmy Lou, "Where is Hayden?"

"This is Hayden," Emmy Lou turned to this Anglo woman with her. Oh, my God, I was so embarrassed, although I tried not to show it. I had just assumed that Hayden Herrera was a Chicana or Latina. Perhaps this was based on a certain kind of gendered nationalism.

But you can't judge a book by its cover. I learned that Hayden was Anglo, but married to a Latino man by the name of Herrera. The more I thought about it, none of this mattered. What mattered was that Hayden was writing about Frida, which would culminate in her wonderful biography published in 1983. On the other hand, God, I wished that she was a sister.

I don't remember what Hayden thought about our homage, but she seemed to enjoy herself as did everyone else. Everybody just loved the show for a variety of reasons, including for many their first introduction to the art and personage of Frida Kahlo.

■II■

That same year in 1978, I also got to meet a giant in Mexican art—Manuel Alvarez Bravo. He was the greatest photographer in Mexico and in the world. He had international stature. He was part of the Mexican Renaissance linked to the Mexican Revolution of 1910, and he knew all of the artists associated with it, including Los Tres, and he photographed many of them. He also photographed everyday life and culture in Mexico in an exceptional way. He was just an incredible photographer. I knew his work and had read books about him and his work. I wasn't a photographer myself; however, photography was very important to my own work. As a graduate student I took classes on photography with photorealist professors Robert Bechtle and Richard McClean. Photographs inspired my paintings. They were the basis of many of my images although I altered them from the real photos.

I met Bravo because he was invited by the San Francisco Art Institute to be an artist in residence and to have a major show of some of his photos. A student of mine at San Francisco State, Juan Garza, became a friend of mine, and Juan had some connection with the Art Institute who asked or hired him to show Bravo around the city. It was through Juan that I got to meet Manuel Alvarez Bravo. I had hoped to meet him at the Institute and do an interview with him; I had a list of questions to ask him. Juan arranged the interview. It was just such an honor to meet Manuel. He was very cordial and pleased that I wanted to interview him. We talked in both Spanish and English, and when his Spanish became too complicated for me to understand, Juan stepped in and translated for me. My lack of proficiency in Spanish did not disturb Manuel and he tried to help by speaking more in English although it was not his native language. In this way we had a great interview, which I taped, and I still have the tape. Manuel was fantastic. One of my questions for Alvarez Bravo was whether he considered himself a surrealist artist. I asked this question because André Breton, the important French surrealist poet and theorist who spent much time in Mexico, promoted Alvarez Bravo as a surrealist. Manuel emphatically answered that he was not. Surrealist artists, he explained, approached art including photography in a way that is consciously based on nonrational approaches to making a picture. Instead of painting a man standing on the ground, they would paint him upside down. By contrast, Alvarez Bravo took pictures of everyday life as it exists. He made no arrangements of the objects to be extraordinarily curious or unbelievable. Bravo just found situations in life and photographed them. On the other hand, surrealists were very interested in doing art that was mysterious, beyond belief; they were challenging rational thinking and were influenced by Freud—the unconscious. Alvarez Bravo was not interested in exploring Freud to find ideas of how to make outrageous pictures as the surrealists were. Breton was wrong even though he considered Bravo to be a surrealist. Manuel strongly denied this.

Alvarez Bravo was interested in all kinds of things, and he always had his camera with him. At the end of the interview when he expressed interest in getting to know more about the Bay Area, including the presence of Chicanos, I instinctively said,

"Why don't you come and stay with me and my wife and we can show you around?"

To my surprise he said he would like that but didn't want to impose on us. I assured him that it would not be an imposition and that we would love to host him for a few days. And so, one day I picked him up and drove him to our house. It was a wonderful opportunity to get to know this great artist even better. He was so unassuming. You'd think he had never made a photograph in his life. He was also a very sharp man, intelligent, very well read, and more. But he didn't have the stereotypical trappings of the so-called fine artist. Not at all. His trappings were of everyday life. I was very impressed with this. He was likewise never demeaning in any fashion or judgmental.

In turn, Manuel asked me questions especially about Chicanos. He was very interested in the figures of the pachucos and especially their street language, *caló*. Although I had never been a pachuco myself, I did know some of their language, which some also referred to as *pochismos*. The term comes from *pocho*, which was a derogatory term used by Mexicans in Mexico against the U.S.-born Mexican Americans. It incorrectly suggested that Mexicans in the United States had lost their Mexican culture; they were decultured pochos. Mexican elites, including in the art world, expressed this snobbishness towards Mexican Americans. There are those who don't like us in Mexico. Manuel Alvarez Bravo was not one of these. He was very interested in Chicanos and understanding of our experiences in the United States. I arranged to take Manuel to La Galeria and introduce him to some of the artists there.

We were sad when Manuel had to leave; he actually stayed with my wife Sammi and me for almost a week. We took him around and went to different restaurants, and we just got along so well together. After Manuel had returned to Mexico, one day I received a package in the mail from Mexico. It was from Manuel and with a short handwritten note thanking me and Sammi for our hospitality. To thank us

for this, he included a photograph that he had taken of Diego Rivera when he was still a young artist. It shows him working on a mural. We were floored. How wonderful! I couldn't believe we had a Manuel Alvarez Bravo photograph of Diego Rivera. Whew! Wow! I'll never forget Manuel's visit with us and cherish the memory.

■II■

Nineteen seventy-eight seemed to be when all these things were happening to me. This included my getting married in April of that year. This was Sammi, the love of my life. I actually met her in 1976, and it was funny how we came together. Sammi grew up in Los Angeles and after school became a model and also did some work in the film industry. At the time that I met her she was working for CBS Radio in San Francisco although she got unjustly fired from this job and then became quite involved in the National Alliance Against Racist and Political Repression that had been started by Angela Davis. Sammi was friends with the Davis family, including Angela.

The second time I met Sammi was at a meeting I hosted at my apartment with a group of other artists. The nature of the meeting was to organize artists to support the "March on Raleigh for Labor and Human Rights." Sammi came representing the National Alliance Against Racist and Political Repression. She came early and I opened the door and I didn't remember meeting her earlier. I invited her in and my heart jumped out of my chest, and I just said to myself "wow!" I couldn't believe this extremely beautiful woman had just come into my home. Lord, have mercy! However, because of my insecurities with women, I projected that she probably was married and was madly in love with her husband. So, I played it business-like with her that evening even though I was very attracted to her. Sammi later told me that she did remember seeing me at Angela's place with Angela's sister, Fania, and thought that Fania and I were an item. We were for awhile until I realized that Fania only wanted to be friends not lovers. This hurt me, but I accepted this, and Fania and I remained good friends.

Finally, Sammi and I really met when we both went to a party of a mutual friend who was helping to raise money for the rent of a warehouse to be used as a studio by various artists. At first, I didn't feel like going but finally did. Sammi also didn't want to go, although her friends finally convinced her. So, we both went reluctantly. We saw each other at the party and realized that we weren't with someone else. I couldn't believe I was seeing Sammi alone and she probably thought the same thing. We started dancing and talking and all along I was falling madly in love with her. I think I had fallen in love with her already the first time I met her at my place. From the party, we started seeing each other until we got married in 1978.

The idea of getting married was foreign to me. I had never wanted to get married and never thought that I would. I believed in marriage as an institution of commitment and the sharing of each other's lives. For me getting married meant that it's real love and it's passionate. Still, it was scary for me.

To be honest, it was Sammi who asked me to get married. I didn't ask. I probably wouldn't have asked anybody. I say this because as far as I was concerned, I was married to my art. To me the most important thing was being an artist. That was always number one in my mind. I actually told Sammi this even after we agreed to get married. "You're marrying a guy who's a very serious artist and totally committed to my art. It's never not on my mind. And it's important for you to know this."

Sammi understood this because she also had her career and her commitments as an activist. We were on the same page. But we were also madly in love with each other and came to believe that getting married was the way of expressing this love. I'm very glad she took the initiative and asked me to marry her!

But we also talked about children. I know that some people won't understand this, and I know our own families didn't, but we decided not to have children. It was a decision that we both agreed to, and it proved to be absolutely beneficial for both of us. No question about it. We made this important decision based on our lives and our work and what we wanted to accomplish in life. When you have children, you have to make a full commitment to them if you want to raise them the right way. It's a demanding commitment. If you can't do this, then you shouldn't have children. We both

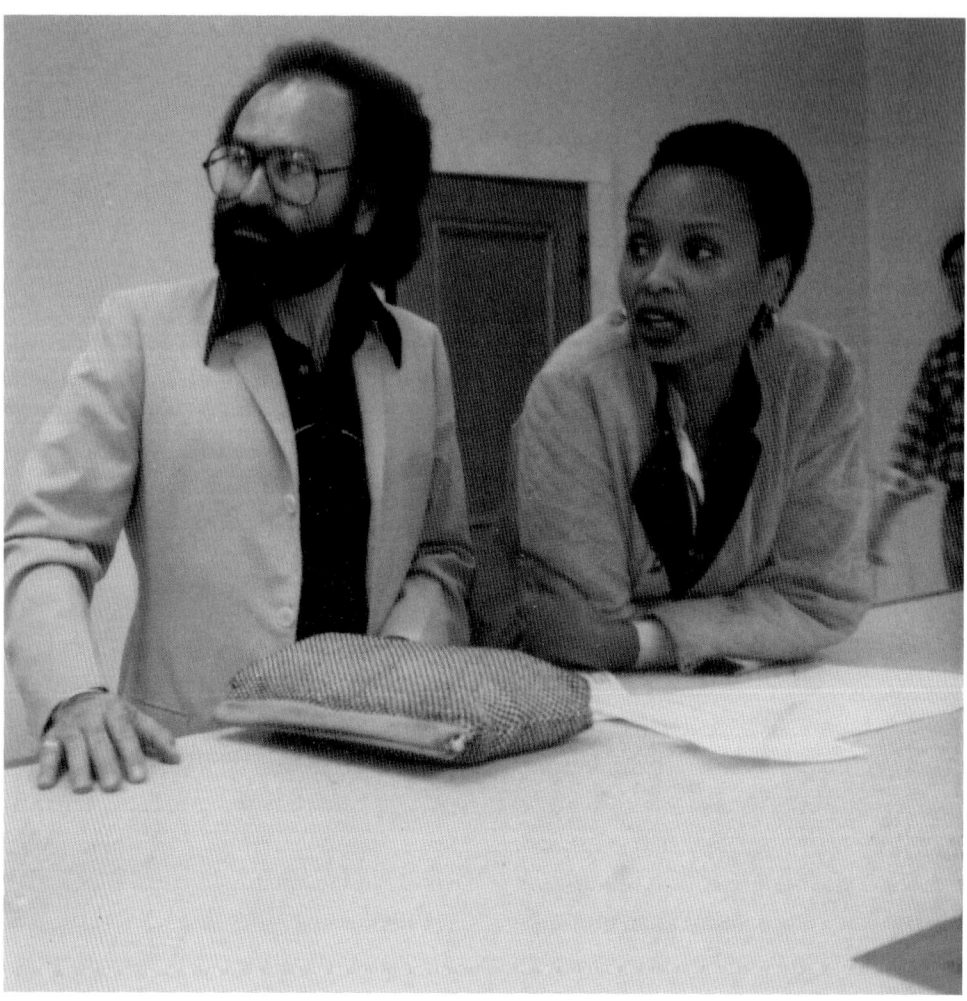

Civil marriage of Rupert García and Sammie Madison, San Francisco City Hall, April 18, 1978. Photo courtesy of Rupert García.

decided to prioritize our lives and careers. Speaking for myself, being an artist is a way of life and children don't fit into it. Sammi felt the same way. All this may sound callous and selfish, but this is how we felt.

—||—

At the time I got married, I was making an income by teaching part time. I continued in La Raza Studies at San Francisco State for a few more years, but I also taught a class here and there at the San Francisco Art Institute and in Ethnic Studies at UC Berkeley. I was not averse to selling my art and, in fact, when I had my exhibit at the Modern Art Museum, I sold my first painting. Still, I was cautious about becoming a commercial artist. I knew it would be difficult to make a living as an artist, but to me most importantly was my sense of integrity. That's paramount in my work. The work has to speak in the most honest fashion about me. I would never knowingly compromise my art in order to make it commercially viable. I knew that the art market is fickle and arbitrary. This is true of any marketplace, whether Wall Street or used car places. I didn't want to depend upon something that's undependable. I didn't want to be part of this. I never showed in galleries on purpose for a long time because I wasn't interested in that. I knew that this was how I was to approach being an artist, and this was to maintain my integrity.

To make an income, I fell back on teaching. I had always had the desire to teach even when I was in high school. I liked the idea. I thought it was an important job. I was inspired by great teachers that I had in high school and also in junior college. I learned a lot from them and they made us work and have pride in our work. So, it made sense to me that I would pursue teaching. It did not supersede my passion for art, but it was a way of making a living. I liked teaching, and I'm very good at it. Perhaps not the best, but still very good. I feel very good about how I teach because I see the results. At the same time, I didn't want to have a full-time tenure track position. I feared the loss of studio time by being overly absorbed in academia such as committee work and departmental politics. I didn't want to deal with that.

■ii■

In 1979 I applied and was accepted to the MA program in the History of Art department at UC Berkeley. I had always wanted to go to Cal to study art history. I had also grown to love art history. I learned how important it is. I wanted to understand the methods and theories behind it. In addition, I wanted to learn what the traditional perception of art history was so I could subvert it. Finally, I never received an MFA, and yet I realized if I wanted a more permanent faculty position that I might need that degree. However, I figured that with the MA I already had from San Francisco State that was on art practice, I could add the MA in art history and that this would be equivalent to an MFA, perhaps even more. So, going for the degree in art history was a practical decision on my part, yet this was balanced by my attraction to the field.

I knew that going back to school would take up some of my time from painting. Anything other than making art bothers me. It doesn't matter what it is. If it's mowing the lawn, I'm worried that it will take away from my work. At the same time, I really felt compelled to go back to school and study the history of art. Fortunately, I was accepted for an MA in art history where you along with your adviser defined the course of your work, including your thesis and the language you will be tested on. I chose Spanish and also chose to do a thesis on pre-Chicano Movement murals.

Before working on my thesis, I had to first take several seminars. These included one on contemporary art. Another seminar that I especially recall was one on German Expressionism that included studying fascism and modernism. I did a paper for that seminar on something like "The Twisted Cross," in which I studied the attempt by the Nazis in the 1930s to eliminate the avant-garde in Germany. Hitler hated the avant-garde, which he considered to be Jews and Communists. Instead, he promoted this boring work that I call the art of totalitarianism. I really enjoyed doing this paper.

I also took a class from T. J. Clark, a visiting professor from London, who taught nineteenth-century European art in a social context. He brought the understanding of art and artists within the context of where the artist lived and the historical factors that make up what I call the "art context." As a Marxist art historian, he understood art as ideology within a historical and social environment. It was never art for art's sake. This class reinforced my own view of art production.

In fact, I enjoyed the whole MA program at Cal. This in large part had to do with working with two great faculty advisers. One was Professor Herschel Chipp, who had written an important book in 1968 called *Theories of Modern Art*, which was used all over the country and which I read. It was Chipp who told me "if you want to get your Master's from our department, you have to jump through six hoops. Not seven, not five, but six. If you don't jump through these hoops, you're not going to graduate." I wasn't intimidated. I said, "Let's go, let's do it!" By six hoops, he meant passing your language exam, passing your seminars, and doing your thesis among other things. With Chipp, I took a seminar on European and American

art after World War II. Besides Chipp, I was fortunate to also work with Professor Peter Selz. In a way, Selz proved to be more of my mentor than Chipp. Peter had written a book on German Expressionism in the 1950s which looked at art in a way that I thought it probably should be looked at not only culturally, but socially and politically. This included looking at the individual artists and their surroundings. I very much agreed with this and learned much from Selz. Eventually, he became a Rupert García supporter and later wrote several essays in art magazines and catalogs on my work.

What I also found in the Art History department was the total lack of appreciation of Latin American art. It had no faculty member in this area. They just didn't think it was important. It would take years before they hired a Latin Americanist.

For my MA thesis, I chose to write on murals in California prior to those of the Chicano Renaissance in the 1970s as part of the Chicano Movement. I was part of the renaissance, but not as a muralist. However, I did appreciate the murals and had written about them in *El Tecolote*. I came upon this thesis quite by accident. One day I went to a Mexican restaurant in the Mission with Francisco Camplis. It was called El Azteca on Mission near Twentieth Street. While eating, Francisco said, "Rupert, look at the mural on the wall." I turned to my left and saw this mural that depicted a battle between Aztec warriors and the invading Spaniards. The painting covered one entire wall. I got up and went to take a closer look. I saw that at the edge was the artist's name, Oscar Caraveo, and the date of the completed mural which was 1963. It was entitled *Atardecer de un Imperio* or *The Waning of an Empire*. It is an example of what is called *pulqueria* art in Mexico. Pulquerias are bars; however, the wall paintings within or outside the bars are also found in restaurants, bakeries, grocery stores, meat markets, barbershops, and other businesses throughout Mexico, especially in rural areas or urban working-class barrios. I thought that this was really interesting. It got me thinking about other murals in other Latino establishments. I remembered seeing a bank mural in East Los Angeles that I later discovered was done in 1966 at the Pan American National Bank by José Reyes Meza and entitled *Our Past, Our Present, and Our Future*. This stimulated me to consider doing my MA thesis on these pre-Chicano Movement murals. I presented this idea to my professors, and they thought it was also a good project and approved it.

Actually, I was already aware of pulqueria art in the Mission because I had written an article in *El Tecolote* in 1977 titled "Pulqueria Art: Defiant Art of the Barrio." I brought attention to the many contemporary examples of pulqueria art in the Mission. In part, I wrote:

> What is noticeable in the Mission, and quite unlike the impersonal, slick and "professional looking" corporate advertisements are numerous paintings on the outside and inside walls and windows of restaurants, stores, Mexicatessens,

and bars that colorfully and personally draw our attention to the variety of goods available to us in the neighborhood. These paintings are among the best and truest examples of people's visual art presently existing in the Mission district and can be viewed as gestures of cultural resistance to the dominant racist and culturally chauvinist anglo [*sic*] culture, for these paintings use pre-Hispanic designs and motifs, and scenes of Latin America, and immediate reality within the United States.[2]

As I embarked on researching my thesis, I found still other pre-movement murals. On a trip to East L.A., I found another mural at the Casa Carnitas restaurant done by Alfredo Matamoros in 1967. These and other such murals that I discovered were similar to ones done in Mexico in similar establishments. These were murals in places frequented by everyday folks. I also found some murals done by Chicano artists but prior to 1970, which was my cutoff point since most of the Chicano Renaissance murals were done after this date. There were also two murals done by Antonio Bernal in 1968 for the Farm Workers Cultural Center in Del Rey, California. Both were untitled. In East Oakland, Malaquias Montoya had painted in 1969 an untitled mural for the East Oakland Development Center. Esteban Villa in Sacramento did a mural which he titled *Emergence of the Chicano Social Struggle in a Bi-Cultural Society* in 1969–1970. He painted his mural for the Washington Neighborhood Center.

Finally, at the UCLA Chicano Studies Library, Eduardo Carrillo, Ramses Noriega, Sergio Hernández, and Salud Solache had done a mural entitled *Chicano History* in 1970. I was excited about these discoveries. We knew about the murals of the 1970s, but not about those that predated these better-known murals. No one had studied or brought attention to these earlier murals, and that's what I wanted to do. I wanted to write about these precursor murals.

I found in researching these murals that they were done by artists who were more or less self-taught, with the exception of Reyes Meza. Their murals were readable, meaning that it was easy to see the stories being depicted. Because they were done by artists who had no training, the murals appear awkward to a more trained eye. However, they were not awkward to the artists or to the people who enjoyed them. In all cases, the themes of the murals were mexicano, Mexican themes, ancient and contemporary. In the case of the East L.A. restaurant mural done by Matamoros, the mural is about the restaurant itself. The mural shows the exterior of the restaurant and was placed on one of the interior walls. The style and themes of these murals reminded me of the early twentieth-century artists in Mexico who did pastoral scenes depicting ranchos and caballeros. The pre-Chicano Renaissance murals come out of this tradition and genre. This genre is also found in the *calendarios* in Mexican bakeries in the United States that not only show such pastoral scenes, but

also the pre-Columbian ones of Aztec warriors. All of this, to me, suggested that prior to the Chicano Movement, there were cultural artifacts such as the murals and calendars that passed on a kind of Mexican cultural nationalism and that helped to perpetuate a sense of *mexicanidad* in the barrios of California and the Southwest. The Chicano Movement consciously and unconsciously built on this influence.

I concluded my thesis by writing:

Building upon these early La Raza mural activities of California during the 1960s, a state-wide and community-based Chicano mural movement emerged by the early 1970s and peaked by the mid-1970s. Hundreds of murals appeared on a variety of surfaces such as fences, garage doors, windows, and most frequently on walls. These painted surfaces were covered with a profusion of images and symbols in bright colors relating to gang warfare, drugs, the Catholic Church, police brutality, oppression, Mexico, nationalism, war, education, the family, the farmworkers, revolution and Chicano independence.[3]

I really enjoyed researching and writing my thesis, which I titled "La Raza Murals of California, 1963–1970: A Period of Social Change and Protest." I was also very thankful that my professors in art history allowed me to do this kind of thesis. It made my experience in the program very exciting and worthwhile. It wasn't like I was writing a whole book. It only took me a couple of months to do the thesis.

It was just 169 typed double-spaced pages, including footnotes and illustrations of the eight murals that I analyzed. Still, to me, it was a major project. It was approved in November 1981. I felt good about the knowledge and information that I amassed in my thesis. I thought it perhaps laid the basis for someone else to built on my study and carry it further. I thought of actually expanding my thesis and turning it into a book. I started some additional research and discovered more of these murals. But it takes a lot of time to write a book and, in the end, I prioritized my art. I'd rather make pictures than reflect on those already made.

I was very proud of myself in obtaining my MA in art history from Cal, so much so that I decided to participate in the graduation ceremonies in the spring of 1982. I was proud of myself because I completed my program at the same time I was still doing my art, teaching, and developing my marriage relationship. It was very difficult to maintain all that. Very, very demanding. That's why I wanted to go through the graduation as a symbolic gesture of what I had accomplished. I was very excited to be in the ceremony. I invited my mom and my family, and she and my sister attended along with Sammi. I wore my robes and went through the whole commencement ceremony. I felt that I had earned every goddamn thing I got because I had worked my butt off. I had really wanted to study art history and to attend Cal. I felt good about accomplishing both. I should also say that I was helped by obtaining some minority graduate fellowships that augmented my income and allowed me more time to focus on my studies.

—II—

In the late 1970s, I began to have more contacts with the Department of Ethnic Studies at UC Berkeley and, in particular, with the Chicano Studies component. My key connection was with Carlos Muñoz, an activist political scientist. Carlos was also very much involved with the National Association of Chicano Social Scientists (NACS) that had been formed in the early 1970s. Carlos helped to host the conference in the spring of 1977, and he asked me to do the poster for it. I agreed and even though I was doing mostly pastels by this time, I went back to offset printing to do the poster. I wanted to do an image of a Chicana activist. I discovered the recently published book *500 Years of Chicano History* edited by Betita Martínez, who was a long-time political activist. As I looked at the various photos in the book, I found one of Emma Tenayuca from San Antonio, whom I had never heard of before. I learned in the book that she as a teenager led in organizing female pecan shellers in that city and that she was also a member of the Communist Party. "Man," I said to myself, "what a woman!" She reminded me of Dolores Huerta and of my mother, both strong no-nonsense women. I decided to do her image from the photo in the book. In the photo, Emma is behind prison bars after having been arrested for her organizing work. I decided to do her portrait with her in front of the bars, suggesting her

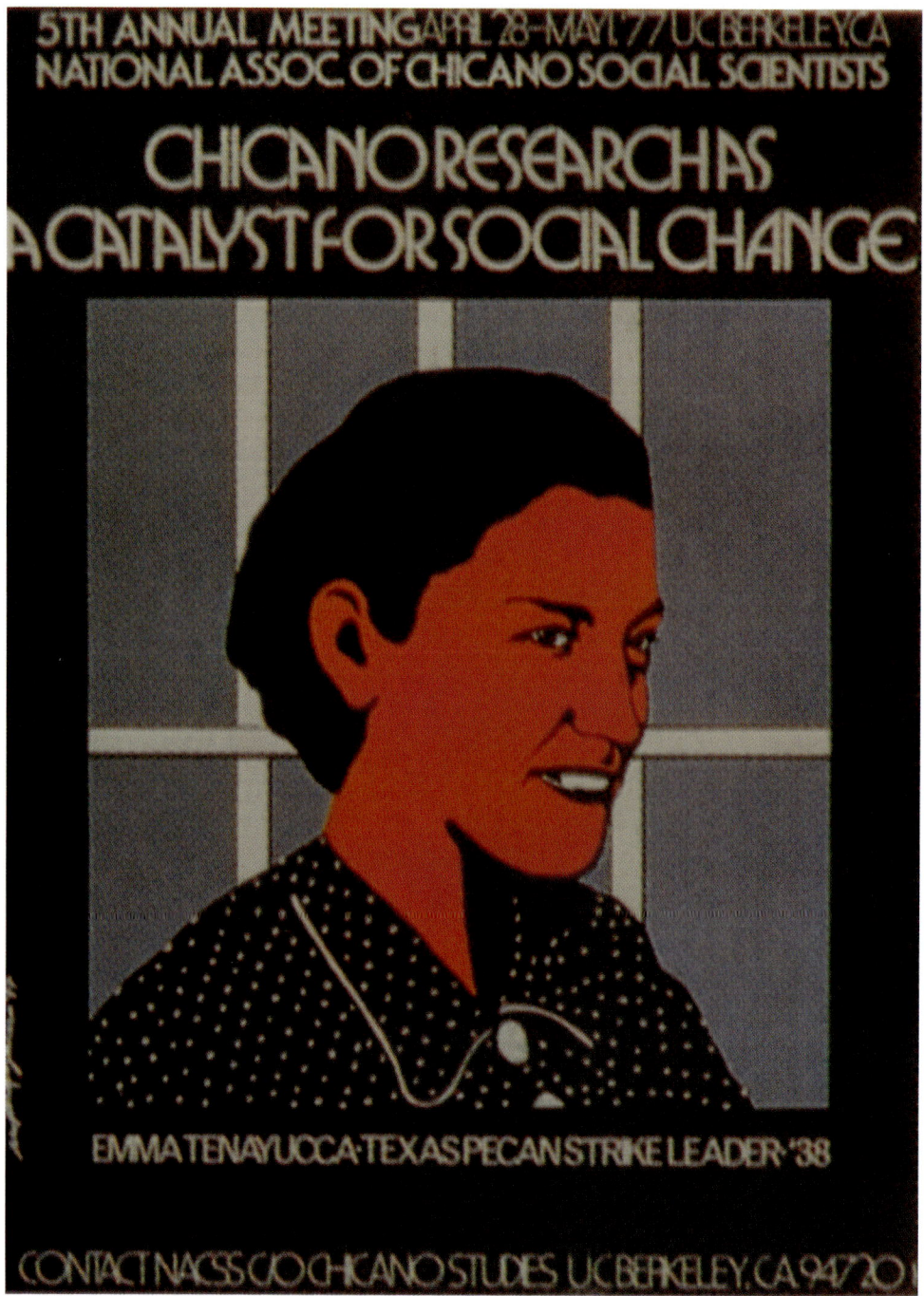

Chicano Research as a Catalyst for Social Change, 1977. Color offset lithograph on white wove paper, sheet size: 20 x 15 inches, image size: 19-1/4 x 14-1/4 inches. Copyright © Rupert García.

unwillingness to be silenced. Although Emma was light-skinned, I painted her face a copper brown to link her with the cultural nationalism of the Chicano Movement, which asserted that Chicanos were a people of color. The poster is entitled *Chicano Research as a Catalyst for Social Change*, which was the theme of the conference. We printed five hundred copies of the poster, which was highly received especially because it featured a Chicana historical figure who had been recently discovered.

Marissa Provenzino:

[Rupert García] brings heroines of social justice that are normally identified as Chicana into the master narrative. By doing this he recognizes their importance in the development of social justice for all Americans.[4]

Because of my connection with Carlos Muñoz, I began teaching part-time in Chicano Studies at Berkeley. I taught both a studio course at first and then added a course on Chicano culture that I was asked to teach. The studio course with just a few students was a natural for me and similar to my course at San Francisco State that I was no longer teaching. However, I had to work harder for the culture course, since I didn't know the full complexity of Chicano culture. I worked my butt off for this class. I also employed a critical approach to the examination of the culture. I didn't romanticize it or glorify it. I raised questions about different aspects of it and contradictions

such as on class and sexism and confronted stereotypes that Chicanos had created for themselves, especially out of the Chicano Movement. This meant that I critiqued the cultural nationalism of the movement while still upholding the importance of it. As at San Francisco State, I had mostly Chicano/Latino students. They seemed to enjoy my cultural course and even though I raised critical questions, they seemed to appreciate this. I actually found that the students at Cal were more prepared. I enjoyed my classes in Chicano Studies and continued teaching them into the 1980s, which helped my income. I later was also hired part-time to teach some classes in the School of Environmental Design at Berkeley. Here, I taught freehand drawing for architecture, graphic design, and figure drawing for architecture.

In doing my particular class on Chicano art history, I benefited from the work done by Professor Jacinto Quirarte at the University of Texas at San Antonio. Quirarte was a pioneer Chicano art historian, and his syllabus for his class was very instructive for me in organizing my own classes.[5]

◼️❚◼️

Although Sammi and I had individually and collectively been living in San Francisco for many years, we decided to move across the Bay to Oakland in 1981. This was a big decision on our part. There were three main reasons for the move. First of all, we were asked to move from the house we were renting. The owners wanted to move in themselves. The second reason was that we tried to find a house to actually buy in the city, but we found out it was too expensive for us. So, we decided to see about Oakland. We got a real estate agent and she found us a three-bedroom house next to the Oakland Zoo which was just perfect for us. It was quiet and very importantly it had space for a studio for me. In the rented house, I had been using one of the rooms for my studio, and it wasn't really adequate. The new place had a downstairs space away from the rest of the house. I could even set up a small office away from what would become my studio. It was a big studio space with high ceilings, which I really needed because I was now doing very large paintings, such as ten to twelve-foot-long ones. They were big suckers. Finally, we moved because we could afford the mortgage. We wound up living there for ten years.

The move to Oakland for me was traumatic. I loved San Francisco. It hurt to leave. It reminds me of Tony Bennett's classic song, "I left my heart in San Francisco." Well, that's how I felt. My whole frame of reference and thinking had become San Francisco and still is. After we moved, we even still shopped in the city at the stores we were familiar with. Of course, in time I became adjusted to Oakland, and that also became part of my reference.

—||—

I took a big step in 1982 when for the first time I became a commercial artist—meaning that I began to exhibit my pictures for sale. That year I had an exhibit of some of my pastels at the Simon Lowinsky Gallery in downtown San Francisco. It was among the best galleries in northern California and certainly among the top five in the city. I had met Simon much earlier around 1969–1970 in Berkeley. He then had a gallery on College Avenue called the Phoenix Gallery, and I had gone there to see an exhibit. Someone introduced me to Simon, and we talked a little bit. Several years later, he opened a gallery in San Francisco called the Simon Lowinsky Gallery on Grant off of Geary. I saw him again and soon we became friends along with his wife. We didn't discuss an exhibit of my work because that wasn't why we had become friends. Simon's gallery was a beautiful, slick, elegant gallery space. It was just a gorgeous design. He primarily exhibited photographs.

Eventually, we did talk about an exhibit for me. This was a few years later at a point where Simon was considering closing his gallery. He asked me one day if I would like to show some of my work before he moved to New York. It would be his last exhibit in the gallery. I was delighted and immediately agreed. Simon's gallery was a commercial venue of art. The art was for sale. I had never been in that kind of a context. Certainly not in a high-end gallery. So, I knew what I was getting into and I had no problem with this.

I selected some of my pastels to exhibit. The show looked fabulous. We had an opening event, and although the gallery which was a big space wasn't full, there were many of my friends and others who attended. I wasn't yet known through the "proper channels." This meant being connected to mainstream art collectors, curators, museum directors, and art critics. None of these people attended, and I frankly didn't care. For me it wasn't about that anyway. It was about this great space and my friends being there to see my work.

My pastels looked great and we did sell a piece. It was my image called *Abanderado*. It was bought by David Peoples and his wife Jan. They became friends. Both worked in movies and David was big time. He cowrote one of my favorite movies of all time, *Blade Runner*, which when I saw it I was just stunned. I later told David, "what a beautiful piece of work that was." David also wrote a filmscript which hung around a long time. Nobody wanted it. Until finally Clint Eastwood wanted it and made the film, *The Unforgiven*, which won the Oscar for best picture.

I had no hesitation in moving into commercial art. Hell, no. None whatsoever. I've never had an either-or kind of consciousness and this applied to being or not being a commercial artist. I didn't feel that I was giving up something to gain something else. I didn't feel that at all. I wish I had sold all my damn paintings! I heard indirectly that some others were criticizing me for going commercial as if I was giving up my political views. I didn't see it this way, and the fact is that such criticisms didn't affect me at all. I knew that I wasn't giving up my principles. It wasn't like I was going to become super-rich. Artists have to make a living in a capitalist society that makes a commodity out of anything that might sell. This includes art. However, if you are aware, as I was, that we live in a capitalist society, then you have some level of control of your product. You can make intelligent choices and understand what compromise really means and that "selling out" isn't as simple as some people like to think. It's much more involved because we live in a very complicated society and economic and political culture. It's not either/or if you understand the various layers of internal contradictions of our society and culture. Understanding all of this means you can make better decisions.

Going commercial, at least in my case, didn't lead to a de-politicization or de-radicalization of my art. It could mean that, but not necessarily, because I still did and showed the same kind of art that I did before going commercial. Simon didn't ask me to change my art and I didn't. I exhibited some very strong and tough pictures. In fact, the one that David and Jan bought shows a man carrying a Molotov cocktail. There are some artists who have abandoned their political commitments in order to sell their art which becomes de-politicized or at least conforms more to a capitalist culture. They metaphorically remove the thorns from their "nopales" (cacti) and make them very smooth, and the green is easy to enjoy and the red on the flowers of the nopal is softened. That's possible. However, you can also make those points on the cactus sharper and you can make that red stronger and brighter and make that green of the nopal richer.

The fact is that I didn't think that moving into the marketplace meant that my art lost its critical edge. Why? Because I don't make art to be political. I don't have an ideological agenda that determines the type of work that I make. My work does resonate with politics and criticality and that's true. But I don't make art to be political. It comes off that way, sometimes very clearly. However, at the same time, there are many layers going on, and the metaphor perhaps has a lot of meanings. I think that I'm a person who is and always has had an edge to myself. Earlier it wasn't quite clear what the edge meant or felt, but it meant and felt something. Now the edge has a bit more understanding of itself and it cloaks itself in a certain kind of politics. It does, but it doesn't mean to be only political.

The other thing about going commercial is that it was premised on my believing that my work was good and even terrific. I didn't need the owner of a gallery or a curator and certainly not a critic to tell me this; I know it. Nothing can or will interfere with this dimension of how I understand my work. As a consequence, I will show in any gallery that appreciates my position and promotes my work for what it is and not for what they want it to be in order to sell it.

For my first commercial show, as noted, I displayed several of my pastel paintings. One of them was *Assassination of a Striking Mexican Worker*. This was based on an incredible photo by Alvarez Bravo which he took in the 1930s and which I knew about even before I met Manuel. I loved that photograph. It is so powerful. I had wanted to use it for something, but never felt quite prepared to do so. This changed after I met Alvarez Bravo. I felt more comfortable afterward in tackling the photograph. I did the painting after Manuel returned to Mexico. I did it in 1979. Because the photo is small, I really exaggerated my image to scale making it monumental. I cropped the photo and made some changes in it. The photograph showing a striking Mexican worker dead on the ground was so impressive, how could I expand upon it, be consistent, and honor the graphic emotional impact of the photograph? Well, I had to make it as big as I possibly could and use colors that would really resonate with each other. Manuel's photo is in black and white with some gray, so I had no idea what the real colors were of the assassinated worker and had to figure out from the photo what colors to use. I made an educated guess. The photograph is striking as hell; however, in my world color has to define the complexity of experience. My pastels created a wonderful quality in the overall image. I aimed to give the fallen worker a sense of dignity, pride, and elegance. I didn't want people to see him as a poor victim and say "oh, pobrecito." I wanted to make a beautiful if tragic image. I painted in a little bit whiter in the eyes to indicate energy or vitality and a sense of élan of someone who was not giving up. Even though the worker is dead there is still a sense of potential.

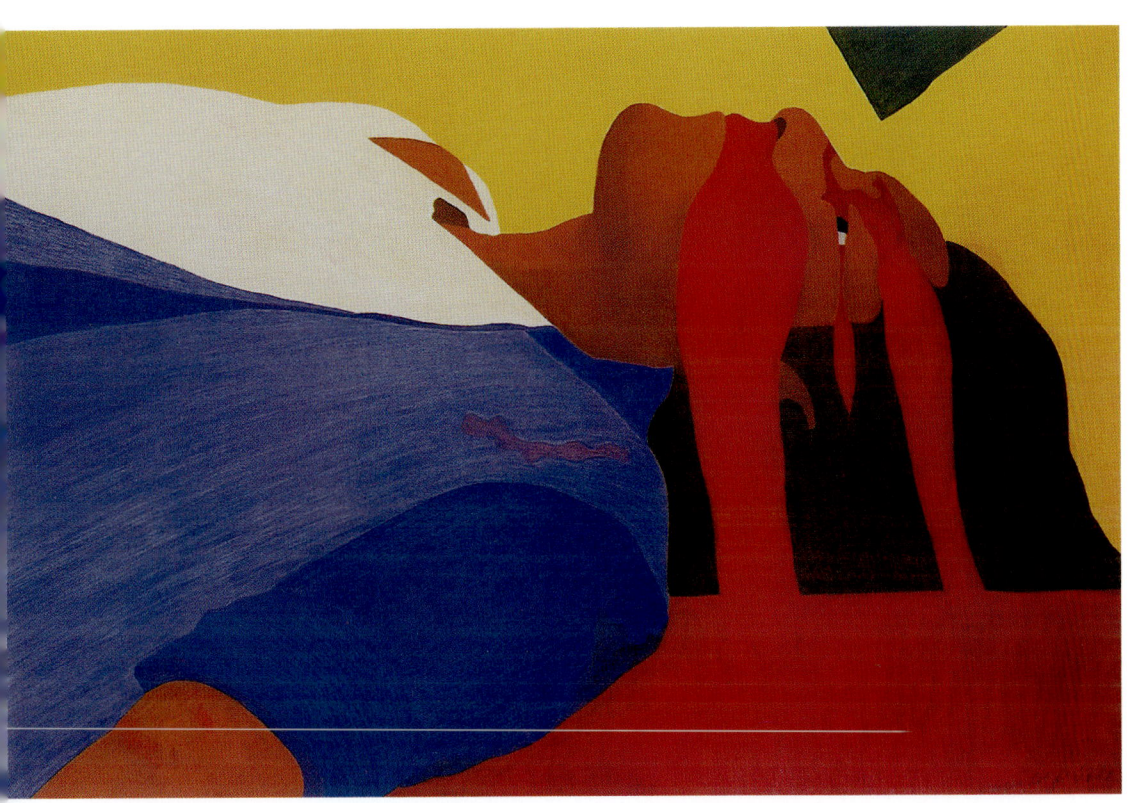

Assassination of a Striking Mexican Worker, 1979. Pastel on illustration board, canvas size: 42-2/5 x 60 inches. Copyright © Rupert García. Courtesy of Rena Bransten Gallery.

I had done a picture of Ricardo and Enrique Flores Magón, the anarcho-syndicalist leaders of the Mexican Revolution of 1910. I saw a documentary on the brothers and was impressed by their story and exploits. The fact that they were brothers led me to think of a pastel painting a diptych showing the two brothers. I painted their images on two separate sheets of paper. One critic has written that in my use of diptych and triptychs, I have the panels in conversation with each other. I leave such views to the critics and the people who see my images. I also did the diptych for economic reasons. It was the economy of space. I didn't have one sheet of paper the size of the finished diptych. But I had two panels of illustration board that when put together would equal a nice area. I did the painting using different colors; however, for later publication of my images, I only had a black and white photograph of it. That's all I had, but in the exhibit, it was in color. This was part of my show.

I added my homage to the great Spanish painter Francisco Goya which I had done and included it in the exhibit. I first became acquainted with Goya in an undergraduate art history class at San Francisco State, and I started to get interested in him and his

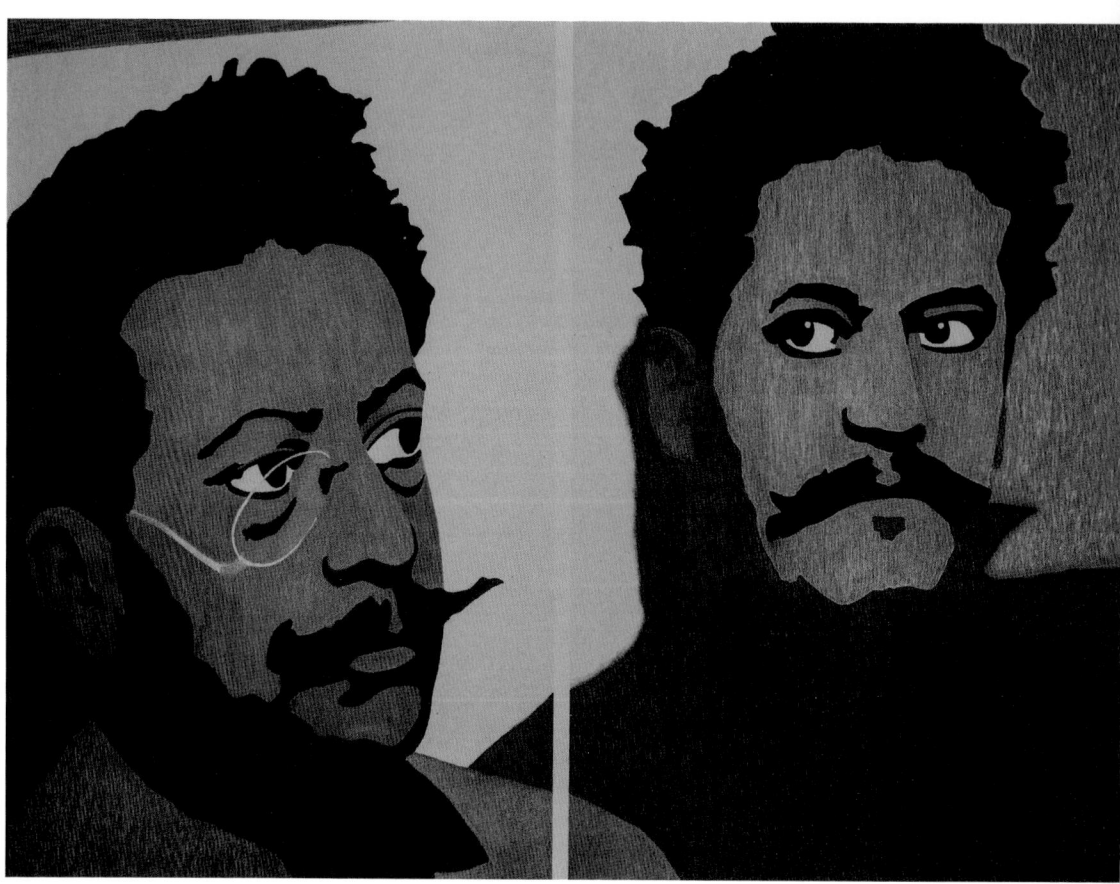

Hermanos Flores Magon, 1979-1980. Pastel on illustration board, canvas size: 60 x 80 inches. Copyright © Rupert García.

paintings. He was an iconic figure; he was the model of an artist who goes through interesting changes in his life and becomes a great artist. The way he used paint and coloring composition was super. His murals are exciting. His series of etchings about the disaster of war are just stunning. Just incredible use of lineage. His work was beautiful and strong. He is an example of an artist who eventually really worked at a sense of integrity and who made works about society and politics. Yet he didn't allow the political realities to overwhelm the aesthetics in making a painting.

I could see myself in Goya. Absolutely. It was that balance of the aesthetics of his art with his political beliefs so that neither of the two dominate. Rather they enhance each other to accomplish, in my estimation, the best picture possible. That's very difficult to do. I really like how Goya was able to do this. That's the challenge of my artistic life. It's not the viewer's challenge or that of the people who sit in a corner with a pad and pencil to see if it's Chicano enough or not. I'm not interested in that. What they have to say is of no consequence to me. What is consequential to me is my making

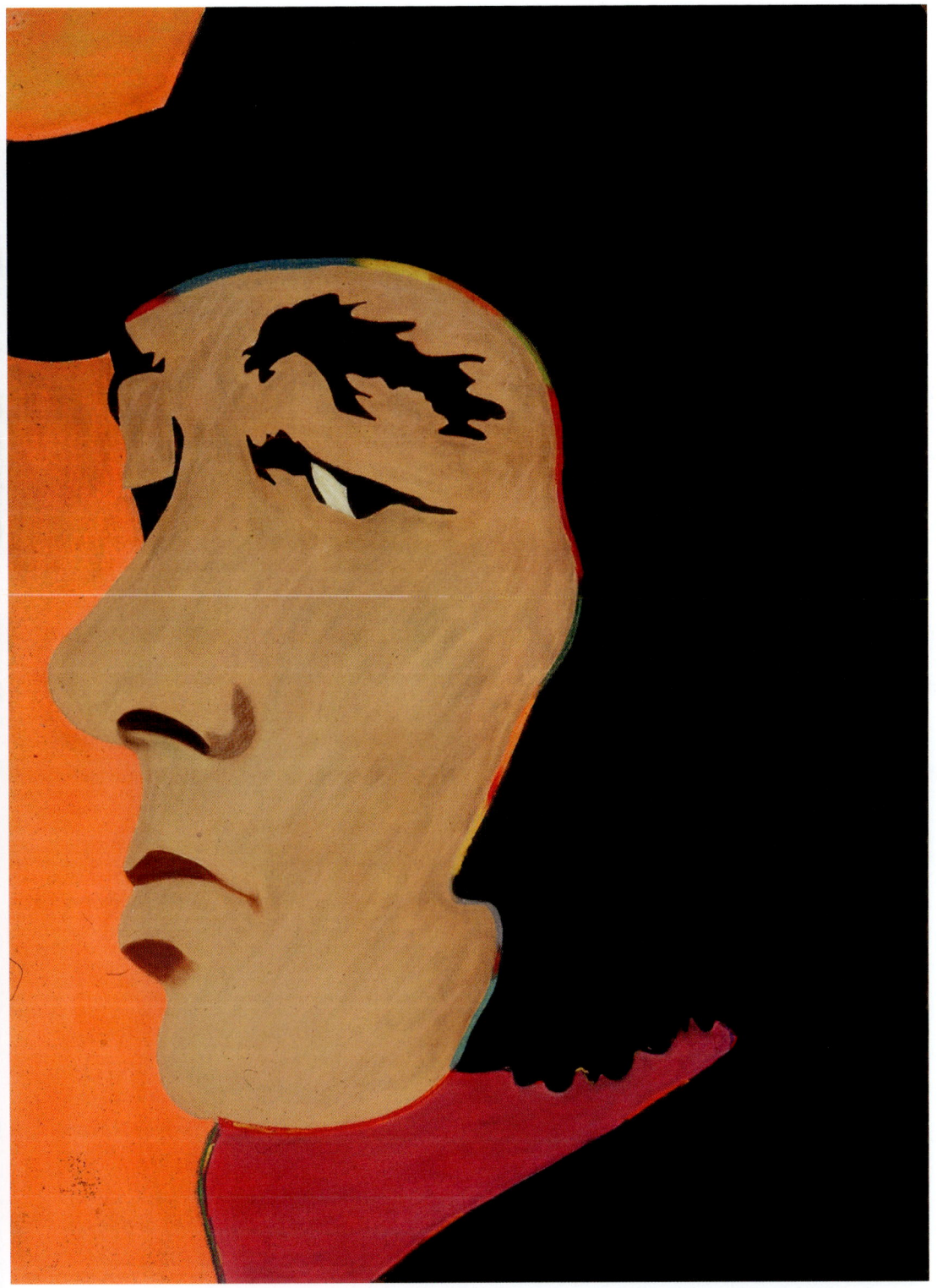

Goya, 1980. Pastel on paper, canvas size: 42 x 29-3/4 inches. Copyright © Rupert García. Courtesy of Rena Bransten Gallery.

the picture. If this satisfies my needs, then what others say doesn't matter. The process which I go through to make the picture is what matters, and how I feel about the process and the picture is what matters.

I also admired Vincent Van Gogh and so I did my homage to him which was also in the exhibit. I love the colors that I used for it. However, no one ever bought this painting. If I had the money, I'd buy it!

Of course, I added my picture *Abanderado* that David Peoples bought. The inspiration for the painting was a newspaper photo of a hooded figure holding a Molotov cocktail. I first saw this image in the late 60s or early 70s, and it really struck me. It actually isn't this image that I used for the painting, but a very similar one in 1982 which was equally as striking. Wow! Should I do a painting of this? Would I be advocating violence? Am I saying that it's the right thing to do? That was one of the few times that I've had to really think about doing a picture. No, Rupert, it's just a picture. It's about something you're interested in. You don't advocate that. But there's something compelling about that situation that would make for an interesting picture about this aspect of people rebelling and protesting. An so I thought, well, okay, fine. I'm not advocating this action. I convinced myself of that. That's not why I'm doing it. I did it.

Still another painting that I showed was one that I did on the scientist Robert Oppenheimer who had helped develop the atomic bomb. I was interested in this but also the fact that later

Oppenheimer was accused of being a Communist and politically persecuted. He was ostracized from the scientific community and denied security clearances. I learned this from a documentary on him (cowritten by David and Jan Peoples) that I saw in a movie theater. I was very taken about how he was red-baited. It enraged me that the government in the early Cold War years was persecuting innocent people, not just Oppenheimer, but many others under McCarthyism and the Red Scare of the 1950s. I was moved to do a painting of Oppenheimer. I went to a theater in Berkeley that was showing the documentary and asked if they had a poster or leaflet on the film that had an image of Oppenheimer. They did and gave me a leaflet. This is what I used to base my pastel of him. The leaflet image showed Oppenheimer smoking his ubiquitous pipe, and that's how I painted him.

Finally, I exhibited my homage painting to Diego Rivera. I had already done some on Frida who was married to Diego, but not of him. I always loved his face, a great face with kind of frog eyes. Some called him "El Sapo" or the frog.

Almost all of my paintings then are facial images. I have always been fascinated by faces. This fascination goes back to my teenage years, when I loved to peruse movie magazines to see the faces of movie stars. I think too in my family face-to-face contact was very meaningful. It was as if the face carries with it a lot of information, emotional information, and intelligence. Also, going to the movies and later watching

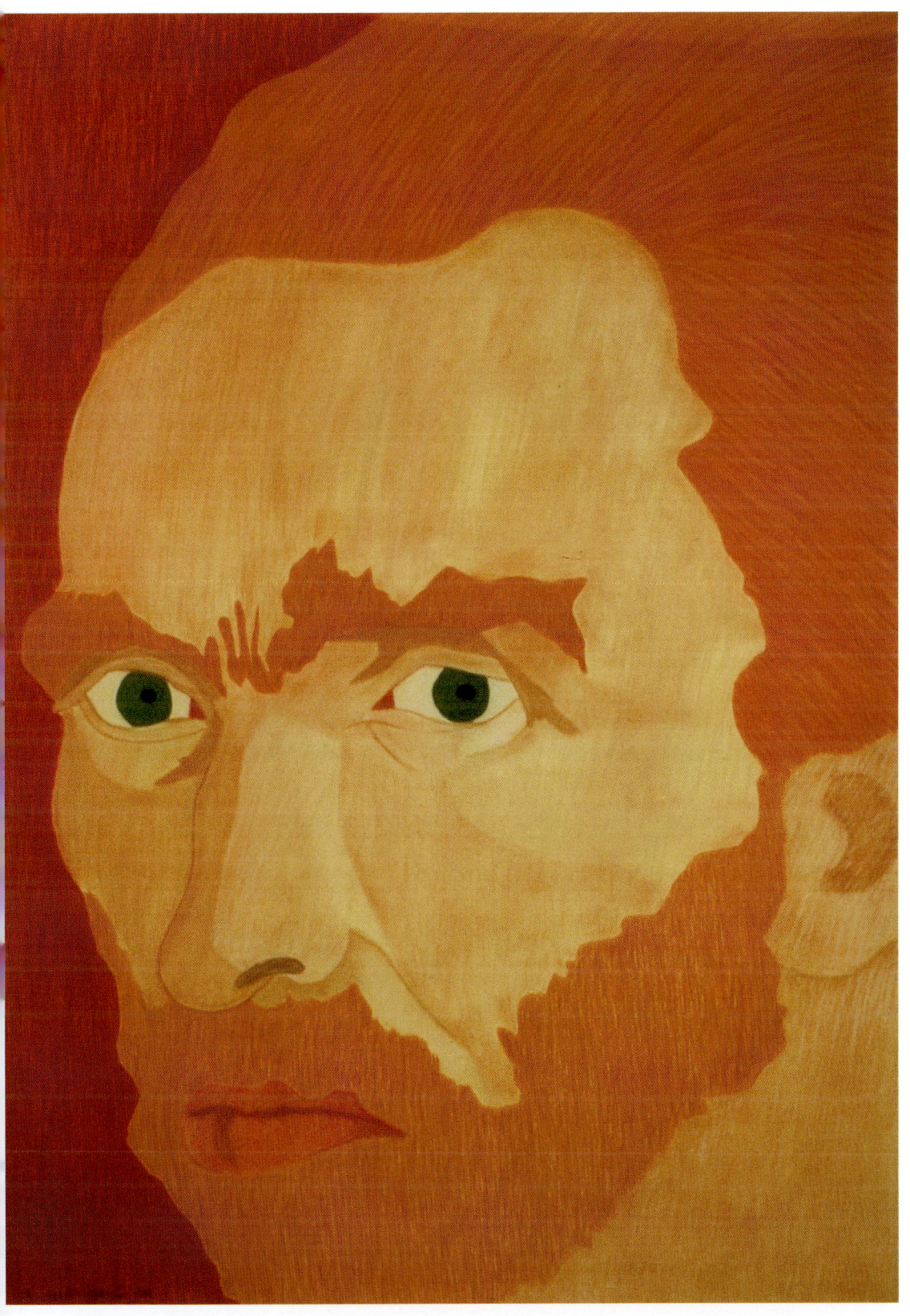

Vincent, 1980. Pastel on paper, canvas size: 42 x 29-3/4 inches. Copyright © Rupert García. Courtesy of Rena Bransten Gallery.

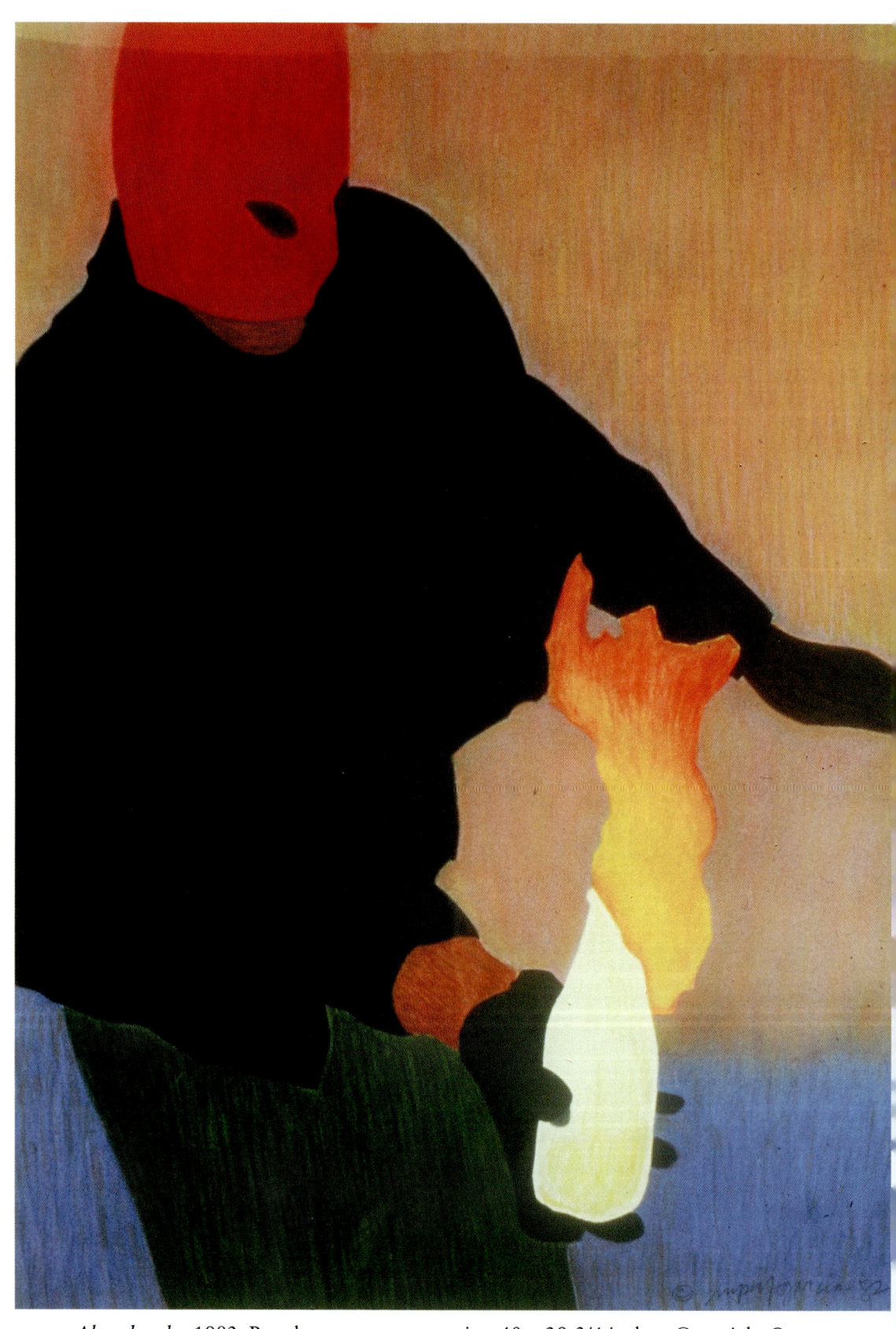

Abanderado, 1982. Pastel on paper, canvas size: 40 x 29-3/4 inches. Copyright ©
Rupert García. Courtesy of Rena Bransten Gallery.

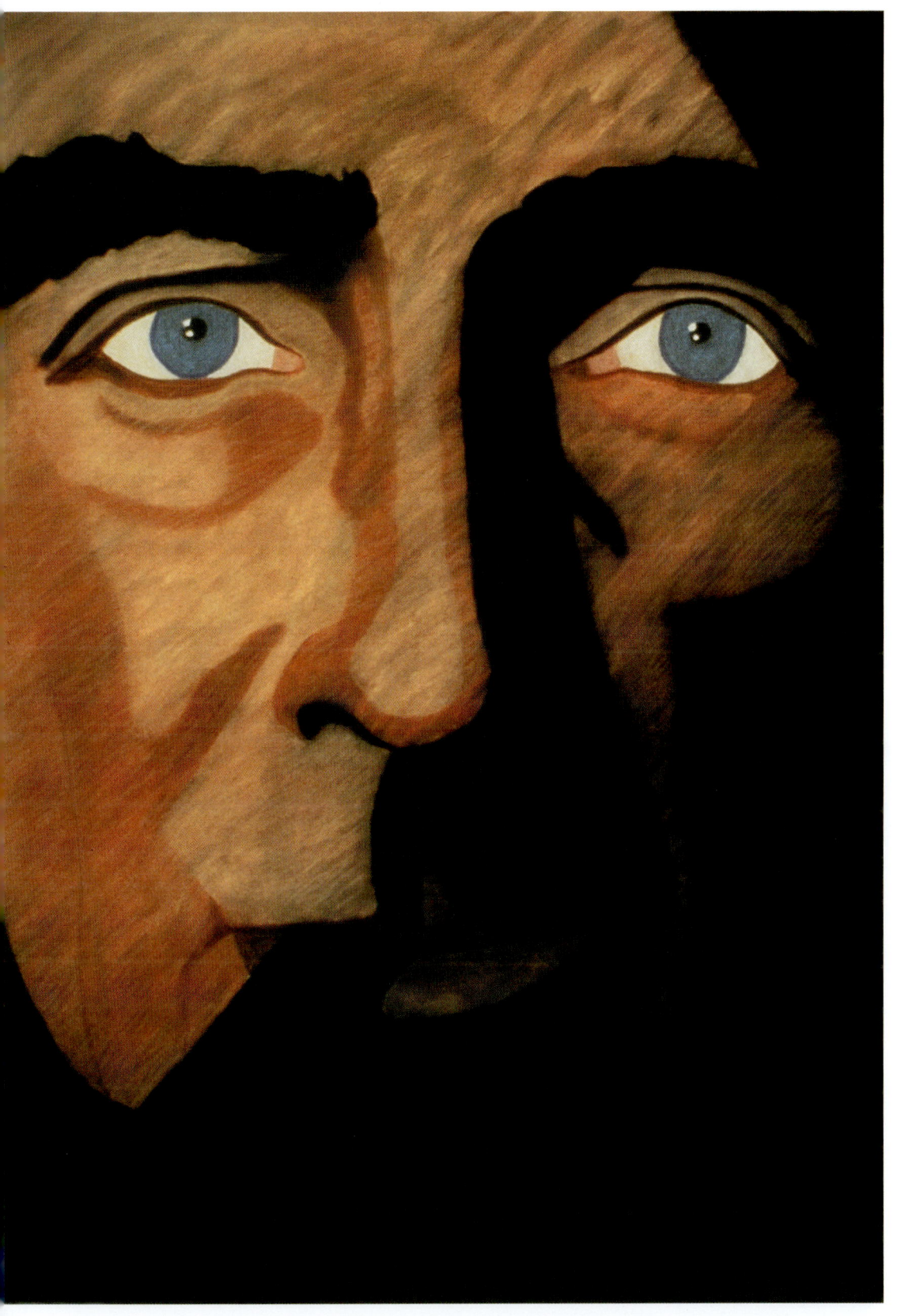

J. Robert Oppenheimer, 1982. Pastel on paper, canvas size: 41-1/2 x 29-1/2 inches.
Copyright © Rupert García. Courtesy of Rena Bransten Gallery.

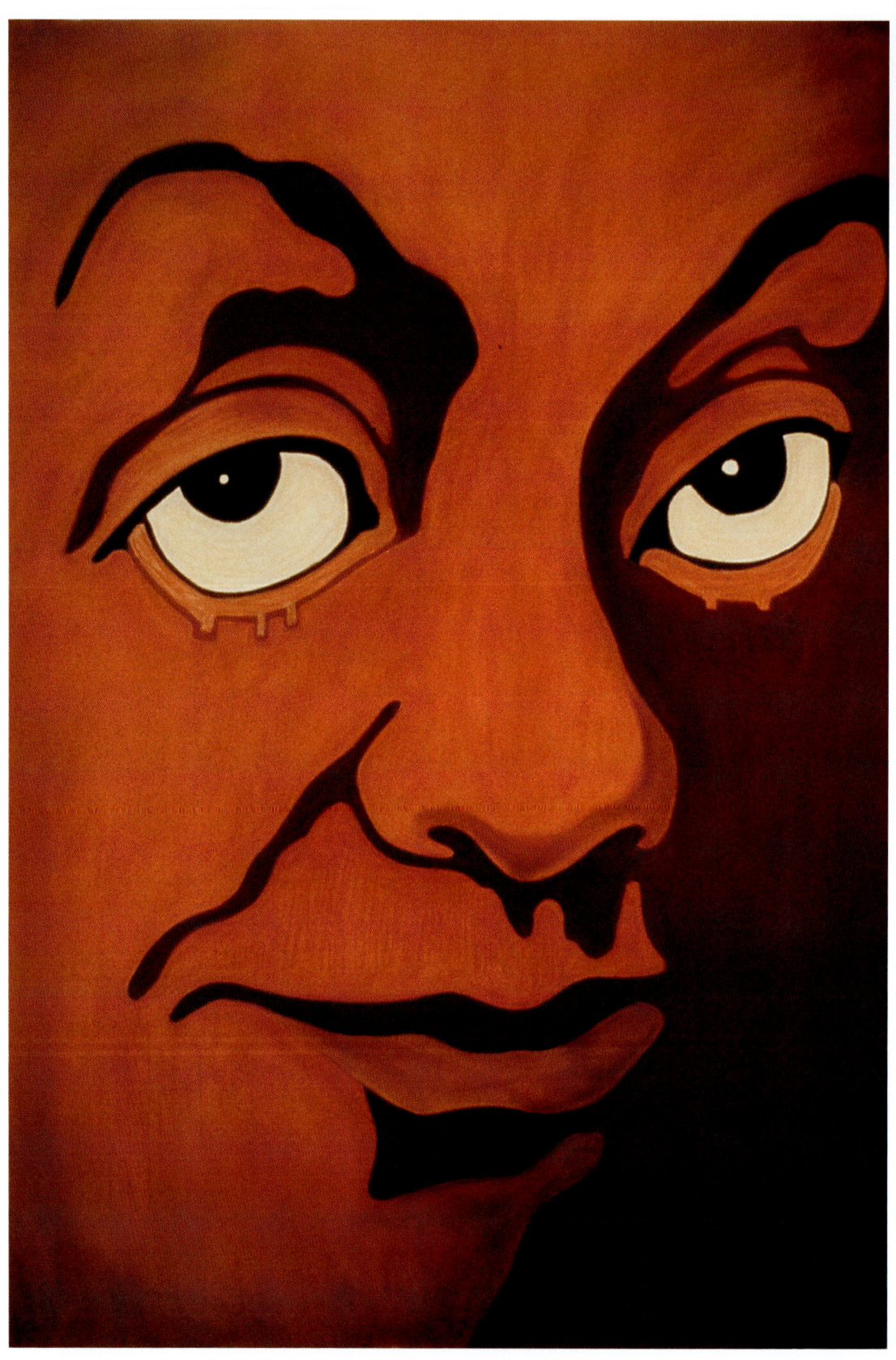

Diego Rivera, 1982. Pastel on paper, canvas size: 41-1/2 x 29-1/2 inches. Copyright ©
Rupert García. Courtesy of Rena Bransten Gallery.

TV with the faces right in front of me. Even going to church, I was impressed at looking at the face of Jesus and the different saints, including the Virgin Mary, depicted in paintings and statues. So, it's not as much of a surprise that I eventually painted faces, because they have always been very important to me; it's a kind of intimacy of face-to-face discussion and showing of warmth to someone whom I love, whom I admire. All of this influenced me to focus on portraits of different people. Thomas Albright, an art critic for the *San Francisco Chronicle*, referenced my portraits as political icons. I think that's true. They are images of people who were politically and socially engaged in a way that made sense to me and with whom I agreed. I have never done a homage to people who I think are reactionary or who are fascists or abusers of women and children. I would never do a portrait of Donald Trump.

▬▐▬

Some might raise the question about some of my portraits—"but Rupert this isn't Chicano art because there's nothing Chicano about this." My response is that not all Chicano art has to depict some kind of Chicano reality. There are different ways to represent this reality or realities. You can do it representationally; you can do it abstractly; you can do it nonobjectively. You don't have to do it in one way and it doesn't always have to depict certain icons. I've always felt this. I think it goes back to my childhood and how I was raised in Stockton. Being raised a

Mexican didn't preclude me from liking rhythm and blues, Mickey Mouse, Bugs Bunny, Daffy Duck. It didn't preclude me from liking peanut butter and jelly sandwiches. It didn't preclude me from liking Chinese food made by one of my best friend's mom. It didn't preclude me from a lot of things. So how in the hell is being a Chicano going to preclude me from all of these things? It can't and never did for me. Isolating what Chicano culture meant didn't make any sense to me. I understood why this had to be done in the Chicano Movement, even though this essentialism neglected the heterogeneity of Chicano culture.

Much of the art associated with the movement essentialized Chicano culture. I chose to be an artist who expressed the heterogeneity of Chicano culture. I didn't see doing Chicano art only one way. There were, in fact, all kinds of ways. I remember reading articles about how the representation of Chicano culture and art had to only be represented in one way. I found these articles to be suffocating. I couldn't breathe when I read these pieces, because it seemed to limit the imagination and intelligence. I have no interest in any "ism" that wishes to do that. I don't give a damn what the end is. If you're asking me to cut up my toes so I can meet what the end is, I have to ask you why do I have to cut off my toes? Why do I have to limit my imagination and intelligence for this goal that I may be in general agreement with such as the Chicano Movement but disagree with the means in part. Let's talk about the means. If there's no dialogue open, then I have to say goodbye or go around you or else ignore you. For me that was a healthy path. The same is true, for example, after World War II in the avant-garde art movement. Abstract expressionism was considered the "ism" of all "isms," and if you didn't make art that looked like abstract expressionism, then you weren't making meaningful art. You were making something else. That was a pretty domineering perspective, but it was held for a long time.

So, these kinds of "isms" happen in all movements, including social movements such as the Chicano Movement. Certain perspectives on Chicano art were too narrow. The fact was that even during the movement, there were all kinds of art being done that didn't necessarily fit this narrower view of what constituted Chicano art with its emphasis on indigenous symbols, genuflections to the Mexican Revolution, or barrio motifs. These other expressions of Chicano art, however, were just as genuinely Chicano art as any other. We have to reflect on this and become more accepting and tolerant of a variety of art that emanates from particular communities. We can't have a litmus test as to what is really Chicano or Latino art. My art has never bowed to any master narrative and it won't.

8

Fluorescence

The 1980s politically was a scary decade. It started with the election of Ronald Reagan. I felt threatened and scared by his election. People talked about the Reagan Revolution, but it was really the Reagan Counterrevolution. His unraveling of what had happened in the 1960s and into the 1970s worried me from the time he got in to the time he got out as president. Reagan had previously been governor of California and so I knew of his reactionary conduct and points of view. I also recalled the awful movies he did when he was an actor. I knew of his mediocre talent, and knowing that someone of his low level of creativity was president was troubling. It seemed to me that he was a shell whom others would manipulate. He would act—literally—as if he was doing things, but in reality, he was a puppet. I also felt threatened because I felt that he would get us into a war at any time. Everything he said seemed so absurd. I had little to no faith in his two terms. In retrospect, you could see where he was laying the foundation for the resurgence of a new rightwing conservatism in the country. He was giving voice to white supremacists composed of angry white men and women, but especially men who were angry, insecure, embittered, and frightened by the changing demographics of the country, including Blacks, Chicanos, Latinos, and Asian Americans. Does this sound like Trump? You better believe it. I think that Reagan laid the foundation for Trump and his reactionary followers.

━▮━

Reagan, unfortunately, did get us into a war. This was in Central America. It was a proxy war, but a war nevertheless. We didn't send military troops, but we sent a hell of a lot of military armaments to the Contras, who were supported by the CIA and the U.S. military in their counter-revolution against the Sandinistas, who had overthrown the dictatorship of the Somoza family in Nicaragua. Reagan considered the Sandinistas to be Communists and stooges for Fidel Castro in Cuba. At the same time, the Reagan administration was sending additional military support to prop up the reactionary government in El Salvador, which was repressing the people, including the use of Death Squads. I was against all of this stuff. It seemed so obvious what was going on. After having been a part of the U.S. war in Indochina where, like in Central America, the United States fought an undercover war in Thailand where I was based, I understood the nature of proxy wars. Hence, the intervention of the United States in Central America seemed to me just a repeat of what had happened in Vietnam. It's almost as if whatever the United States does, you know it's wrong. You don't even have to investigate; it's wrong! Of course, there's a long history of these kinds of interventions, including when the CIA directed the overthrow of the democratically elected president of Guatemala, Jacobo Arbenz, in 1954, or when again the CIA encouraged and assisted in the overthrow of Salvador Allende in Chile in 1973. If corporate America feels some kind of crunch in Latin America, or anywhere in the world for that matter, the United States will initiate covert operations. The American intervention in Central America came out of the same playbook.

I protested in marches and rallies against this intervention. Not as a member of any group, but by myself. I can't be a member of any group that has a point of view that if you have any difference with it, you'll be ostracized. At the same time, I'm not an anarchist. I think that the role of an intellectual in these kinds of circumstances is unique. I was and still am very much influenced by the thoughts of Edward Said about the role of intellectuals. Said wrote that the intellectual has to have in mind the betterment of humanity. And the work of the intellectual is to make sure that the sacredness of the human being is protected. You can strategically and tactfully take sides including joining a group, but in the end, you might have to criticize that group which is allegedly democratic but in fact is not democratic. You have to highlight that. So, the role of an intellectual is not to become popular or to be liked. It has nothing to do with that at all. You have to always possess a critical edge; you can't be compromised by one group or another. If you are compromised, you lose the role that Said defines as the role of the intellectual. I identified with this because as an artist, I'm also an intellectual. It's funny how people often distinguish between intellectuals and artists. This is a false binary. It's as if they're saying that an intellectual uses one side of the brain and an artist uses the other side. Nonsense! Artists are intellectuals.

Some of my work in the 1980s was influenced by what was happening in Central America. One good example is my pastel painting that I titled *The Horse in Man* that I did in 1985. This picture is of an individual who has been cut in half and separated to create three areas of space on the sheet of paper. In the center is a hobby horse which I borrowed from a photograph by Alvarez Bravo. Flanking the play horse on the left is the front portrait of a man and on the right side is the man's ear and the back of his head and the collar of his shirt. The man who I depicted is that of a Central American dissident who was beaten up by

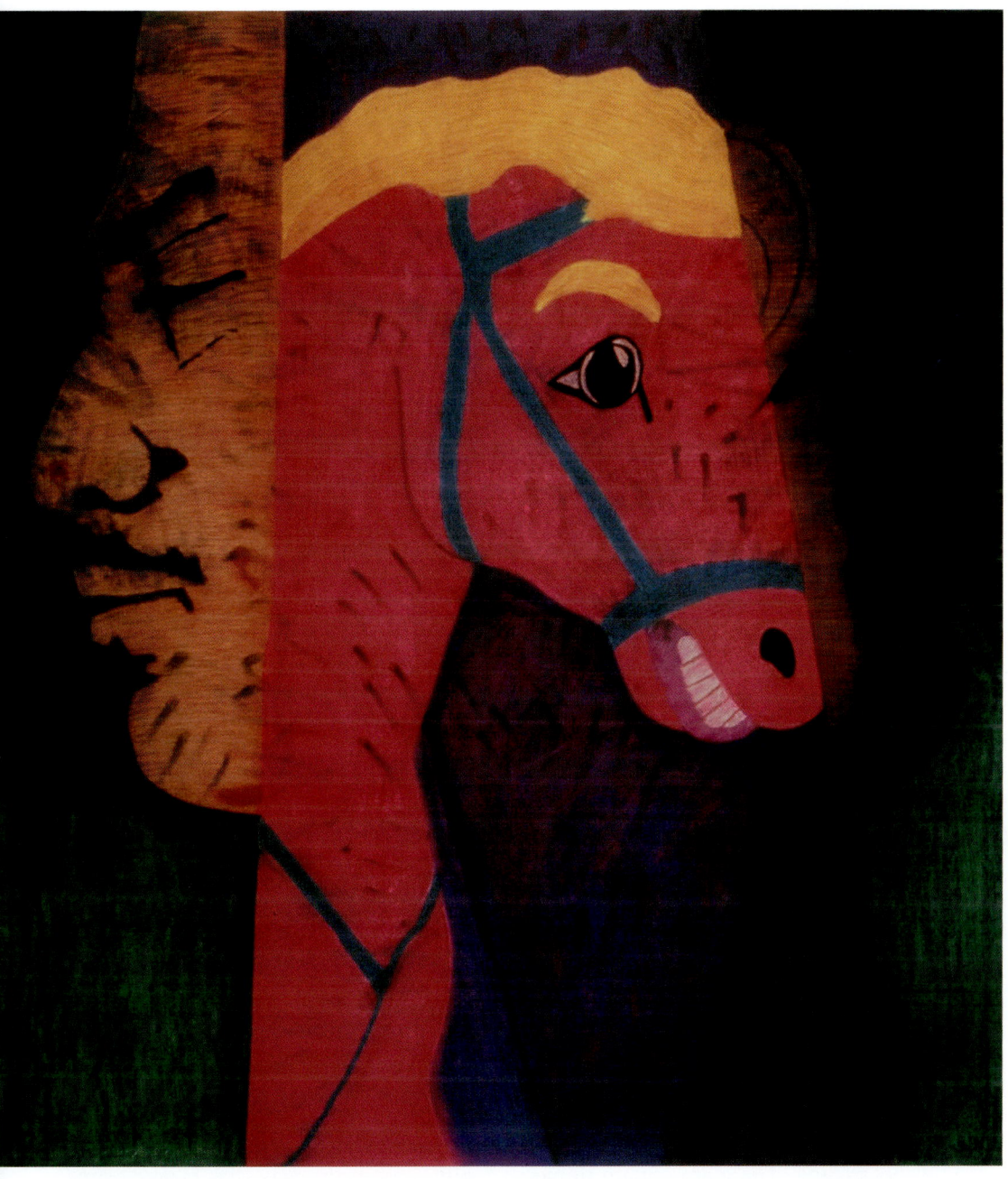

The Horse in Man, 1985. Pastel on paper, canvas size: 60 x 54 inches. Copyright ©
Rupert García. Courtesy of Rena Bransten Gallery.

soldiers because of his outward protest against army rule. I took the image of the man from a photograph, or it might have been a drawing in a publication from Guatemala, where the army ruled with vengeance against the people.

My image comes from that particular moment, but it also speaks of something that I strongly believe in which is the inherent goodness of human beings, even though it may seem ironic given the image of the persecuted man. Nevertheless, I believe there is an inherent goodness in human beings. I recognize that people can be led to the point of committing massacres or dropping an atomic bomb and killing millions of people. But these actions by some, I believe, is not necessarily innate in human beings. I believe that the overriding presence in all human beings is love and a sense of goodness. But I also recognize that we have a survival mechanism which can sometimes be manipulated by different kinds of societies and which can be channeled in ways that are abusive of others, as in the case of fascism and white supremacy. We are basically good, but we have to struggle against this survival instinct. What has been going on in American society is the interplay between these two opposite poles. Unfortunately, I believe the latter is winning to the point that we have, I believe, a perverse culture where it's difficult to distinguish between what's good and what's evil. We have to struggle to make sure that, as they say, our better angels prevail.

I loved my painting *The Horse in Man*. I had a great time doing it. It was simultaneously exhilarating and disheartening. There are certain things that we produce as intellectuals that we sometimes step back and admire and even think, "this is great! I can't believe I did it!" To some people they would think this guy is full of himself. But this has nothing to do with that, because it's possible to amaze oneself with one's own work. There's nothing

wrong with that. What's wrong? Many people think that this is self-indulgent, egotistical, and all that kind of nonsense. But it isn't because it's possible to fascinate oneself with one's work. It's magnificent no matter if you made it or someone else did. One's work isn't always magnificent. It may be very damn good, but it may not be magnificent. But then again, sometimes one's work is magnificent. I thought this about my *The Horse in Man*.

I also did a second painting in 1985 that related to Central America. I was asked by the film director and cinematographer Haskell Wexler to do the poster for his film *Latino* about a Chicano U.S. soldier sent to help train and organize the Contras in Nicaragua. I actually had known Haskell already for several years. His son, Jeff, was at San Francisco State when I was there, and we both participated in the strike. On one occasion when Jeff was back home in Hollywood with his family, he invited me to visit him. This was like in 1969. My then girlfriend, Liz, was from L.A., and on a trip there I arranged to visit Jeff who coincidently was home. I didn't know much about Jeff's father, although I was aware that he had filmed the movie *Who's Afraid of Virginia Wolf*. It's a great-looking film, and in the way that Haskell shot it, the camera seems to become another character in the film. In his career, he won several Academy Awards. He was also a very politically progressive person.

Haskell was a very nice man. I would get to see him several more times. One day, I foolishly asked him how he could make such politically committed films and yet live in this mansion in Hollywood. "Isn't there a problem with this?" I asked. I forget what his response was, but it definitely was not defensive. My question said more about me than him. Who was I to pontificate how anyone should live? This was ridiculous. The problem was me not Haskell. I was then caught up in that either/or binary of you're either for us or against us. And how can you be for us if you're living in this beautiful house which is contrary to those we wish to support and free? This was silly of me and very anti-intellectual and apolitical. But I didn't know this then.

Haskell didn't hold this against me. We actually engaged in some very serious discussions about art. But this discussion on his part did resonate with my stupid question. Haskell said that if he or I couldn't take another person seriously, how could we possibly take that person's work seriously? That strongly resonated with me. I had to pound my head on some bricks because it made absolute sense. If I ask stupid questions, how can anyone take me seriously? So, it begins with me taking myself seriously and maturing in my views of others and of the world. This was a very important moment for me. I use the Haskell Wexler anecdote with my students. You have to shape up and work on your mind and sense of self. You have to understand what you value and believe in it. You have to take a position and do the best you can. I love Haskell for his discussion with me on these issues.

Several years later around 1984, Haskell was making the film *Latino* which he financed, produced, and filmed. He and his team were in post-production work at the George Lucas film studios in San Rafael in Marin County. One of Haskell's actors, Peter Bonerz, had a party at his house and somehow invited me. Haskell was there and we started to talk.

"Rupert, how would you like to do the poster for my film?"

"I'd love to do it and it would be an honor."

I went to the studio and got to see some of the rushes of the film to acquaint myself with it. I also talked to the composer of the music for the film. I got a real inside view of filmmaking. It was very exciting. The film editor also showed some photos of the film. I went through them and selected one photo that appealed to me. It was of the nude backside of the main character, a Latino, a Special Forces guy who was from East L.A. He was changing to disguise his identity as a U.S. soldier. He was told that he needed to get rid of whatever he had that identified him as such. This included his dog tags, which contained personal information. It was this process of a Latino losing his identity as a U.S. mercenary that I wanted to capture in my poster. How can you be Latino when you are supporting a counterrevolution against other Latinos in Nicaragua? What does it mean to be Latino in this context? My poster is about the war in Central America, but it's also about an individual having a dialogue with himself about who he was and what

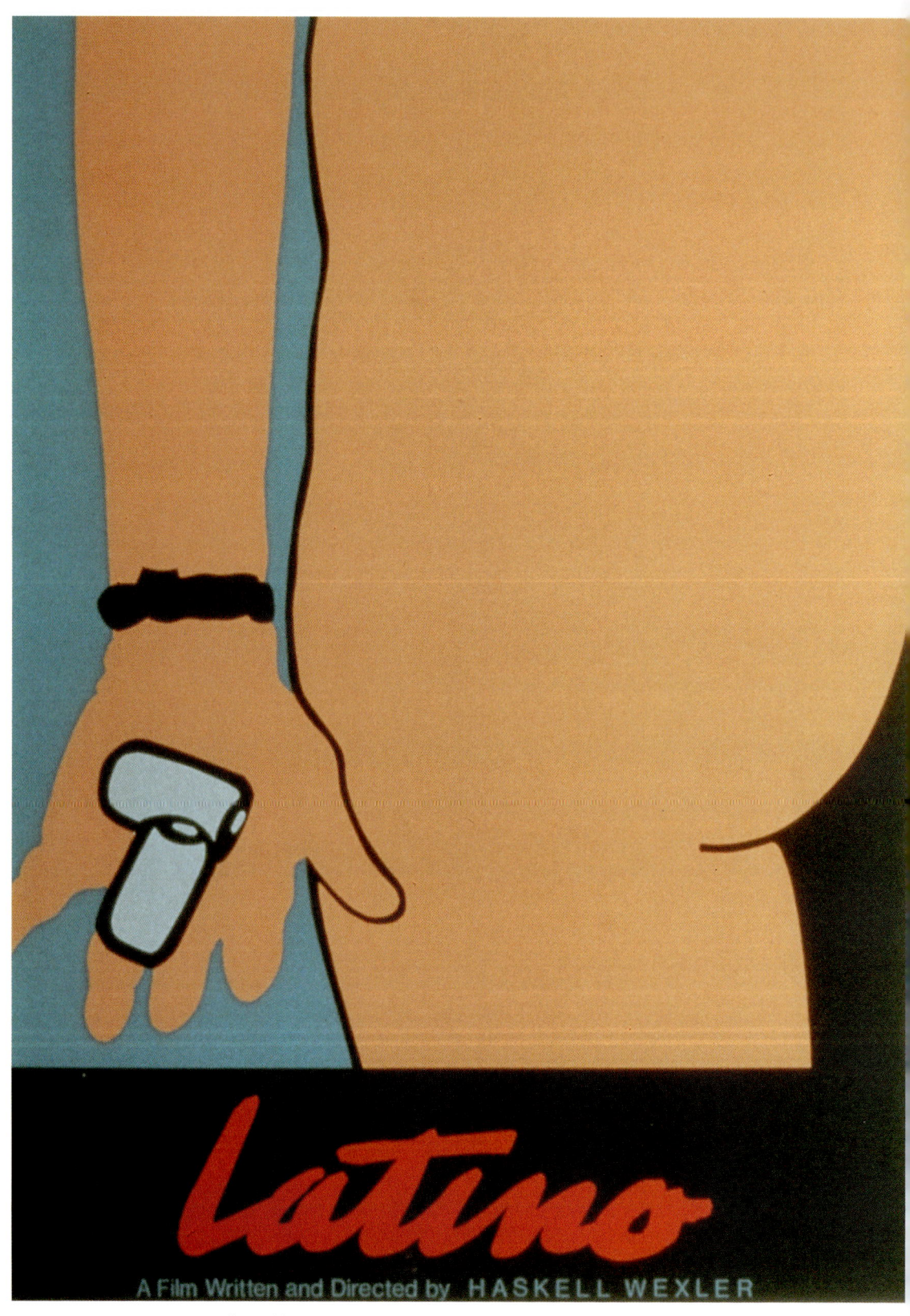

Latino, 1985. Color silkscreen on white wove paper, sheet size: 26 x 20 inches, image size: 25-3/8 x 19-1/4 inches. Copyright © Rupert García. Courtesy of Rena Bransten Gallery.

he was doing in Nicaragua. So, this is what I depicted in my silk-screen image. It shows the backside of the Latino soldier that I printed in a tan color, and it shows him holding his dog tags in his left hand but behind him so that it cannot be seen from the front. He's hiding his dog tags like he's hiding his identity as a Latino. At the bottom, I printed "Latino." This is the only film poster that I've ever done, and I'm indebted to Haskell Wexler for letting me do it. It was shown in many theatres throughout the country and in other countries as well.

■||■

In 1981, I watched a TV interview with a black South African on apartheid. For me, to even say a black South African is almost an oxymoron, but it was because of the domination of Blacks by white Europeans in South Africa. I had to distinguish by color. I knew something about apartheid, but listening to this interview enlightened me more and enraged me. This was just too much, this apartheid stuff. It's just obvious to anybody that it's wrong. You don't need a PhD to know this. I knew about Nelson Mandela, the leader of the anti-apartheid movement in South Africa and who had been unjustly imprisoned. I had read about him in *Tricontinental*, a publication in Cuba. I was so moved by the TV interview with this black South African who worked with the U.N. Center Against Apartheid. The Liberation Support Movement in the United States working against apartheid contacted me to produce a poster. I

proposed that I would do a poster with the image of Mandela to assist in their efforts. They agreed and requested that the wording in the poster be trilingual: English, French, and Spanish. This was because they hoped to distribute the poster around the world. They hoped to produce thousands of copies of my poster. I was delighted at their enthusiasm and support for my proposal. The Liberation Support Movement had some publications, and they let me use one of their photographs. I used this to do my image of Mandela. I wanted to focus on him because he represented a people who were struggling against fascism and white supremacy and a Eurocentric view of the world. This struggle registered with me. I printed the image of Mandela and included at the bottom the wording: "Free Nelson Mandela and All South African Prisoners." On the right side of the picture, I inserted the same wording in Spanish and French. I got some friends to help me with these two languages to make sure I didn't make any mistakes. It was an impressive-looking poster, and it received wide distribution. People thanked me for doing this and I appreciated this, but it had to be done and I did it. To be honest my ego was flattered when I was praised for the poster, but I didn't do it to be praised. I did it to support a fundamental human rights cause. I did this the best way I could through my art.

Rupert García:

Art plays many roles in the struggle. But art is not going to win; art and culture never overcome repression. People do that, but art

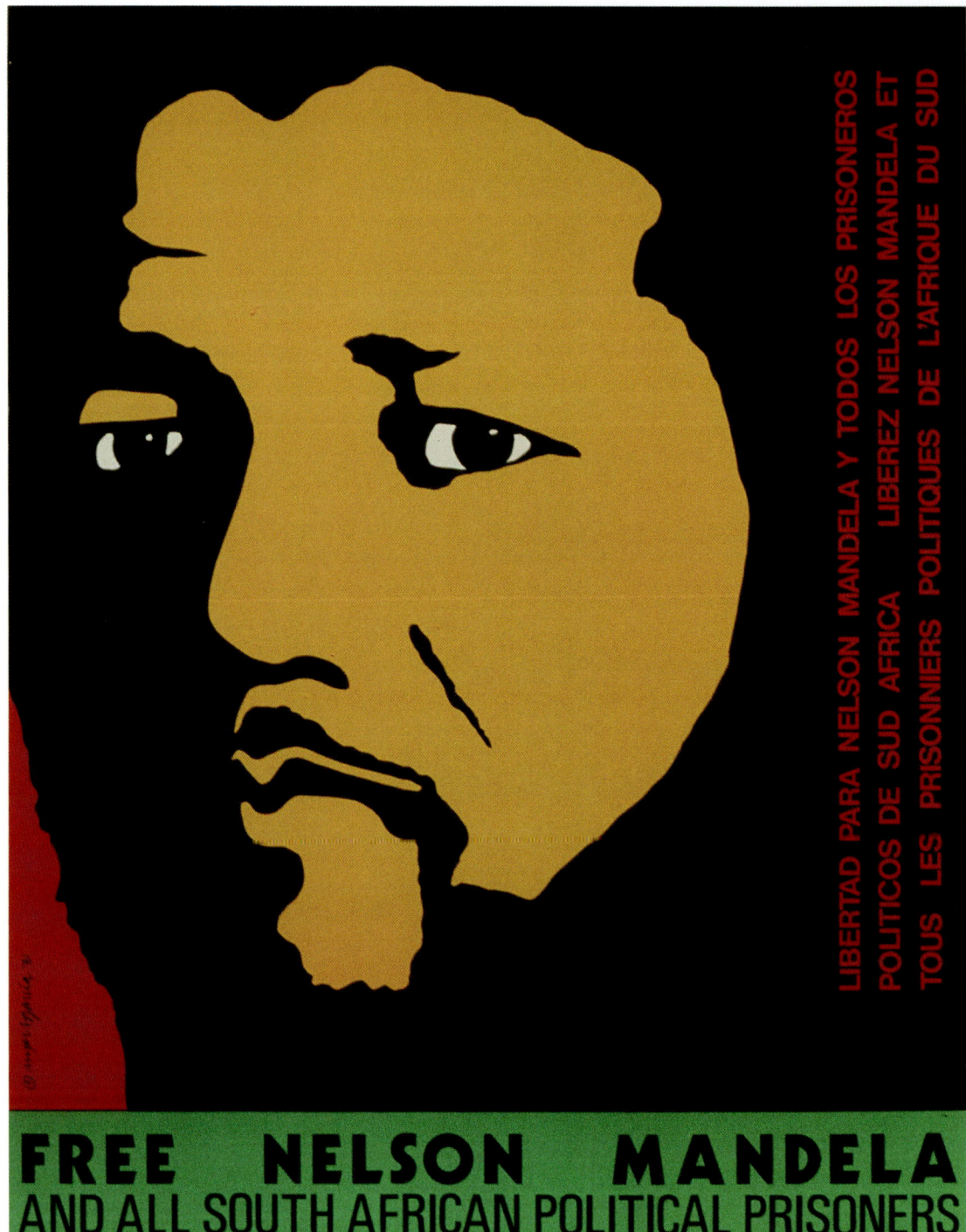

Free Nelson Mandela and All South African Political Prisoners, 1981. Color offset lithograph on white wove paper, sheet size: 22-1/2 x 17-1/2 inches, image size: 22-1/2 x 17-1/2 inches. Copyright © Rupert García. Courtesy of Rena Bransten Gallery.

can contribute and can be very helpful.[1]

■▮■

By the early 1980s, Chicano art was receiving more attention. Curiously, this seemed to be more the case in Mexico than in the United States. The first international exhibition of Chicano art occurred in Mexico, whereas there had yet not been a national exhibition in the United States on Chicano art. In Mexico, this had a lot to do with former President Luis Echeveria, who through his organization made concrete outreaches to Chicanos including artists. The result was the 1983 *A Traves de la Frontera* exhibit in Mexico City. He also organized an accompanying conference on Chicano art. I was very excited and honored to be part of the exhibit and also to be asked to contribute an essay for the catalog. My essay was on Chicano wall art. I wrote it in English and they translated it into Spanish. Unfortunately, I was not able to attend the opening of the exhibition. I contributed mostly some of my posters and one or two of my pastels. Other Chicano and Chicana artists also exhibited such as Yolanda López, Malaquias Montoya, Ester Hernández, Carlos Almaraz, Carmen Lomas Garza, Willie Herrón, Santa Barraza, and Gronk.

Although I couldn't attend, I heard that it was a beautiful exhibit. It was well-received by many except for those that I would describe as "fancy-pants intellectuals." These included those who didn't appreciate the Mexican presence in the United States and looked down on Chicanos. They expressed Eurocentric views and an elitist racism against Indigenous and mestizo people in Mexico and across the border. They had no interest in Chicano art or anything else related to Chicanos. It didn't matter to those who were openly political and artistically welcomed the exhibit.

While I didn't attend the exhibition, from what I knew of the art being displayed, I thought it was too narrow a perspective. It represented primarily Chicano Movement art and did it well, but it didn't show other artists not as closely associated with the movement or whose art was not directly related to it. The exhibit wasn't expanded sufficiently to consider the complex experiences of Chicanos. This problem wasn't unique to the Mexico City exhibit; it was also pervasive in the United States. Too many associated Chicano art as being the art of the Chicano Movement. It excluded many other non-movement artists who also needed to be recognized.

One of my paintings exhibited in the show was my *Assassination of a Striking Mexican Worker* which I had based on an Alvaro Bravo photograph. In fact, it was used as the cover of the catalog and the promotional poster. Unfortunately, this became controversial not because of the image, but because Alvarez Bravo, who had not seen the painting before, was led to mistakenly believe that I had not asked for permission to use his photo image. I heard that Don Manuel was very upset with me. This really hurt. The last thing in the world that I wanted

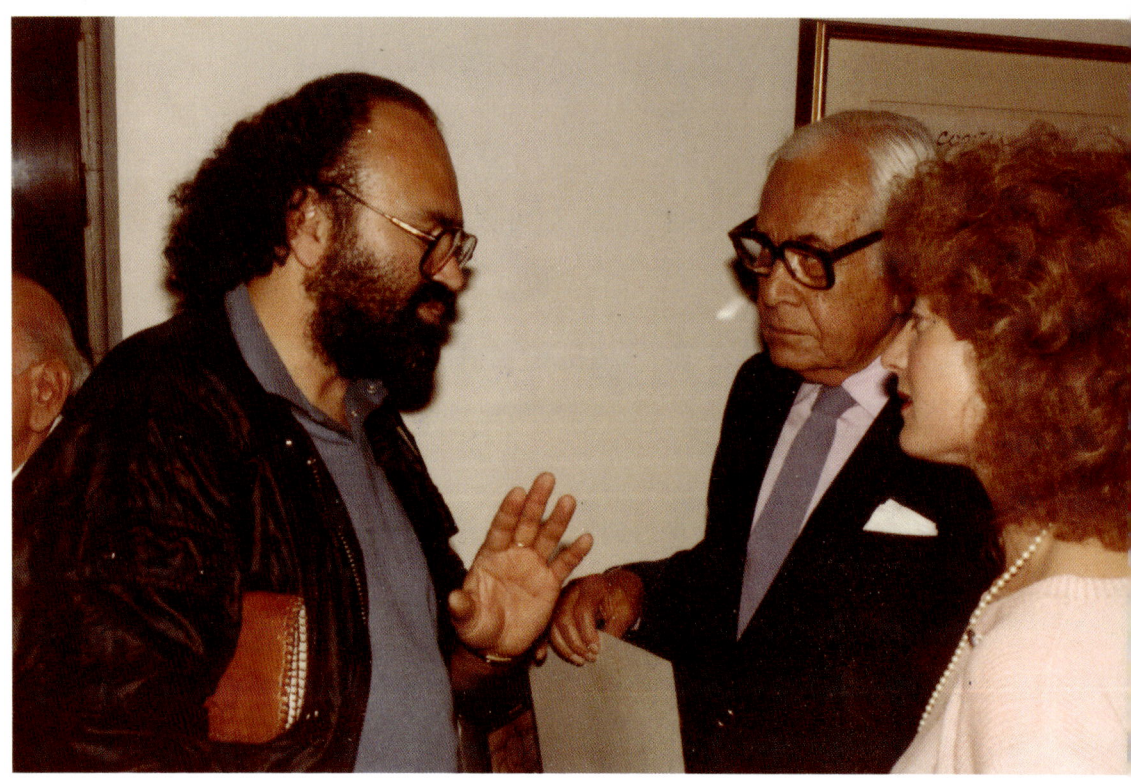

Rupert García and Rufino Tamayo, San Francisco, 1983. Photo courtesy of Rupert García.

was to make him angry with me. I had made this painting as an absolute homage to this great man. I felt really bad about this. Some years later, I was in Mexico and attended a big show of Alvaro Bravo's photos. I saw Don Manuel and tried to talk to him, but he was aloof with me. I took it to mean that he didn't want anything more to do with me. I was so crushed. Then, however, in 1990 when the Fine Arts Museum of San Francisco and the Centro Cultural/Arte Contemporáneo from Mexico organized an exhibition of my prints and posters from 1967 to 1990 in San Francisco, they included the Manuel Alvarez Bravo photo on which my pastel version was based to complement the exhibit of that particular painting. On the photo was a statement by Don Manuel in which he gave permission for this image to be used by other artists. He had obviously forgotten about this and had mistakenly assumed that I had no permission to use his image. But he was wrong. I didn't know this at the time I did my image, but knowing it later made me feel better that I had not betrayed Don Manuel and even though I never saw him again, I hoped that he had become aware of this mistake.

━╍━

Although I was now a "commercial artist" in that I was open to selling my work, I didn't belong to any gallery. This changed in the mid-80s when I joined the UPB Gallery as part of the University Press Books Bookstore in Berkeley on Bancroft right across from the U.C. campus. Adrian Fish, who had once been married to the literary scholar, Stanley Fish, who taught at Duke, ran the bookstore/gallery. I came to know her because my MA thesis advisor, Peter Selz, who had always been in the Rupert García corner, said to me that he wanted to introduce me to Adrian. He did and she expressed an interest in my work. We got along immediately very well and we became good friends. She offered to organize an exhibit of my paintings, and we did a couple of shows. I included my large pastels. This was the first time I had ever joined a gallery, and Adrian Fish came to represent me at least with respect to the shows I did in her gallery. She wasn't really an agent, but she would represent me with respect to anyone wanting to buy some of my work. I actually did sell a couple of paintings. My commercial relationship with Adrian only extended to these shows and not beyond. As far as my having an agent, I wasn't actively looking for one, and the fact was that nobody was running to beat down my doors from a commercial gallery.

I met Fred Banks, the president and CEO of the Harcourts Gallery in San Francisco, at what was called a Matrix show at the University Art Museum in Berkeley where my picture *The Assassination of a Striking Mexican Worker* was exhibited. Actually, the Matrix was an important venue for artists. I was really honored when I was asked to show my paintings for this display. Banks attended the opening and really liked my picture. He was very excited about it and right away said,

"I want to buy your picture; I want to buy it tonight. I also want to talk to you about being part of my gallery."

I was like "wow!" I couldn't believe this was happening. After talking more with Fred, I decided to take up his offer and join Harcourts Gallery. There was no problem leaving UPB because Adrian Fish knew that our arrangement was only temporary, and she couldn't promote my work the way Harcourts could. The contract with Harcourts was only for two years, and Fred said we would see how things were in that period of time. Harcourts was my first major engagement with the world of galleries. Harcourts was not one of the top galleries in San Francisco; it was more of a middling one. Still, I felt great about being represented by an important gallery in the city. I did sell my painting to Fred, who later donated it to the Mexican Museum in San Francisco.

What I really appreciated from Fred is that he very soon arranged for me to have a showing at the gallery in September 1985. It also came with a full-fledged catalog that Peter Selz wrote the introduction for. I was very appreciative of Peter agreeing to do this for me and for the catalog. I appreciated Fred's sponsorship, which might have led to fame and fortune, but I wasn't necessarily interested in this. If fame and riches came along, hey, that was great. But it wasn't the carrot that

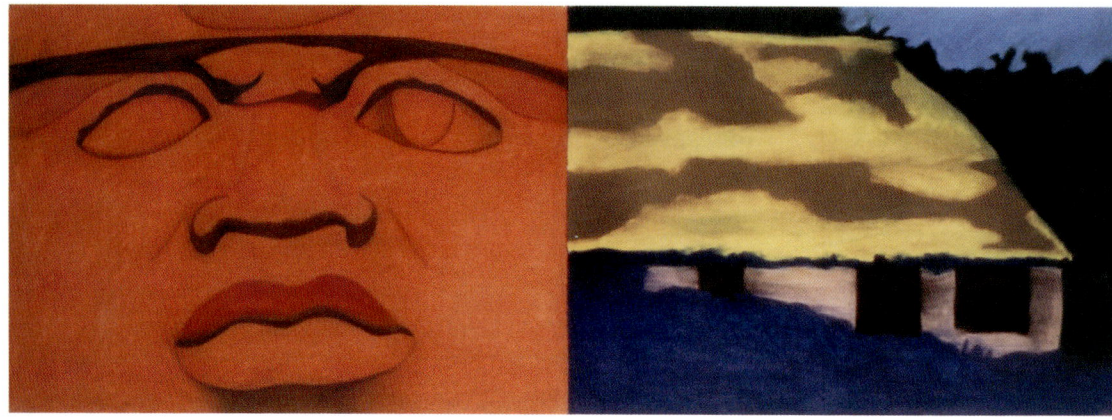

Raices, 1984. Pastel on paper, canvas size: 26-1/8 x 80 inches. Copyright © Rupert García. Collection of the Hood Museum, Dartmouth College, NH. Courtesy of Rena Bransten Gallery.

drove this horse. I don't paint to sell paintings. I paint because that's who I am—an artist.

At my exhibit, I selected fifteen of my large pastels to be shown. They were all historically based and were from photographs or references to images that were photographed. None of my paintings were done for the show. I don't do art for showings. I do art and then I along with the gallery select those to be exhibited. The show was very well received and got some positive reviews.

One of the paintings exhibited I titled *Raices* or roots. It links the Indigenous past with the Mexican Revolution of 1910. This is an expression of my connection to something that makes sense of who I am. It's not all of who I am but a part of it. One is the ancient people of the Americas, in this case the Olmecs, and so on the left side of the painting is an Olmec head. Then linked to the Mexican Revolution is the figure of Zapata and his political

ideas and concerns for social change that I hold dearly, and so on the right is my rendition of Zapata's house.

This is a superficial rendering of these images, but it's more complex. As for the Olmec head, which is very African in appearance, I've always been interested in anti-Black racism in Mexico and the lack of discussion of a link with Africa. I've always found this problematic not only with respect to Mexico, but also based on my own childhood experience in Stockton, where there were fights between Mexicans and African Americans. I never understood why we were fighting each other.

I chose the cover for the catalog. It's my image called *For Caravaggio and the ALB*. It's based on a famous photograph *The Falling Soldier* by Robert Capa of a Spanish Republican soldier who was shot during the Spanish Civil War of the 1930s. I always liked the photograph a lot. It's a very dramatic one in black and white. I did my version in color and coupled

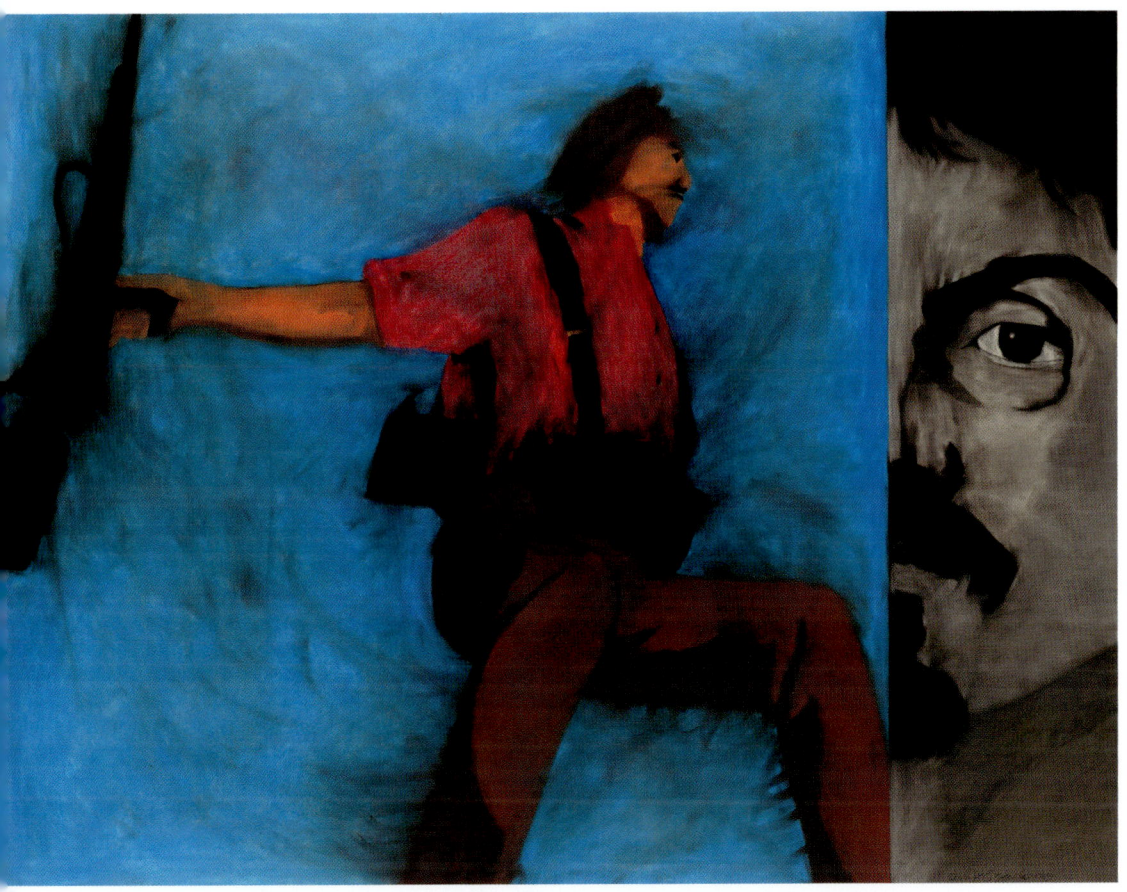

For Caravaggio and the A.L.B., 1985. Pastel on paper, canvas size: 48-1/2 x 63 inches. Copyright © Rupert García. Courtesy of Rena Bransten Gallery.

it with an image of Caravaggio, the Italian painter of the seventeenth century who revolutionized painting in content and style. He painted mainly religious iconography, Catholic, such as of Jesus and the saints. But it's the way that he painted them that is fascinating. Instead of choosing people who appear otherworldly, he picked everyday people such as peasants with dirty muddy feet and dirty clothes to represent Christian figures as well as Christian events such as the Annunciation. His Christians are not all clean and shiny like most religious paintings

are. He did not idealize the poor but painted them as they were. He gave his figures a sense of gravity, of real space and time linked to their period. He also gave a sense of dimension that also was of our time. His figures appear three dimensional and like his images are coming out of the painting, which connects with us today. I appreciated his concern with the populace as in the photo by Capa which depicted the Spanish civil war. I didn't learn about Caravaggio in my art history classes but on my own. I liked his paintings and read up on him. So, the convergence of the two made total sense in my mind's eye to juxtapose Caravaggio who favored the poor and dispossessed along with the symbol of an attempt to change society for the better, which is the Capa image. In both images, it's my response to both Capa and Caravaggio. The ALB which I include in the title is my homage to the Abraham Lincoln Brigade composed of Americans who went to fight in support of the Spanish Republicans against the fascist forces of Francisco Franco. They were fighting for freedom too.

Another of the paintings in the exhibit which was particularly meaningful to me, although all of my images are meaningful or otherwise I wouldn't have done them, is my *La Virgen y Yo*. I associate the Virgin of Guadalupe with my maternal grandmother whose name was also Guadalupe. As mentioned earlier, I always loved the image of La Virgen more than that of Jesus Christ. I used to get confused when I was younger when I thought that my grandma was La Virgen. My grandma was a wonderful person. She always had an image of Guadalupe at home. I later realized that I had to do my own painting of La Virgen. However, I couldn't just reproduce the image based upon the story of the miraculous appearance of La Virgen to the Indigenous Juan Diego in 1531. I had a long battle with organized religion, in particular Catholicism. I knew that if I was going to make a picture of Guadalupe it couldn't be straight; it had to be full of problematic concerns, both pictorially and conceptionally. I first decided

to it as a diptych. I chose to only use part of the traditional image and so I truncated her, only showing her from the waist up, and I also changed the traditional colors of the image a bit. I painted in a necklace around her neck that is not in the original. This necklace is connected to the Aztec earth goddess Tonántzin. Many of the Indigenous believed that Guadalupe was Tonántzin. On the other side of my image is a long and thick black shape that is supposed to be me! That's me all messed up and hanging by my ankles from who knows what and swinging around and being made topsy-turvy by organized religion.

I guess I was the among the early Chicano artists to reinterpret La Virgen, although my image still sticks close to the original one. Other artists have also done this. In fact, over the years, the image of Guadalupe has become kind of a commercial icon from t-shirts to key chains. The commodification of the image is almost to the point of the denial of the profound spirituality therein. My picture has nothing to do with denying the majesty and spirituality of what Guadalupe represents. I'm not out to destroy it at all.

Patrick Burnson, *People's World*, September 21, 1985, 10:

> The staid, well-appointed and rather hallowed wall of San Francisco's Harcourts Gallery seems at first glance to be an unlikely place to find the canvases of Rupert García. But when one considers it carefully the venue is an entirely appropriate locale to showcase

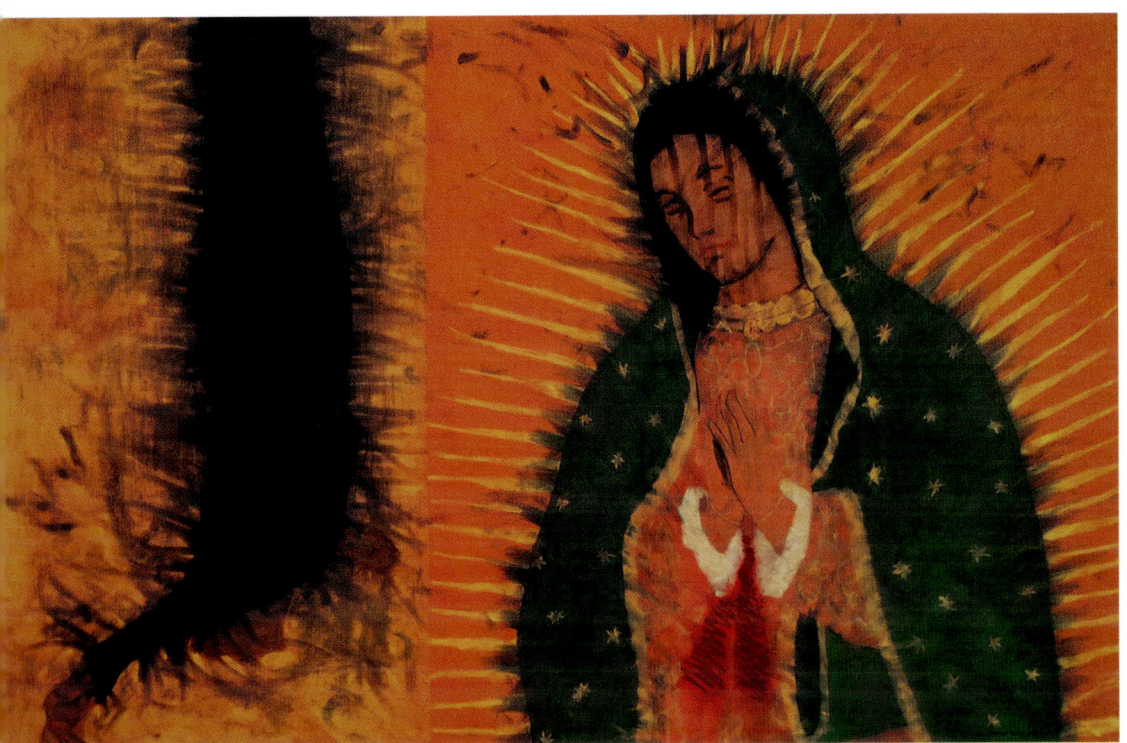

La Virgen y Yo, 1984. Pastel on paper, canvas size: 48 x 72 inches. Copyright © Rupert García.

the work of a man who so reveres tradition and history. What makes this exhibition such a radical departure, however, is the fact that García's paintings and pastels pay homage to Hispanic culture while addressing contemporary Latino issues.

Another artist who has revised the traditional image is Yolanda López. I think it's great how she shows Guadalupe as a runner and as her grandmother. It represents a feminist critique of the Virgin as a symbol of the power of womanhood. I think that Yolanda's paintings are among the most interesting ever done on La Virgen because they're very complex. She personalizes it, extends it to her family, but always

connects it simultaneously with the past and the present and doing so in a way that seems to be necessary for her. Yolanda's work has many layers of meaning, not just one. I don't think it can easily be reduced to a Chicana feminist picture. It's that but also more. If it was just a Chicana feminist image, then it would be just a common piece of art and very boring. But, it's not very boring.

Yolanda's depictions of La Virgen were criticized by some critics as being anti-Catholic and sacrilegious. I don't agree because this begs the question about sacredness and that sacred images such as La Virgen transcend historical time and because of their purity you can't mess with them. I don't know if I accept this because if it's true, then there's so much out there that artists can't work with. I will say that there are some images of religious figures that are done in a way which I find problematic, but I don't think I can stand up and say that artists can't depict such images in a different way. At the same time, I do think that artists have to approach something like La Virgen within the complexity of making a picture with some sense of responsibility. It's a fine line.

Yolanda and I are contemporaries but we didn't know each other personally. We knew of each other and we would see each other at events and we were always cordial to one another. It wasn't until later when she became quite sick that I visited her.

Still another revised image of Guadalupe is one done by Ester Hernández, who depicts the Virgen as a karate figure. I love that piece. If you look at it, Ester is not negating the Virgen, but empowering her. Both Ester and Yolanda use the image of Guadalupe in incredible kinds of ways, and only they can do it in those ways. I think that they're using a religious image to empower themselves, Chicanas, and women in general and male Chicanos too for that matter. Now there are some who will see these revisions, including my own, as being sacrilegious. They believe that you're making profane that which is sacred. They see it as a sin. They see the image of La Virgen as a pictorial prayer and so to "disfigure" it is to commit a pictorial sin. It's one of those either/or situations, but I and many other Chicanos, men and women, don't buy into that either/or kind of thinking. Art is a lot of things and one can't control who is going to perceive something as sacrilegious or not. At the same time, the artist has to be held responsible for what they do. The artist cannot be overly self-censored because the role of the artist/intellectual is many and among them is to be inside and outside the society at the same time, to go back and forth and not to remain static. In this case, artists like Yolanda, Ester, and I have to be concerned about sacred images but not trapped by them.

The performance artist/writer Guillermo Gómez-Peña did an interview with me some years ago, and in it he refers to the fact that he sees much spirituality in my work. My response to this is that I have always felt since I was a little boy the importance of just being alive. I have appreciated the wonderment of being able to feel, to think, to listen, to taste, to smell, to touch, and to move through space and time. I've always had that kind of connection with existence that seems to be profound and wondrous. I have fought like hell to maintain this to this very day. It's the joy of life which is combined with ups and downs. It's not either/or. It's a combination of the two. So, it's the spirituality of that kind which I bring to my work. That's why I try to imbue my subjects with a sense of hope, of beauty, and of purpose in life. My use of colors in a way are part of the spirituality of my paintings. They represent a spirituality which is a profound life force, which to me is inherently good.

Since I was a little boy, I've been taken by the vitality of color—orange, reds, yellows, and sometime the juxtaposition of orange colors against blue colors, and sometimes real dark colors against bright colors. There's a sense of life there in these colors. As a kid, I liked to wear shirts that were colorful. I didn't know why I did, but I just liked the colors. I loved the colors at *jamaicas* and other festivals as well as at birthday parties where you hit the colorful piñata and all of the colorful lights. It was fantastic! It made me feel alive and involved in the moment. And seeing the Ballet Folkloricos with the colorful wardrobes was amazing. Spirituality is involved here because of the sense of excitement of being alive and the wonderment of the world around us—the stars, nighttime, daytime, to me that can be a high level of spiritual experience not coming from the Bible or any religious readings. Things in themselves are just really exciting, and color really captures that excitement.

━ǁ━

In 1985 I was fortunate enough to receive a three-year artist-in-residence award from the California Arts Council. This was very important to me because it paid me a nice salary. I had been earning a living by teaching part-time in different colleges and universities in the Bay Area. Now this fellowship paid me a full salary. It helped me and my wife survive economically. So, the award was crucial, no question about it. It helped us plan our life better.

The stipulations of the award were that I needed to be sponsored by a nonprofit art institution. In my case, I chose the Mexican Museum, which provided me space to teach classes in pastel painting. During these three years the museum moved to Fort Mason where it acquired greater space. I had great students. It was a really good three years. Under the award, I didn't do any of my own paintings at the museum. I just taught my classes. I never do my work where I teach. I never do that because it's not about me. It's about the students. I also never talk with the students about my own work. I shy away from this because if an instructor talks about his or her work, it can be intimidating for the students because they worry that they can't come up to my standards or live up to my expectations. It can be debilitating to the students. I will talk about my work with graduate or advanced students, but not undergrads.

It was during my fellowship when I did my image of Vincent Chin. This was in 1986. It was based on a brutal incident of racial violence in 1982 in the Detroit area against a young Chinese American man by some white autoworkers who blamed their hard times on the success of the Japanese auto industry. They thought that Chin was Japanese. They beat him to death with a baseball bat. I read about it and later saw a documentary on it, which really pissed me off. The documentary was very profound. The incident scared the hell out of me. It really scared me that there were and are people who are racists who will reduce someone to a nonbeing and allow them to beat

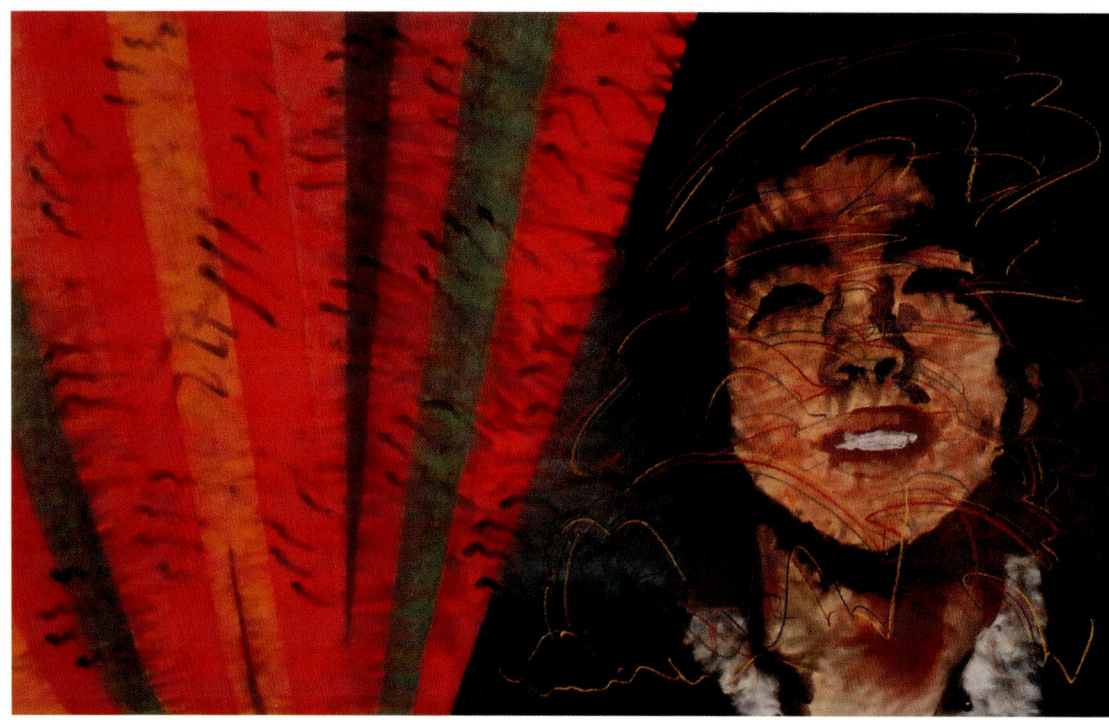

For Victor Chin, 1986. Pastel on paper, canvas size: 43-3/4 x 72 inches. Copyright © Rupert García.

the shit out of him and kill him. It's unbelievable. I personally identified with this situation. Man, I've been in a few of these things although not as bad, but it still scares the hell out of you. I felt that I had to do something about the killing of Vincent Chin. This is Emmett Till from the 1950s all over again, which really depressed me then as a young man. But now, I felt that I shouldn't feel helpless about this killing. I had to make a picture of it and in this way express my love for Vincent and his family. I wanted to make the image hopeful to maintain a certain spirituality about hope and that Vincent didn't die in vain. I wanted to respect him as a human being. I got a leaflet from a protest in San Francisco about the killing and it had Vincent's

photo. On the day that I was working on the picture, I had a book on Mexico open that was upside down. I looked at it and it was a picture about a Mexican blanket with these beautiful striped colors, and so I painted these on one side of my picture. But I also felt that I needed to integrate the bat that killed Vincent within these stripes, which I did. I married the colorful stripes with the bat. Using the photo of Vincent, I painted him with a wonderful smile and seeming to look upward. There is a sense of hope on his face and of the future. It was a senseless killing of a young man with his whole future ahead of him. I wanted to give him back his future. The picture exudes energy and joy. I titled my pastel *For Victor Chin*.

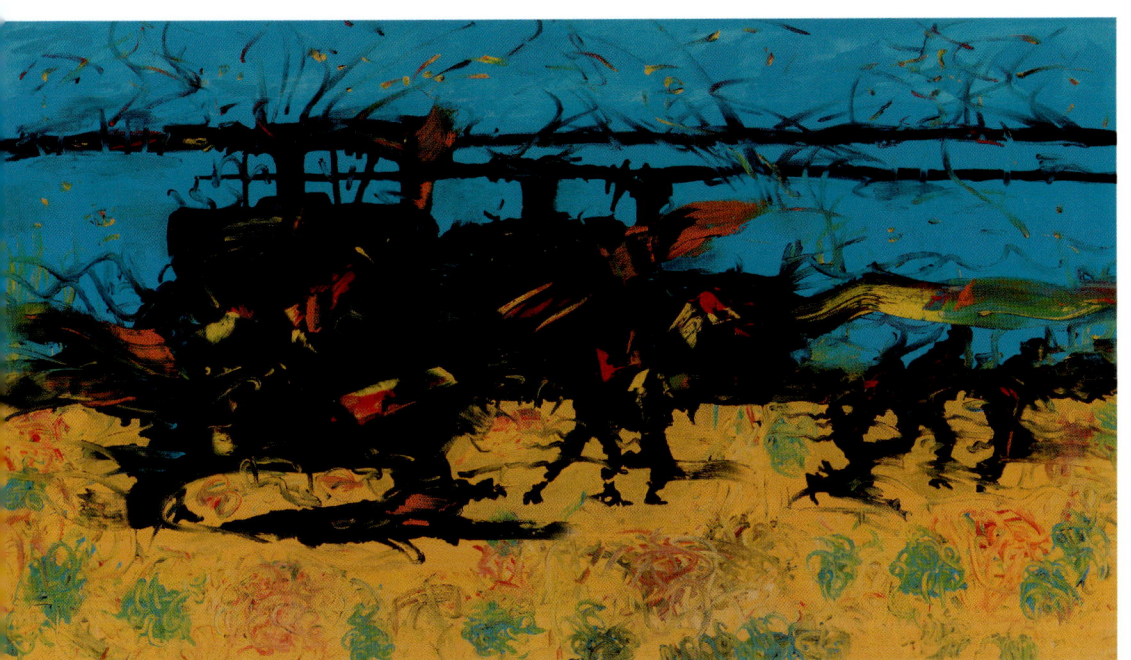

Goliath over David or the U.S. Invasion of Grenada, 1987. Chalk, linseed oil, & oil paint on cotton canvas, canvas size: 49-1/4 x 90 inches. Copyright © Rupert García. Courtesy of Rena Bransten Gallery.

In the 1980s, the issue of Central America was a hot-button issue. The civil war in El Salvador, for example, led to thousands of refugees attempting to find safe haven in the United States. Unfortunately, the Reagan administration rejected them and falsely claimed that they were "illegal aliens" who needed to be deported back to El Salvador. Nevertheless, many entered without papers. While the government rejected them, many good Americans embraced them in what came to be called the sanctuary movement. Led by religious groups, they reached out to the refugees and attempted to help them in any way possible, such as providing food, shelter, clothing, medical assistance, and legal support. In addition, Reagan ordered an invasion of the Caribbean country of Grenada in 1987, claiming that pro-Soviet forces had seized the government and needed to be overthrown, which was done. Moreover, in 1989 under the new George H. W. Bush administration, the United States invaded and overthrew the government of Panama which the United States claimed was led by drug dealers. Still, it was a violation of international law and recalled earlier U.S. military interventions in Central America.

Although I was not an activist in the Central American protest groups in support of the refugees, against the U.S. efforts to overthrow the Sandinistas, or in protest against the Grenada and Panama invasions, I supported them and used my art to express this. I painted a picture showing U.S. soldiers and helicopters invading Grenada. I entitled it *Goliath over David or the U.S. Invasion of Grenada.*

Two years later, I did a silk screen about the Panama invasion that showed attack helicopters as part of the scene. I printed the helicopters in black with a dark background. At the top of the poster I painted in bold red letters *¡Fuera de Panama!* This latter picture I did for the group CISPES (Committee in Solidarity with the People of El Salvador) and the Nicaraguan Information Center. I completely rejected what the United States was doing in Central America and in the Caribbean and was glad that my art could help in the protest efforts.

In doing these pictures, I can reflect that the body of work in various ways is connected to a lot of issues. Sometimes it is blatantly clear as in these two posters, but sometimes the images are not as clear and sometimes the allusion is a bit askew to some, although I don't care. For me it's not askew. Sometimes it is more readable for the viewer. However, I'm not doing it to be that way for the viewer. It is true that in my earlier work from the sixties and seventies, the images seemed to be more obviously a representation and connected to certain kinds of issues. Later, however, into my pastel period, that kind of pictorial representation started to change because I started to change. Different kinds of needs were being fulfilled, which hopefully is the case with all human beings. Being static to me is really problematic.[2]

John Zarobell:

> García's work is fundamentally concerned with raising consciousness, but he rarely approaches this in an overt way.[3]

It was during my residence at the Mexican Museum that the museum organized a retrospective of my work in 1986 titled *The Art of Rupert García.* It was just wonderful! It was wonderful for a lot of reasons. First of all, the museum was founded in 1975 by someone whom I had known since I was a child in Stockton, Peter Rodríguez. He and his family were friends of my family. I used to see him when he worked at a local clothing store and gallery. He was among the first artists that I knew. Of course, my mother was an artist in her own way as well. Knowing Peter and his history with the Mexican Museum made this retrospective of my work very special. What was also special was that the retrospective would cover the first seventeen years of my work as an artist. Not all of my work would be exhibited but enough to show people the trajectory of it. Finally, it was also special because as part of the show, the museum published a beautiful catalog with an insightful essay by Dr. Ramón Favela, who at that time had just been hired as an assistant professor of Chicano Studies and art history at UC Santa Barbara. Ramón was also the curator of the exhibit, and he did a great job in both capacities.

I was overwhelmed when I saw the exhibit before it opened to the public. The installation of the show looked unbelievably beautiful. I walked in and it looked like a jewel. The lighting was special and the way they organized my paintings was incredible. I was so elated. I just felt great. I couldn't believe it! It was the first retrospective of my career.

When I saw my work in different mediums, I never thought, gee, I might have done something differently or better. I don't look back on my work and think of how I could have changed it. What was important to me about the retrospective was that it represented a record—a historical record—of my work. It was like an archive. It showed seventeen years of my using my mind and imagination. I was overwhelmed approaching it this way and felt very honored by what the Mexican Museum had done. If anything, while looking at my paintings I wished I had done even larger ones to really fill the space of the exhibit. Of course, my paintings over the years have become bigger. Personally, bigger is better. This sense of bigness comes from two influences. One is the big motion picture screens that I saw as a kid. Second, I'd always been impressed by the vastness of the sky, beginning when I was a kid in Stockton. The sky was amazing, overwhelming, and just beautiful. It would be simultaneously infinite and then it would appear to be a flat sheet of blue. My mind wondered forever looking at this dual glass ceiling. That was a wonderful thing to experience as a kid. It was great.

I didn't select the paintings by myself for the retrospective. I did this with Favela as the curator. Some things I wanted to have in and he didn't agree. We would talk about it. As the curator, Ramón had the final word, but he did consult with me. I had no problem with this because the curator should have the final decision because sometimes the artist can't see the forest for the trees. For the artist, including myself, every piece is fabulous. If left up to me, I would have included all of my work and completely filled the museum and more.

The retrospective included a few that I had done in the late 1960s. One which I have not commented on is titled *Unfinished Man*. Ramón Favela got it right when he wrote about the image in the catalog:

> This seventeen-year survey exhibition begins with a rare acrylic painting title *Unfinished Man* (1968). The painting was done two years after the artist's return from military service in Indochina and during his art studies at San Francisco State. According to the artist, the source for the image was a photographic reproduction of an unknown black man, a newspaper clipping, one of many from the artist's growing "picture morgue." Placed starkly against a thinly painted field of evanescent sky blue, the man's head, mouth half-open in the pain-ridden gesture of an impending scream, has been dramatically and radically cropped. To the question "In what way is the man unfinished?" García responded: "Well, the condition of racism made it [in 1968], makes it today, still, very difficult for black people and other oppressed people to feel complete, to fulfill their

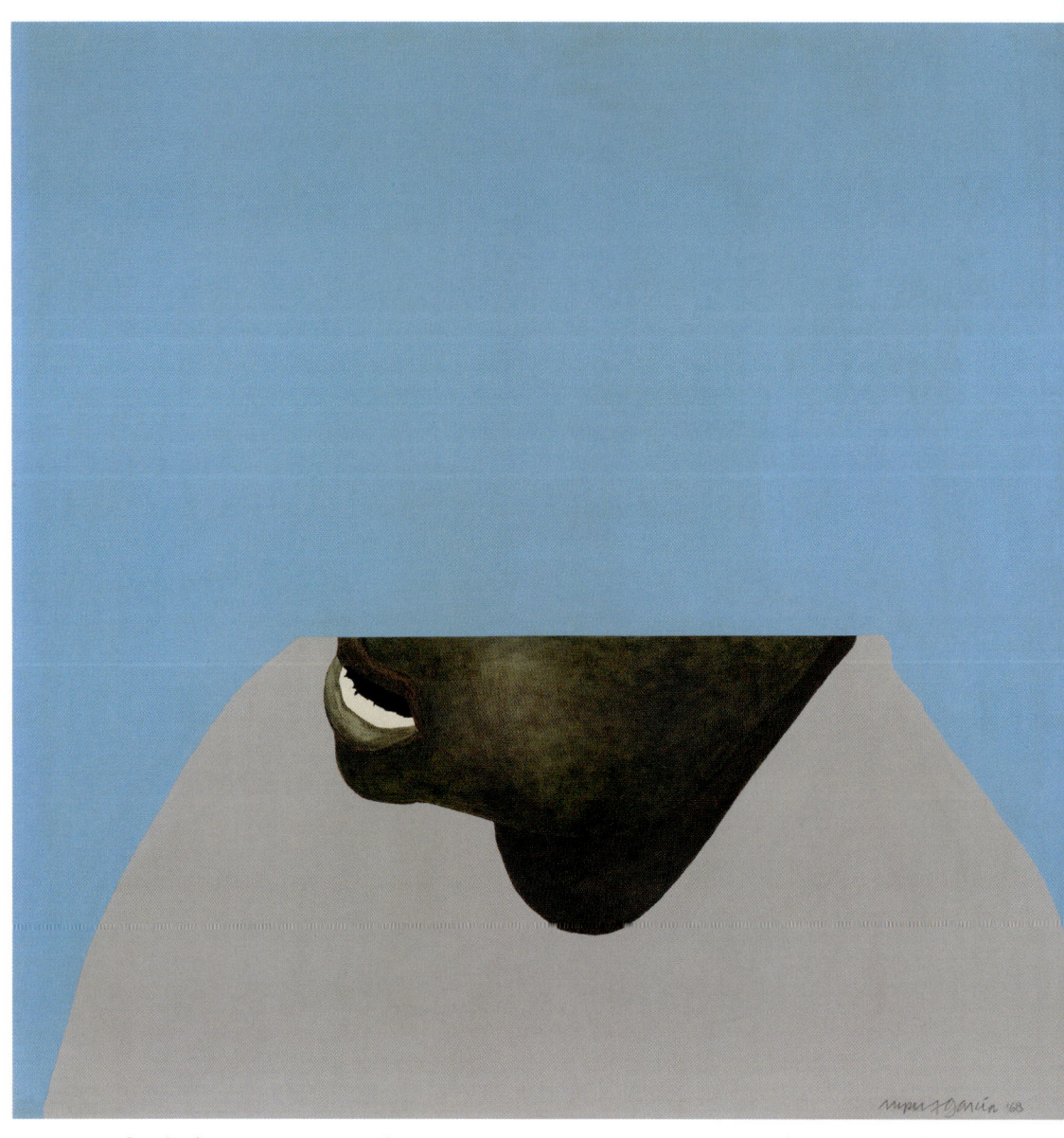

Unfinished Man, 1968. Acrylic on canvas, canvas size: 48 x 48 inches. Copyright ©
Rupert García. Collection of the Museum of Modern Art, New York, NY. Courtesy
of Rena Bransten Gallery.

human potential. That's what the
picture is about, a human "unfin-
ishedness" that has been imposed.[4]

In 2004, The Museum of Modern Art
in New York added this painting to its
permanent collection.

Some of my other pictures in the
exhibit included my images of Che
Guevara, Zapata, Ruben Salazar, An-
gela Davis, Orozco, Picasso, Siqueiros,
Frida Kahlo, Inez García, Mao, the
Magón brothers, and Diego Rivera.
The non-portraits included *Down*

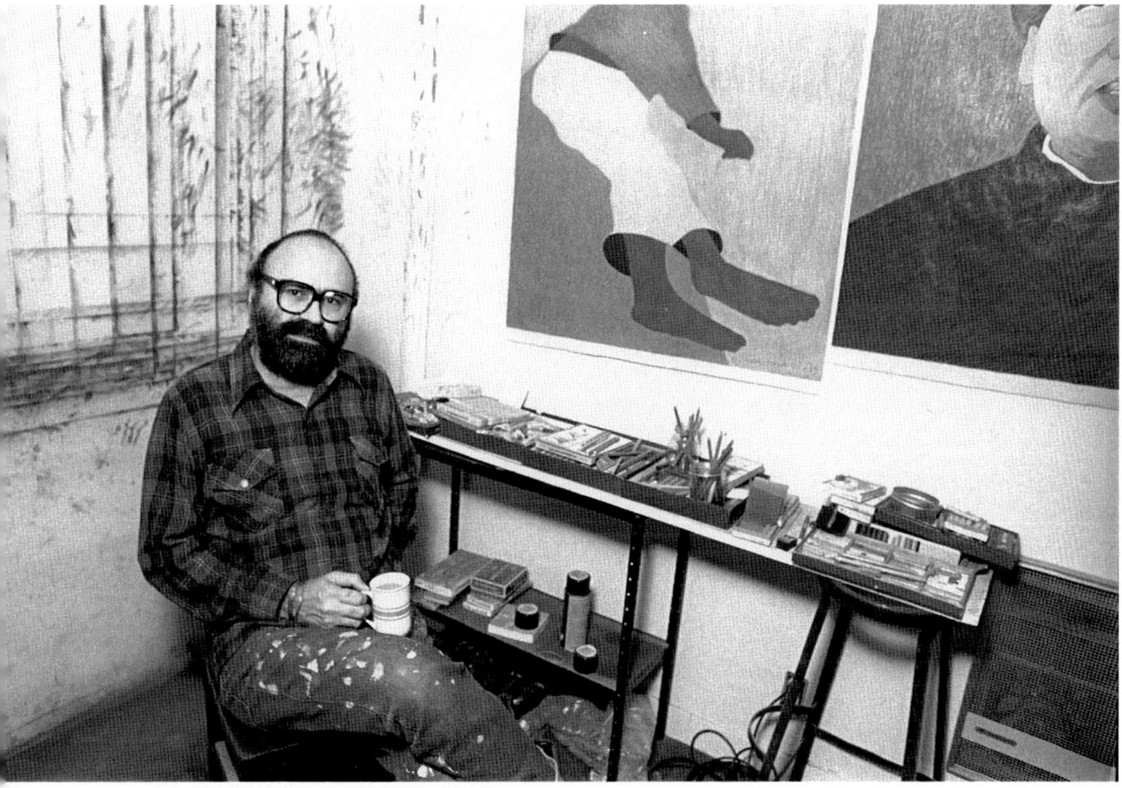

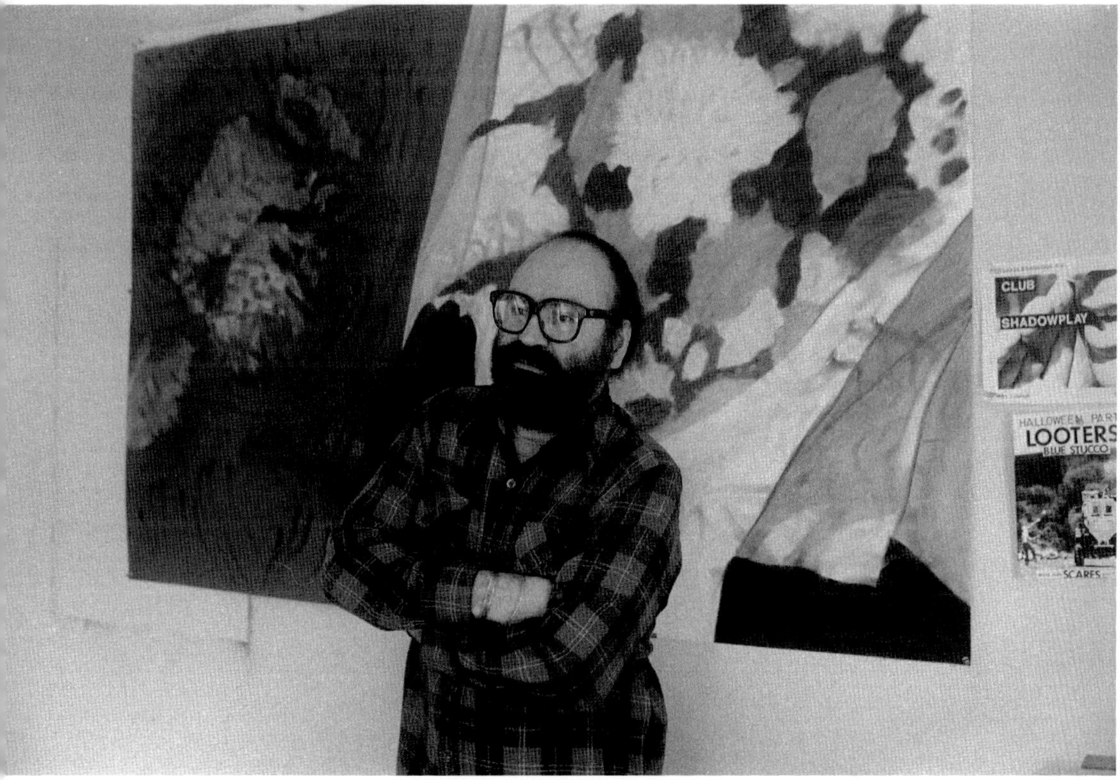

Rupert García in his Oakland studio, 1986. Photos courtesy of Terry Lorant.

with the Whiteness; *Attica is Fascismo*; *The Bicentennial Art Poster*; *Mexico, Chile, Soweto*; *El Grito de Rebelde*; *Assassination of a Striking Mexican Worker*; *Prometheus Under Fire*; and *La Virgen y Yo*. In total fifty-five of my works were exhibited. For the catalog cover, Favela chose my image of *The Horse in Man*.

The retrospective lasted from August 20 to October 19 of 1986. It was very well reviewed by the local press. Unfortunately, the retrospective did not travel to other venues. I had no say in this, but I was disappointed that it was not sent to other museums. I think this was a major mistake, although I didn't blame the Mexican Museum; I was the only artist that was being exhibited. At least the catalog was done, and it's a beautiful one with all of my images reproduced in color, except for my image of the Magón brothers that I did in black and white. It's expensive to do a catalog with so much color. Fortunately, the exhibition was supported by Los Amigos del Museo and the National Endowment for the Arts. Overall, I felt very honored.

What was also special about the exhibit was that many of my friends and relatives attended. I don't remember my mother being there but she probably was. My mother is interesting when it came to my work. She saw a number of them but she wouldn't say much about them. But that was how my mother was. She was always the peacekeeper in the family and as such would often not take a position one way or another. This was a technique of survival. I know she appreciated that I was doing what I wanted to do and in her own way also appreciated my work. Someone once asked me if I ever gave my mother or any in my family some of my paintings. "No," I responded. "Only if they paid for them. I need the money." But no, I never give my paintings to anyone. I don't know what that's about. It's not because they're so precious to me, because when my work is done, I almost don't need to see it anymore.

—‖—

It was also in the 1980s that I begin to receive some awards for my work. One was a San Francisco Art Commission Award for Outstanding Achievement in Print Making in 1986. Then another surprise award was the Purple Globe Award from San Francisco State that honored different people in the Bay Area for their cultural contributions. This included musicians, actors, writers, and artists like me. I was in good company with some of the other awardees, which included Alice Walker, Danny Glover, the film director Wayne Wang, and the great Latin musician Pete Escovedo.

Also, in 1986, another honor was when I learned that I had been awarded a two-month resident art fellowship at the East–West Center at the University of Hawaii. I had to commit to being there for the two months. They paid me a stipend, gave me a huge studio to myself, and provided a nice nearby apartment. The only other stipulation is that whatever painting I did there, I had to give one of them to the East–West Center. I accepted right away and made my travel plans. Sammi couldn't go with me because of her work, but she visited me for a week or so.

My residence was terrific. All of the paintings I did were about Hawaii. I painted a variety of images such as a portrait of King Kamehameha, which is the one I gave to the center. I did some scenic ones such as a representation of Diamond Head and some also based on Hawaiian postcards. I gave these postcards a much deeper and more complex meaning. I tried to depict the reality of Hawaii and not the fantasy connected with tourists. I also while at the center did a lot of reading about the history of Hawaii, which is incredibly filled with conquests, colonization, resistance, big business, and big military.

For my Hawaiian paintings, I decided to paint only in acrylic in order to expedite the process. I had begun using more oil, but oil takes weeks if not months to dry and I didn't have that kind of time. Acrylic takes just a few hours. I wanted to take my paintings back home and so using acrylic would allow me to do this. Acrylic is a water-based material and its base is a plastic-like substance, but it's not plastic. There is a binder that holds together the dried powder color that makes it possible to apply the acrylic paint to a canvas surface. It's different from both oil and pastels.

What was also nice was that while I was in residence, the Center had an exhibit of some of my posters and pastels. At the end of my stay, I had an exhibit of what I had painted in the two months. It was very well received and I got a nice review in the local paper.

■❙■

It's also in Hawaii where I decide to change galleries. Harcourts Gallery was good for me. Before I went with them, I had no options with respect to galleries. I couldn't pick and choose the kind of gallery I wanted to be in. No gallery expressed an interest in my art until Harcourts came along. During my two years with Harcourts, I started to get some acclaim and recognition in the art world and my work was selling well. However, I felt after those couple of years that I had to decide what I wanted to do. I decided that I wanted to be in a gallery that could present me in a context in which I wanted to be perceived. That context is a gallery whose physical presentation is serious. It wouldn't be a gallery like Harcourts where my work was exhibited along with a bunch of eclectic totally commercial paintings. I wanted a new context where when you walked into it you knew the gallery had a sense of integrity and belief in their artists and that the work being exhibited there was serious, important work. That's what I wanted and Harcourts couldn't provide this for me. This was not the kind of gallery that Harcourts was. I was with Harcourts because the owner loved my work and eventually loved me. That's why I was there. Harcourts was a mismatch for me and my work, but at the time I had no choice. I had no other options.

However, while I was in Hawaii, I had an option when another gallery approached me about representing me. This was the Iannetti-Lanzone Gallery in San Francisco. I thought it had the context that I wanted. I had to decide before I returned to the Bay Area. I chose to accept their offer. So, when I returned I asked for a meeting with Fred, the owner of Harcourts. This was painful for me, but I told him that I wanted out. That I had to move on and that this was strictly a business decision. It wasn't personal because the staff all treated me very well. Fortunately, I didn't have a written contract with Harcourts. It had been a Gentleman's Agreement.

It was hard but I told Fred that I was leaving and I did. I then signed on with Iannetti-Lanzone in 1988, which was a beautiful gallery. The way this connection occurred was when the director of the contemporary section of Harcourts also left and went to Iannetti-Lanzone and through him the gallery made me an offer to transfer to it. This worked out very well. An artist should have someplace to go before they leave a gallery. It just makes good business sense. I was invited to join the new gallery and I said, man this is where I want to go. I could envision my work in this beautiful gallery space. It was a brand-new gallery located at Grant and Sutter on the corner. What attracted me to the new gallery was the physical structure of the gallery, which was just beautiful. Absolutely gorgeous. This is where I wanted my work exhibited. The gallery was also representing other important artists, which impressed me. The owners and staff likewise had connections with various collectors who might be interested in my work. By comparison, Harcourts was very limited, and this included its exhibition space. I had two solo shows in the new gallery, and they both were very well received. They were wonderful exhibits, really just killers, and the reception for my first show was amazing. I was selling some of my work. Everything seemed just right and made me feel that I had made the right decision.

Unfortunately, it was not to be. The gallery soon thereafter went bankrupt. They weren't paying their bills, and the investors and artists in the gallery were owed money. I later learned that the owners were also involved in illegal activities. They owed someone in New York almost a million dollars. It became a big scandal and was covered by the papers and media. They had paid me for the sale of my paintings the first year, but then they started cutting back and I got nothing the second year. They owed me a lot of money, which I never got. I hired a lawyer and he was able to recoup some of the sales owed to me but not much. The gallery closed. It's unusual for a gallery to go bankrupt. Actually, it was the corporation behind the gallery that went bankrupt. The fact is that galleries are a business, and some don't succeed. It's also the case that for the most part there is an adversarial relationship between the gallery and the artist. Most artists have a vision of art and don't focus on the profitability of their work, while the gallery focuses on what is going to sell. I had not seen the red flag go up because I was doing well that first year. At least, I got more recognition from my exhibitions with the gallery.

Fortunately, I was able to join another gallery almost right away. This was the Rena Bransten Gallery just a few blocks away on Geary and Grant, and they have represented me since. Bransten was one of the top galleries in northern California, and I was very happy to be part of them. It had vision and support for its artists.

━ⅠⅠ━

In between changing galleries in the late 1980s, I got an opportunity to exhibit in Paris in 1987. It was a solo exhibition and my first in Europe. It was an amazing experience. I was invited by the Galerie Claude Samuel. The owner of the gallery had seen some of my work in a group exhibit of American art in an art fair in Switzerland that Harcourts had helped arrange. The Parisian owner contacted me and said that he would like to do a show of some of my pastels. They would also do a catalog, and they would pay for me to spend two weeks in Paris as the gallery's guest, including my airfare and hotel. I couldn't believe it! I had never been to Paris much less any part of Europe. The exhibit would be from March 3 to April 4. I was excited as was Sammi and my whole family. Sammi couldn't go because of her work, but my family in Stockton all decided to accompany me. This included my mother, my brother, my sister-in-law, and two of my tías. From Stockton to Paris! We were all thrilled. We flew over on Air France, which is a great airline. Just terrific. Everyone was treated like royalty, man. I'm telling you. The people in first class must have been treated like I don't know what because we were treated really well. Just great. Our hotel in Paris was also very nice. Not the top but it was top enough. Very beautiful. We all were in seventh heaven!

After we settled into our hotel, I took a cab to the gallery and met the owner and some of his staff. It was a beautiful gallery. I was just very excited number one for being in Paris and number two having a solo exhibition in Paris. All this was just too much. At the gallery, I helped install the exhibition. The paintings selected for the exhibit were boxed and transported to Paris at the expense of the gallery. After the exhibit, they sent back the paintings to my Oakland studio. I was just on a high taking the taxi back to the hotel. However, after I exited the taxi, I realized that I didn't have my bag with me that contained my wallet with my money and credit cards and my passport. At first, I thought I could stop the cab, but it quickly got lost in a sea of other cabs. Oh, man! I was like all of my feelings were numb. I got nauseous. I just stood there thinking what the hell am I going to do now? I went from a high seeing the gallery and the installation to the bottom. Oh, man! Finally, I walked into the hotel and went to the front desk to ask what I could do.

"Are you Monsieur García?"

"Yes, I am."

"Is this your bag?"

Oh, my God! Here was my bag with everything in it. Nothing was taken. The clerk explained to me that apparently when I opened the cab door, my bag fell in the gutter. I didn't realize it because I was busy paying the cabbie. Someone saw it while I was still standing in shock outside of the hotel and turned it in to the front desk. Oh, God was I relieved! There is no worse feeling than losing your wallet and passport in another country. My Aunt Mary said "es Dios." It was a miracle. In this instance, I believed it.

The opening the next evening was marvelous. I and the gallery chose eleven of my pastels. They were fairly recent paintings done either in 1985 or 1986, including my image on Vincent Chin. All were pastel on paper. The catalog included in color many of the pictures in the show. Some of the other paintings included some that were inspired by paintings by Manet. Two of the Manet images had religious connotations, although most people are not aware of this connection. One of my Manet-inspired pictures I called *The Geometry of Manet and the Sacred Heart*. There is this religious connection in the Manet painting but no Sacred Heart. I decided to put in my painting the Sacred Heart. I did it as a diptych with an image of Manet on the left-hand side and on the other the traditional image of Christ showing His Sacred Heart. I had seen the Manet image in an exhibition in Chicago. It was of Christ sitting on a throne. I didn't know that Manet had done any religious paintings because his work seemed to depict non-religious images. I was awed by his religious painting. I remember seeing images of Christ and the Sacred Heart growing up, since many Mexican American Catholics had this image in their homes. I was always struck by the redness of the traditional image including Jesus's robe and that of the Sacred Heart. Consequently, I painted my version with saturated reds, oranges, and greens. The colors are just incredible. The geometry that I refer to in my title concerns that on the left-hand image there's a green triangle and then on the right-hand image there's another triangle that is in yellow, orange, and red. So that's the geometry; it's just a technical term for my composition and as a way of helping make the picture appear to be flat in some areas.

We also exhibited another of my paintings inspired by a French connection. This is my image of *Libertad y las Americas*. It's also a diptych. On the left-hand side is an image of a woman. Libertad refers to the woman wearing a green dress toting a shoulder weapon and the flag of black and red and wearing a red cap. This I took from a painting by Delacroix called *Liberty Leading the People in the Revolution*. This is a reference to the French Revolution. I changed the colors somewhat from Delacroix's image. On the right-hand side is a portrait of a twentieth-century Latin American revolutionary. The image of the revolutionary I took from my 1985 picture *The Horse in Man*.

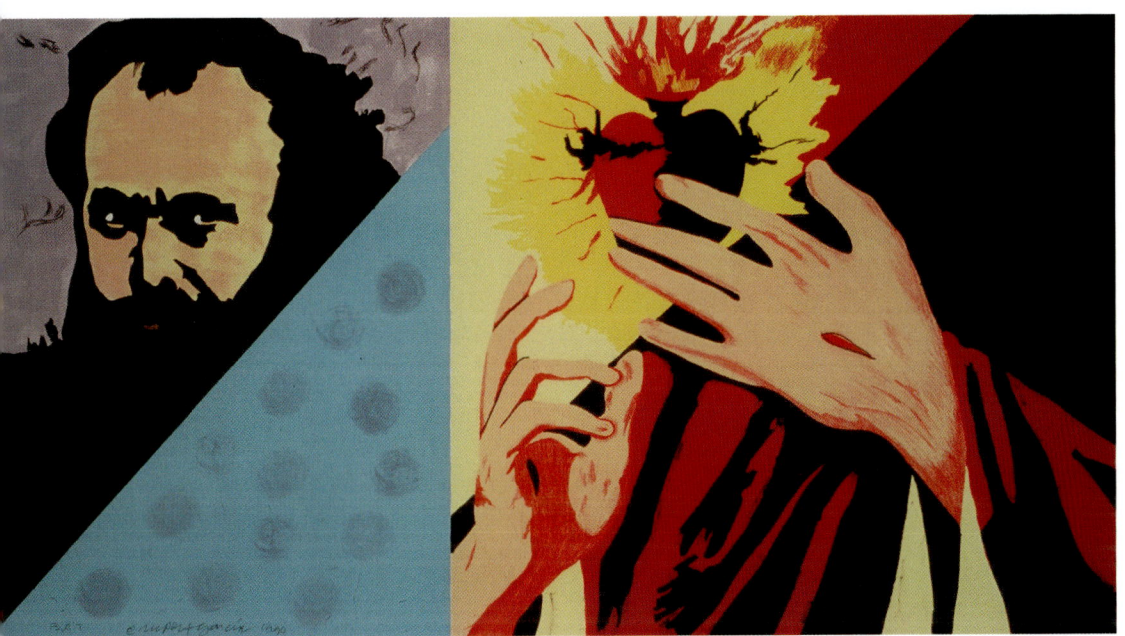

The Geometry of Manet and the Sacred Heart, 1990. Lithograph, sheet size: 19 x 35 inches, image size: 19 x 35 inches. Copyright © Rupert García. Courtesy of Rena Bransten Gallery.

The only other of my paintings which I will mention here is still another image of Frida Kahlo that I did in 1986. I called this image *The Snow in Frida Kahlo*. It is the same image of Frida that I used in my previous Frida paintings; however, this version is done in very light colors except for her bright red lips. I have no idea why I linked it to snow although I painted in snow falling on Frida. I'm sure that at some time in her life she experienced snow. I think snow is wonderful and so I wanted to surround Frida with it which I did using an eraser to make the white marks. It has lighter colors because I pressed very lightly on my pastel crayon. I wanted a light quality to this picture. It's a very different image of Frida.

A number of people attended the opening including a representative of the Mexican consulate in Paris. The gallery had just recently opened, and so it was just developing a reputation. The gallery was located in *Place des Vosges* which is one of the oldest squares in Paris. It's a beautiful area and a very expensive one for those who live there. It's also a big tourist site. The gallery was not big but small and intimate in typical Parisian style for galleries. It was a beautifully designed space and elegant. Still we had a nice turnout. Some were artists, but most were not. The buzz at the exhibit seemed to be positive. My whole family were in support of me and they loved the reception, even though they went back to the hotel earlier. I stayed and met many of those who had come to the show and then had dinner with the owner and some of the staff.

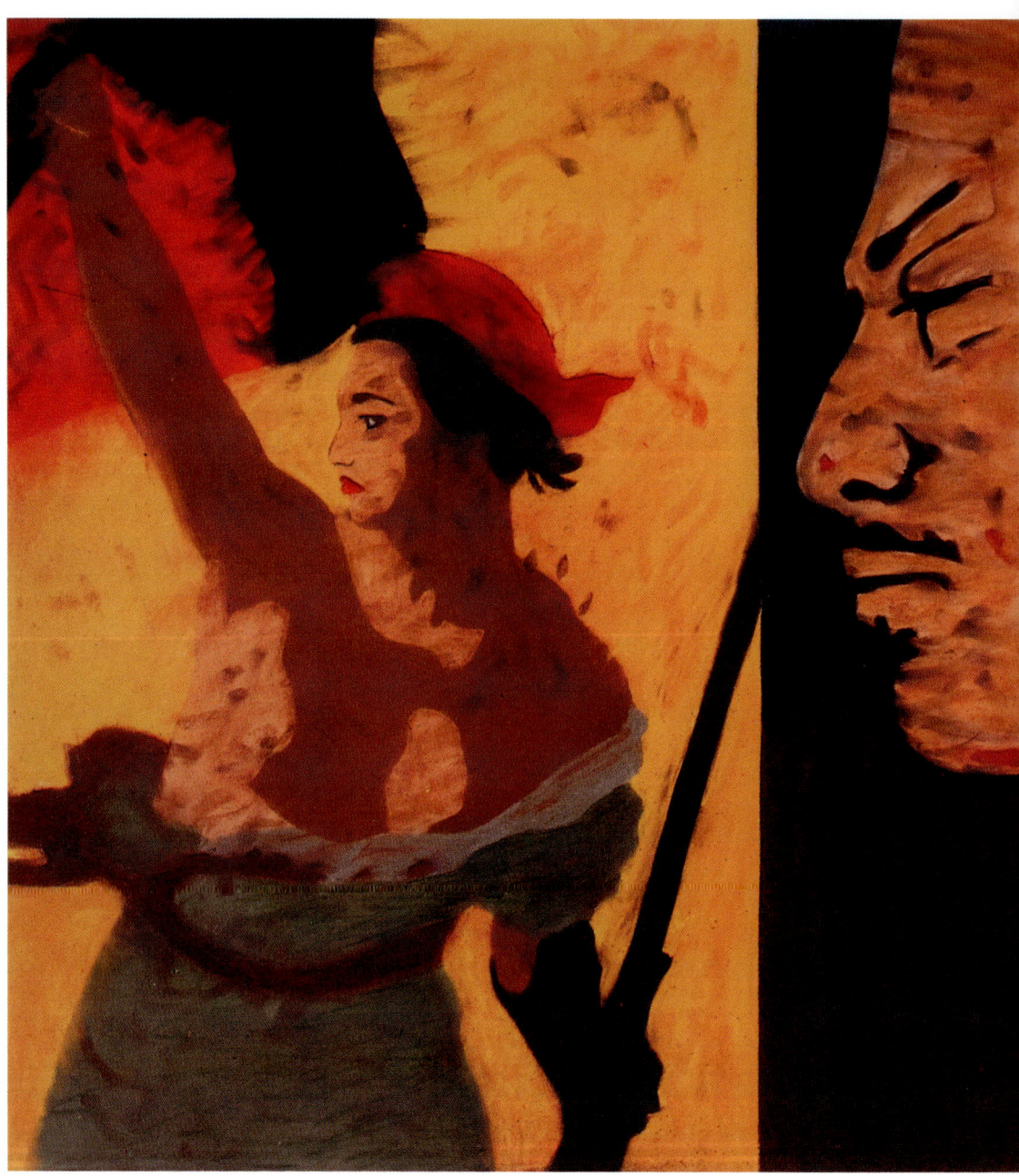

Libertad y las Americas, 1986. Pastel on pastel cloth, canvas size: 40 x 37-1/4 inches. Copyright © Rupert García.

My family also had a great time in Paris, but they left after a few days to fly to Rome. My mother and aunts had to absolutely go to the Vatican and pray at St. Peter's Basilica. I stayed in Paris and visited many of the museums. I had a bad experience once riding the Metro subway trains. I had a feeling that people were looking at me strangely. They must have thought

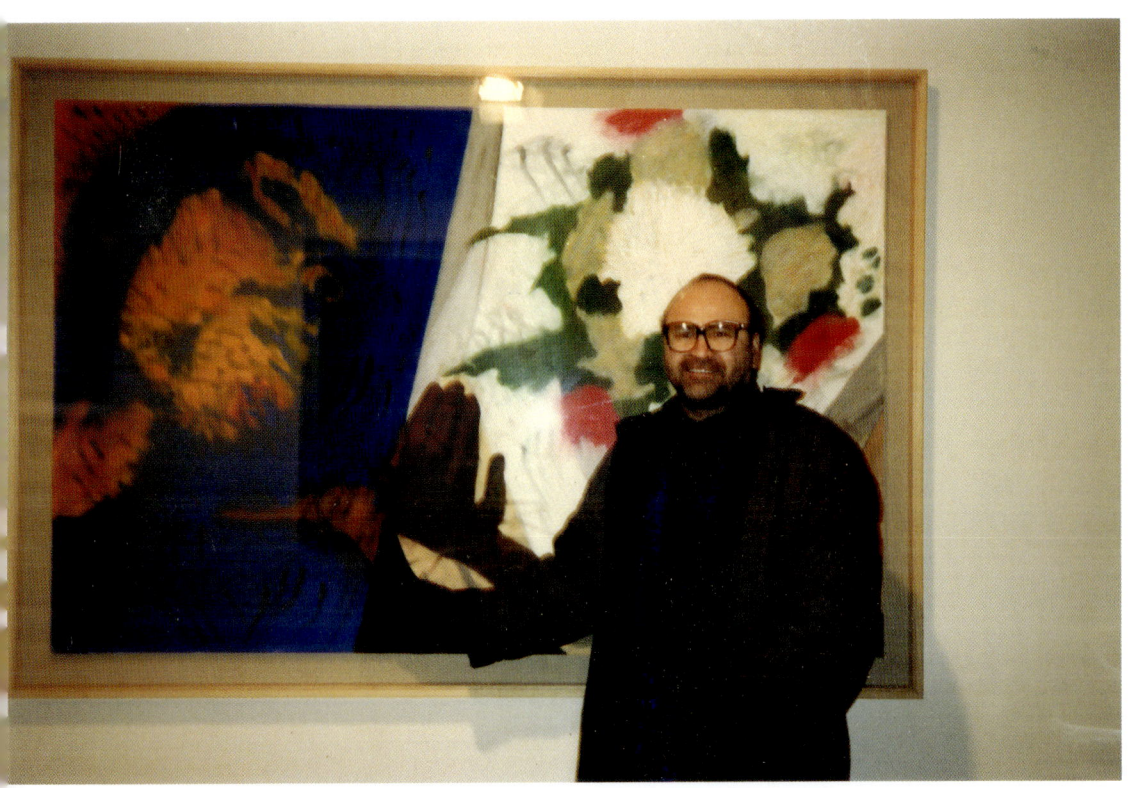

Rupert García in Paris at solo exhibition at Galerie Claude Samuel, 1987. Photo courtesy of Rupert García.

I was an Arab and because of the Algerian War of the 1950s there was still racial tension between Parisians and Arabs. I could feel this kind of unease. Maybe I was overly suspicious, but I felt something.

I played tourist although I didn't go to the Eiffel Tower. I spent most of my time in the museums. The city itself was a cultural education. I'd been in a few cultures other than the one I was raised in such as in Indochina and Mexico, and whenever I go to these different cultures everything is an experience. Going to the museums or going to the corner store is an experience. It's just all wonderful. Everything matters. I was probably one of the most open tourists ever to go to Paris. I was open to everything. And it was great. I didn't necessarily have a favorite museum. I liked and appreciated all of them. As an artist, I just loved to see the paintings of such masters as Monet and others like Gustav Courbet. I wanted to see how Manet put the paint on with his brush and to look at the texture of his painting, the thinness and the thickness of it, the transparencies of color. These technical aspects are very interesting to see. What I liked about Courbet was that unlike other painters of his time who fixated on kings, queens, princesses, and wars, Courbet turned all of this upside down. He painted everyday people, which was scandalous among other artists and art patrons. His stress on everyday people, of course, interested me very much. These artists knew how to put paint on, move it around, and develop fabulous shapes of color and nice lights and darks as well as deal with content. So, to see them in person and look at them closely was just wonderful. I had only seen these paintings in books and slides and here I was standing in front of the actual paintings.

Having said that, I was very disappointed when I went to the Louvre and saw da Vinci's *Mona Lisa*. I wasn't impressed. The hype is better than the picture. I mean, it's not a bad painting, but it's not a great painting. Not everything that da Vinci touched turned to gold. I couldn't believe that there had been so many centuries of applause whose sound was louder than the actual image. I couldn't believe it. I kept looking at it hoping that somehow, I would feel otherwise, but nothing happened.

Unlike the other smaller museums, the Louvre was overwhelming. I had a mixed reaction to it. I had to remind myself that it was a depository of conquests and looting. You go downstairs and see art from other countries that the French stole art from. It was painful. On the one hand, it was overwhelmingly beautiful to see the gorgeous art pieces, but then you realize where did they get all of these things? How'd they get here? Imperial wars and pillage, that's how they got here. So that was the pain especially at the Louvre—a monument to the French empire. I also found the size

of the Louvre to be too much. The size of it almost takes away from the appreciation of art because it's so immense.

Even though I am critical of what the Louvre represents as evidence of the French and European colonization of the Third World, I never into the 1990s bought into the anti-Eurocentric attitudes expressed by some in the U.S. Third World movements, especially in the academy including in Chicano Studies. I agreed with this position to the extent that I do not believe that everything of value and of aesthetic beauty emanates from Europe. What I disagreed with was the additional view that dumped on all aspects of European art as being racist and therefore to be discarded or ignored by Third World people. I have no affinity for this ridiculous and absurd view. It didn't make any sense to me. It's a narrow ideology. I never had an anti-European cultural perspective. I studied European art and I appreciated much of it as I did on my visit to Paris. I had this view even during the most nationalist period of the Chicano Movement where some Chicanos dumped on everything that was of European origins, including the art. This got me into some trouble with extreme Chicano nationalists. I never agreed, further, when some Chicanos asserted that they were non-European people, which was an absolute lie. Chicanos cannot say they are of a non-European background. Some mexicanos can who are much more Indigenous. But most Chicanos and mexicanos are mestizos, meaning that they have both Indigenous and Spanish genes. So, I never bought into this extreme racial nationalism. I never fell into this type of anti-Eurocentrism at the same time agreeing that Europe did not represent the epitome of human cultural advancement.

After a great two weeks in Paris, I flew back alone because my family had returned from Rome. I left on a pretty good high from the trip and, as a matter of fact, I think I got back to this country without using a plane! Going to Paris made me excited about seeing the art there and about my being an artist. I saw artists such as Picasso who I had admired from a distance, and to see their work in person just blew my mind. It was emotionally stimulating and my imagination took off and my intellect expanded. It was a wonderful experience. It was as wonderful as when I first went to Guadalajara and Mexico City. I'd advise anyone to go to Paris if they can. I'm ready to go again.

■ꓲꓲ■

It was around the time I went to Paris that I returned to oil painting. I say return because in junior college I painted in oil. So, this is why some years later, I returned to oil. I returned because I always saw myself as a painter since I was in high school. When I thought about being an artist, it meant making paintings. This is a love I still have today. So, when I went through the experience of doing pastel, it got me closer to being a painter. But it was also a reminder that if I wanted to I could make some paintings with a wet medium like oil. And so, I did. A friend of mine, Oliver Jackson, was a very good painter in oil, and I asked him once how he did his oil paintings. He said that he got some chalks and soaked them in linseed oil and then painted with them like a paint stick using oil. I experimented with this and was just bowled over. The oil I painted with was fabulous. The medium of oil carries the pigment, which is whatever color you want. The color is like dust. Colored dust. I combine the dust with linseed oil, and what holds it together is called the binder. The result is an oil with elasticity to move around the chalk sticks that I used. Man, the oil gives a luster to the color that is amazing. It's remarkable what you can achieve with oil. Besides the chalk sticks, I also used brushes. I said, man, this is it. I love it. I loved the richer texture and color of the oil and the way it smelled. This gives the painting a deeper quality. Unlike pastel which is fragile, oil by comparison endures more abuse. Oil when it dries really stays there. At the same time, unlike pastels, oil takes much longer to dry. When I was doing pastels, the immediacy was important. I needed the results right away. This speaks to my earlier career when I wanted to turn out a number of pictures one right after another, and pastel allowed me to do so. However, by the late 1980s when I was older, I was at a place in my life where I didn't mind waiting for an oil painting. I had time. It also speaks to my becoming more complex as a painter and demanding more of myself. I was giving myself more time to figure a painting out. It was no longer a matter of doing a picture in a few days. Now with oil, it would take me a few weeks or even months. It involved patience just like writing a book.

Even though I turned primarily to oil painting in the late 1980s, I never accepted a hierarchy about mediums or the idea that oil painting is more sophisticated than other mediums. The fact is that I continued to do some posters and prints while I was doing pastels and oil painting. I never turned my back on my earlier forms such as silk-screening. I didn't see oil painting as more sophisticated, but it was a turn to a new kind of freedom in expressing my art. Oil painting felt more open and free, but I wouldn't say that it was more sophisticated than silk-screening or pastels. Sophisticated suggests a kind of hierarchy, and I don't believe too much in hierarchies.

In my oil paintings moving forward into the 1990s and beyond, some continued to label me as a political artist, which I am not. I'm not trying to convey a political message in my paintings. For example, I didn't set out to make a political statement when I painted my image of a stealth bomber. I'm not a political artist. I'm an artist who sometimes deals with political issues. But if I were a political artist, I would be exhausted trying to illustrate so many political issues that I would want to confront. There may be some political artists. I don't know, but if there are they're probably not very good artists. One of the reasons I was attracted to Los Tres in Mexico was that they could marry image, subject, and form in a way which made good things to look at that were complex. This was instructive for me. It made me realize that you can do issues of social concern in creative ways in which the image will not be superseded by content and the wonderfulness of form, but rather that they all work together. In this way, I'm not separating art from politics, yet politics does not dominate the creative process. That's why I'm not a political artist. On the other hand, if some look at my stealth bomber painting and take away a political message, I can't help this. It doesn't bug me. I can't control that and, frankly, I don't care. If I were concerned about this, I would be arrogant, meaning that I would do the painting with the idea of shaking up an audience believing that I could do this. I only aim to shake myself up. I know what I get from the painting and that's all that matters. What you get from the painting, I have no control over. I didn't do the painting for you to experience. It was done for me to experience.

◼�█◼

Nineteen eighty-eight was an important year for me because I agreed to a tenure-track appointment at San Jose State University. This marked another important junction in my life and career. That year as I was finishing my three-year California Arts Council Fellowship, I was invited by the School of Art and Design at San Jose State to give a lecture on silk-screening. As part of a campus-wide effort to hire minority professors, the school had been given a position which they chose to focus on silk-screen printing. When they told me this, I told them that I was not interested in teaching about silk-screening. I don't do silk-screening any more, and I have never taught a course on it and I never will.

"Well, Mr. García, we would still like you to give a lecture on any topic you wish," the director of the school kindly replied. "You never know what other positions may come up in the future."

"Of course," I said.

So, I went down to the campus and made a presentation about my paintings. At my talk there were a number of faculty and students. The dean as well as the chair of the painting department were also present. My talk seemed to go well and that was that. However, to my pleasant surprise a few days later, the dean called and invited me to become part of their faculty. He said that they had been very impressed with my talk and that he and the Art Department chair had in addition seen my show in San Francisco at the Iannetti-Lanzone Gallery and were very impressed.

"We want you as part of our faculty to teach whatever you want," the dean said, and this was later seconded by the chair and the head of painting. "We want you. We want you."

I couldn't refuse. I knew that part of the appointment was to have someone who would work with minority students such as Latinos. I ignored that. I wasn't going to play the affirmative action card. I support affirmative action, but I'm no one's monkey. I'm not. I was going to teach as a professional artist and if I had minority students that would be great, but I wasn't going to be some kind of affirmative action counselor or recruiter. I made that very clear to them. They agreed and offered me a tenure-track position as an associate professor. I was not hired with tenure; however, in order to provide me a much higher salary than an assistant professor, they gave me the higher rank. They also promised me a faster track to tenure and promotion to full professor, which came to be. I also stipulated that I would teach painting and drawing classes, including undergrad and grad seminars. I had taught part-time at other schools, but the position at San Jose State was full-time and with a very good salary. It would help very much with our household expenses. Being an artist is not always a lucrative career. It's not. I loved to teach and this would give more of an opportunity to do so in addition to the financial support.

I enjoyed my teaching at San Jose State. It was great. I loved the students and I had good and decent colleagues. When I joined the department, the overall quality was very good. It's become a better program over the years. When I started, there were about three hundred majors in art. This included the fine arts, industrial design, graphic design, illustration. Fine arts, which was my program, dealt with painting, sculpture, printmaking, drawing, photography, computer fine arts, and installation performance. What initially impressed me about the students was that they didn't have the pretense of being artists, generally speaking. I had taught at the San Francisco Art

Institute and their students had a big attitude about being artists. This was not the case at San Jose State, and I preferred the latter one. The students there reminded me of how I started my art education at San Francisco State. They had a limited understanding about art and one that was usually distorted by movies and TV. They didn't have this notion of being artists who are above other people. They had a kind of innocence and even naivety, and I found this refreshing because the students didn't have false expectations. This was nice and very real. It can sometimes be a problem, because every now and then you have to develop an attitude of what it means to be an artist. However, these students will develop such an attitude, but one that is not snooty and apart from real people's lives. Students who take my classes with this more open attitude will get a lot out of my classes. The occasional few who already have a preconceived notion of being an artist will only get what they already bring. Most of my students are down-to-earth students from mostly working-class families, and so they have few if any pretensions. I appreciate that.

I find that students have different reasons for majoring in art. It's difficult to generalize. But I can say that many students who are art majors want to become illustrators, graphic designers, or industrial designers because that's where the jobs are. It's a practical step toward gaining an income. It's more predictable and stable. Whereas in the fine arts, it is not predictable. However, many students who are taking design and graphics really want to be artists. They really want to be in fine arts, but they're afraid and they have reason to be afraid. They are sure about what they have to do to get a job, but that's not the same thing as what they would like to do.

I think that what I bring to my students compared to my own art education is a sense of insight. To be an artist, you have to use your mind, including an awareness of the spiritual and the wonders of the imagination. I always talk about this and show my enthusiasm for these things. The students need to develop these and be very conscious of that. I also stress the integrity of the artist. You have to be yourself and be true to your principals. Don't sell them out for fame and fortune. Always strive to do the right thing. You can fight for what you believe is valuable. Because if you don't, you lose your integrity. It's gone. You just become another cog in the wheel of "progress" and you'll be run over. You may have a nice house, car, etc., but if you don't have a true sense of who you are and what you believe in, you don't have very much. Artists can work against this malaise and rise above it if you have integrity. Where does one go for a sense of self? A true sense of self? TV? Movies? All this is mostly commercially based and so it won't allow you to think critically or individually. The fine arts can be an alternative and oppositional space. I say these things in my classes without sounding preachy or in a dogmatic way.

I tell my students that I am proud to be an image maker. When they hear this they practically fall out of their chairs or desks. "What do you mean, you're proud?" they want to know. I tell them that I'm proud and honored to be a person who makes images, because I don't see myself in isolation. I see myself as part of a world history of image makers and how magnificent that is. It's wonderful! It's exciting! But it's demanding, arduous work. It just kicks your butt. Yet to be part of the human tradition of making images, wow, that's great. You can't be willy-nilly about being an image maker. You've got to take your self seriously.

Among my students, I've had some Chicanos and Latinos. I work hard with all of my students, although I'm particularly interested in young Chicanos and Latinos. I try to dispel them of not getting caught up in myths about who Chicanos are and what is expected of them as artists. They don't have to just make paintings of *calaveras* and Aztec warriors. They need to get away from such stereotypes about what it means to be Chicano. It's not necessary for you to do that, I tell them. Being a Chicano artist is not replicating what Chicano artists did during the Chicano Movement. That was then and this is now. You have to be true to yourselves and to your own historical moment. There is no or there should not be a prescription about being a Chicano artist. You are who you are and you have to be true to yourself and your feelings and thoughts. For the most part they take my advice, and it's wonderful to see them develop with a sense of integrity. It's painful for some of them to change, but most do. They have to become independent. I encourage them to leave home, get divorced, and rob banks! Well not all that, but be yourselves and not have someone else tell you who you are and how you have to identify.

As I said, getting a full-time position and getting tenure was a new junction in my life and career. At some earlier point, I might have thought that I could be a full-time artist and a full-time teacher, but as I matured and especially when I began at San Jose State, I realized that I couldn't do this. I had to compromise and I did. This also coincided with my shifting to oil painting. I think this all reflected a certain security as an artist that allowed me to branch into full-time teaching. I was confident of myself as an artist that I could cut back some in order to teach full-time. I realized that on my teaching days I couldn't paint. Teaching took all of my energy and attention for me to live up to high standards at school. On the days that I taught, I would come home physically and mentally exhausted and all I could do was watch TV. I could paint on my nonteaching days and on weekends. I followed this schedule for over twenty years while at San Jose State, and not only was I a successful professor in my opinion, but my productivity as an artist was not curtailed much. This artistic productivity would take various directions into the end of the twentieth century and into the new millennium.

━ ‖ ━

At the end of the decade of the 1980s, there was a major exhibit of Chicano art. This was the CARA exhibit at the Wight Gallery at UCLA in 1990—*Chicano Art: Resistance and Affirmation*. It focused on Chicano art from 1965 to 1985. It was organized by two art graduate students, Holly Barnet-Sanchez and Marcos Sanchez, along with a number of scholars on an advisory committee. I was asked to be part of the committee, but I turned this down because I felt it would take up too much of my time which I needed to devote to my own art work. I consulted a bit but not much. It took two years to organize the exhibit. Many artists were included, going back to the Chicano Movement. They selected some of my posters from my earlier period, such as the ones on Zapata, Ruben Salazar, and Frida Kahlo. I attended the opening of the show and it was packed with artists and dignitaries. I felt a sense of community with my fellow artists, many of whom I met for the first time. It was an important moment in American cultural history. I was proud of being part of these male and female artists who struggled to create their visions. It was beautiful.[5]

At the same time, I have to say that I was quite critical of the organizing theory and strategy behind the exhibit. To me, it looked like the art of twenty years was being put into a mold. It was the mold of Chicano cultural nationalism reflected in the ideology of Chicanismo. I found this problematic. It was like there had been little to no change in how Chicano/a artists did their work in two decades! The show reflected no complexity in Chicano art production. In fact, it reduced that complexity for the sake of an organizing theme. Everything shown had to reflect Chicanismo and El Plan de Aztlán. This was supposed to be Chicano art. But this was too limiting. It didn't register, for example, the Third World and international influences and connection within Chicano art. Not all of this art in this period was a nationalistic one. The organizers used ideology—Chicanismo—to determine culture and in this case what they defined as Chicano art. Chicano art was steeped in social struggles but did it reflect only a singular identity? The answer was and is no! Not everyone embraced Chicanismo, or some had different interpretations of it.

But CARA didn't reflect this diversity and complexity. The show was exclusive rather than inclusive. There was no effort to show art that suggested an African influence in Mexico, and Chicano abstract art was excluded. Instead, the organizers only wanted art with a clinched brown fist. I rejected this perspective because I and other artists had evolved from strict cultural nationalism. The exhibit was too restrictive of Chicano art and didn't reflect the intelligence and imagination of Chicano artists. It was a preconceived notion of what constituted Chicano art, and then images were selected to support this. I considered this to be a vulgarized cultural nationalism.

Unfortunately, there existed a running notion that Chicano art equaled posters and murals. And what went into these mediums were largely images of the Virgen de Guadalupe, skulls, pyramids, images of native peoples of the Americas, and popular images of Mexican and Chicano culture. These obvious elements by some were considered to be necessary to be recognized as Chicano art. However, to reduce Chicano art as such was a major problem for any people. I understand the issue and the then necessity for the development of a certain kind of nationalism. The United States, for example, has always done that. All nations do that. Even people within nations who are unhappy with their condition will oftentimes revert to some form of nationalism as a way to organize resistance. I understood all of this in the heat of the moment. My problem with CARA was that years later after the heyday of the Chicano Movement, it was still promoting this static view of what Chicano art represented. It wasn't a retrospective show. It was a show that said that this in 1990 is still what Chicano art is. It provided no room for a more diversified Chicano art that had evolved up to 1990.

Despite my criticisms of CARA, it still represented an important recognition of Chicano art, a recognition still not prevalent in most of the country. In fact, Europe was ahead of the United States in recognizing the importance of Chicano art. One year prior to CARA, the first major European traveling exhibition of Chicano art, Les Demous des Anges, took place at the Centre de Recherche pour le Developpement Cultural in Nantes, France. Some of my work was included, although I didn't go to any of the showings. It was a big show with a heavy focus on

L.A. artists such as Carlos Almaraz, Gronk, Patsi Valdez, and others. I was included as part of the Bay Area artists along with Amalia Mesa-Bains.[6]

—||—

Almost in contrast, I was honored to have another major retrospective of my work also in 1990, the same year as the CARA exhibit. It wasn't planned like this; it just happened. I had had a retrospective show a few years earlier at the Mexican Museum, but this one was much larger and included my graphic work from 1967 to 1990. It was called *Rupert García: Prints and Posters, 1967–1990*. It was cosponsored by the Fine Arts Museum in San Francisco and by the Center for Creative Arts in Mexico City. It was a wonderful show, and it produced a beautiful catalog. I participated in selecting the pictures and consulted on the catalog. For me, the exhibit was important because it was an example of an artist who had varied experiences from Stockton to Indochina to San Francisco State and beyond. The show reflected my evolution as an artist with respect to themes and technique. It showed my changes over twenty-three years. It revealed an artist whose vision was open-ended and didn't follow a prescribed ideology or cultural influence. I took Chicanismo into consideration, but along with other perspectives. I am proud of this type of evolution.

The opening exhibit was great and I was bowled over when I saw this huge banner hanging above the entry to the courtyard with my name and the title of the show. It seemed almost absurd. The San Francisco critics loved it. It was one of the few times that my work was reviewed by these critics who tend to be elitist and Eurocentric.

I think this exhibit was important because it represented who I am and was after years of working and thinking connected to social concerns, politics, and aesthetics. The exhibit further showed different stages of my work, including prints and posters. They were different modes of expression, and all of my works need to be seen as a whole. They are me and I am them. Not only one expression is me; all of them are me.

My exhibit was not done to counter CARA, but it did show an artist who was part of CARA, but there presented only in one dimension. By contrast, my show revealed all of me and my complexity. If anything, my show was in a state of dialogue with CARA.

■■■

The end of the 1980s also proved to be a good time for me. I received additional awards that were near and dear to my heart. The first involved my being inducted into the Edison High School Hall of Fame in 1989. I loved this because I loved my high school, and so this award was a high moment in my life. It was also special because my friend, Maxine Hong Kinston, was inducted with me. This was the first time I had gone back to my school in years. Edison was special because it was the school "on the other side of the tracks" with many Chicanos, Blacks, Asian Americans, and poorer whites.

We weren't expected to succeed, and yet many of us went on to important careers. One interesting and moving part of receiving my award was that I, along with the other awardees, had to select a song from the time when I was in school that would be played when I received my award. I chose one of my favorites, "In the Still of the Night" by the Five Satins. The song brought tears to my eyes. I gave a short speech thanking the school for this great honor. I also said that I was receiving this award on behalf of my friends who had died because of shootings or overdoses or who were in jail. The evening was also special because my mother and my family were in attendance. I cherish this award, and the ceremony was one of the highlights of my life.

In addition, I was thrilled when the Haggin Museum in Stockton in 1988 for the first time invited me to have an exhibit of some of my work as part of its distinguished artist series. I had received other invitations to show my work in Stockton, but the venue I really desired was the Haggin, which was *the* art museum in Stockton. All of my family came to the opening of the exhibit. I gave a little speech in which I said that the Haggin had never had so many Mexicans in its museum. This was a joke but probably true. After the event, one of my cousins, Gus, organized a wonderful dinner for me and my family and friends at the Civic Auditorium. There must have been a few hundred people.

In the exhibit, I showed some of my more recent paintings in oil with one pastel. I have already discussed some of

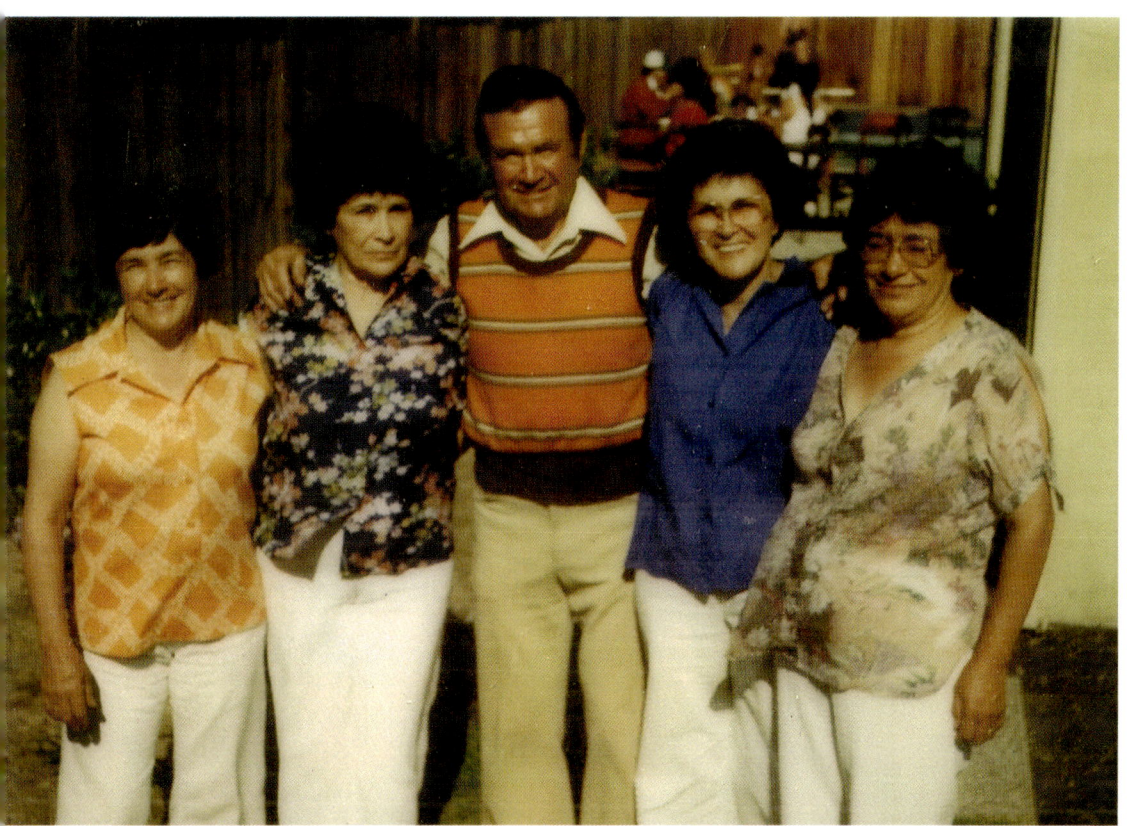

Rupert García's mother (in the blue blouse) and her siblings, circa 1970s. Photo courtesy of Rupert García.

these images, but the one that I particularly want to mention is entitled *For Tia Juana Y Mi Abuelita Guadalupe De Jalostotitlán*. Although I did the painting one year before the exhibit, it was a family picture. This was a homage to my grandmother Guadalupe who had helped raise me and to her sister Tía Juana whom I had met on that family trip to her village Jalostotitlan in Mexico in the 1970s. Both had passed by the time of the exhibit. I paid them tribute as artists in their own right. On that trip Tía Juana gave me some of her artwork made of clay and painted with water-based paint. Out of these and other materials such as cardboard,

clay, and cloth, she made these statues of people and animals. I still have them in my studio and cherish them. My grandmother as I have noted made images out of tissue of various animals and people. I thought this was magical. I got the inspiration for my painting from an old book that I had and which had a picture of a deer. I loved the way it looked, and it reminded me of both my tía and grandmother because they made images of deer. So, on the left-hand side of the picture I painted in a deer. Then on the right-hand side I painted in these different colored dots. Actually, I didn't paint them in with a brush but with my fingers. I dipped my

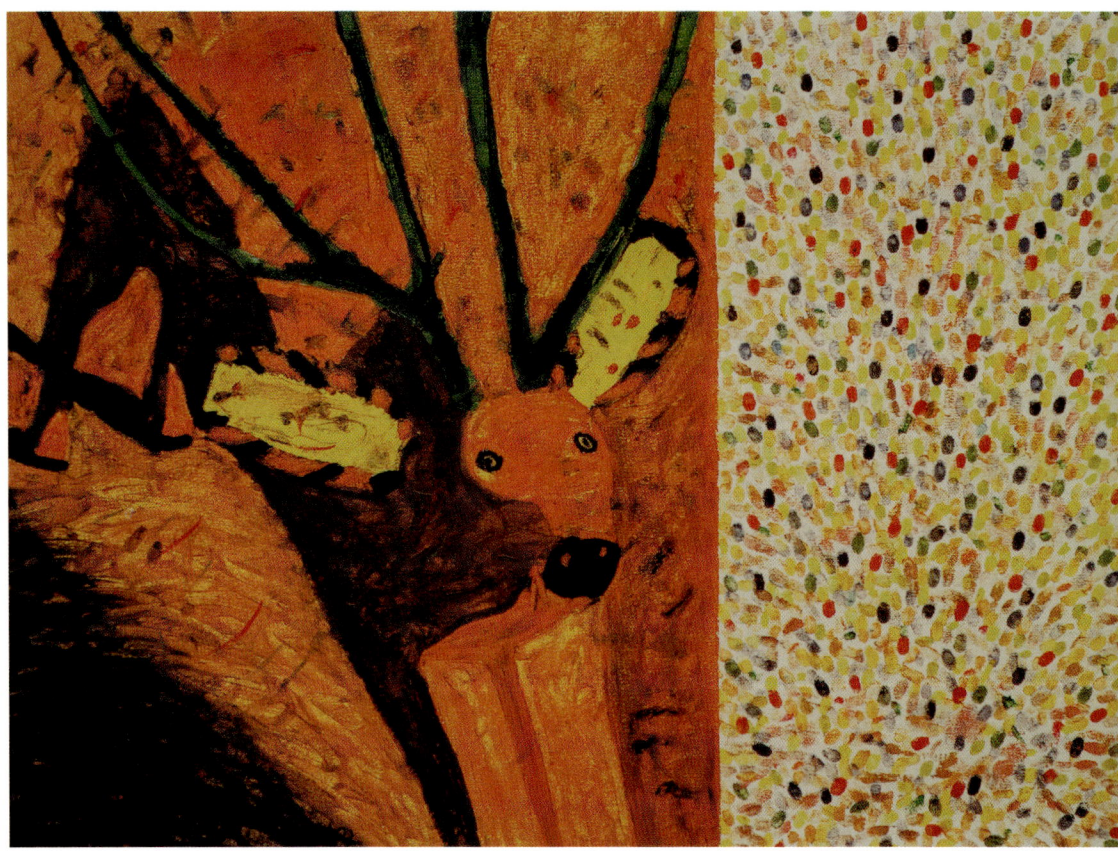

For Tia Juana y Mi Abuelita Guadalupe de Jalostotitlán, 1987. Chalk and linseed oil on canvas, canvas size: 38-1/8 x 52 inches. Copyright © Rupert García.

fingers into the paints and put them on the canvass. These are my fingerprints, and they pay homage to my Tía Juana and my Grandma Lupe, because they used their fingers and hands to do their art.

In the published catalog, I was honored that the museum asked my childhood friend and fellow student at Edison High School to write a short recollection. In her essay, Maxine Hong Kingston wrote that Rupert García "draws with [a] . . . passion for social justice, and whether hung in a gallery or distributed in the streets, Rupert García's art is powerful and beautiful."[7] I very much appreciated Maxine's comments.

I in particular value the awards that I have received with a Stockton connection. It's very important to me. It's my hometown, and I lived there for twenty-one years. It molded me and who I became. I experienced good things and bad things in Stockton; still it is the deepest emotional connection I have. It's my place and whatever has happened in my life, Stockton was the start. I had a great time in school. I think about Stockton all of the time. I had a great time growing up with my brothers and my mom and my grandmother and my tías and tíos. This was just all fantastic. So, I cherish being recognized as one of Stockton's own.

—II—

In 1992 I became involved in the Counter Columbian Quincentenary. That year, of course, marked the five hundredth anniversary of Christopher Columbus "discovering" America. Although some still celebrated this fiction, many by 1992 in the Americas did not. Instead, they saw conquest, genocide, and colonial exploitation by Europeans over the Indigenous peoples of the Americas. I agreed with this counternarrative. My participation was focused by my involvement in *The Columbian Quincentenary: A Reappraisal* exhibition organized at the Lang Gallery of Scripps College and the Claremont Graduate Humanities Center in Southern California. I was invited to exhibit my image of Columbus which I didn't do specifically for the exhibition, but which I had done in 1989 in anticipation of the Quincentenary.

I tried to make my image of Columbus intriguing and engaging. I titled my oil painting *El Día de la Raza, or the Cristobal Enterprise*. El Día de la Raza is the substitute term for Columbus Day that many in Latin America observe. "The Cristobal Enterprise" symbolizes the imperialist colonialist conquest unleashed by Columbus. This was a painting that I really wanted to do as part of the critical revisioning of Columbus and what he stood for as an imperialist colonizer. What's interesting is that we have no image of Columbus produced while he was alive.

There is a famous image made posthumously by Sebastian del Piombo in 1519 (the same year Cortez invaded Mexico) on which I based my image of Columbus, but with major changes. For example, I think some people even today wouldn't like the way I painted Columbus, but that doesn't bother me. I was not trying to talk to anybody with my artwork. I was talking to myself and I was trying to understand myself in the world. Making such an image was a very important way to do this. If I think too much about who the viewer is going to be, I get very confused.

On the right-hand side of my picture there are images painted in red, yellow, orange, and brown on a blue background with black spots. These images represent the dismembered hands, arms, and feet of the Indians committed by the Spaniards in their conquest of the Americas following Columbus's "discovery." Then on the left-hand side is my image of Columbus but with his head severed from his body. I don't recall that I intentionally set out to do this. I was expanding the light blue background that you see in the picture, and as I did this the paint went underneath Columbus's chin, dismembering the head from the body. I guess subconsciously I was getting back at the "bad guy" for what happened to the Indians after 1492. One could say that it represents the revenge of the Indigenous.

In addition to having my image of Columbus exhibited in the Columbian Quincentenary exhibit, I was also asked to write a short reflection on

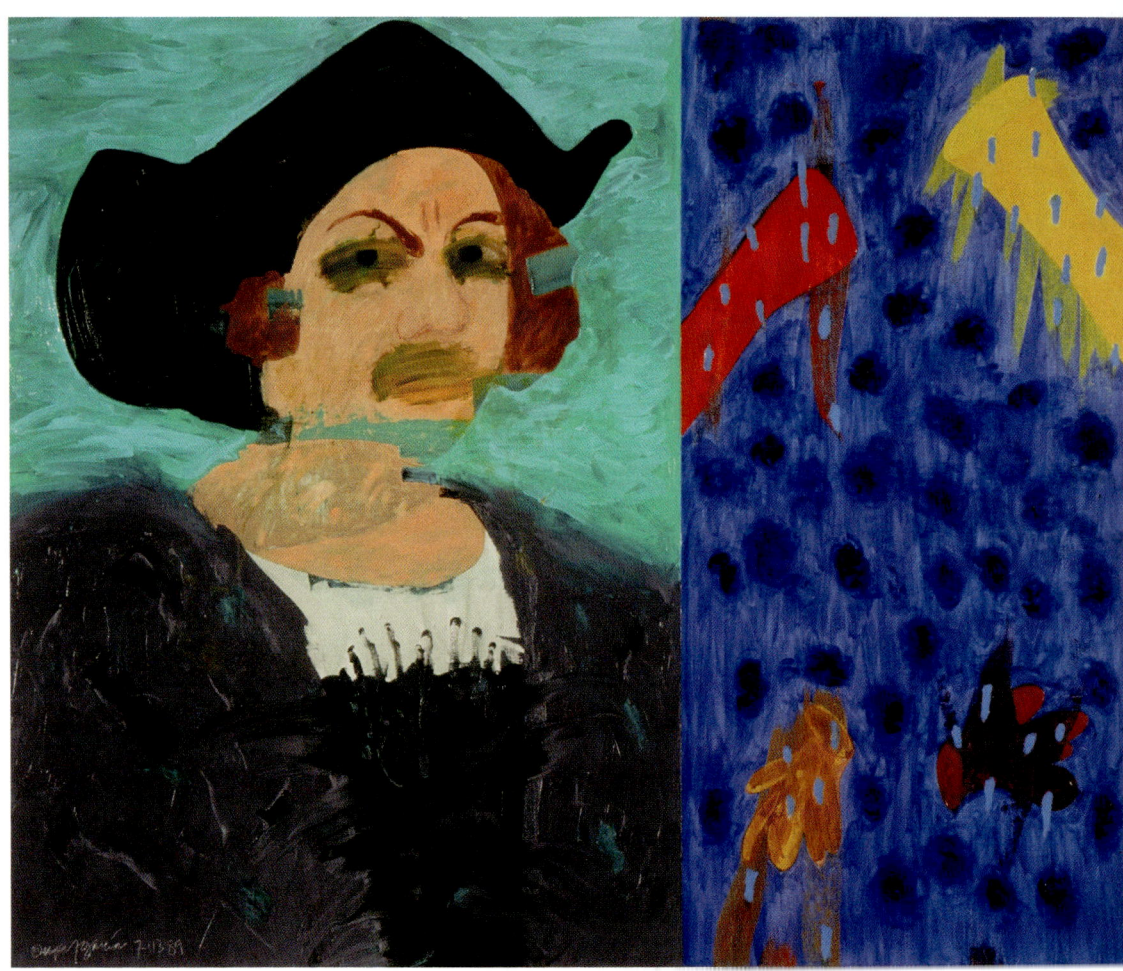

El Día de la Raza, or the Cristobal Enterprise, 1989. Oil paint on linen, canvas size: 74-1/4 x 90 inches. Copyright © Rupert García. Courtesy of Rena Bransten Gallery.

my painting. I observed that I see my counterimage of Columbus as a metaphor. It is a metaphor for any kind of invasion that has taken place and still takes place such as colonialism, imperialism, slavery, and any kind of exploitation of human beings. Columbus, to me, represents all of these types of exploitation.

—॥—

A year after the Quincentenary exhibit, I was asked to do a solo show at the Alternative Museum in New York. Jos Sances, who was on the museum board, suggested the show and the museum thought it was a good idea. It included my paintings, prints, and posters. The show was called *Aspects of Resistance* and ran from December 1993 to February 1994. It was a wonderful show and was done very well. The installation was right to my expectation.

Geno Rodríguez and Andrew Perchuk, cocurators:

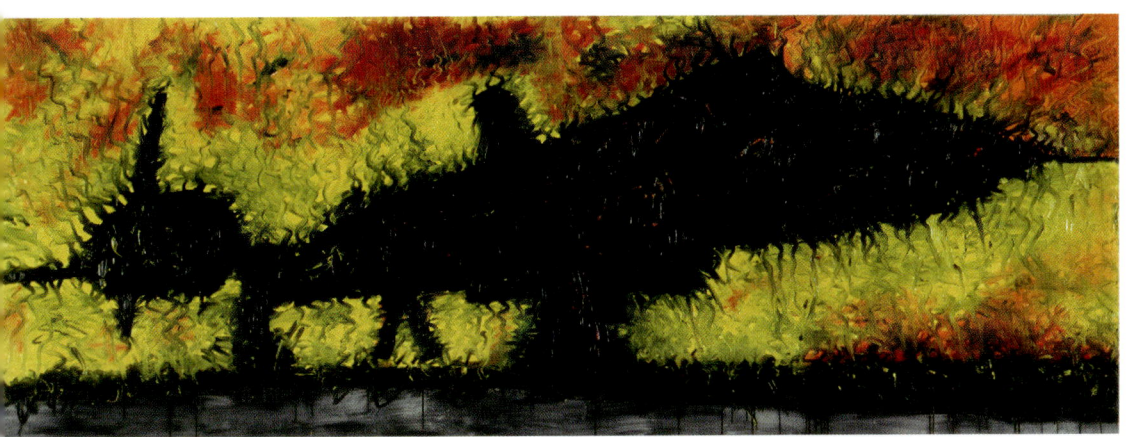

Ominous Omen 1987. Chalk, linseed oil and oil paint on canvas, canvas size: 47 x 130 inches. Copyright © Rupert García. Courtesy of Rena Bransten Gallery.

The Alternative Museum is particularly pleased to present *Aspects of Resistance* by Rupert García. García has long been known on the West Coast for his passionate, superbly executed works on paper but these recent works demonstrate how García has extended his unique vision to works on canvas as well. Rupert García in his work and in his actions throughout his career has stood for the type of socially committed art that the Alternative Museum has tried to foster for the last eighteen years. . . . [García] has been as he describes himself a critical artist, meaning primarily a concerned human being. His career is proof that artists who are not enfranchised in our society because of race do not create or exist in a context unconnected to American history, but rather that these artists and individuals have always been creators of American history and culture.[8]

One of my paintings in the exhibit reverted back to my depiction of the U.S. jet fighter that I guarded in Thailand during the U.S. war in Vietnam. My image of one of these planes I titled *Ominous Omen*. The planes on their own were beautiful kinetic sculptures. They had beautiful lines and shapes. On the other hand, the planes represented killing machines that would release deadly bombs including napalm. It was a symbiosis of aesthetics and death. The plane was not just one thing but two things at the same time. I chose the title *Ominous Omen* because I liked the poetry of the two words. At the same time, it was a picture about death. It's an omen about death caused by the fighter bomber. Although the plane is beautiful, I felt I had to destroy it because of what it represented. In the image the jet is self-destructing because it's on fire and is melting. In the picture, the orange and reddish colors represent fire and the black lines that are emanating from the plane is melting metal exploding. The plane is self-destructing almost as if it's guilty of what it does—kill people. I wanted to

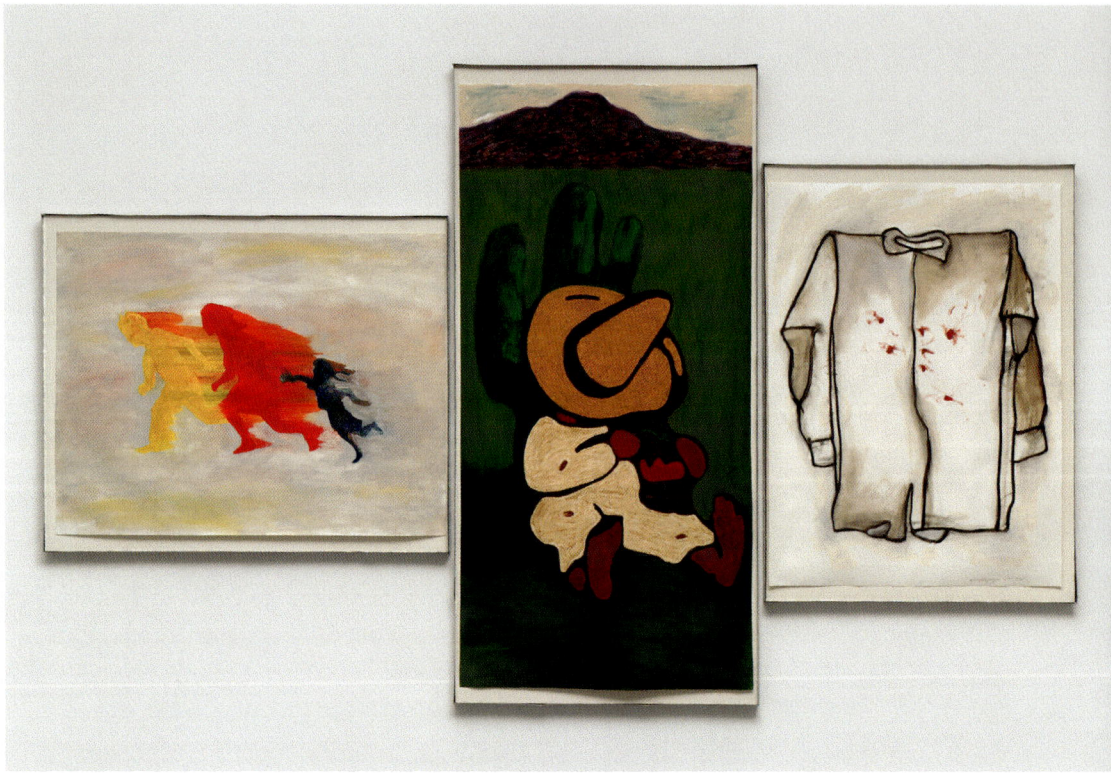

¡Hello, Goodbye, Hello!, 1992. Oil on paper, canvas size: 72 x 120 inches. Copyright © Rupert García. Courtesy of Rena Bransten Gallery.

destroy this machine because I didn't have any love for what it was intended to do. I didn't want to be part of that. It's a beautiful painting in oil where the oil moves around to produce the striking colors.

Even though there were many more of my paintings in the *Aspects of Resistance* exhibit, some of which I have already discussed, I want to mention one more picture that was shown. It's a tryptic entitled *¡Hello, Goodbye, Hello!* done in 1992 in oil. This date is important in California because of growing hysteria about "illegal aliens" coming across the border and right-wing Republican politicians such as

Governor Pete Wilson exploiting the issue. My painting was a response to this hysteria and its implications. For one, the nativists all addressed stereotypes about Mexicans to suggest that immigrants of this background were undesirable. Part of my picture addresses stereotypes and another is about combatting such stereotypes and the repression that flows from them. For example, in the middle section I painted the stereotype of the sleeping lazy Mexican with a big sombrero. I always hated that image. On the left is a picture that later became the face of Proposition 187 in 1994. The stereotypical image shows a man, a woman,

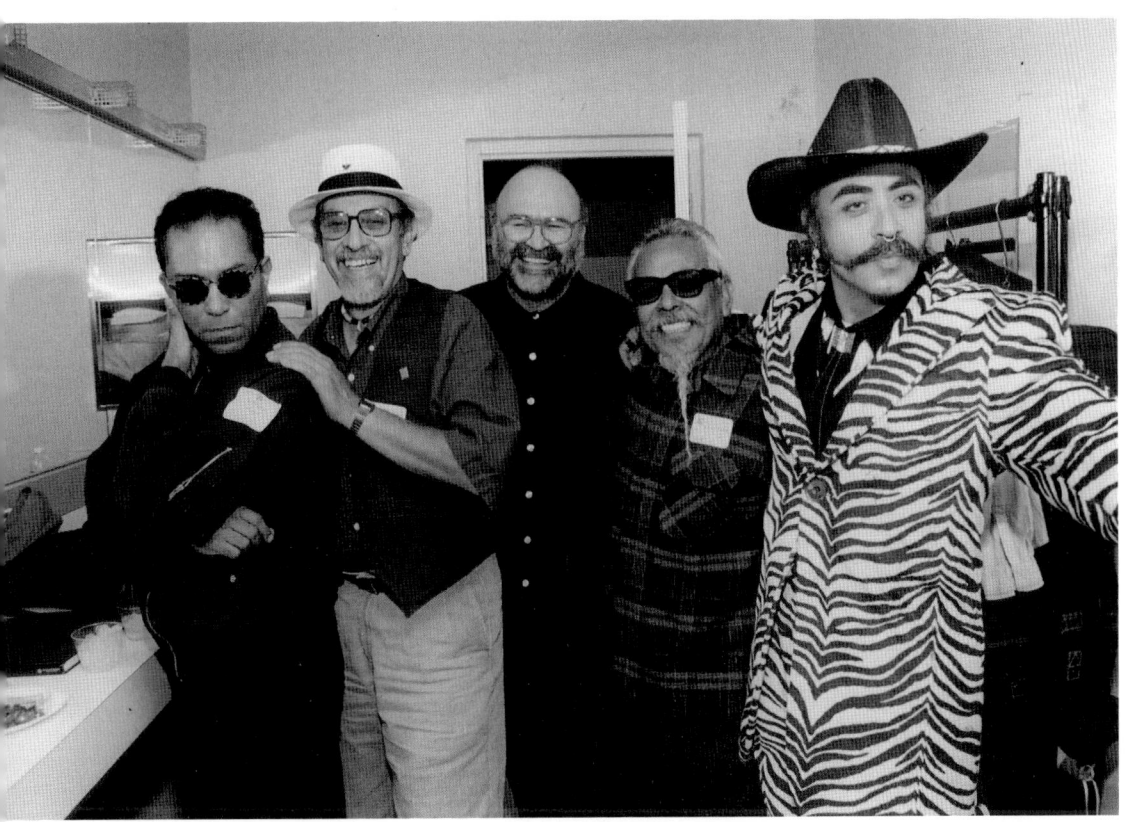

Rupert García with other major Chicano artists, 1995. Left to right Gronk, José Montoya, Rupert, Dr. Loco, and Guillermo Gómez-Peña. Photo courtesy of Bob Hsiang.

and a child racing across the freeway. Usually this image was accompanied by a text that read "They keep coming!" This was to unfairly suggest a horde of Mexicans racing across the border and that something needed to be done. Prop 187 addressed this by denying the undocumented any public services such as in education and health. It was an inhumane proposition. To counter this image, I painted my version on the left-hand side which does show the same people running, but with the use of colors I try to give them some dignity and to suggest that they are coming to achieve a better life,

especially for their children. They were the same as all other immigrants who have come to the United States, including the ancestors of the very people pushing Prop. 187. Finally, on the right-hand side I did an image based on a photo of the Emperor Maximillian's shirt after he was captured and executed by the Mexican army led by Benito Juárez in 1867. Juárez had temporarily defeated the intervention by the French on May 5, 1862 (Cinco de Mayo) although the French went on to impose a foreign emperor to rule Mexico with the French. This was Maximillian of Austria. The bloodied shirt that I painted suggests that repression then and now can be defeated, including things like the racist stereotyping of Mexicans and Proposition 187 which was passed by voters in California, but fortunately declared unconstitutional by a federal court. Interestingly, the last panel with Maximillian's shirt is in the possession of the wonderful writer Richard Rodriguez. Having said all this, I want to also stress that while you can read a certain interpretation of this painting and of all of my paintings, all this is not the totality of why I did this painting or any other painting. There are a lot of innuendos in my paintings here and there. It's not just one thing; it's a lot of things.[9]

■ll■

The 1980s and into the 1990s was an important period in my artistic development and evolution. I became more experimental in themes and techniques. I broadened myself as an artist and as a person. I was not afraid to explore new challenges and opportunities. I began to receive more recognition, both nationally and internationally, for my work. I might still be considered in some circles a Chicano/Latino artist, but I had developed into much more than that. My art reflected this complexity and diversity. I looked forward to still more challenges in the new millennium.

9

Millennial Artist

I didn't pay much attention to the fact that by 2000 we were entering into a new millennium. I don't think this change affected my art. At least at the time, I didn't think so. However, as I reflect back, you can detect certain changes in how I painted and what I painted. The most significant change was that I started not only to experiment with digital art, but I became fascinated by it and started to do various digital images, so that by the first two decades of the new century, I was fully engaged with this new way of painting. I think that while I revised some earlier images through digital art, I also did new subjects that did not always reference Chicano/Latino images or topics but yet, in my opinion, constitute Chicano/Latino art, to say nothing of American art. If I had blossomed as an artist in the 1980s and 1990s, I continued to grow in the new millennium so that my art has a more mature appearance. I think too that as I went up in age I felt that what I was painting or printing would perhaps be the last phase of my legacy.

◼◻◼

I had never had an interest in digital art or what some call computer art or new media art and, in fact, didn't pay much attention to what digital art was happening. Most digital art was mainly used for commercial purposes. I was very hesitant about digital art; I found it too mechanical. I really fought it. This, however, changed when I was introduced to Don Farnsworth in the early 1990s. Don was an early pioneer in digital art as an artist himself and as a producer of digital art for other artists. He encouraged artists such as myself to experiment in digital art, but more importantly, he had the facilities to show artists how to do digital art and the equipment to actually produce the art. Don founded what would be Magnolia Editions in 1981 in San Francisco and then moved to West Oakland, where he leased an 8,000-square-foot warehouse on Magnolia Street, hence the name of his operation. This large space resembled a factory. It was through Don that I started a new phase of my art—digital art.

I forgot who introduced me to Don or if he reached out to me. I just

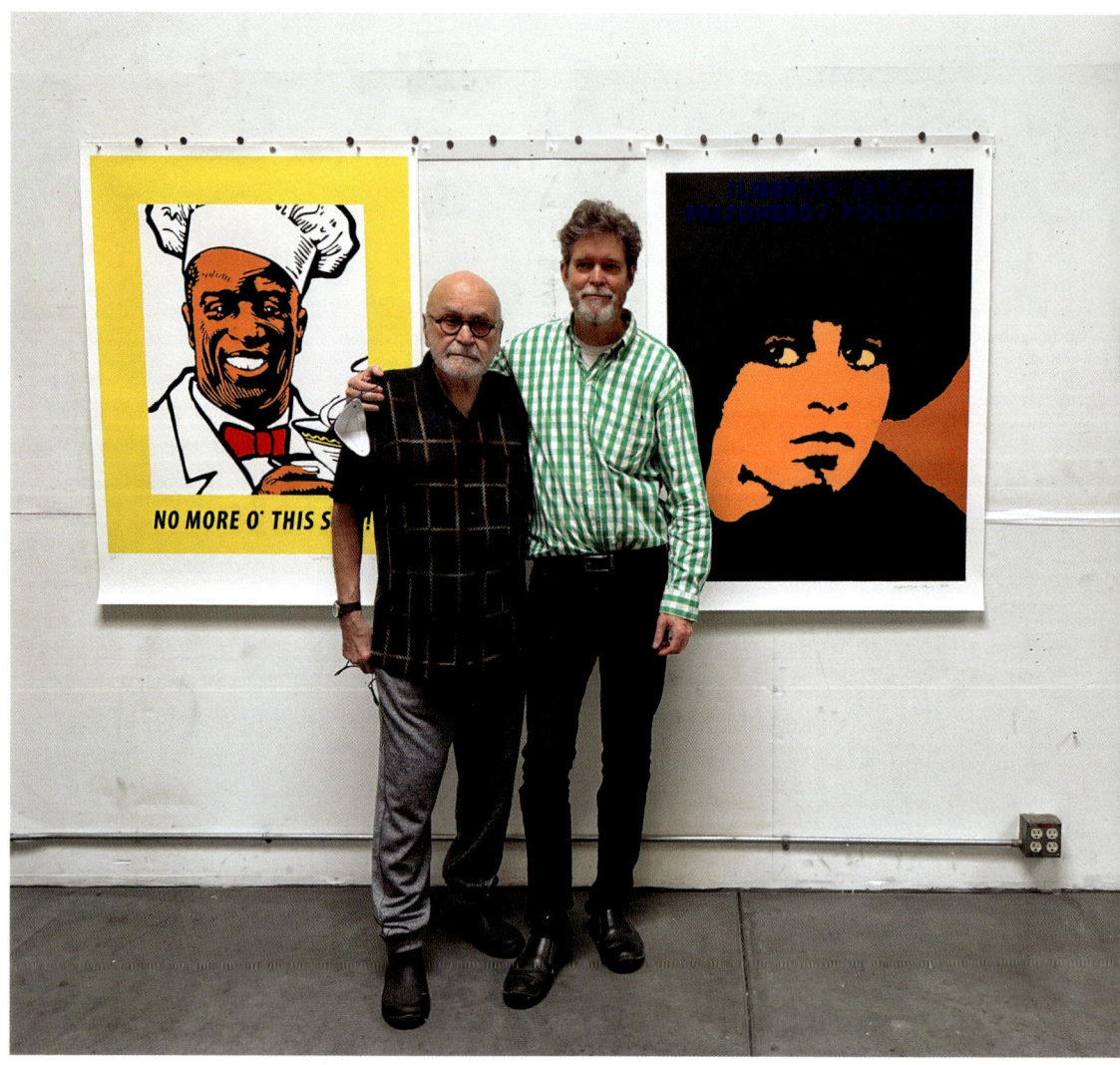

Rupert García with Don Farnsworth at Magnolia Editions Studio, Oakland, California, 2021. Photo courtesy of Don Farnsworth and Magnolia Editions.

remember going to his facility where Don showed me how digital art is produced. I was blown over! I was fascinated by how you could do a painting digitally or even revise an earlier image. I'm not someone who is technically inclined, but Don made it possible for me to understand the process. "Let me contaminate your art," Don joked. Moreover, he alleviated any anxiety I had about venturing into this new format by saying that he or one of his assistants would always work with me on producing my digital pictures. I would not be alone. In addition, I would have to do these images at the Magnolia facility, because they had all of the needed equipment.

I was still initially cautious about venturing in this new art, but Don made it easy for me to learn and how to appreciate how much richer the colors came out digitally. This involved software, computers, and other electronic devises. Your picture can be printed on canvas or special paper and even on wood. This results in your prints. The prints can be quite large, which is what I prefer. Magnolia has high-quality printers. This process can be very technical, and it's hard for me to explain it all in detail. What I can say is that what is involved is scanning an image or a sketch and putting it into a computer. Once inserted, you can begin to fill in and augment your image. Of course, part of this process is selecting the colors you will use and through the computer accessing them. The program you use can provides examples of all kinds of colors. Digitally I can think more quickly about color, because the computer is like an extension of my mind.

My initial digital images were some pencil drawings I had done in the late 1960s and which I experimented on. I couldn't believe how real these images looked digitally. During the next few years while still doing my oil paintings, I started to warm up to what was possible in doing digital art. As a result, I started producing particular paintings by the end of the decade and into the new century.

■||■

I did one of my first major digital images in 2000 with my picture of Sor Juana Iñes de la Cruz, one of the great Mexican poets of the colonial era. She became a nun as one of the only ways for women to be educated then. I titled the image *Untitled for Sor Juana*. I was motivated to paint Sor Juana after I had seen a recent book on her by Octavio Paz. I found an image of Sor Juana and used that as my model. Sor Juana, of course, has become seen as a proto-feminist, especially by Chicana artists and intellectuals, but that wasn't why I did her picture. I did it because I was inspired by her story.

Using the computer, I also did a new version of La Virgen de Guadalupe in 2002. Guadalupe, of course, was the name of my grandmother, and she had a strong devotion to La Virgen as I explained earlier. So, in honor of my grandmother, I have done various images of Guadalupe over the years. This digital picture was one of them. I called it *La Virgen and Colored Boxes*. I scanned my earlier *La Virgen y Yo* and then introduced various colored boxes which have no particular meaning other than for aesthetic reasons. These boxes do, however, provide a fragmented Virgen that one can interpret in any way. I love my images of La Virgen because they remind me of my grandmother but also of my mother, who had her own strong devotion to Guadalupe. As a matter of fact, on one occasion my siblings and I organized a birthday party for my mother. I designed place cards using one of my images of La Virgen. Although I'm not a practicing Catholic, I always honor the image of Guadalupe. She is always with me.

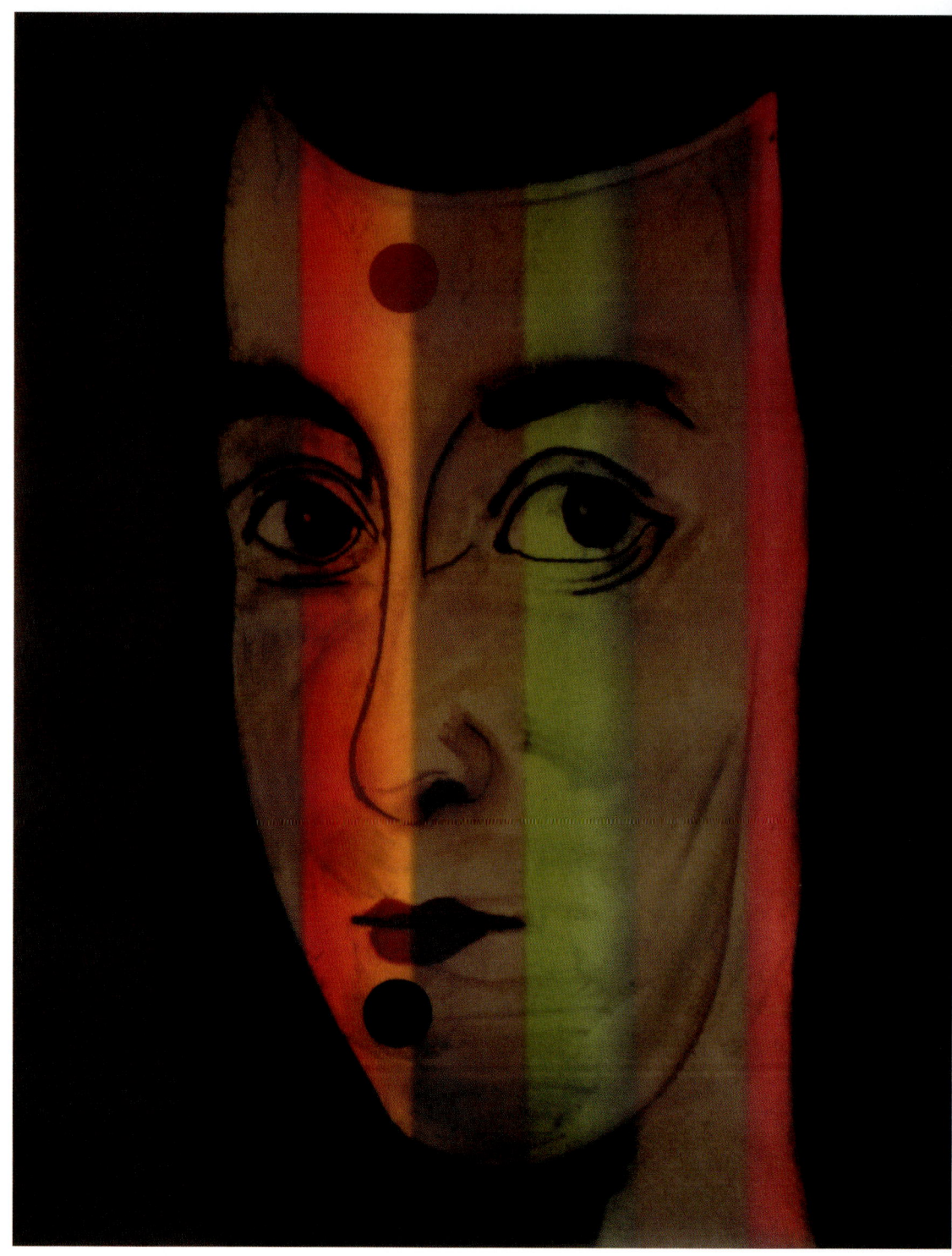

Untitled for Sor Juana, 2000. Pigmented inkjet print, sheet size: 40 x 33 inches, image size: 40 x 33 inches. Copyright © Rupert García. Courtesy of Rena Bransten Gallery.

Between 2000 and 2011, I produced about eighty digital prints and paintings all at the Magnolia facility. Most of these became the nucleus of my first major exhibit of digital art held at the de Young Museum in San Francisco in 2011. Don Farnsworth and I had been talking about such an exhibit.

"Where do you think we could have it?" Don asked.

"Well, I've been on the board of the de Young Museum and they might be interested," I responded. "I'll check."

It was a lot of work to make the exhibit happen, but we did it. It was a limited one occupying only one main room, but it was worth it. There was an opening reception where I gave a lecture on the work and talked about doing digital art. The exhibit ran from February 19 to July 17, 2011. It was titled *Rupert García: The Magnolia Editions Projects, 1991–2011.* The catalog was by the same title, and it was a beautiful production. I was very pleased and thankful to Don Farnsworth and Magnolia Editions for doing it.

One of my digital pictures, a triptych, I named *Untitled for Manet, Zapata Et Che.* For this one, I was inspired by the paintings of Manet, who is one of my favorite painters. What I admired about Manet was not only his Impressionist style and his sharp criticism of what he considered to be bourgeoise painting, but also that he was not afraid to state his political positions and was often opposed to his government's policies. It fascinated the

hell out of me to learn all of this. I love this guy and I love his paintings. So, in a way this particular digital image is a homage to Manet. In my print, both on the left and right-hand side, I have an image of Manet in black, white, and gray. In the center there are four cubes in pink, green, orange, and red in squares. Within these squares, I have two images of Che Guevara. The one on the left is his face after he had been killed by the CIA in Bolivia in 1967. However, on the right, I printed Che alive and smiling. Overlaying the Che images is a figure of a horse outlined in white but filled in with the colors I used for the Che cubes. This is Zapata's horse. Hence, the painting is also a homage to Che and Zapata, whose images I had done back in the early 1970s.

In previous paintings before I started to experiment in digital art, I did some images related to war inspired by my experiences in Thailand, in particular images of the type of jet fighters used, which as a security guard I protected. Based on this influence, in 2002 I did an image which I called *1819, 1962– 1966, 2002.* This painting in part is based on a famous 1819 one by the French painter Théodore Géricault. I was fascinated by Géricault and other French painters of the nineteenth century who critically approached their work and their themes. In Géricault's painting there is a large raft with several men on it lost at sea. It caused a big scandal in France. The painting is focused on a man standing and waving a piece of clothing to try to get the attention of what we assume is another

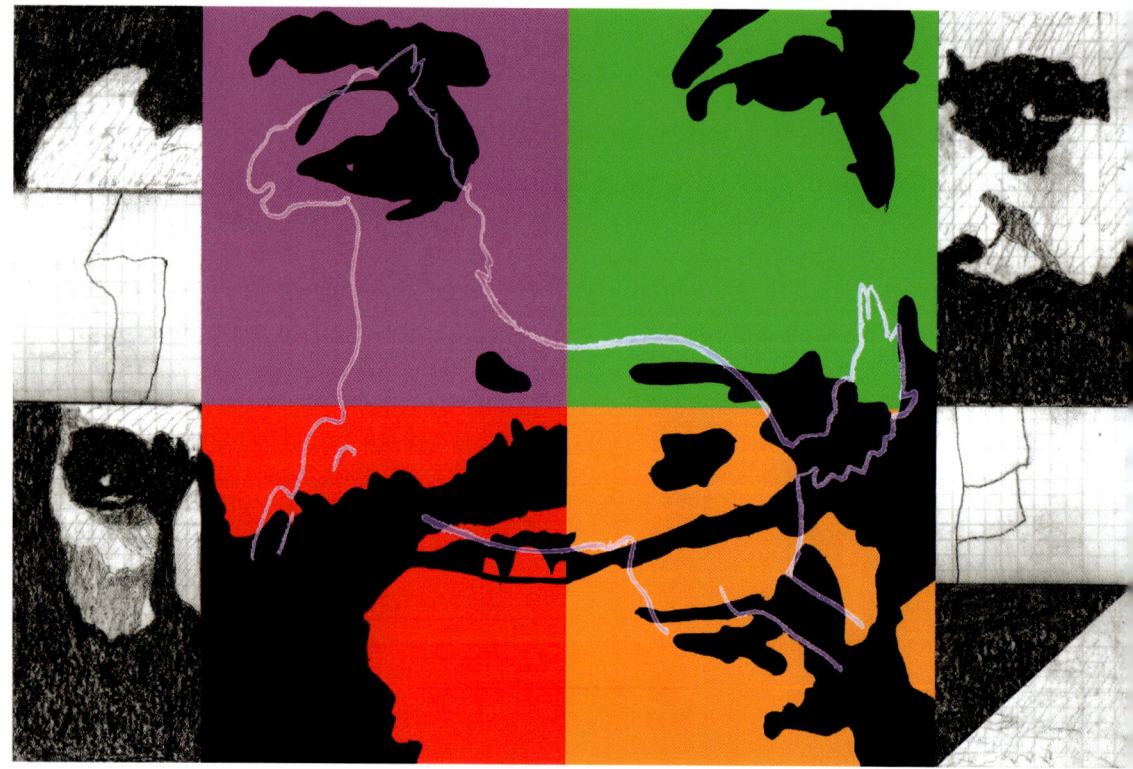

Untitled for Manet, Zapata Et Che, 2000. Pigmented inkjet Japanese micropolyester, canvas size: 35 x 57 inches. Copyright © Rupert García. Courtesy of Rena Bransten Gallery.

ship. In researching this painting, I further learned that the man standing is an African. I said "wow! Wouldn't it be great to do something with that!" So, I did. In my version, I cut out the others on the raft and focus only on the African waving. However, on the right-hand side of what amounts to a diptych, I painted a U.S. jet bomber of great deadliness. I created this magnificent-looking instrument of war in the same dark shade that I did the African and with the same ominous reddish dark sky as in the other image. I reduced the likeness of the man on the boat and enlarged the image of the bomber. In this composition, I used the

computer, but when the picture was printed, I colored in some parts with acrylic. Actually, for some of my other digital images, I also would paint on them after the image was printed out. This is not unusual in doing digital art, and so you have a mixed medium. You can do this because the ink in the printer is acrylic and when it dries you can paint on the digitized images, and it won't necessarily obstruct any of the color or any of the composition.

For the de Young exhibit, I included two images both entitled *Hiroshima*. These two are very personal. When I was a kid I had a very good friend who was Japanese American. A few

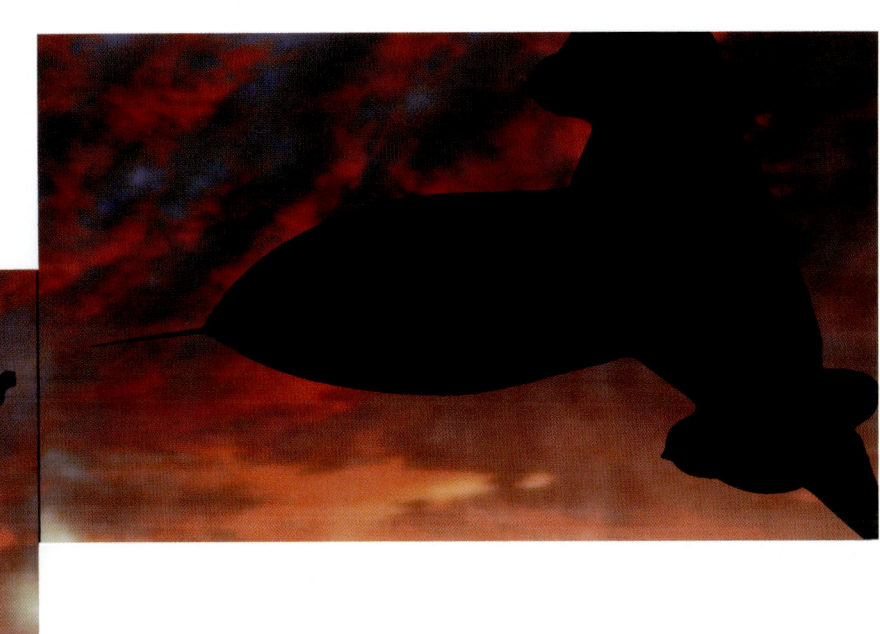

1819. 1962–1966, 2002, 2002. Pigmented inkjet with acrylic on canvas, canvas size: 58 x 93 inches. Copyright © Rupert García. Courtesy of Rena Bransten Gallery.

years later I learned about the atomic bombs dropped on Hiroshima and Nagasaki by U.S. planes. I remember linking it back to my Japanese American friend. I wondered if perhaps he had family in either city and what may have happened to them. I was horrified by this thought, which was only worsened as I would see the actual explosion of the bombs in newsreels or documentaries. But I held these feeling inside of me even though at some point I wanted to do a painting about these horrific events. I finally did two images in 2009. It may have been the U.S. bombings in the Iraq War that Bush and Cheney unleashed without any justification that inspired this painting. Sometimes I'll make a work whose reference is complex and which may include something from my childhood or something I saw or somebody I met. So, in the Hiroshima paintings, I made them because of my feeling about Hiroshima. In the first painting when you look at it you think you see only two squares. The left-hand one you see in white and the right-hand one in red. However, the closer you look you see in the red section the planes that dropped the bomb and the image of the bomb exploding. However, this is not very obvious. I wanted to slow down my interaction with what I was thinking and painting. The white section stands on its own because in Japanese aesthetics white is death and red is the opposite. At first this painting looks like a solid

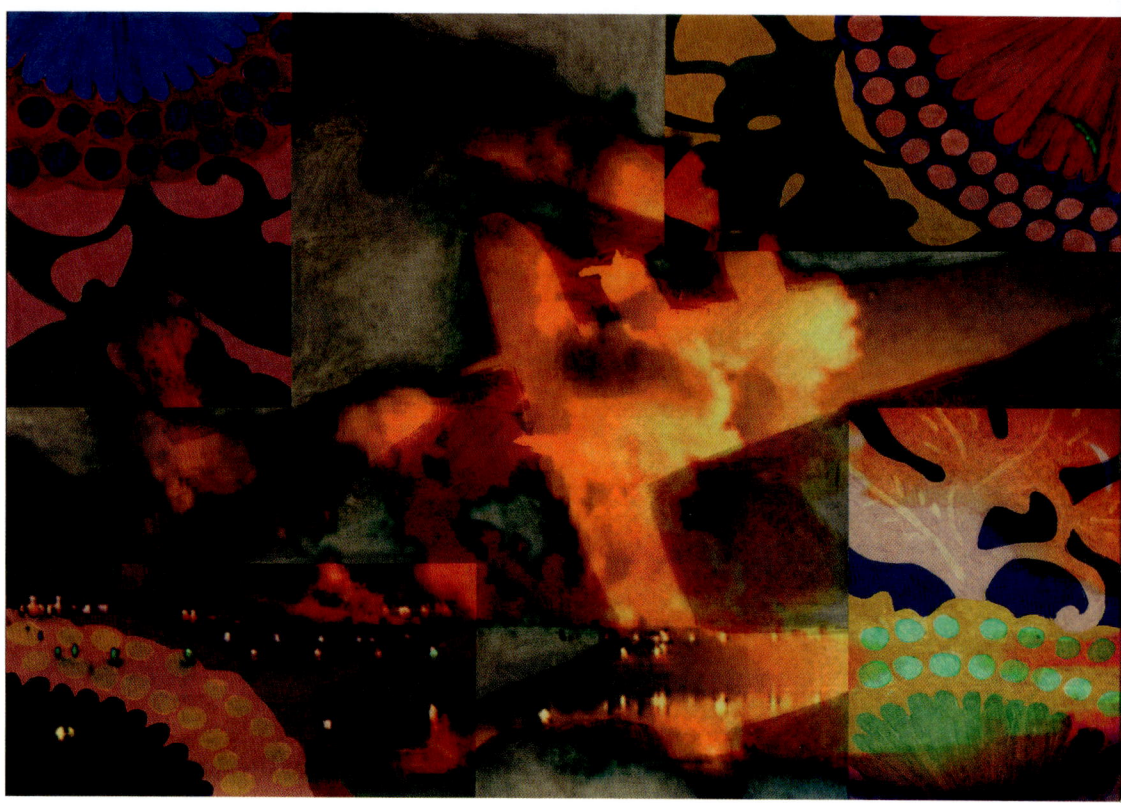

Hiroshima II, 2009. Mixed media on paper, canvas size: 22-3/8 x 30-1/8 inches. Copyright © Rupert García. Courtesy of Rena Bransten Gallery.

geometric image, but if you stay with it, it becomes more complex, and I just love that experience. I did this digitally but also painted in some of the image, so it is a mixed-medium picture.

My second Hiroshima digital piece was also mixed medium. In this one you clearly see the outline of the bomber, and below it and above are the atomic clouds as the bomb explodes. It came out pretty good and is in a way more visual and dramatic than the first Hiroshima. These two pictures all began with that feeling I had linking my Japanese American friend with the horror of the attacks on Hiroshima and Nagasaki. Sometimes I don't mind

not knowing where everything is going and just follow my feelings and do the picture.

Of course, I did other digital paintings, but I will discuss these in other sections of this chapter. It is fair to say, however, that the new millennium brought forth a new and exciting medium for the art of Rupert García.

◼▮◼

Besides the de Young exhibit in 2011, I also participated in other exhibits into the new century that focused on my work. One that I really appreciated was at the prestigious Corcoran Gallery of Art in Washington, DC called

Politics and Provocation: The Posters of Rupert García in 2000. This was my first show at the Corcoran. I didn't seek this out. I have never sought out exhibits. Organizers of exhibits come to me. This is exactly what happened in the Corcoran case, which focuses on portraits.

We selected about twenty prints and posters, all from my earlier days. The exhibit was to occupy one room at the gallery. Although no catalog was produced, they did do two digital posters using my 1973 silk screen of Picasso and my 1974/75 silk screen that I revised as digital images for the posters. The exhibit ran from March 3 to March 23 in 2001. Almost all of my images were posters and not prints. Although I don't agree, the traditional view in the art world is that posters are not really art because they contain words which, according to them, contaminate the image and therefore do not constitute a print which has no words. So, a print is acceptable as art but not a poster. This is all nonsense, and thank God the Corcoran didn't buy into this definition. It accepted my posters with words as art, and I was very grateful for this.

What I further found interesting in the exhibit was the emphasis on my earlier work and the title of the show, *Politics and Provocation: The Posters and Prints of Rupert García*. Over the years too much attention has been paid to only these earlier images and not the greater body of my work. I have no problem with the title of the exhibit linked to these early posters because here I was deliberately being

political and being provocative. I had to be given the politics of the late 60s and early 70s and the influence on me of the San Francisco State Strike. I was angry then not only about the conditions on campus but about what was happening in the country and the world. I could not remain silent, and I spoke through my posters as a critique of the status quo. The problem has been, however, that from this earlier period, I have been stereotyped and reduced to doing just "political art" and being a "political artist." This is true but not true. This ignores my evolution as a more complex artist and doing work that can be considered political but in a subtler way. In a way, the Corcoran was reducing me as an artist; I did the show because it was at least important to call attention to my work, even though it was only a very small portion of it. I have gone beyond this and done much more.

The same essentialism applies to those who see me only as a Chicano or Latino artist. I see my myself as an American artist because Chicanos and Latinos are Americans. I was raised as a mexicano and then I discovered being a Mexican American and then Chicanismo came along. The human brain multiples things and so you can have multiple identities. I'm all of these but in the end I'm also an American artist. We shouldn't allow anyone to monopolize the term American. We have paid our dues in this country through our blood, sweat, and tears, and no one can or should deny that we are Americans. In the art world, there is sometimes a tendency to type artists, including ethnic ones, as being Chicano or Latino artists. This is not so much a racialized thing, but an attempt to market ethnic art.

There was one exhibit that I personally appreciated. This was a homage to me at La Galeria de La Raza. This occurred in 2014 and paralleled my receiving the Southern Graphics Council International Conference's Bay Area Lifetime Achievement Award. The exhibition at La Galeria included the prints and posters along with the images done for the calendarios when I was a member of the Galeria during the 1970s. A former student of mine and an excellent artist, Juan Fuentes, came up with the idea of the homage to me by La Galeria. It wasn't a large exhibit given the limited space of La Galeria, but I thought it was great. I had not been involved with La Galeria for some years and so I was moved that it still appreciated the work I had done as one of the early artists involved in this historic collective. The fact of the matter is that La Galeria was very significant in my development as an artist.

Another exhibit that I participated in was not one just on my work but on Latino art in the United States. It was called *Our America: The Latino Presence in American Art* held at the Smithsonian Museum of American Art in 2013. I had only one picture in the exhibit, which was a pastel that I had earlier donated to the Smithsonian in 1978. The exhibit was composed of all Latino artists, men and women, and it made me think about the concept of Latino art. The exhibit impressed me about the diversity of Latino art

of which I was a part of. It's true that early on artists were influenced by Chicanismo and the Chicano Movement, especially in doing a kind of neo-Indigenous art. This early art was also connected to important movement pronouncements such as El Plan de Aztlán. However, even during the heyday of the movement, some artists such as myself were influenced by the movement but were not captives to it, and we expressed some independence from Chicanismo. We didn't always follow the rules of what Chicano art should look like and be about. I was fortunate because La Galeria was very broad-minded about what constituted Chicano/Latino art. I began to see this more artistic independence in the 1980s and 1990s, and it only accelerated into the new century. Latino art became more complex. Some complained that it was becoming too intellectual and too remote from *la gente*, but I disagree. It has certainly become more diverse as the *Our America* exhibit revealed, but it is still grounded in the Chicano/Latino experience, although it has expanded that experience.

At the *Our America* exhibit, I was one of the older artists in the show. Some there and elsewhere consider or may consider me to be a senior statesman of Chicano/Latino art. But I don't see myself in this way at all. Yes, I'm in my early eighties, but I haven't retired from making art and still very creative art. I'm not part of an older school of art; I think that I still represent a vanguard in Chicano/Latino art, especially now that I'm doing digital art, which many Chicano/Latino artists are not.

So, I reject profusely that categorization of me as an "elder artist," which suggests that you're done as an artist and so let the new generation express itself. I think that I'm actually still ahead of this new generation.

—||—

After the Bush-Cheney administration unjustly invaded Iraq in 2003 under the lie that Saddam Hussein possessed weapons of mass destruction—a war of choice—I was enraged at this. Although I didn't participate in the protest marches before or after the invasion, I did react by doing several paintings critical of what the United States was doing. I let my art speak for itself. One picture I called *¡No War For Oil!* (2004). It expressed my belief that the real reason for the invasion was to take over Iraq's extensive oilfields. The painting which I did digitally shows an image of a stealth bomber all in black of the kind used in the bombardment of Bagdad, which Bush called "Shock and Awe." Beneath the bomber is a layer of red and above it is blue with some white. It is a striking image that is anti-war.

During the invasion and occupation of Iraq, American soldiers and CIA agents captured and tortured a number of prisoners. This included the

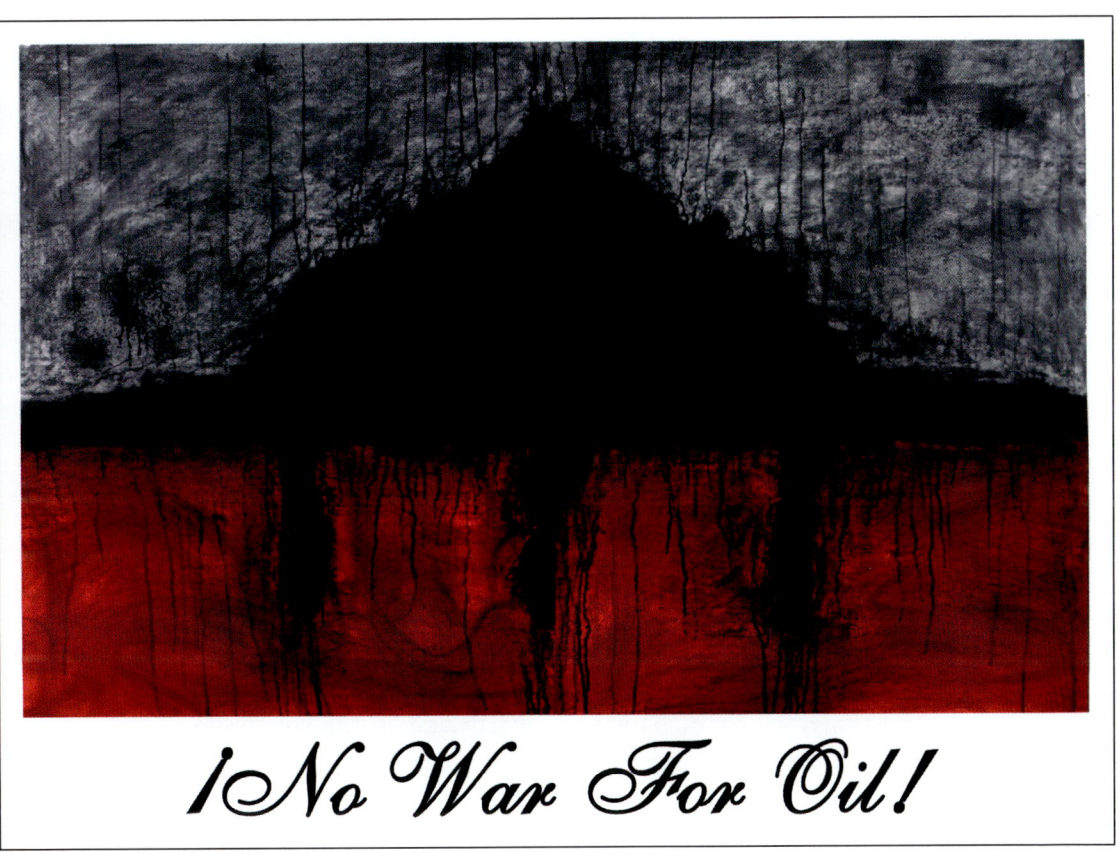

¡No War For Oil!, 2004. Pigmented inkjet with acrylic on canvas, canvas size: 29 x 40-1/4 inches. Copyright © Rupert García. Courtesy of Rena Bransten Gallery.

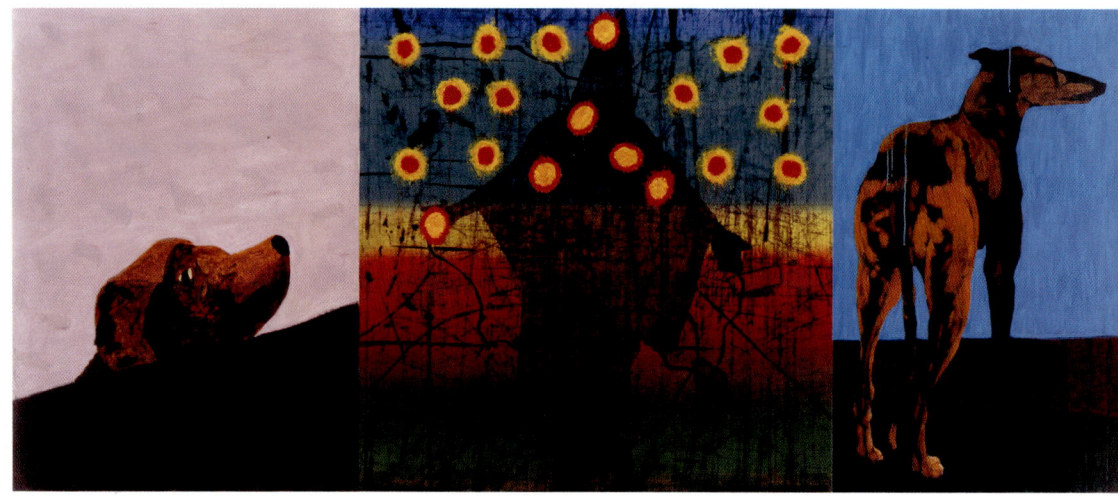

Los Dos Perros y Abu Ghraib, 2005–2006. Pigmented Inkjet with acrylic on canvas, canvas size: 53 x 119-1/4 inches. Copyright © Rupert García. Courtesy of Rena Bransten Gallery.

infamous water boarding interrogation technique that was clearly a violation of human rights. The media exposed these horrendous torture techniques including a now famous photo of a hooded Iraqi prisoner standing on a bench or platform being tortured. The torture took place in a detention center called Abu Ghraib. It is an amazing picture. It motivated me to do my own image of this figure, which I called *Los Dos Perros y Abu Ghraib*. It's a triptych with the center piece showing my version of the hooded prisoner and the left and right panels showing two *perros* or dogs. In reality, U.S. soldiers at Abu Ghraib used dogs to guard and intimidate the prisoners. They were part of the torture. However, in my painting the dogs are there to protect the tortured prisoner from further abuse. This was my testimony of such torture. The dog on the left was completely hand-painted while the dog on the right is a combination of digital and hand-painted technique. The prisoner in the center is also a combination of digital and hand painting. I really love using mixed medium, and actually a number of my digital images also include hand painting. I find this approach very exciting.

▬▮▬

In 2008, I became very interested in the campaign of Barack Obama for president of the United States. I didn't know much about him, although I knew he was a senator from Illinois. As his campaign developed, I learned more about him and saw in him a fresh wind within the Democratic Party and in the country. I also was excited that he could become the first Black president. I was always a supporter of the Black Power Movement, and some of my early images related to it. Moreover, Oakland where I lived is a very Black city, and I had over the years supported and voted for various Black candidates. I saw in Obama a movement for social change, and this complemented my politics. I was not a political activist, but as in the San Francisco State Strike, I put my art in support of Obama.

I approached his campaign about doing a poster of Obama for them. I never got a direct answer, and so I did the image on my own. I did it to raise money for the campaign. I actually did two digital pictures, and one of them I put up for sale with my gallery on a special night. Someone bought it and I don't know what they paid for it, but all of the money went to the Obama campaign. This was my way of supporting it. Both had a kind of pop art look to them which I liked. The first one is a profile of Obama which I titled *Obama Hope*. At the top of the picture is his name "Obama" and at bottom is the word "Hope." In the image, Obama looks very serious and is not flashing his famous smile. However, in the second picture he is. I simply called this one *Obama 2008*. At the top is his name and at the bottom I put in 2008.

They were not converted into posters. My images did not become the iconic one used in the campaign. That was done by Shepard Fairey.

I never met Barack Obama but like many other Americans voted for him and was delighted when he won. I thought he was a good president under difficult circumstances. To show my continued support of him, but also to bring attention to his historical and complex relations with the past, I did

a third digital image of Obama called *Obama From Douglass* in 2010. I love this print, but it's a very complex one. I wanted to link Obama to Fredrick Douglass the great Black emancipator, but at the same time I wanted to raise questions about that proposed relationship. I chose Douglass because he was a man of consequences. Is Obama the inheritor of Douglass's politics or not or somewhere in between? As the first Black president is Obama an emancipator and liberator of Black people? I don't provide the answer but want people to think about it, which is something I try to do with many of my other pictures. I also wanted to humanize Obama. To raise these questions, I inserted on the left the smiling image of Obama that I had done for the campaign but eliminating the wording. On the right is the classic image of Douglass captured in a photograph by George Kendall in 1879. I received permission to replicate that image into my print. In my image, it looks like Douglass is looking at Obama in a stern and quizzical way.

There is an interesting comparison between the two portraits. The Obama one is very flat in shapes and color and appears almost cartoonish and very poster-like. There is no nuance but there's that great smile. By contrast, the Douglass image appears to depict a very serious no-nonsense man. The black and white photograph looks like parchment and gives you a sense of something aged and not of our time, and that's how I used it. The Obama image seems to be of the moment and pop art while the Douglass

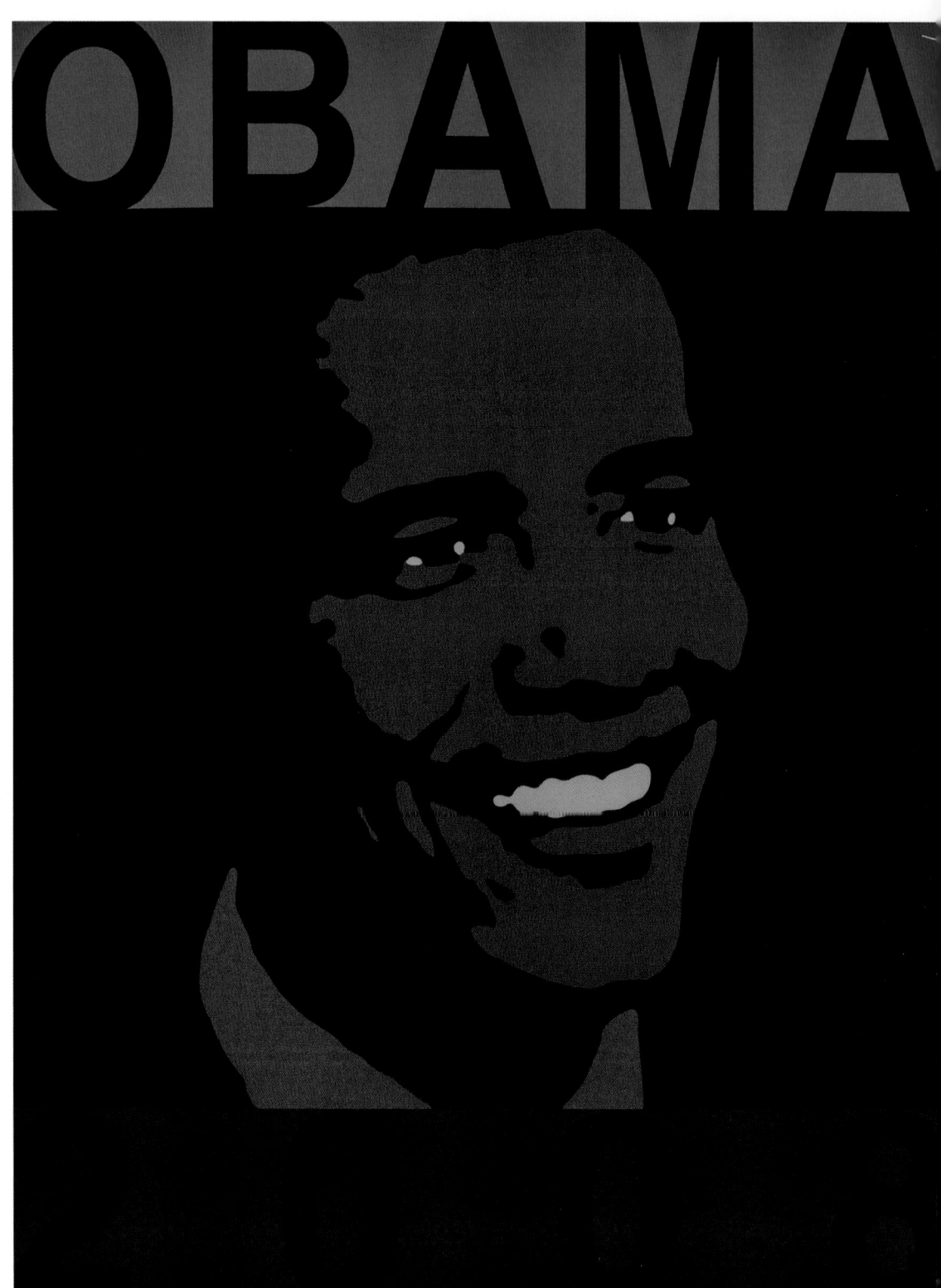

Obama, 2008, 2008. Pigmented inkjet print, sheet size: 30 x 22-1/4 inches, image size: 25-1/8 x 19 inches. Copyright © Rupert García.

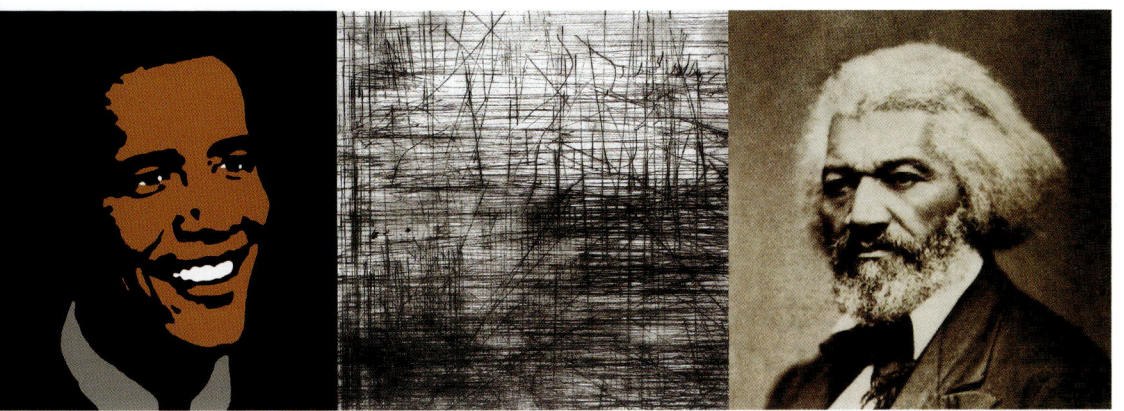

Obama from Douglass, 2010. Pigmented inkjet print, sheet size: 44 x 96 inches, image size: 31 x 90 inches. Copyright © Rupert García. Courtesy of Rena Bransten Gallery.

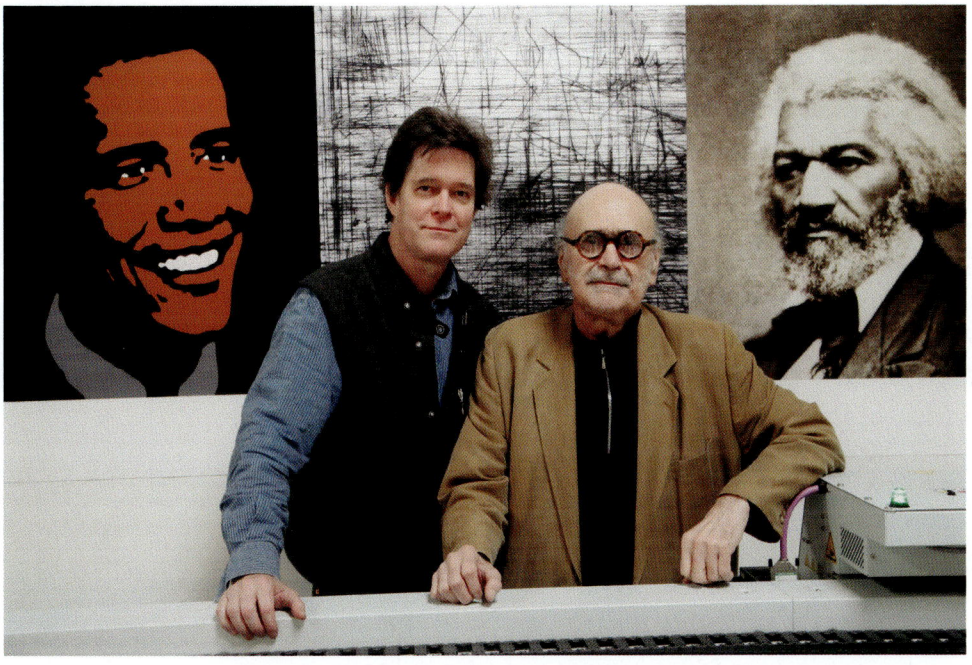

Rupert García with Don Farnsworth at Magnolia Editions Studio, Oakland, California, 2018. Photo courtesy of Don Farnsworth and Magnolia Editions.

one is transcendental, of the ages. But then to complicate the relationship, in the middle dividing Obama from Douglass, I added in these black lines going vertically and horizontally with a white backdrop. I say dividing but one could also say that the lines represent a bridge. The lines are meant to raise questions about the relationship and to instill nuance and complexity. The lines can be troubling. There is no simple way for me to comprehend this picture, because there is so much going on. I like that complexity. Who

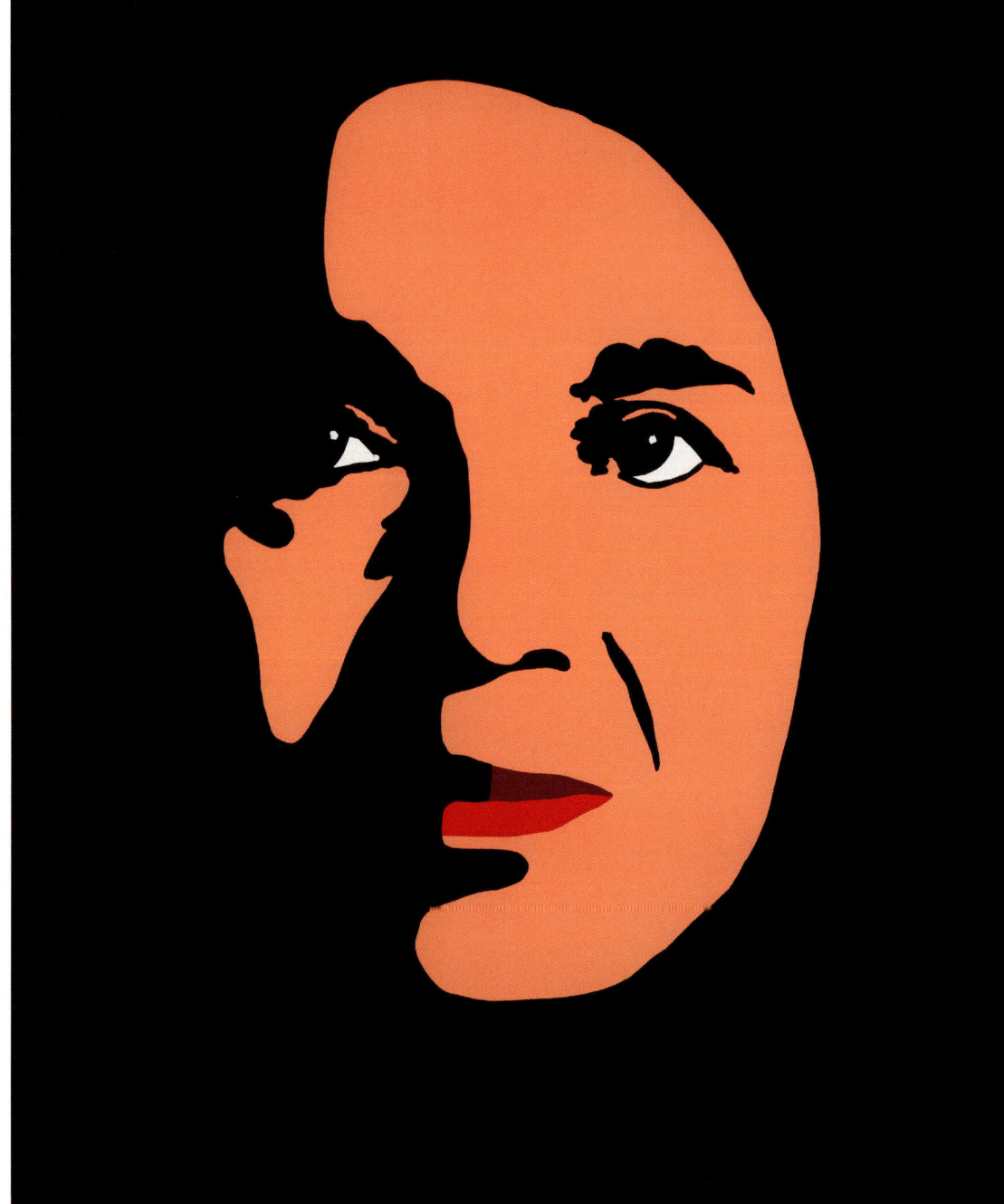

VIVA DOLORES HUERTA
65TH BIRTHDAY CELEBRATION
APRIL 29, 1995 DELANCEY STREET FOUNDATION SAN FRANCISCO

Viva Dolores Huerta, 1995. Screenprint, sheet size: 26-3/16 x 19-13/16 inches, image size: 22-7/8 x 15-15/16 inches. Copyright © Rupert García. Courtesy of Rena Bransten Gallery.

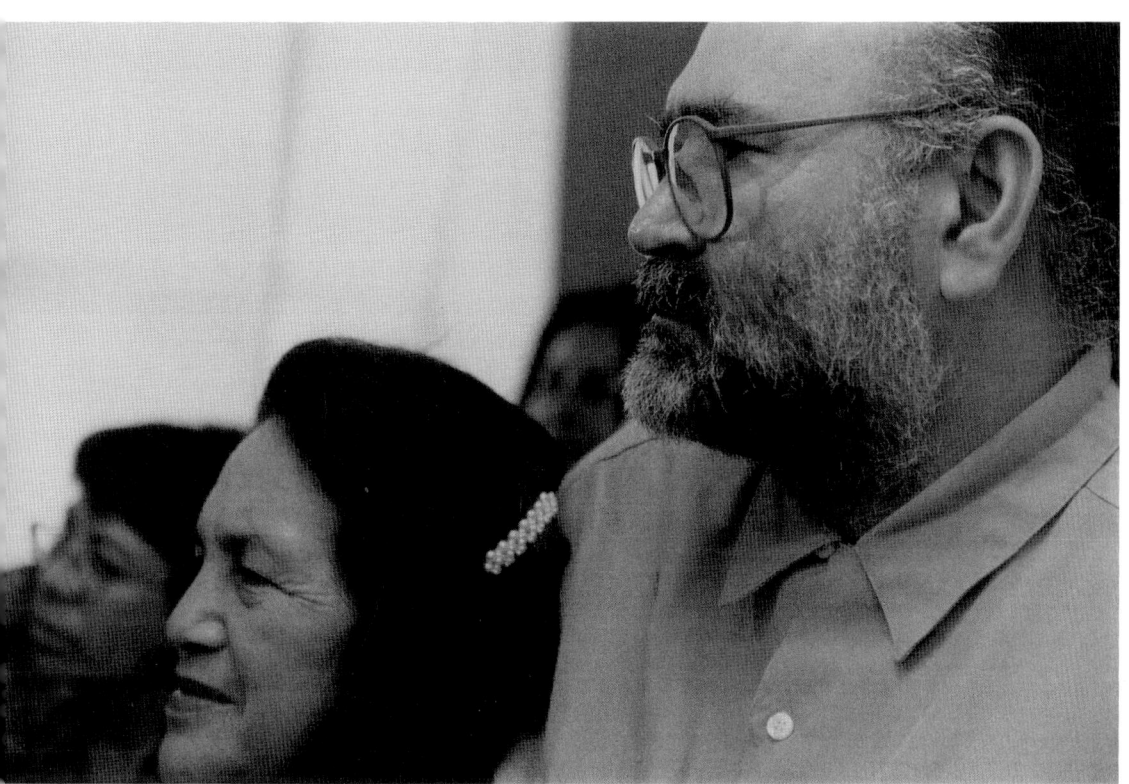
Rupert García with Dolores Huerta, 1996. Photo courtesy of David Bacon.

is Obama? Is his smile genuine? And similar questions could be raised about Douglass. Was he a saint or a sinner or both? I wanted to do a triptych that would problematize Obama and not accept him 100%, which you shouldn't do for anyone, especially a politician. When the images are separate, it may be easier to understand each one of them. But that isn't the case when they are together. Divided as they are in my picture by those black lines, it problematizes the relationship. I'm forcing myself to think about this relationship and to come to my own conclusion. I'm not trying to think for other people. I have enough to think on my own. When I finished the piece, I had just what I wanted. I was just thrilled.

Besides Barack Obama, another icon that I produced is Dolores Huerta. She is an amazing person who besides struggling with César Chávez to bring social justice to farmworkers has also struggled on many other fronts for Latinos, women, peace, and voting rights among others. On the occasion of her sixty-fifth birthday, I was asked by her family to do an image of Dolores. "Are you kidding?" I said, "of course I will." I've known Dolores all of my life. She is also from Stockton, and my aunt Romana, my mother's sister, is married to Dolores's brother. So, this makes Dolores part of our extended family. Although I don't see her often enough, we keep in touch. Dolores is now in her 90s but still going strong. Her energy is very intense and her clarity of thought continues. She's quite something![1]

By contrast, I never did a picture of César Chávez, whom I never met. There were so many images already of César that I didn't feel like I had to. I only paint something when I feel the need to; that's how I work.

◼ⅠⅠ◼

Rupert García:

> I do not believe that war is the way to solve human problems. The cost of human life is too high. The social and political exchange between adversaries is the only humane way to resolve conflict.[2]

One of my more recent exhibits was in 2018 at the Rena Bransten Gallery called *Rolling Thunder*. In speaking to my curator who is the gallery's director and owner of the gallery, Trish Bransten, at one point we discussed how over the years one theme that kept recurring in my work was that of war. I didn't realize that I had done so many war images.

"Why don't we do an exhibit with these paintings?" Trish said.

"That would be great!" I responded.

And so in 2017 we worked to put this exhibit together with images that included some fifty years of work. We also decided to title the show *Rolling Thunder*. In some military actions, a name is attached to it. When I was in Indochina, the effort that I was assigned to was called "Operation Rolling Thunder." This was the official nomenclature for what I was involved

with. This operation was already underway when I got to the secret Air Force base in Thailand. The jet fighters that I was assigned to protect were part of the decision by President Lyndon Johnson to bomb North Vietnam to get it to cease its support of the Viet Cong in South Vietnam. All of this bombing operation was called "Rolling Thunder." This was Johnson's bright idea to end the war, which didn't work.

I wanted to make a very personal statement about the exhibit and bring attention to my own role in America's wars. Of course, my father was in World War II and my two brothers also joined the service, one in the Marines and one in the Army. From when I was a boy there was always a war that the U.S. was actively involved in. In my case, it was the U.S. war in Vietnam. For the exhibit and for the cover of the catalog, it was decided to use my Air Force photo when I was in Thailand and also the Vietnam service commendation I received. My picture was taken in Ubon right outside the air base in 1965 and so I had it since then. My photo served as a memento for me and I thought I might share it with my family when I got home. At first, I didn't know what I really wanted to do with it artistically, but I knew I was compelled to engage with that photo. I kept looking at the photo and trying to figure out how to use it. I had to use it because it meant many things for me. I had actually used my military photo once before in a 2003 painting, but in that one I didn't cover my eyes. But for *Rolling Thunder* I wanted to use it differently. The more I looked back on my service in Thailand as part of "Operation Rolling Thunder," the more I came to see how I and others were lied to. I began to think "oh son of a bitch I was bamboozled!" Some of these thoughts I had after I returned from Thailand, but I had never fully concretized them. The exhibit forced me to do so. The war in Vietnam was not winnable and our military and civilian officials knew that, as was revealed in part by the Pentagon Papers. Yet in order for LBJ and the Democrats not to be criticized for "losing" Vietnam, they poured half a million of us into the war and still didn't win. Americans were deceived and sixty thousand Americans including Latinos lost their lives, and many came back physically and psychologically wounded. I wanted to focus on this big lie.

Lowery Stokes Sims:

> The glaring fact that black men and those of Latino heritage represented a disproportionally high number of draftees in the war is particularly relevant as we view the work by Rupert García in the exhibition.[3]

I got the idea of incorporating the image of my Vietnam Service Medal and ribbon into the picture. This award had nothing to do with any heroics on my part. Anyone who served in direct support of operations in Vietnam received a service medal and ribbon upon being discharged. I decided to bring attention to how this commendation was part of the big lie. I scanned my photo and then covered my eyes with the war service ribbon. The ribbon's tricolors represent South Vietnam. I titled my self-portrait *Hoodwinked* because I was hoodwinked into believing we were fighting for freedom and to protect democracy. This was untrue. We were fighting for American imperialism in Indochina. Putting the ribbon over my eyes was to show how I was blinded to this reality. I was using the ribbon as a hoodwinked mechanism. I was using the ribbon in a way that contradicted what it was supposed to represent—loyalty to the service, where in reality I and others were servicing the U.S. ruling class and its attempt to control the resources of Southeast Asia. The ribbon by itself would look like I supported the war and that America was the greatest thing since ice cubes. But no. I had to say that's not true. I had to critique the war, and my picture with my eyes covered by the ribbon was my critique. I liked the way the image appeared: The authenticity of the photograph and the authenticity of the Vietnam service ribbon put together add up to something more than the two. For me, it reaches the heights of a poetic experience—but based in history and in a personal history. Of course, we can go back in history to see how the United States has hoodwinked Americans in going to other wars, overthrowing and invading countries or governments that we didn't like. My *Hoodwinked* image in a sense introduced the exhibit and became the cover of the catalog.

We then structured the exhibit beginning with a small print etching that I did in 1967 called *The War and*

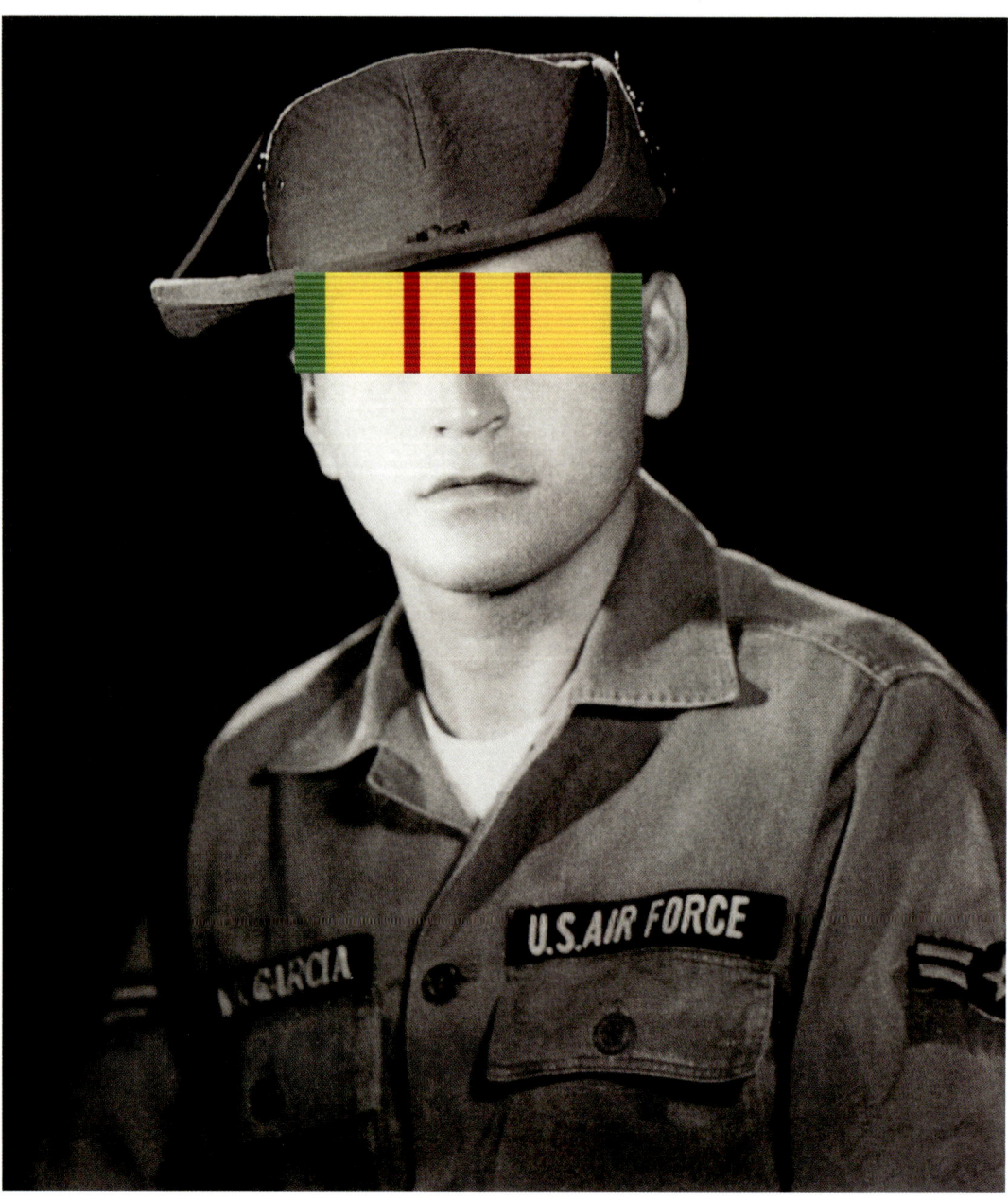

Hoodwinked, 2017. Pigmented acrylic inkjet on paper, sheet size: 36-5/8 x 30-1/4 inches, image size: 29 x 25-3/4 inches. Copyright © Rupert García. Courtesy of Rena Bransten Gallery.

Children and which I have already discussed.

In the catalog, we decided to start with this little 1967 print and then couple it with a new picture I did in 2017 called *Rolling Thunder 2017*, which is a mixed-media image, both digital and painting. This was done specifically for the show. It's a triptych. On the left-hand side is a depiction of dark

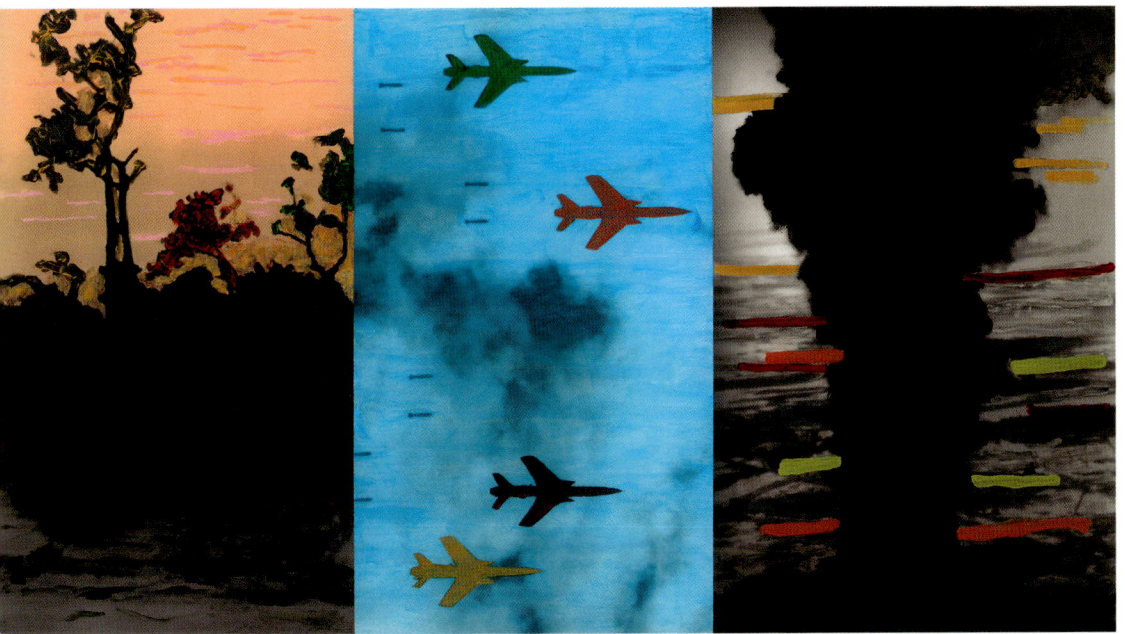

Rolling Thunder, 2017. Mixed media, sheet size: 60 x 100 inches, image size: 52 x 96 inches. Copyright © Rupert García. Courtesy of Rena Bransten Gallery.

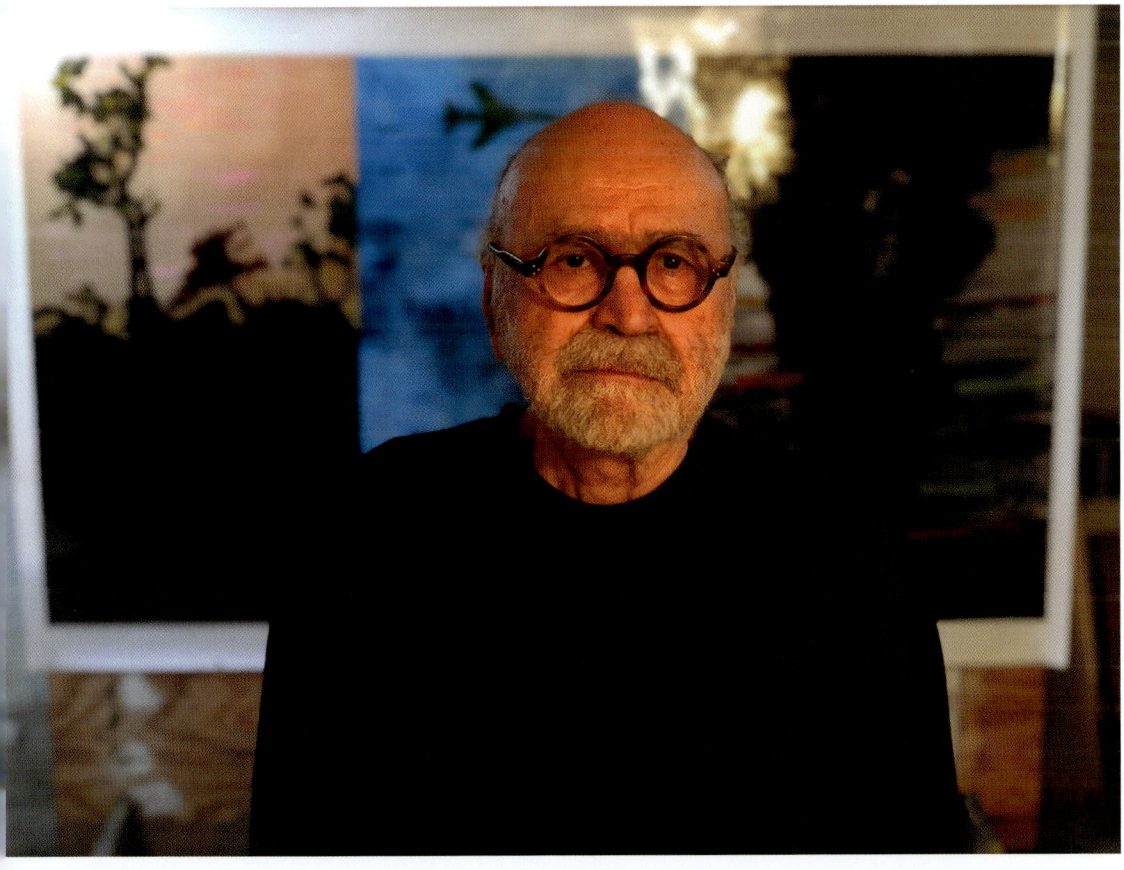

Rupert García in front of *Rolling Thunder 2017*, 2017. Photo courtesy of Don Farnsworth and Magnolia Editions.

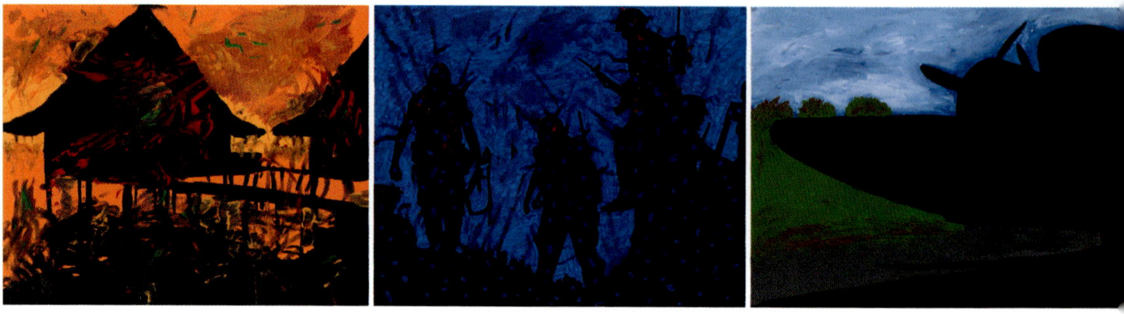

Memorias de Honolulu, las Filipinas y Ubon, 1987. Acrylic on paper, canvas size: 30 x 120 inches. Copyright © Rupert García. Courtesy of Rena Bransten Gallery.

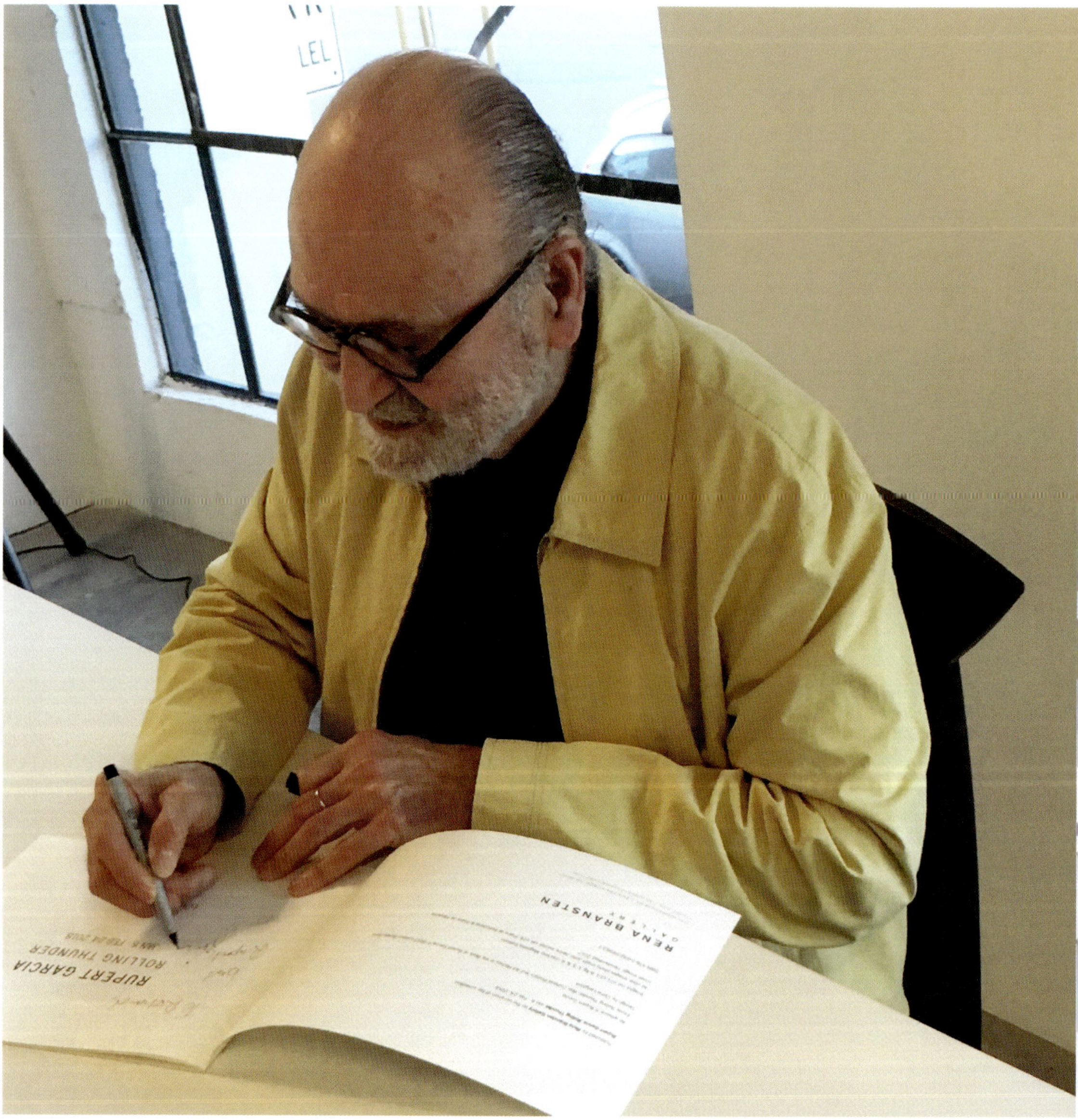

Rupert García signing catalog *Rolling Thunder* at Rena Bransten Gallery, San Francisco, 2018. Photo courtesy of Rena Bransten Gallery, San Francisco.

jungle that I experienced in Thailand. In the middle image there are four F-105 Thunderchief jet fighter bombers in different colors of the kind that I guarded at the base. You also see the bombs coming down from the planes. I used different colors for the plane as an aesthetic choice. It's to make the picture more exciting. The bombs are falling over a petroleum, oil, and lubricant facility in Hanoi which leads to the third panel on the right, which I took from a photograph showing the explosion of the bombs. I did this in very dark colors, which contrasts with the very blue color of the sky in the second panel. I think it's a very powerful painting and just perfect for the show. This is the first picture I had ever done that directly concerns my own involvement in the Vietnam War. It is also a very large painting on paper.

We also used for the exhibit a 1987 acrylic tryptic painting called *Memorias de Honolulu, las Filipinas y Ubon*. Each reference is a place that I had been to. On the right panel is an image of a World War II plane on an airfield. This is Honolulu where I stopped in 1965 on my way to Thailand. Over on the left-hand side are images of thatched structures, which are of the kind I saw in Ubon in up-country Thailand near the Laotian border where my base was located. And in the middle are dark images of American Air Force personnel with weapons of which I was a part of. So, the painting is autobiographical and related to my war experience. This is one of the paintings that I did as part of my being a resident at the East–West Center in Honolulu and as part of my fellowship.

Altogether we used thirteen of my war-related paintings and work on paper, some of which I have discussed elsewhere in my testimonio. *Operation Rolling Thunder* meant very much to me at a personal level. Perhaps it was even therapeutic to get rid of whatever Indochina ghosts I still had. I'm very proud of this beautiful exhibit.

━ıı━

In 2010 I became professor-emeritus at San Jose State after teaching there twenty-two years. I loved all of those years. I think over time I became a better teacher; however, my philosophy of teaching art didn't change. I started teaching there to have students understand how to make a painting. All the way from mixing colors, mixing tints, mixing shades, how to compose, what the different brushes are, to design when you apply paint. I got really technical. I even taught them how to clean a brush the proper way. I really wanted them to be prepared to make paintings of consequence, but paintings that the surface wouldn't crack. "If you don't know what you're doing," I told my students, "that will happen." By the time that some moved from beginning painting to advanced painting, I expected them to know how to mix colors, how to use grays and whites and blacks with colors. They had to think about the size of the canvas. Very importantly, they had to know what their paintings were supposed to do and what the painting was for. Most students at first couldn't

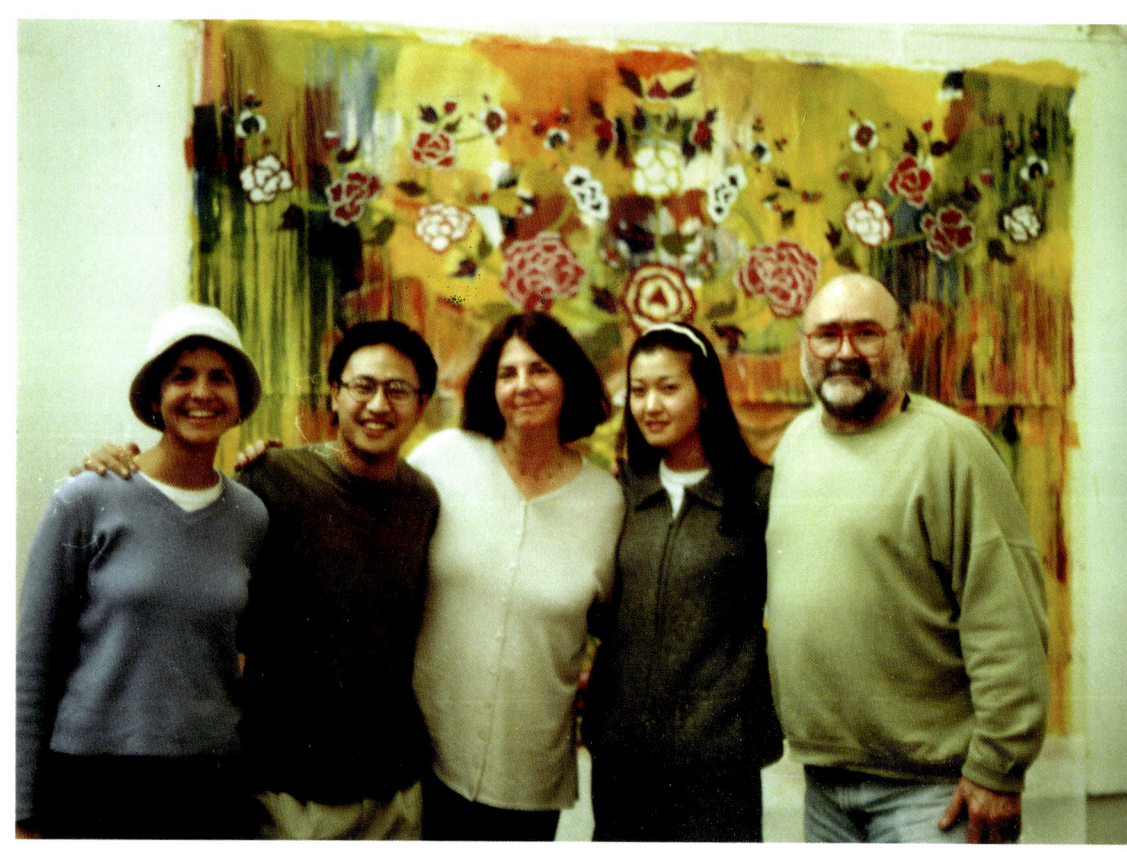

Rupert García at painting studio at San Jose State University with two students and fellow instructor Gale Antokal, third from left, 2000. Photo courtesy of Rupert García.

answer this because they had never been asked such questions. For most, they just wanted to paint, just paint. When I was in junior college, I had a really nice art professor, but he didn't teach me a damn thing. He just said paint. I was not going to be this kind of professor. I was going to teach my students not only how to paint, but what was the purpose of their painting. I wanted them to think, not just paint. They had to become intellectuals, not just painters.

I was sixty-nine when I stopped teaching and I felt that I needed to devote full-time to my paintings with what years I still had left. I was ok with retiring. I didn't look back because I was like my students pursuing my true love, which was painting.

I think I was a good and inspiring teacher. If asked what my legacy might be as an art professor, I would say that I impressed upon my students that art is serious, very serious, and being an artist can be a very serious way of life if you choose this route. I think students saw this in me and recognized that being a serious artist can be a great life. You might not get rich but you'll be very, very happy. Every class that I taught I began by going over a list of items that if students followed, they would hopefully become good artists and people. This list included not smoking, no drugs, getting enough sleep, not too much booze, love people, and that kind of stuff. Following such instructions, I told them, you might get to the point where you know that your work is good and you're on your way to being safe from evil ideas promoted in the art world that say, "you can't paint and what you're painting now has been done already." I want my students to get to the point that they know that they're doing what they should be doing and that they don't have to listen to anyone else—except me, of course! My legacy is that I gave my all to my students and encouraged them to do the best they could and more. I wanted to instill pride and confidence in them and their work. I asked of them as much as I ask of myself. I wanted their art and my art to be extraordinary.

—ii—

Pensamientos

As we come to the close of my testimonio, I would like to share some thoughts or *pensamientos* that shed more light on my sense of self and who and what I represent.

One of these is that despite many challenges that I have had to face and those that we as Latinos and as a country have had to confront, I still consider myself an optimist. Even going to my childhood and coming of age years, I have been optimistic, and this has held true for my adulthood. When you think everything is just shit, sometimes you become pessimistic for a moment, but my optimism sees through what caused that pessimism. It's a momentary thing. I'm an optimist because I believe in the magnificence of life, and it's just amazing to me. I have always felt that existence is great; it's fantastic. And I don't let those who think the worst of things and feel the world is going to hell influence me. I think that I express my optimism in my art. The joy of making art is a sign of optimism.

I've often been asked if there are things in my life that in retrospect I would do differently. The only thing I can think of is not going into the military. I wouldn't have volunteered. To me those four years in the Air Force were just a job, but the wrong job. I did it because I didn't want to stay in Stockton and work in the meat plant or in a gas station. I think that's the only thing, because everything else I did I'm very satisfied with. Of course, I made mistakes but overall, I'm comfortable about my life and career.

I've also been asked who is Rupert García and is there a private Rupert and a public Rupert? What I can say is that I am a guy who wishes to the best of my ability to use my imagination and intelligence to try to understand myself, my history, and my future. Of course, there is a private Rupert García. But what I do with my family, my wife, and friends is private. No one needs to know about this. It's none of someone else's business. I tell my students that just because someone asks you a question, you don't need to answer it. You reveal what you want to reveal to the public on your own terms. Some people have an incredible misconception of who I am because they judge me not by knowing me but by what they see and project.

I would also like to say that while I'm not an angry person, I am bitter about some things. I'm bitter about my mom's retirement because she worked so hard for JC Penney, and they didn't give her anything when she retired. I'm bitter about my maternal grandparents having to leave Mexico, their homeland, and then having to struggle so hard in this country. I'm also bitter about so many people from different lands who came to the United States in pursuit of the American Dream and then only found discrimination and exploitation. And I'm bitter about how many people in the world have to endure conquest, domination, and racism. Finally, I'm bitter about sexism.

How do I want my art to be remembered? That it's complex. That it's seemingly wonderful and beautiful, but that it's more than that. It's multilevel in terms of significance and meaning. It's not a one-shot deal. You have to work with it to truly understand it.

What it means to be an artist is a lifetime of practice, growth, and reflection. Being an artist is the one thing you devote your life to. There is no plan B to being an artist, there's only plan A, because if you have a plan B, then you can rationalize yourself out of the intense practice necessary to be the kind of artist that you want to be. As a growing and developing artist, I had to develop a sense of when a

painting is successful. I have to determine this by myself, and I can't allow art critics, museums, galleries, or those who want to buy my art determine this for me. But this takes discipline and even a sense of superiority in yourself. You have to be self-confident. I don't make art to acquire money or to support my livelihood. That's why my jobs have been to teach art, and that has been my main income. This has allowed me to be free to be an artist on my own terms.

I don't try to see myself in a spectrum of American art. That's a demanding chore and perhaps an unnecessary one. I'm interested in thinking about things that make me a better artist, and I don't think saying where do I see myself in the scheme of American art is helpful, and so I don't think like that.

I also don't attempt to describe my art. Some artists do that but all I can say is that I want my art to be wonderful, fantastic, and complex. Even if some consider my art to be political, I want that art to still be beautiful. If I do a painting about war, I still want it to be beautiful.

My art would have probably been very different if it hadn't had a connection with the Chicano and Latino social movements. It was these movements along with that of the Black Power movement and Third World movement that significantly affected me as an artist and my art. These movements changed my thinking about what art is. The critical views of these movements influenced my critical thinking about art and society. In this context, I developed a critical mind. If I hadn't experienced the San Francisco State Strike along with the protests of that period, I don't know what kind of art I would have made. For me these actions opened up my mind, and the rules concerning what art is changed, and I continued in that way to this day. El movimiento and other critical activities changed me forever, and I came to realize this change was absolutely true for me and about what I was doing and thinking. At the same time, I don't want to be remembered just as a movement artist. I am that but *mas* (more), and that *mas* is very important.

Sometimes I'm asked what my normal work patterns are since I've been consistently productive over the years. I don't know what a normal working day is. I work when I have a lot of time to do a project, and sometimes I would just do things because I felt like doing it then. It was never just one mathematical laid-out working day plan. Sometimes I work all day and into the evenings, even into the early morning hours. I lose all track of time when I'm into my painting. Another thing about my work habits is that I never show my work while it is in progress to anyone. What I am producing is a secret, and only I know it. I love this mystery. When it is finished I show it to my agent or dealer and to Sammi. I won't talk about my work until it's finished, and then you can't shut me up.

I also never do a painting spontaneously. Some artists do but I don't. I never start a painting without having done a sketch first. I have to have a layout about what I want to do and sometimes knowing where I'm going to put certain colors. In the process, I allow myself to make changes, perhaps making something bigger or smaller or making the green a little darker. Making changes is easier now that I'm doing digital art.

Back in 1991 I said the following to an art critic, and what I said is still true today:

> The process of making a picture is one I experience with delight, as well as pleasant uncertainty. It's sexual, it's intellectual. I recall memories and project the future. When I'm working, I feel I have absolute control of the universe, not in a dominating sense, but in a way in which whatever I'm doing feels perfect.[4]

I've also been asked where are our future Latino artists going to come from? They're going to be coming from wherever they live, like me from Stockton. But what I also say is that hopefully they will be artists who have been exposed to Chicano/Latino Studies and Ethnic Studies so they can be exposed to big issues about Chicanos and Latinos living in America. They can learn our history from a critical perspective. They will have a critical perspective as well about art and art history and be willing to challenge the status quo and produce an art that is influenced by becoming ethnically and politically aware.

Whether it's Latino art or any other type of art, all I know is that there can't be a world without art. A world

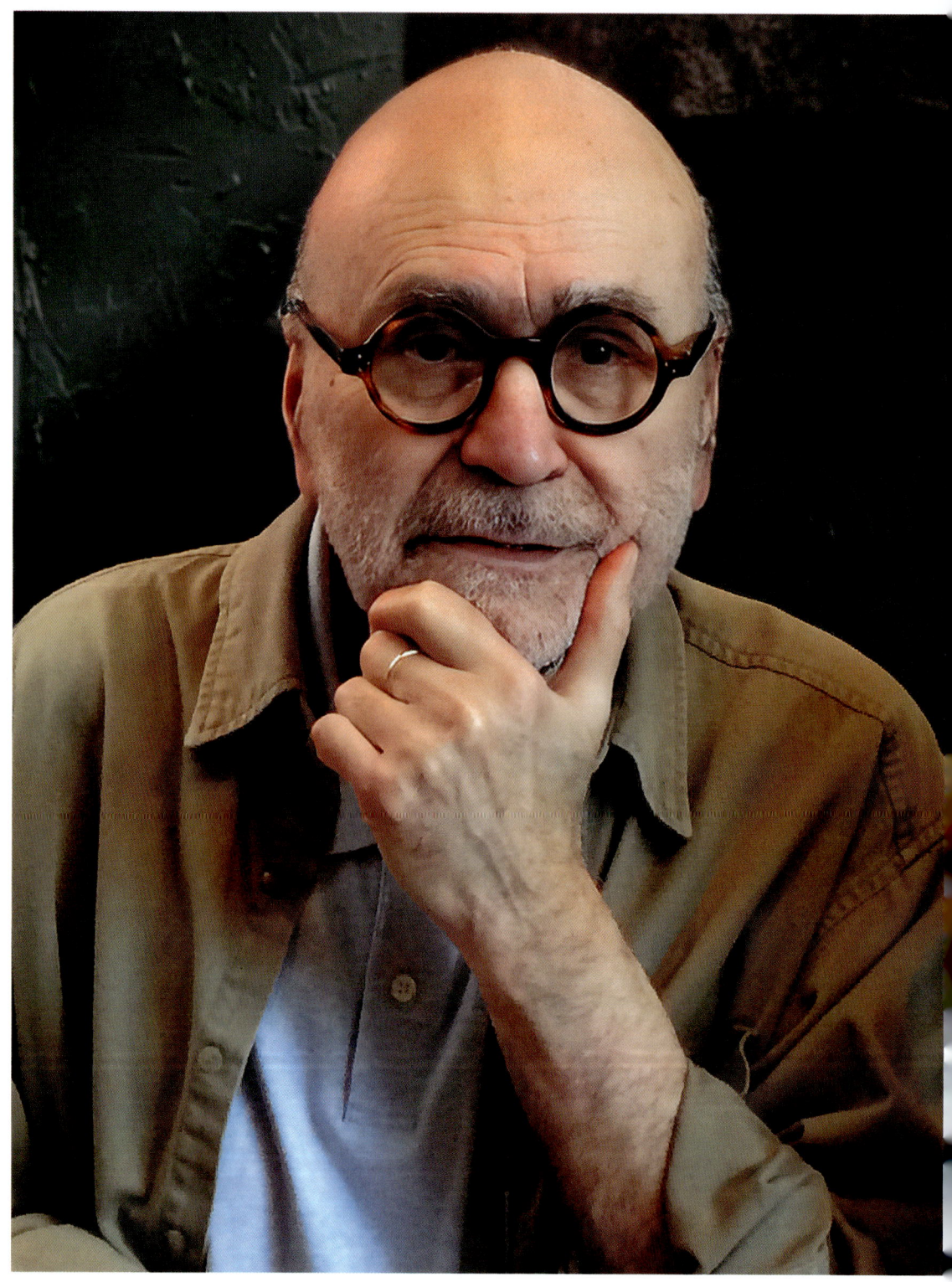

Rupert García, 2018. Photo courtesy of Don Farnsworth and Magnolia Editions.

without art is a world without human beings. So long as there are human beings, we're going to have art of all kinds and stripes. Art is not some abstract thing that floats around. It's concrete and is produced by people. To be a human being is to make art. Art represents the existence of human beings and throughout time; wherever there have been human beings, there have been people making art.

I have often been asked what is the trajectory of your work? Well, the answer is that I am trying to express the truth of being alive and experiencing my moment and the moment of human beings and situations in the world. I want to embrace this and to express it as if it's absolute truth. And that's the end goal. Every painting I make or every picture I make, I am after my truth. I am not saying it's an objective truth. I'm after my truth. I want to experience that truth and so each work that I do I'm pursuing that truth.

How do I want to be remembered and what is my legacy, the good professor asks me? First of all, I have no regrets about my life and what I have done. I always wanted to be an artist and so I want to be remembered as a man who enjoyed making art and found it to be a way of being in the world and a way of sensing myself in the world. What I have done is of consequence to me. I didn't do my art because of the world and for others. I'm arrogant and self-centered but not when it comes to making my art and making it complicated. I have tried to make my art exciting but not to change people's minds. I am an artist who loved his art, but I don't think about what a great artist I am. That's where I control my ego. I just want to make decent, deep, complex, and exciting work. For me. Does my art make people think? I didn't set out to do this but if people respond in ways that they feel enlightened or whatever, that's wonderful, because I'm trying to enlighten myself.

Afterword

Mario T. García

It has been a long journey to this Afterword. To be exact, twenty-seven years since I started interviews with Rupert García for this testimonio. I still feel a pang of guilt for having put aside his story for a number of those years. However, what is important is that I came back to it and it is now completed. As mentioned in my Introduction, it is somewhat fortuitous that it worked out this way, and so Rupert's story now contains so much more of his life than would otherwise have been the case if I had written up my 1996 interviews. I would have left off so much more of Rupert's evolution as an artist. It is the story of a major American artist of Chicano/Latino background.

No other Chicano/Latino artist, in my opinion, can rival Rupert's productivity and national and even international acclaim. And this prominence continues. In March and April of 2023, Rupert had still another showing at the Rena Branston Gallery in San Francisco. It was titled *Rupert García Architectonics*. What is architectonics? I asked Rupert. He explained to me that this show was influenced by the curator and art critic Lowery Stokes Sims who asked Rupert if he would let her see three 1968 paintings that had never been exhibited. Rupert consented and after she saw them was struck that these early works seemed to convey certain visual techniques that are apparent in his later work. Sims suggested that these early images used a technique of planning of where to put shapes and figurative elements as if Rupert was using building blocks to make a composition, in the way that an architect would build a structure. Everything has to fit in, nothing can be too big or lean and there should be no space in between different shapes of color. Everything had to be tight like an architect's plan. This is how Sims proposed this approach in her online essay that accompanied the exhibit:

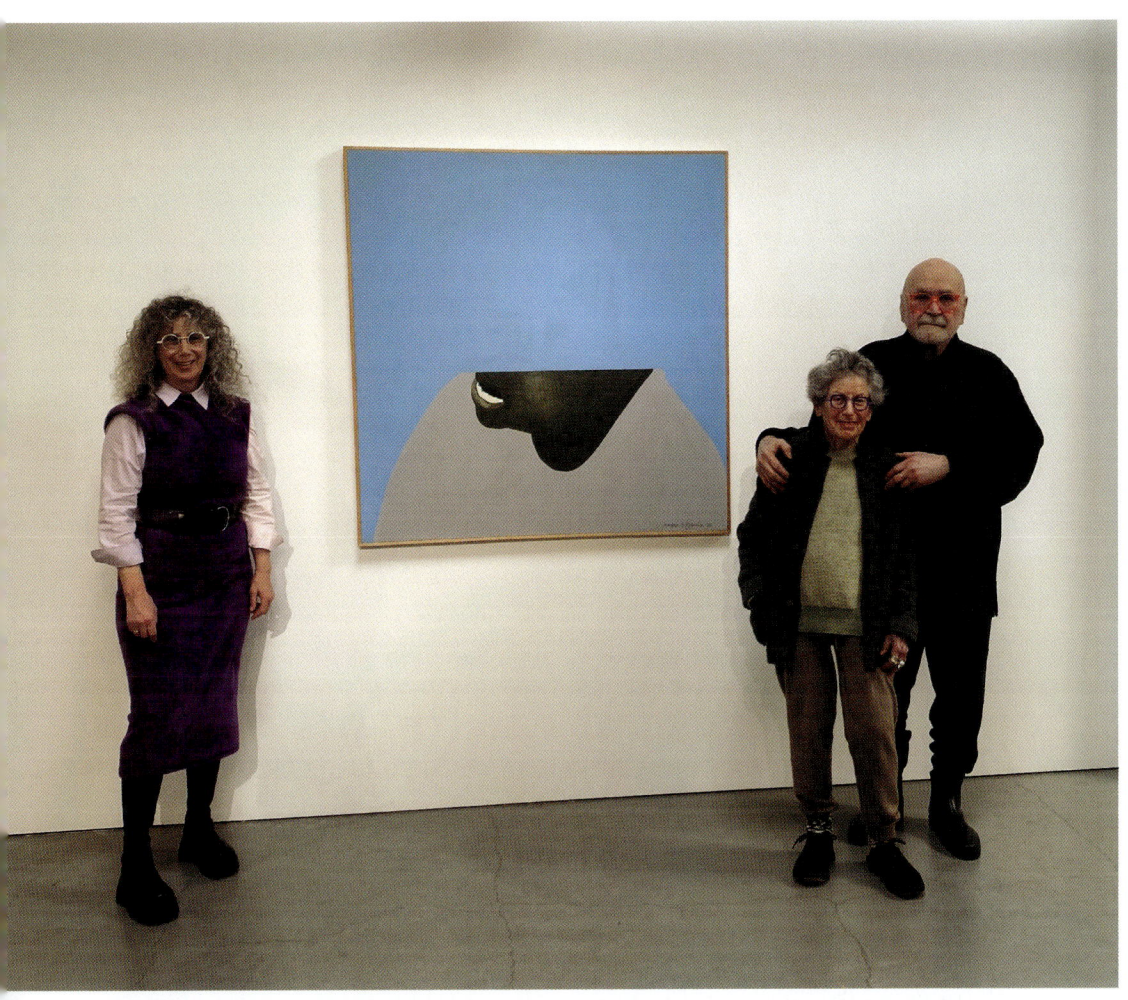

Rupert García with Trish Bransten (left) and Rena Bransten (center) in front of *Unfinished Man*, at Rena Bransten Gallery, San Francisco, 2023. Courtesy of Rena Bransten Gallery, San Francisco.

The visual and visceral impact of Rupert García's work has consistently been achieved by means of a clarity of form and design that bridges "graphic" and "fine" art. He engages the basic building blocks of image making—color and shape—drawing on the modalities of Color Field painting, Minimalist forms, and Pop Art. The focus of this installation are four paintings from 1968 that demonstrate that these impulses were evident in García's work even while he was studying at San Francisco State College.[1]

The four pictures that Sims refers to of which three had never been exhibited before included *Woman and Elephant*, *Japanese Master*, and *Woman, Lips, Tongue*. One other 1968 piece, *Unfinished Man*, had been previously exhibited and was included along with several other later images such as *The Bicentennial Poster*, *Down with the Whiteness*, and *El Grito de Rebelde*, among others that curator Sims believed reflected the "architectonics" character of García's work.

Among other reasons, I think that Rupert García's testimonio is important because there is no biography of him. The significant A Ver series of biographies of Chicano/Latino artists by the UCLA Chicano Studies Research Center is impressive, but to date none of its publications include García. It's my hope that my testimonio of him will encourage at last a full biography of Rupert. But what is important about his testimonio beyond a biography is that Rupert gets an opportunity to tell his own story and what he wants others to know. Of course, as is the case with any autobiography or memoir, sometimes what is important is not what the author reveals but what he doesn't. As the author of the testimonio there were certain constraints on the type of questions I felt I could ask that did not impinge on Rupert's privacy. A biographer would have less constraints to probe other areas of Rupert's life not covered in this testimonio. At the same time, what is also important about the testimonio is that we are getting from Rupert García his own interpretation of his art not mediated by the art historian. It is rare to find an artist analyzing their own work and playing the role of art critic with respect not only to their work but to their thinking about being an artist. This is what I think is most valuable in Rupert's

testimonio, that we hear his own voice concerning his role as an artist, his ideals and principles, and about his evolution as an artist. As much as possible, Rupert is opening his mind and heart to us in a way that a biography cannot achieve. I am proud of my collaboration with Rupert and of this testimonio. I believe I was a good listener and interviewer of his story, and the result is a unique first-person narrative of a major Chicano/Latino artist—an American artist.

I am struck by the many different art portraits that Rupert García did over the course of his career, ranging from Zapata to Angela Davis to Dolores Huerta. In a way, as a historian, I share Rupert's fascination with faces—historical faces. I have likewise produced not artistic portraits like Rupert, but scholarly ones including Bert Corona, Fran Esquibel Tywoniak, Luis Leal, Raymond Telles, Sal Castro, Dolores Huerta, Raul Ruiz, Gloria Arellanes, Rosalio Muñoz, and Fr. Luis Olivares. These are my portraits that hang in my historian's gallery. Both Rupert and I further share a fascination about people's lives, especially those who have had an impact on society, and this made our collaboration more meaningful. I was interested in Rupert's life and he appreciated this.

What Rupert and I also share is the aspiration for social justice and of addressing this not only to our Chicano/Latino communities but to other Americans. Through his amazing critical images that in one way or another touch on social justice, Rupert is attempting to convey this theme to all who witness his art and may be motivated by it. In a way, Rupert in a kind of Paulo Freire way and a Liberation Theology way is asking his audience to observe his images, reflect about them, and then, most importantly, to act on what they have observed and reflected on—join the struggle for social justice and democratic rights in their communities and countries. In my own way, that is what I hope readers get from reading and reflecting on my work, which includes my many testimonios.

Finally, I further hope that other historians will be motivated to join me in the use of the testiminio method to produce other such life stories not only of other Chicano/Latino artists, but also of other figures in this history, especially those who have struggled for social justice. Many of these artists and activists (artists are also activists) are still alive, and many of their stories like Rupert's are waiting to be told. I don't know how many other testimonios I am capable of, but even if I don't do another one I am proud that I did Rupert García's story.

Rupert, it's been a long way to publishing your testimonio, but I think it has been well worth it. I thank you for your patience, your collaboration, and your friendship. Take care y abrazos.

Acknowledgments

First and foremost, I want to acknowledge the cooperation of Rupert García in the making of this book. Obviously, without Rupert there would be no book at all. It is his story and a very powerful one. It took many years, too many, to finally produce his testimonio, and I am grateful that he remained patient with me. Rupert not only provided me his story but also copies of art catalogs of his work and unpublished material from his own archives. Rupert further provided photos from his personal collection for the book. We were true collaborators.

I want to also thank Nicole Solano from Rutgers University Press. As an acquisitions editor she enthusiastically embraced Rupert's story from the very beginning. I am grateful for her enthusiasm and support for the book. Nicole always and professionally addressed my queries. She is one of the very best editors that I have ever worked with.

A big thanks to Darla McDavid for transcribing the first part of my interviews and to my undergraduate research assistant Bethany Sahagun for transcribing the second part of the interviews, and Lori McCracken for transcribing the second part of the interviews.

The Academic Senate of the University of California, Santa Barbara, provided important research funds for this project.

The Chicano Studies Research Center (now the Chicano Studies Institute) provided space for the first part of my interviews with Rupert.

Tony Mastres and Jeff Liang from Photo Services at my campus, UC Santa Barbara, expertly provided me and the press with high-resolution images of Rupert's art, and I am very grateful to them. Without Rupert's incredible art images, we would have no book.

I also am very grateful to Rena Branston Gallery in San Francisco for providing the press their scans of many of Rupert's images. I particularly want to thank Trish Branston, China Langford, and Kira Lyons at the gallery for locating and providing the scans. On the side of the press, I am thankful to Emma-li Downer for working with the gallery on this matter.

Thanks to Bob Hsiang for the photos

I am additionally grateful to Joe Ramos, Terry Lorant, David Bacon, and Don Farnseorth and Magnolia Editions for additional photos used in the book.

I also want to thank the whole production staff of the press for their expertise in producing the final book product.

I want to acknowledge Professor Ella María Díaz, Professor Terezita Romo, and Juan Fuentes for sharing their reflections on the art of Rupert García that aided me in writing my Introduction.

Melinda Gandara, my former graduate student and art historian, provided important insights on the art of Rupert García.

Finally, I want to thank my wife, Professor Ellen McCracken, for allowing me to bounce off of her my thoughts on producing my testimonio of Rupert García and for her love and support over the years. She is my true emotional and intellectual companion.

Doing my many interviews with Rupert, researching his story and that of Chicano/Latino art, and then writing the testimonio was made easier by the many pleasurable times with my family, including my daughter and son Giuliana and Carlo; my daughter-in-law Calista; and my two grandchildren, Luca and Emery. They are what life is or should be all about.

Notes

Introduction

1. In addition to my testimonios noted in note 2 also see Mario T. García, *The Chicano Generation: Testimonios of the Movement* (Oakland: University of California Press, 2015).

2. Frances Esquibel Tywoniak and Mario T. García, *Migrant Daughter: Coming of Age as a Mexican American Woman* (Berkeley and Los Angeles: University of California Press, 2000); Mario T. García, *Luis Leal: An Auto/Biography* (Austin: University of Texas Press, 2000); Mario T. García and Sal Castro, *Blowout! Sal Castro and the Chicano Struggle for Educational Justice* (Chapel Hill: University of North Carolina Press, 2011).

3. See Tomas Ybarra-Frausto, "Raquachismo: A Chicano Sensibility," in *Chicano Aesthetics: Rasquachismo*, 5–8, Catalog MARS (Movimiento Artistico del Rio Salado, 1989).

4. On the Chicano Movement see note 10.

5. Karen Mary Davalos, *Yolanda M. López* (Los Angeles: UCLA Chicano Studies Research Center Press, 2008), 4.

6. On the Chicano Moratorium see Lorena Oropeza, *Raza Si! Guerra No! Chicano Protest and Patriotism During the Viet Nam War Era* (Berkeley and Los Angeles: University of California Press, 2005); García, *The Chicano Generation*.

7. On Ruben Salazar see Mario T. García, *Ruben Salazar: Border Correspondent—Selected Writings, 1955–1970* (Berkeley and Los Angeles: University of California Press, 1995).

8. Interview with Juan Fuentes, April 24, 2023.

9. Interview with Fuentes, April 24, 2023.

10. Mario T. García, *Católicos: Resistance and Affirmation in Chicano Catholic History* (Austin: University of Texas Press, 2008).

11. On the Chicano Generation see Mario T. García, *The Chicano Generation*. Also see Carlos Muñoz Jr., *Youth, Identity, Power: The Chicano Movement* (New York: Verso Press, 1989); Ernesto Chávez, *"Mi Raza Primero!" Nationalism, Identity, and Insurgency in the Chicano Movement in Los Angeles, 1966–1978* (Berkley and Los Angeles: University of California Press, 2002);

David Montejano, *Quixote's Children: A Local History of the Chicano Movement, 1966–1981* (Austin: University of Texas Press, 2010); Jorge Mariscal, *Brown-Eyed Children of the Sun: Lessons from the Chicano Movement, 1965–1975* (Albuquerque: University of New Mexico Press, 2005); Maylei Blackwell, *Chicana Power! Contested Histories of Feminism in the Chicano Movement* (Austin: University of Texas Press, 2011); Ignacio M. García, *United We Win: The Rise and Fall of La Raza Unida Party* (Tucson: Mexican American Studies and Research Center, University of Arizona, 1989); Alma M. García, *Chicana Feminist Thought: The Basic Historical Writings* (New York: Routledge, 1997); Frank P. Barajas, *Mexican Americans with Moxie: A Transgenerational History of El Movimiento Chicano in Ventura County, California, 1945–1975* (Lincoln: University of Nebraska Press, 2021); Guadalupe San Miguel Jr., *In the Midst of Radicalism: Mexican American Moderates During the Chicano Movement 1960–1978* (Norman: University of Oklahoma Press, 2022); Oropeza, *Raza Si! Guerra No!*.

12. On the Mexican American Generation see Mario T. García, *Mexican Americans: Leadership, Ideology & Identity, 1930–1960* (New Haven: Yale University Press, 1989).

13. On the pachucos see Luis Alvarez, *The Power of the Zoot: Youth Culture and Resistance during World War II* (Berkeley and Los Angeles: University of California Press, 2008); Catherine Ramírez, *The Woman in the Zoot Suit: Gender, Nationalism, and the Cultural Politics of Memory* (Durham: Duke University Press, 2009); Mauricio Mazón, *The Zoot-Suit Riots: The Psychology of Symbolic Annihilation* (Austin: University of Texas Press, 1984); Eduardo Obregón Pagán, *Murder at the Sleepy Lagoon: Zoot Suits, Race, and Riot in Wartime L.A.* (Chapel Hill: University of North Carolina Press, 2003).

14. On the Third World Liberation Strike see Kay Boyle, *The Long Walk at San Francisco State* (New York: Grove Press, 1970) and Tomás F. Summers Sandoval Jr., *Latinos at the Golden Gate: Creating Community & Identity in San Francisco* (Chapel Hill: University of North Carolina Press, 2013).

15. On Chicanismo see Ignacio M. Garcia, *Chicanismo: The Forging Militant Ethos Among Mexican Americans* (Tucson: University of Arizona Press, 1997) and Mariscal, *Brown-Eyed Children of the Sun*.

16. Shifra M. Goldman and Tomás Ybarra-Frausto, eds., *Arte Chicano: A Comprehensive Annotated Bibliography of Chicano Art, 1965–1981* (Berkeley: Chicano Studies Library Publications Unit, University of California, Berkeley, 1985), 3.

17. Karen Mary Davalos, *Exhibiting Mestizaje: Mexican (American) Museums in the Diaspora* (Albuquerque: University of New Mexico Press, 2001), 21.

18. Terezita Romo, *Malaquias Montoya* (Los Angeles: UCLA Chicano Studies Research Center Press, 2011), 7.

19. Bill Berkson, "Questions of Moment: Rupert García" in exhibit catalog *Rupert García* (Stockton: The Haggin Museum, 1988), 7.

20. Robert Flynn Johnson, "The Composition of Conscience," in exhibit catalog *Rupert García: Prints and*

Posters, 1967–1990 (San Francisco: The Fine Arts Museums of San Francisco, 1991), 11.

21. Lucy R. Lippard, "Rupert García: Face to Face," in *Rupert García: Prints and Posters*, 28.

22. Carla Stellweg, "Rupert García: Chicaneidad, Art and Cultural Politics," in exhibit catalog *Aspects of Resistance* (New York: Alternative Museum, 1993), 9.

23. Claudia E. Zapata, "Chicano Graphics in the Digital Age," in *¡Printing the Revolution! The Rise and Impact of Chicano Graphics, 1965 to Now* (Washington, DC: Smithsonian America Art Museum and Princeton University Press, 2020), 133.

24. Maxine Hong Kingston, "Introduction," in *Rupert García* (Stockton: The Haggin Museum, 1988), 5.

25. Karin Breuer, "Foreword," in exhibit catalog, *Rupert García: The Magnolia Editions Projects 1991–2011* (Oakland: Magnolia Editions, 2011), ix.

26. John Yau, "Images Are Not Neutral," in *Rupert García: The Magnolia Editions*, xvi.

27. Ramón Favela, "The Pastel Paintings of Rupert García: A Survey of the Art of the *Unfinished Man, Inside-Outside*" in exhibit catalog *Rupert García* (San Francisco: Chronicle Books and The Mexican Museum, 1986), 26.

28. Harry S. Parker III and Robert R. Littman, "Directors' Foreword," in *Prints and Posters*, 7.

29. Alicia Gaspar De Alba, "From CARA to CACA: The Multiple Anatomies of Chicano/a Art at the Turn of the New Century," in Jennifer A. González, C. Ondine Chavoya, Chon Noriega, and Terezita Romo, eds., *Chicano and*

Chicana Art: A Critical Anthology (Durham and London: Duke University Press, 2019), 456.

30. Catalog supplement to *Rupert García, The Magnolia Editions*, 1.

31. Peter Orsi, "Rupert García, Artist," in a clipping in *California History* in Rupert García and Sammi Madison Collection in California Ethnic and Multicultural Archives (CEMA 101) in Special Collections, Library, University of California, Santa Barbara.

32. Parker and Littman, *Prints and Posters*, 7.

33. Favela, "Pastel Paintings," 11, 17.

34. Favela, "Pastel Paintings," 21.

35. Jennifer A. González, "Introduction," *Chicano and Chicana Art*, 4.

36. Peter Selz, "Rupert García: The Artist as Advocate," *Artspace* 15, no. 3 (March–April 1991): 60.

37. Stellweg, "Rupert García," 10.

38. Favela, "Pastel Paintings," 19.

39. Davalos, *Yolanda Lopez*, 52.

40. See video "Meet the Artist: Rupert García on the Influence of Social Justice Icons on His Printmaking," Smithsonian American Art Museum. Also see video "Latinopia Art—Rupert García on Public Art" (2015) and video "Decade of Dissent—Rupert García," Center for the Study of Political Graphics.

41. Malaquías Montoya and Lezlie Salkowitz-Montoya, "A Critical Perspective on the State of Chicano Art—1980," in González et al., eds., *Chicano and Chicana Art*, 37.

42. Mark Van Proyen, "Rupert García at Rena Branston," *Art in America* 95, no. 2 (February 2007): 156.

43. Tanya Wyatt, "Rupert García: Art for the Chicano Movement" in *Shifting Perspectives*, Mills College on internet.

44. As quoted in Favela, "Pastel Paintings," 9.

45. Lippard, "Rupert García: Face to Face," 41.

46. Linda Nochlin, "Rupert García: The Power of the Image," in exhibit catalog *Rupert García* (San Francisco: Rena Branston Gallery, 1997), 5.

47. David Levi Strauss, "García's Rebel Yell," *California*, January 1991, 30.

48. Katherine Cook, "Insider as Outsider: Rupert García in Retrospect," *Visions* 5, no. 3 (Summer 1991): 38–39.

49. William T. Henning, "Foreword," *Rupert García*, 3.

50. Favela, "Pastel Paintings," 8.

51. Neery Melkonian, *Arts Magazine*, January 1982, in Rupert García's personal collection.

52. Lippard, "Rupert García: Face to Face," 34.

53. *Cal Poly Report*, January 7, 1993, 2.

54. Peter Selz, "Rupert García," in program for art exhibit *Rupert García: New Pastel Paintings* (Paris: Galerie Claude Samuel, 1987), 1.

55. Lowery Stokes Sims, "Rolling Thunder: War, Cultural Politics and Art History" in exhibit catalog *Rupert García: Rolling Thunder* (San Francisco: Rena Branston Gallery, 2018), 5.

56. Geno Rodríguez and Andrew Perchuk, "Foreword" in exhibit catalog, *Aspects of Resistance: Rupert García* (New York: Alternative Museum, 1994), 5.

57. As quoted in Francisco X. Camplis, "La Raza and Films: Four Interviews," Communications Department, Stanford University, 1976, 28.

58. Tatiana Reinoza and María del Mar González, "The Island as Bridge: Rconceptualizing the Trienal Poli/

gráfica de San Juan," *CAIANA: Revista Académica de Investigación en Arte y Cultura Visual*, no. 11 (Fall 2015), 185.

59. Selz, *Rupert García*, 2.

60. Rodríguez and Perchuk, "Foreword," 1.

61. Camplis, "La Raza and Films," 26.

62. Terri Cohn, "'Oakland Icons' at the Craft & Cultural Arts Gallery," *Artweek* 33, no. 9 (November 2002): 16.

63. Parker and Littman, "Directors Foreword," 7.

64. As quoted in Dewey Crumpler, "Rupert García," *Shift* 5, no. 5 (1991): 43.

65. Antonio Prieto, "Border Art as a Political Strategy," *Isla* (2014): 1.

66. Nochlin, "Rupert García," 7–8.

67. Lippard, "Rupert García," 42.

68. David J. De la Torre, *The Art of Rupert García: A Survey Exhibition* (San Francisco: Chronicle Books and the Mission Museum), 5.

69. Cohn, "'Oakland Icons,'" 16.

70. Johnson, "Composition of Conscience," 9.

71. *San Francisco Chronicle*, March 15, 1978, 4.

72. Statement by Smithsonian Art Museum in Rupert García personal collection.

73. Email from Terezita Romo to Mario T. García, May 12, 2023.

74. Shifra Goldman, "A Public Voice: Fifteen Years of Chicano Posters," *Art Journal* (Spring 1984): 54–55.

75. Some key sources for getting a sense of the history and contemporary status of Chicano/Latino art are the following in no particular order of importance: Chon A. Noriega, ed., *¿Just Another Poster?: Chicano Graphic Arts in California* (Santa Barbara: University

Art Museum at University of California, Santa Barbara, 2001); E. Carmen Ramos, ed.,¡*Printing the Revolution!: The Rise and Impact of Chicano Graphics, 1965 to Now* (Washington, DC: Smithsonian American Art Museum and Princeton University Press, 2020); Jennifer A. González, C. Ondine Chavoya, Chon Noriega, Terezita Romo, eds., *Chicano and Chicana Art: A Critical Anthology* (Durham and London: Duke University Press, 2019); Shifra M. Goldman, *Dimensions of the Americas: Art and Social Change in Latin America and the United States* (Chicago and London: The University of Chicago Press, 1994); Alicia Gaspar de Alba, *Chicano Art: Inside Outside the Master's House—Cultural Politics and the CARA Exhibition* (Austin: University of Texas Press, 1998); Guisela Latorre, *Walls of Empowerment: Chicana/o Indigenist Murals of California* (Austin: University of Texas Press, 2008); Karen Mary Davalos, *Exhibiting Mestizaje: Mexican (American) Museums in the Diaspora* (Albuquerque: University of New Mexico Press, 2001); Karen Mary Davalos, *Chicana/o Remix: Art and Errata Since the Sixties* (New York: New York University Press, 20017); Cary Cordova, *The Heart of the Mission: Latino Art and Politics in San Francisco* (Philadelphia: University of Pennsylvania Press, 2017); Carlos Francisco Jackson, *Chicana and Chicano Art: ProtestArte* (Tucson: University of Arizona Press, 2009); Ella María Díaz, *José Montoya* (Los Angeles: UCLA Chicano Studies Research Center Press, 2020); Karen Mary Davalos, *Yolanda M. López* (Los Angeles: UCLA Chicano Studies Research Center Press, 2008); Terezita Romo, *Malaquias Montoya* (Los Angeles: UCLA Chicano Studies Research Center Press, 2011).

1. Stockton Boy

1. As quoted in Dewey Crumpler, "Rupert García," *Shift* (San Francisco, 1991), 40.

5. San Francisco State

1. Peter Berger and Thomas Luckman, *The Social Construction of Reality: A Treatise in the Sociology of Knowledge* (Garden City, NY: Doubleday & Company, 1968).

2. Tatiana Reinoza and María del Mar González, "The Island as a Bridge: Reconceptualizing the Trienal Poli/Gráfica de San Juan," *Caiana* no. 11 (2017): 185.

3. Carla Stellweg, "Rupert García: Chicaneidad, Art and Cultural Politics," *Aspects of Resistance: Rupert García* (New York: The Alternative Museum, 1993), 10.

4. Sign used in the strike; see Kay Boyle, *The Long Walk at San Francisco State* (New York: Grove Press, 1970), 16.

5. Quote taken from Calisphere Rupert García Interviews, video tapes 155, 156, 157 done in 1983 by Philip Brookman, Department of Special Collections, University of California, Santa Barbara.

6. García notes that one of the activist Black students was Danny Glover, who would go on to be a big film star, especially in action films. García met Glover and they became friends.

7. Rupert García, draft of essay, "The Mexican Muralists & The School of Paris," 1976, in possession of Mario T. García.

8. Terezita Romo, "Aesthetics of the Message: Chicana/o Posters, 1965–1987," in E. Carmen Ramos, ed., ¡Printing the Revolution!: The Rise and Impact of Chicano Graphics, 1965 to Now (Washington, DC: Smithsonian American Art Museum in association with Princeton University Press, 2020), 79.

9. For influence of Cuban poster art on García see Shifra M. Goldman, Dimensions of the Americas: Art and Social Change in Latin America and the United States (Chicago and London: The University of Chicago Press, 1994), 166.

10. Carol A. Wells, "La Lucha Sigue: From East Los Angeles to the Middle East," in Chon A. Noriega, ed., ¿Just Another Poster? Chicano Graphic Arts in California (Santa Barbara: University Art Museum, University of California, Santa Barbara, 2001), 177.

11. Romo, "Aesthetics of the Message," 80.

12. See Shifra Goldman, "A Public Voice: Fifteen Years of Chicano Posters," Art Journal (March 1984): 52.

13. As quoted in "Zoot-Suit: The Triumph of El Pachuco," New West, September 11, 1978, in CEMA 101, Box 4, Fld. 5, Dept. of Special Collections, University Library, University of California, Santa Barbara.

14. As quoted in Joe Bower, "Rupert García: Portrait of the Artist as a Social Activist," SF 3, no. 2 (February 1991): 35.

15. George Lipsitz, "Not Just Another Social Movement: Poster Art and the Movimiento Chicano," ¿Just Another Poster?, 75.

16. As quoted in Claudia E. Zapata, "Chicano Graphics in the Digital Age," in Ramos, ed., ¡Printing the Revolution!, 130.

6. The Mission Cultural Renaissance

1. As quoted in Philip Brookman, "Looking for Alternative: Notes on Chicano Art, 1960–1990," in Jennifer A. González, C. Ondine Chavoya, Chon Noriega, and Terezita Romo, ed., Chicano and Chicana Art: A Critical Anthology (Durham and London: Duke University Press, 2019), 23–24.

2. For a discussion of some of these centers see Tatiana Reinoza, Reclaiming the Americas: Latinx Art and the Politics of Territory (Austin: University of Texas Press, 2023).

3. See John Bryan, "Posters for La Raza," The San Francisco Phoenix, September 20, 1976, 9 in CEMA 101, Box 2, Fld. 20 in Rupert García and Sammi Madison Collection.

4. On Salazar see Mario T. García, Ruben Salazar: Border Correspondent—Selected Writings, 1955–1970 (Berkeley and Los Angeles: University of California Press, 1995).

5. David Pagel, CSP 6, Center for the Study of Political Graphics, online.

6. "Turning It Around: A Conversation Between Rupert García and Guillermo Gómez-Peña" in Aspects of Resistance, 14.

7. See Tómas Ybarra-Frausto, "Notes on the Chicano Mural Movement," unpublished paper in CEMA 101, Box 4, Fld. 18, García-Madison Col.

8. Tim Drescher and Rupert García, "Recent Raza Murals in the U.S.," Radical America 12, no. 2 (March–April 1978): 17.

9. Drescher and García, "Recent Raza Murals," 18.

10. Rupert García, "Wall Art of the Chicano Movement: Posters and Murals

from the 1960s to the Early 1970s," unpublished paper (1983), 6 in García-Madison Col., CEMA 101, Box 2, Fld. 25.

11. Drescher and García, "Recent Raza Murals," 20.

12. As quoted in Rupert García, "This mural is not for the bank. It's for the people," *El Tecolote*, June 10, 1974, 8–9.

13. As quoted in "Talking Walls," *Newsweek*, January 1, 1979, in García-Madison Col., CEMA 101, Box 4, Fld. 13.

14. Rupert García, "Death in Art and Society," unpublished paper, 1975, in possession of Mario T. García.

15. See Malaquias Montoya and Leslie Salkowitz-Montoya, "A Critical Perspective on the State of Chicano Art," *Metamórfosis* 3, no. 1 (1980), 3–7; and Shifra M. Goldman, "Response: Another Opinion on the State of Chicano Art," *Metamórfosis* 3–3, nos. 1–2 (1980–1981), 2–7.

16. Drescher and García, "Recent Raza Murals," 23–24. Also see Guisela Latorre, *Walls of Empowerment: Chicana/o Indigenist Murals of California* (Austin: University of Texas Press, 2008) and Cary Cordova, *The Heart of the Mission: Latino Art and Politics in San Francisco* (Philadelphia: University of Pennsylvania Press, 2017) and Davalos, *Exhibiting Mestizaje*, 64–66.

17. Karen Mary Davalos, *Yolanda M. López* (Los Angeles: UCLA Chicano Studies Research Center Press, 2008), 31.

18. Interview with Rupert García for exhibit "The Fifth Sun: Contemporary/Traditional Chicano & Latino Art," University Art Museum, University of California, Berkeley, 1977 in possession of Mario T. García.

19. Romo, *Malaquias Montoya*, 6.

7. Moving On

1. Rupert García, "Community Art-Murals," 11, in possession of Mario T. García.

2. Rupert García, "Pulqueria Art: Defiant Art of the Barrio," *El Tecolote*, December 1977, 7.

3. Rupert García, "La Raza Murals of California, 1963–1970," MA thesis, 1981, 74.

4. Provenzino, "Rupert García," online.

5. A Sample of Quirarte's syllabus can be found in "Meeting of Historians and Critics of Chicano Art," July 11–12, 1980, San Antonio, Texas, in García-Madison Col., CEMA 101, Box 4, Fld. 7.

8. Fluorescence

1. Quoted in "The Soaring Spirit of Chicano Arts," *New West*, September 11, 1978, in García-Madison Col., CEMA 101, Box 4, Fld. 5.

2. See Rupert García, "The State of Art in California," *The Arts Biweekly*, December 15, 1976, 1–5.

3. Interview with Rupert García by John Zarobell, "Studio Sessions," Rena Bransten Gallery, January 30, 2018.

4. Favela, "The Pastel Paintings," 7.

5. Alicia Gaspar de Alba, *Chicano Art: Inside Outside the Master's House—Cultural Politics and the CARA Exhibition* (Austin: University of Texas Press, 1998), XV.

6. On the CARA exhibit see Richard Griswold del Castillo, Teresa McKenna, and Yvonne Yarbro-Bejarano, eds., *Chicano Art: Resistance and Affirmation, 1965–1985* (Los Angeles: Wight Art Gallery, 1991), and Gaspar de Alba, *Chicano Art*.

7. Maxine Hong Kingston, "Introduction," in catalog *Rupert García* (Stockton: The Haggin Museum, 1988), 5.

8. Quoted in catalog *Aspects of Resistance*, 5.

9. In the 1990s, García did two murals. The first was at the San Francisco Airport and the other at the San Francisco General Hospital.

9. Millennial Artist

1. On Dolores Huerta see Mario T. García, ed., *A Dolores Huerta Reader* (Albuquerque: University of New Mexico Press, 2008).

2. As quoted in *Rupert García—Rolling Thunder* (San Francisco: Rena Bransten Gallery, 2018), 22.

3. Lowery Stokes Sims, "Rolling Thunder: War, Cultural Politics and Art History in the Work of Rupert García," in *Rupert García—Rolling Thunder*, 5.

4. Joe Bower, "Rupert García," 37, in possession of Mario T. García.

Afterword

1. Lowery Stokes Sims, "Rubert García Architectonics," in online announcement of exhibit.

Index

About the Author

Mario T. García is distinguished professor of Chicano Studies and History at the University of California, Santa Barbara. A native of El Paso, Texas, he received his B.A. and M.A. in history from the University of Texas at El Paso. He received his Ph.D. in history from the University of California, San Diego. A Guggenheim fellow, he is the author or editor of over twenty books in Chicano history. These include *Desert Immigrants: The Mexicans of El Paso, 1880–1920*; *Memories of Chicano History: The Life and Narrative of Bert Corona*; *Blowout! Sal Castro and the Chicano Struggle for Educational Justice*; and *Father Luis Olivares—A Biography: Faith Politics and the Origins of the Sanctuary Movement in Los Angeles*. His books have won numerous awards and he is the 2016 recipient of the Stetson Kennedy Vox Populi Award for linking oral history to social justice issues given by the Oral History Association. He recently retired from UCSB after 47 years of service.